VISUAL BASIC 6
Object-Oriented Programming

Gold Book

Gene Swartzfager, Ramesh Chandak,
Purshottam Chandak, Steve Alvarez

Publisher
Keith Weiskamp

Acquisitions Editor
Stephanie Wall

Marketing Specialist
Gary Hull

Project Editor
Meredith Brittain

Technical Reviewer
Andrew Indovina

Production Coordinator
Meg E. Turecek

Cover Design
Anthony Stock

Layout Design
April Nielsen

CD-ROM Developer
Robert Clarfield

Visual Basic 6 Object-Oriented Programming Gold Book
Copyright © Ramesh Chandak, 1999

All rights reserved. This book may not be duplicated in any way without the express written consent of the publisher, except in the form of brief excerpts or quotations for the purposes of review. The information contained herein is for the personal use of the reader and may not be incorporated in any commercial programs, other books, databases, or any kind of software without written consent of the publisher. Making copies of this book or any portion for any purpose other than your own is a violation of United States copyright laws.

Limits of Liability and Disclaimer of Warranty
The author and publisher of this book have used their best efforts in preparing the book and the programs contained in it. These efforts include the development, research, and testing of the theories and programs to determine their effectiveness. The author and publisher make no warranty of any kind, expressed or implied, with regard to these programs or the documentation contained in this book.

The author and publisher shall not be liable in the event of incidental or consequential damages in connection with, or arising out of, the furnishing, performance, or use of the programs, associated instructions, and/or claims of productivity gains.

Trademarks
Trademarked names appear throughout this book. Rather than list the names and entities that own the trademarks or insert a trademark symbol with each mention of the trademarked name, the publisher states that it is using the names for editorial purposes only and to the benefit of the trademark owner, with no intention of infringing upon that trademark.

The Coriolis Group, Inc.
14455 North Hayden Road, Suite 220
Scottsdale, Arizona 85260

602/483-0192
FAX 602/483-0193
http://www.coriolis.com

Library of Congress Cataloging-in-Publication Data
Swartzfager, Gene
    Visual Basic 6 object-oriented programming gold book / by Gene Swartzfager...[et al.].
      p.   cm.
  Includes index.
  ISBN 1-57610-255-6
    1. Object-oriented programming (Computer science).   2. Microsoft Visual BASIC.
I. Swartzfager, Gene.
QA76.64.V573   1999
005.1' 17 — dc21   98-38266
                                                                                             CIP

Printed in the United States of America
10 9 8 7 6 5 4 3 2 1

an International Thomson Publishing company

Albany, NY • Belmont, CA • Bonn • Boston • Cincinnati Detroit Johannesburg • London • Madrid
Melbourne • Mexico City • New York • Paris • Singapore • Tokyo • Toronto • Washington

14455 North Hayden, Suite 220 • Scottsdale, Arizona 85260

Dear Reader:

Coriolis Technology Press was founded to create a very elite group of books: The ones you keep closest to your machine. Sure, everyone would like to have the Library of Congress at arm's reach, but in the real world, you have to choose the books you rely on every day *very* carefully.

To win a place for our books on that coveted shelf beside your PC, we guarantee several important qualities in every book we publish. These qualities are:

- *Technical accuracy:* It's no good if it doesn't work. Every Coriolis Technology Press book is reviewed by technical experts in the topic field, and is sent through several editing and proofreading passes in order to create the piece of work you now hold in your hands.

- *Innovative editorial design:* We've put years of research and refinement into the ways we present information in our books. Our books' editorial approach is uniquely designed to reflect the way people learn new technologies and search for solutions to technology problems.

- *Practical focus:* We put only pertinent information into our books and avoid any fluff. Every fact included between these two covers must serve the mission of the book as a whole.

- *Accessibility:* The information in a book is worthless unless you can find it quickly when you need it. We put a lot of effort into our indexes, and heavily cross-reference our chapters, to make it easy for you to move right to the information you need.

Here at The Coriolis Group we have been publishing and packaging books, technical journals, and training materials since 1989. We're programmers and authors ourselves, and we take an ongoing active role in defining what we publish and how we publish it. We hope that you're happy with the book in your hands, and that in the future, when you reach for software development and networking information, you'll turn to one of our books first.

Keith Weiskamp
President and Publisher

Jeff Duntemann
VP and Editorial Director

Look for these books from The Coriolis Group:

Visual Basic 6 Black Book

Visual Basic 6 Core Language Little Black Book

Visual Basic 6 Client/Server Gold Book

Visual C++ 6 Programming Blue Book

Visual C++ 6 Core Language Little Black Book

XML Black Book

I would like to dedicate this book to Kavita and Rajita.
—Ramesh Chandak

I would like to dedicate this book to Mayuri.
—Purshottam Chandak

Dedicated to Lisa, Michael, Anthony, and Clayton.
You are my inspiration, and I love you all.
—Steve Alvarez

About The Authors

Gene Swartzfager (Seattle, WA) is a freelance Visual Basic developer, Help file guru, and technical writer. He's worked with Microsoft on several Visual Basic related projects and taught courses on the subject at University of Washington Extension College. Gene developed the Windows API Browser Visual Basic programming utility. He is the author of *Visual Basic 5 Object-Oriented Programming* and *Creating Visual Basic 5 Add-Ins*.

Ramesh Chandak (Jacksonville, FL) has a total of nine years of experience within the IT industry. Having graduated with a Fellowship in Advanced Engineering Study from MIT, Ramesh has worked extensively with Internet, Microsoft, Sybase, Powersoft, and Java technologies. In addition, he has authored 16 books (including *Advanced PowerBuilder 6 Techniques*, *Oracle8 Bible*, *IIS Exam Prep 4.0*, *IIS Exam Cram 4.0*, and *Dynamic HTML Black Book*), tech edited 15 books, and published 25+ technical articles for several leading publishers on client/server, databases, multimedia, and Internet technologies.

Purshottam Chandak (Jacksonville, FL) has six years of experience in designing and developing client/server and Web applications. A Windows application developer and writer who has worked extensively with Microsoft, Powersoft, Oracle, and Internet technologies, Purshottam has developed corporate applications and products for the niche markets. In addition, he has co-authored three other books (*Advanced PowerBuilder 6 Techniques*, *Oracle8 Bible*, and *Web Programming with Microsoft Tools 6-in-1*). He has also published an article on distributed PowerBuilder application development.

Steve Alvarez (Jacksonville, FL) is a Microsoft Certified Solutions Developer and the Director of Software Engineering at Pathtech Software Solutions, Inc. with more than 15 years of software development and consulting experience. He has worked on software engineering projects for the Air Force, Navy, NASA, and industry in areas such as radar, high-speed communications, space station, knowledge-based systems, sales force automation, publishing, and advanced Internet/extranet/intranet applications. He lives with his wife, three sons, a dog, and a cat.

Acknowledgments

Publishing a book is the result of the combined effort of a number of different people. We would like to thank Stephanie Wall for the opportunity to be part of this book. We would like to thank Meredith Brittain and Martha Kaufman for their support and patience in answering our questions during the book-writing period. Thanks to Robert Clarfield for putting together the CD-ROM for this book, and to the rest of the Coriolis team—Meg Turecek, Anthony Stock, April Nielsen, and Gary Hull. We would also like to thank Steve Alvarez for his valued participation and contribution to this book. Special thanks go to Gene Swartzfager, the author of *Visual Basic 5 Object-Oriented Programming*, for setting the groundwork for this book. Last but not least, we would like to thank Kavita and Mayuri for their unconditional love, care, and support.

—Ramesh and Purshottam Chandak

I would like to thank my wife for putting up with late nights as deadlines neared and finding creative ways to leave me alone to work. I would also like to thank Purshottam Chandak for asking me to join this endeavor and Ramesh Chandak for encouraging and coaching me thorough the writing of this book, especially at the beginning. Thanks also to the editors at Coriolis for their dedication and willingness to work with a first timer. Lastly, thanks to Rob Fitzgerald, whose long technical discussions enlightened and encouraged me.

—Steve Alvarez

Contents At A Glance

Chapter 1 Object-Oriented Programming And Visual Basic

Chapter 2 Designing Objects

Chapter 3 Object Foundations: Visual Basic Classes

Chapter 4 VB's Object Tools

Chapter 5 Advanced Classes

Chapter 6 Object Errors: When Something Goes Wrong

Chapter 7 VB's ActiveX Components

Chapter 8 Implementing ActiveX Components

Chapter 9 Object Applications: Encapsulating System Functionality

Chapter 10 Reusable Application Frameworks

Appendix A Resources For The Visual Basic Developer

Appendix B Third-Party Tools

Glossary

Table Of Contents

Introduction xv

Chapter 1 Object-Oriented Programming And
Visual Basic 1
 The History And Development Of Programming Paradigms 2
 OOP: A Look At The Basics 3
 Object-Oriented Design 11
 Visual Basic Object Specifics 15
 Polymorphism In Visual Basic Applications 21
 The Benefits Of Object-Oriented Programming 33
 The Future Of OOP And COM Components 34
 Conclusion 35

Chapter 2 Designing Objects 37
 The Essence Of Objects 38
 The Importance Of Interfaces 40
 Object-Oriented Design 45
 Other Thought-Provoking Examples 69
 Conclusion 70

Chapter 3 Object Foundations:
Visual Basic Classes 73
 Vocabulary: Defining Our Interface 73
 Class Modules 74
 Keeping Data Private 89
 Public Properties: **Property Let, Get, And Set** 94

Public Methods And Private Procedures 104
Events 110
Conclusion 114

Chapter 4 VB's Object Tools 115
Using The References Dialog Box 117
Using The Object Browser 119
Using The Package And Deployment Wizard 123
Conclusion 129

Chapter 5 Advanced Classes 131
More Vocabulary 131
The Lifetime Of Objects 132
Object Collections 150
Implementing Relationships 159
Data-Aware Classes 166
Polymorphism 171
Conclusion 176

Chapter 6 Object Errors: When Something Goes Wrong 177
Design Of The **Error** Class 177
Initialize/Terminate Events And Declarations 179
The **TrapRunTime** Method 182
The **TrapSyntax** Method 202
Stepping Through The Syntax-Checking Algorithm 210
Making The **Error** Class Stand Alone 212
Conclusion 214

Chapter 7 VB's ActiveX Components 215
ActiveX, COM, And DCOM 215
ActiveX DLLs 217
ActiveX EXEs 221
ActiveX Controls 229
Conclusion 256

Chapter 8 Implementing ActiveX Components 259
Compiling An ActiveX Component 259
Maintaining Compatibility 262
Creating An ActiveX Component's Help File 265

Linking A Help File To An ActiveX Component 267
Conclusion 270

Chapter 9 Object Applications: Encapsulating System Functionality 271
Accessing The Windows API 272
Creating A Registry/INI Object 279
Conclusion 302

Chapter 10 Reusable Application Frameworks 305
Frameworks 305
Designing Frameworks 308
Implementing Frameworks 318
The Future Of Software Engineering 323
Conclusion 326

Appendix A Resources For The Visual Basic Developer 329

Appendix B Third-Party Tools 339

Glossary 363

Index 371

Introduction

This book is written for the Visual Basic developer who wants to be a better—and more productive—developer. Whether you are a corporate developer in the Fortune 500 or just an entrepreneur with a dream of writing a cool new ActiveX control, you and your clients or customers will benefit if you can become a more productive developer.

The easiest way to achieve this goal is to learn the new object-oriented development methodology (or object-based methodology, if you are a purist) that Visual Basic 6 (VB6) supports. Because Visual Basic does not support inheritance, some people mistakenly believe that Visual Basic does not support object-oriented programming. This book will remove all such misconceptions and help you understand how you can best deploy the object-oriented methodology with Visual Basic.

Prerequisites For Using This Book

To use this book successfully, you should be an experienced Visual Basic programmer or an experienced Windows programmer. If you fall into the latter group, and you have never used Visual Basic, you would probably benefit by supplementing this text with a general tutorial on Visual Basic such as *Visual Basic 6 Programming Blue Book* (The Coriolis Group, 1998). You also need to have access to a computer with the Professional Edition of VB6 installed, and you should be willing to work through the sample code that comes with the book in a methodical and detailed manner.

What This Book Covers

This book covers all the major capabilities and features that VB6 supports for object-oriented programming. More specifically, the book explains how to:

- Grasp the fundamental concepts of object-oriented design and programming (class, instance, object, encapsulation, polymorphism, inheritance).
- Use VB6 to write class libraries of reusable code—that is, create ActiveX components that can expose their objects for reuse by other ActiveX programming languages.
- Test and reuse the members of a ClassModule object, both internally and externally.
- Use the VB6 syntax that enables the creation of ActiveX components, including ActiveX controls and ActiveX server components.
- Use ActiveX EXEs and ActiveX DLLs, and more importantly, how to know when to use them.
- Use the VB6 syntax that enables the creation of reusable component frameworks.
- Effectively and efficiently use the integrated tools, including the Object Browser, the References dialog box, and the Package And Deployment Wizard.
- Implement commercial-quality, industrial-strength error-handling and syntax-checking code within the procedures of a class.
- Create a commercial-quality Windows Help file for an ActiveX component's class library and link individual Help topics to an object or an object's members.

What's New With Visual Basic 6

Visual Basic has now matured into an excellent product for enterprise development. The new release provides improved support for Web development as well as better access to the database. The following sections highlight some of VB6's new features.

Integrated Visual Database Tools

Because they are integrated with the development environment, these tools allow you to view, query, design, and diagram database elements, such as stored procedures, tables, diagrams, views, and synonyms.

Data Environment Designer

VB6 provides an interactive, design time graphical interface for connecting to the database using the ActiveX Data Object (ADO). The designer helps you to:

- Add a Data Environment designer to a Visual Basic project.
- Create Connection objects.
- Create Command objects based on stored procedures, tables, views, synonyms, and SQL statements.
- Create hierarchies of commands based on a grouping of Command objects, or by relating one or more commands to each other.
- Write and run code for Connection and Recordset objects.
- Drag fields within a Command object from the Data Environment designer onto a Visual Basic form or the Data Report designer.

WebClass Designer

The new release of Visual Basic provides many powerful features for developing robust Web applications. You can now create cross-platform, cross-browser Web applications from within Visual Basic. With VB6, Microsoft introduces WebClass, a new COM object that resides on the Internet Information Server and is capable of communicating with all of your existing components. To help you design WebClasses, Visual Basic provides a WebClass Designer.

Dynamic HTML Page Designer

VB6 provides support for Dynamic HTML with the new Dynamic HTML page designer. You can now write robust, server-distributed, client-side application logic in Visual Basic while taking advantage of the Dynamic HTML's rich multimedia, typographical, and positioning features.

Package And Deployment Wizard

VB6 replaces the Setup Wizard with the Package And Deployment Wizard. With this wizard, you can create standalone or server-distributed setup packages. In addition, you can remotely post server-packages to distribution servers using either FTP or HTTP protocols.

As you can see, VB6 provides a number of new features that enable rapid application development. At the same time, if you develop objects for your project with the object-oriented design and techniques, you will be able to reuse these objects across applications and even across projects. Also, such object-oriented techniques will help you immensely with the maintenance of your project. This book is aimed at helping you design and develop Visual Basic applications using the object-oriented methodology.

Conventions Used In This Book

The following sections explain the typographic, programming, and naming conventions used in this book.

Typographic Conventions

The typographic conventions used in this book are:

- In code:
  - In syntax, an argument inside square brackets is optional (e.g., [HelpFile]).
  - In syntax, a straight slash or pipe symbol (|) indicates that the parts on either side of the slash are mutually exclusive (e.g., Public | Private).
- Non-code words appearing in quotation marks are one of the following: words to be typed, a quotation, or the title of another section or chapter of the book. (In code, quotation marks indicate a string.)
- Words in bold with the initial letter capitalized (e.g., **TypeName**, **VarType**) indicate VB language specific or class library specific identifiers or keywords.
- Directory and file names are set in all capital letters.

Programming Conventions

The programming conventions used in the sample code listings in this book are:

- An apostrophe followed by a space introduces a code *comment*:

  ```
  ' Create instance of class.
  ```

- All comments are set off by one blank line before the comment and appear above the lines of code to which they are related. No endline comments are used.
- Control-flow code blocks are indented three spaces from the enclosing code and are preceded by a blank line:

```
Private Sub Command1_Click()

    ' Variables.
    Dim Results As Variant

    Results = ClientApp.CheckSecurity

    If Results(1) = "Cancel" Then
        MsgBox "This will close your application"
    Else
        Msg = "Login ID and password you input were:" _
            & vbCr & vbCr
        Msg = Msg & Results(1)
        MsgBox Msg, vbInformation
    End If

End Sub
```

♦ Visual Basic supports the use of a *line-continuation character*, a space followed by an underscore (_). Code statements too long for one line are continued on the next line using the line-continuation character. Each continuation line is indented to line up logically with the code in the line above it. An example is:

```
' Center form:
Me.Move (Screen.Width - Me.Width) * .5, _
        (Screen.Height - Me.Height) * .5
```

Breaking a line in the middle of a quoted string is discouraged, but if it cannot be avoided, an ampersand (&) precedes the underscore, as shown in this example:

```
Msg = Msg & "event procedure of this demo form" & _
      "will unload"
```

♦ When a call is made to a procedure using *named arguments*, the line-continuation character is often used to set off each named argument. Each continuation line contains another named argument and is indented in line with the position of the previous named argument. An example is:

```
List.FillWithDAO(CboOrLst:=List1, _
                 Dbs:=Dbs, _
                 Rst:=Rst, _
```

```
                            Field:="Title", _
                            Sort:=SORT_ASC)
```

- Each variable is explicitly declared. The assumption is that Require Variable Declaration is checked on the Editor tab of Visual Basic's Options dialog box (Tools | Options).
- All variable declarations follow the format

```
Dim Results As Variant
```

where the data type is explicitly stated using the **As** keyword. The only exception to this rule is the declaration of a Windows API function. In this case, the suffix approach is used to conserve space and so, as much as possible, to minimize the use of the line-continuation character. For example:

```
Declare Function LockWinUpdate& Lib "USER32" _
    (ByVal hWndLock)
```

- If a Visual Basic *intrinsic constant* exists, it is used. Examples:

```
' Warn user there will be a delay.
Screen.MousePointer = vbHourglass

' Reset default cursor.
Screen.MousePointer = vbDefault
```

- If a *constant* or constants exist for a Windows API function's arguments or return values, this book uses them. Examples:

```
' Constants for SetWindowPos Windows API function:
Const HWND_TOPMOST = -1
Const HWND_NOTOPMOST = -2
Const SWP_NOSIZE = &H1
Const SWP_NOMOVE = &H2
```

- If no Visual Basic intrinsic or Windows API function constants exist, this book's code declares its own constants and assigns most numeric or string literals and control array index values to these constants.
- Whenever coding steps are listed in this book, the assumption is that VB6 is being used.

Naming Conventions For Code

Naming conventions are akin to religious beliefs. Every Visual Basic developer can give you several good reasons why his or her naming conventions are better than all the rest. Most programmers do not waste time preaching to the unconverted. Still, when you read books on Visual Basic or Microsoft Access programming, you may feel that if you do not adhere to the prescribed naming conventions, you will be excommunicated from the Visual Basic flock.

Some of the most widespread and commonly used naming conventions are identified here:

- The Hungarian conventions are named after and recommended by the legendary Microsoft C developer, Michael Simonyi, who happens to be of Hungarian descent. He suggests using these guidelines as a standard way of developing your C and C++ applications.

- Microsoft's suggested conventions for Visual Basic (VB) and Visual Basic for Application (VBA) are explained briefly in the books *Microsoft Office 97 Visual Basic Programmer's Guide* (Microsoft Press, 1997) and *Microsoft Office 95 Data Access Reference* (Microsoft Press, 1995). (See Appendix A for complete bibliographical information on these books.)

- The Leszynski conventions are used by many Microsoft Access programmers and are based on and expand upon Microsoft's suggested conventions. You can learn about the Leszynski conventions with your *Microsoft Office 95 Data Access Reference*.

For Visual Basic's built-in objects, the naming conventions in this book are based on Microsoft's suggested conventions for VB and VBA. For built-in objects not covered by Microsoft, we use the fundamental Leszynski naming conventions.

The conventions for naming other items in code are based on the assumption that you are going to use VB6 to write encapsulated, object-oriented code that will be compiled into an ActiveX component. When you do this, you want to write members which, when viewed from Visual Basic's Object Browser dialog box, appear the same with regard to names/syntax as VB's and VBA's members appear. To achieve this, this book names:

- A member that is a method with a verb. If necessary, the verb is followed by a noun that specifies a related object.

- A member that is a property with a noun.

♦ An argument with a noun or, occasionally, a verb. The name of the argument is not preceded by a three-letter prefix indicating the data type of the variable because the arguments for VB's and VBA's members do not use three-letter prefixes.

Names For Variables

Variables are given descriptive names when they are explicitly declared and are not given any prefix to indicate their data type. This sounds like heresy of the worst sort compared to the commonly used Visual Basic naming conventions, which all use prefixes of some kind.

Microsoft is increasingly promoting the Component Object Model (COM) to write highly cohesive, encapsulated procedures/modules/classes. If you adhere to the object-oriented programming paradigm, the procedures composing the members of a class library should be relatively short and should not be coupled with the code of other procedures except through message passing. No public/global variables should be used and module-level variables, except for those required in conjunction with Visual Basic's **Property Get**, **Let** and **Set** procedures, should only be rarely declared (and then closely commented to document their use).

For those Visual Basic developers who commit themselves to the object-oriented programming paradigm, programmers who continue to clutter their procedures with elaborate and esoteric variable naming conventions and broadly scoped variables seem out of date.

The scope of variables is specified in this way:

♦ Any variable declared to have ClassModule object-level scope has the prefix **c**. The only exception to this is an object variable that is assigned a reference to one of the ClassModule objects in the class library on this book's companion CD-ROM.

♦ Any variable declared to have form-level scope has the prefix **f**.

♦ All variables of form-level or ClassModule object-level scope are declared with the **Private** statement. Procedure-level variables, declared with the **Dim** statement, are private by definition. This practice conforms with the encapsulation characteristic of object-oriented programming, which forbids the use of any variables declared with the **Public** statement (in Visual Basic 3, the **Global** statement).

Names For Form And Control Objects

All *form* and *control* objects intrinsic to VB are identified by a generic, lowercase, three-letter prefix specifying the class of the object. These prefixes are listed in Table 1.

Controls that are part of a *control array* simply use the control's three-letter prefix as their **Name** property. Their **Index** property value is then identified by a constant. For example, two CommandButton objects for OK and Close which are part of a control array would be identified in code by **Cmd(OK)** and **Cmd(CLOSE)**, with **OK** and **CLOSE** being the constants.

How This Book Is Organized

This book consists of 10 chapters, described briefly here:

- *Chapter 1*—A general overview of the theory and practice of object-oriented design and programming, Chapter 1 introduces the essential concepts that govern object-oriented design and programming and the creation of COM components with VB6. The concepts and techniques involved in subclassing with members from the **Dialog** and **Graphic** classes (included in the class library on this book's

Table 1 Prefixes for Visual Basic's form and intrinsic control objects.

Class/Object Name	Prefix	Example
ADO Data	ado	adoConnector
CheckBox	chk	chkWholeWord
ComboBox	cbo	cboBrowse
Data	dat	datBiblio
DirListBox	dir	dirBrowse
DriveListBox	drv	drvBrowse
FileListBox	fil	filBrowse
Form	frm	frmBrowse
Frame	fra	fraOptions
HScrollBar	hsb	hsbRate
Image	img	imgLogo
Label	lbl	lblHelpMessage
Line	lin	linVertical
ListBox	lst	lstFiles
MDIForm	mdi	mdiEditor
Menu	mnu	mnuEdit
OptionButton	opt	optEnglish
PictureBox	pic	picLogo
Shape	shp	shpCircle
TextBox	txt	txtEmpName
Timer	tmr	tmrGetWindowInfo
RemoteData	rd	rdFetch
TreeView	tre	treEmployee
VScrollBar	vsb	vsbRate

companion CD-ROM) are demonstrated. This chapter also includes an explanation of how to write polymorphic methods, which present a single, consistent public interface to the client application programmer, but which implement different kinds of functionality.

- *Chapters 2 and 3*—These chapters explain the fundamentals of how to create classes, encapsulate data to keep it safe, and design a public interface. They also explain the essence of objects and how to initialize and terminate them, as well as persistence and how to declare, raise, and handle events.

- *Chapter 4*—This chapter covers a number of tools that come integrated with VB6, including the Object Browser, the References dialog box, and the Package And Deployment Wizard.

- *Chapter 5*—This chapter explains object collections, data-aware classes, polymorphism, and how to implement relationships.

- *Chapter 6*—This chapter addresses how to handle errors within your VB6 applications.

- *Chapters 7 and 8*—These chapters discuss the Microsoft Active Platform, including COM, DCOM, and ActiveX technologies. They also explain the differences between an ActiveX EXE and an ActiveX DLL, discuss ActiveX controls and how to create them using VB6, how to implement ActiveX objects, and how to add help for ActiveX objects.

- *Chapter 9*—This chapter discusses the specifics of Visual Basic access to system resources and objects.

- *Chapter 10*—This chapter introduces the concept of reusable application frameworks within object-oriented development and offers Windows-based examples.

In addition to these chapters, this book contains two appendixes, a glossary, and a CD-ROM. Appendix A covers resources for the Visual Basic developer, and Appendix B lists numerous third-party products. The book's companion CD-ROM contains a class library, sample code from the book, and evaluation (or demo) copies of third-party software for Visual Basic.

Chapter 1
Object-Oriented Programming And Visual Basic

Key Topics:

- The History And Development Of Programming Paradigms
- OOP: A Look At The Basics
- Object-Oriented Design
- Visual Basic Object Specifics
- Polymorphism In Visual Basic Applications
- The Benefits Of Object Oriented Programming
- The Future Of OOP And COM Components

This chapter introduces the fundamentals and basic terminology of object-oriented programming (OOP) and development. The computer software industry is notorious for its tendency to hype new programming techniques, approaches, and languages as they come along. However, in the case of object-oriented programming, there's real substance behind the hype.

Object-oriented programming, as Microsoft has implemented it with Visual Basic and COM components, is a methodology and framework for developing programs that, in comparison to procedural programming:

- Are composed of a greater number of reusable modules or objects
- Have fewer bugs
- Are easier to maintain, enhance, and scale up

For the corporate programmer and IS (Information Systems) department, adopting the object-oriented programming paradigm can, over the long term, improve programmer productivity by 50 to 100 percent. Because much of the code written the object-oriented way is reusable and easily maintained, corporate programmers enjoy their work and get to write new code a greater percentage of the time than they would otherwise. For you, the individual programmer or utility developer, using the object-oriented approach (in conjunction with COM components and add-ins) makes it easier to write that one hot utility—and this utility, being so easy for other programmers to reuse, might just sell 500,000 copies at, say, $10 per copy. You could then retire to a life of leisure and game playing!

The rest of this chapter familiarizes you with the basics you'll need to know to understand the material within this book. After a brief look at the history of object-oriented programming, this chapter discusses its terminology, from both the software industry's perspective and Microsoft's viewpoint. This chapter introduces the key OOP attributes of encapsulation, abstraction, polymorphism, inheritance, and modularity, along with the larger OOP-related issues of design methodologies, including Grady Booch's object-oriented design methodology. In addition, this chapter discusses designing two-tier and three-tier client/server applications, Visual Basic Collection objects, the ClassModule object, and a couple of polymorphic methods (**Center** and **Load**).

The History And Development Of Programming Paradigms

Although object-oriented programming has assumed a very high profile among developers within the last few years, it's actually more than 25 years old. The Simula language, developed in Norway during the late 1960s, introduced all the essential concepts of the object-oriented approach to programming. The developers created Simula, an acronym for *simulation language*, to support simulations of real-world processes. Modularization in Simula was based on the physical objects being modeled within the simulation, not on procedures, as in conventional programming languages. The concept of software objects arose from the requirement to model or abstract real-world objects and their relationships.

Microsoft has recently added a new twist to OOP, an attempt to structure all object-oriented programming around the low-level abstraction of a COM component (formerly known as an *OLE Automation server*). A COM *component*, which we discuss in more detail later in this chapter, is an application that exposes programmable objects and their members for reuse by any application containing an OLE Automation-compliant programming language. Microsoft has designed Visual Basic 6 (VB6) to easily create class libraries that, at a lower level of abstraction, are COM components.

The history of software development seems to go through cycles of evolution, with each cycle characterized by a greater degree of abstraction. Some of the major steps within this evolutionary process include:

- Machine language programming
- Assembly programming

- Higher-level language programming (Cobol, Fortran, Basic, C, and so on)
- Procedural language programming (Focus, dBASE, Visual Basic 3, and so on)
- Structured programming techniques (capable of being adhered to in almost any language)
- Pure OOP languages (Simula, Smalltalk, C++, and so on)
- OOP techniques (capable of being added on to almost any higher-level or procedural language—for example, object-oriented versions of Ada, Cobol, Visual FoxPro, Visual Basic 6, and so on)
- COM and ActiveX components

Microsoft is staking its future, and the future of the various versions of its Windows operating systems, on the COM component implementation of OOP. Given Microsoft's dominance and influence within the software industry, it's clear that OOP, as embodied within COM components, is more than just a passing fancy—it's here to stay.

OOP: A Look At The Basics

An *object* is a software package that contains a collection of related procedures and data. Within object-oriented programming, procedures are called *methods*, and the data elements are called *properties*. The concept of an object is simple, yet powerful and flexible. Objects make ideal software modules because you can define and maintain them independently of one another, with each object forming a self-contained, independent unit. You express everything a software object knows within its properties and everything the object can do within its methods.

Software objects interact with each other by sending messages requesting that methods be carried out or properties be set or returned. A *message* is simply the name of an object followed by the name of one of its members. A message can have three parts:

- The name of the receiving object
- The name of the object's member (method or property)
- The values specified by the arguments of the member

In Visual Basic syntax, an example of a message is

```
List.FillWithDAO CboOrLst:=List1, _
                 Dbs:=Dbs, _
                 Rst:=Rst, _
                 Field:="Title", _
                 Sort:=SORT_ASC
```

where **List** is the receiving object, **FillWithDAO** is the name of the member, and the remainder of the code specifies the named arguments of the **FillWithDAO** member and the values passed to them. An object-oriented program consists of some number of objects that interact with each other by passing messages back and forth. Because an object's members express everything an object can do or know (that is, methods and properties), this programming model supports all the possible interactions between objects.

An extremely simple simulation might require only a single example of a particular kind of object, but most real-world simulations require several instances of each kind of object. It is extremely inefficient to redefine and recode the same members for every occurrence of a kind of object. An efficient solution to this problem is the concept of a *class*. A class specifies, once and for all, the members you can include within a particular kind of object. Thereafter, each instance of a class needs to contain only the particular values or settings that differentiate the class from its sibling object instances.

As OOP evolved and developers wrote different object-oriented languages, such as Smalltalk and C++, the classes these languages created came to exhibit four key attributes that define the purest form of OOP: *encapsulation, abstraction, polymorphism,* and *inheritance*. We'll cover these attributes in detail later within this chapter, but at a basic level, they can be defined as follows:

- *Encapsulation*—The process of combining logically related procedures and data within one class/object. In this way, you insulate each object from the rest of the program. Because the object is using only data contained within it or passed to it, and the object executes only internal procedures, an encapsulated object is said to implement data hiding or information hiding.

- *Abstraction*—The process of abstracting logically related procedures and data within one class. A class represents an object's behavior that is separate from its implementation. In fact, an object is an instance of the class. Other objects can interact and communicate directly with the instance, not with the class.

- *Polymorphism*—A characteristic of an object's method that lets a programmer call a single method (for example, **Center**) and apply this method to several different classes/objects. It's not necessary for you to understand the details of how this is implemented within the object's method in order to call and use the polymorphic method.
- *Inheritance*—The process by which all subclasses of a given superclass can make use of the members of that superclass/object. Inheritance results in writing common code within a super-, base, or parent class, and specialized code within sub-, derived, or child classes. The final result of creating an object-oriented application while adhering to inheritance is a hierarchy of classes.

A logical group of classes and objects represents a *module*. Creating modules makes it easy to represent an especially large and complex system. Modules communicate with each other via message passing. Abstraction and encapsulation together provide a modular representation of a system. The principles of abstraction, encapsulation, and modularity are therefore synergistic.

Encapsulation

Now that you have a clear understanding of encapsulation from the previous description, let's examine this attribute in more detail. *Encapsulation* means that an object is not coupled to or dependent on any other object or procedure; instead, the object is independent and internally cohesive. The object does not contain any global or public variables and does not require any external procedures to execute its members. You can access and manipulate the data and behavior of an encapsulated object only through the object's public interface (see Figure 1.1).

In Visual Basic, for example, the public interface of a class library composed of ClassModule objects includes the following items:

- The hierarchy of classes (ClassModule objects) that comprise the class library; these classes expose their public members for reuse
- The arguments of a ClassModule object's public **Event**, **Function**, and **Sub** members
- The arguments of a ClassModule object's public **Property Get**, **Property Let**, and **Property Set** members
- The values, upon success or failure, that a member returns; these possible values include the error codes returned to describe a syntax or runtime error

6 Chapter 1

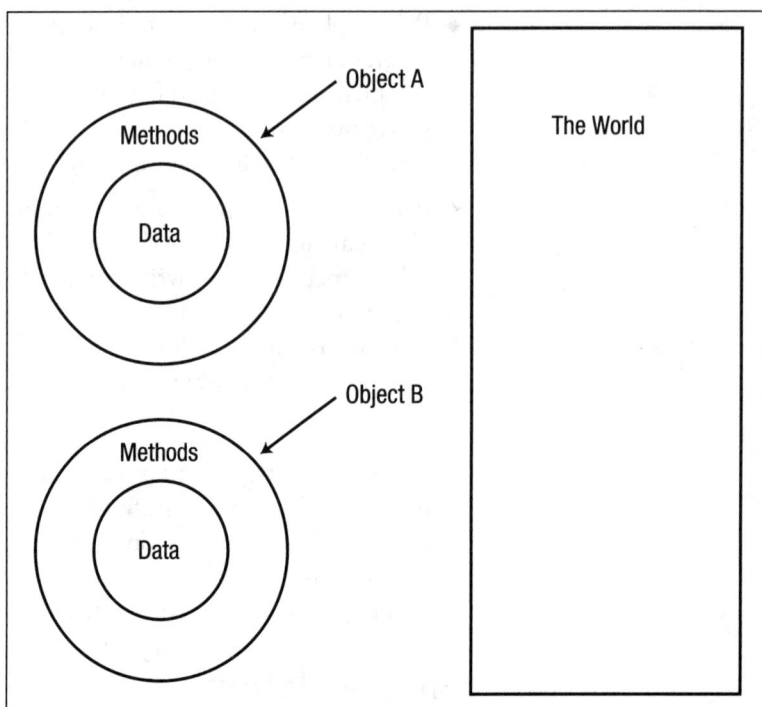

Figure 1.1
Encapsulated objects hide the data from the outside world.

As the previous section indicated, objects are said to exhibit data or information hiding. No one except the programmer who created the object knows the details about what is hidden inside the object. An encapsulated object communicates with another object or part of the program only by receiving and sending messages. Within Visual Basic, this messaging activity is a two-way street. The object accepts values from the calling procedure as arguments for the object's members, and it returns a value (or values) to the calling procedure as the result of a **Function** procedure or **Property Get** procedure.

Encapsulation provides several advantages to object-oriented programmers. Specifically, programmers can perform the following tasks:

- Protect data from corruption by other objects or parts of the program.
- Hide low-level, complex implementation details from the rest of the program and encourage data abstraction, which results in the capability to implement a simple public interface to a more complex set of private members. It's also easier to maintain legacy code or add new members to the object without affecting any procedures that currently call the object.

- Make debugging individual objects easier, as well as ensure that a bug within one object does not affect some other part of the system in an apparently unconnected way.
- Promote reuse of the object by other programmers, thus improving their productivity.

Abstraction

Now that you have a clear understanding of encapsulation, let's look at another object-oriented design attribute. *Abstraction* means separating an object's behavior from its implementation. Abstracting an object from a system description involves building a class for the application (this class is an object that other objects cannot directly act upon). In other words, the other objects cannot communicate and interact directly with the class; you must create instances of the class to enable interaction and communication.

The ClassModule (*filename*.CLS) object is Visual Basic's way of letting you define abstractions and create your own classes. You use a ClassModule object to define a class that can contain members, which you code by using **Event**, **Function**, **Sub**, and **Property** procedures. You can have several different ClassModule objects within a single Visual Basic project. You'll learn more about ClassModule objects later in this chapter.

Abstraction provides several advantages to object-oriented programmers. Specifically, programmers can perform the following tasks:

- Focus on the essential characteristics of the abstracted classes
- Hide low-level, complex implementation details from the rest of the program and encourage data abstraction
- Promote reuse of the class by other programmers, thus improving their productivity

Polymorphism

Moving right along, you're now ready to see a more detailed view of polymorphism. If two or more classes have behaviors that share the same name with the same basic purpose, but you implement them differently, the method/code used to implement the behaviors is said to be *polymorphic*. The ability to hide the implementation details of an object's method behind a common public interface is known as *polymorphism*. If an object's method is polymorphic, a programmer can call

> **NOTE**
>
> Encapsulation and polymorphism are essentially the heart of object-oriented programming. Without them, you cannot design and implement applications the object-oriented way. When designing an application, you should carefully identify and evaluate the objects for the application and determine if one or more methods are common to a set of objects. If so, make these methods polymorphic. For example, you can move objects representing real-world elements, such as a table, chair, desk, computer, and appliance; the design, therefore, calls for a common polymorphic method—*move*—for all these objects.

or invoke that method for any other object the method supports, without knowing or caring about the type of object to which the method is applied.

Within Visual Basic, the **MouseDown** method is polymorphic, because you can apply this method to over 20 different classes. When you apply the **MouseDown** method to a Form object, you pass the method the same number of arguments and the same data types as when you apply the method to a PictureBox object.

For example, as a programmer, you don't need to worry about any of the low-level implementation details of a polymorphic method; instead, all you do is apply the method to a supported object and pass it the correct values as arguments.

As with encapsulation, polymorphism provides several advantages for object-oriented programmers. Specifically, programmers can perform the following tasks:

- Simplify an object's public interface by minimizing the number of its members and hiding low-level, complex implementation details from the client application programmer
- Reduce the size and optimize the speed of the EXE or DLL file containing the object
- Maintain legacy code more easily
- Promote reuse of the object by other programmers, thus improving their productivity

Inheritance

You've conquered the first three attributes without any major problems. This fourth attribute, inheritance, is a piece of cake as well. Although it's possible to define classes independently of each other, inheritance within an OOP language lets you base, or define, one or more classes as special cases of a more general class. These special cases are known as *subclasses*, *derived classes*, or *children* of the original class. The more general class, in turn, is the *superclass*, *base class*, or *parent class* of its special cases.

Through inheritance, a subclass can use all the members of its superclass, override any of the inherited members, and define its own new members. Inheritance increases efficiency, because you program the behavior or methods that are characteristic of larger groups of objects only once, within the superclass. Subclasses add to or modify the behavior of a superclass only as required for their special cases.

There are two types of inheritance: *single* and *multiple*. In single inheritance, a subclass inherits from a single superclass. In multiple inheritance, a subclass inherits from more than one superclass. VB6 still does not support single and multiple inheritance in the classic sense of the term, but you can subclass existing objects with it.

Advantages And Disadvantages

Of course, inheritance provides its own sets of advantages and disadvantages to object-oriented programmers. Specifically, inheritance benefits programmers by enabling them to perform the following tasks:

- Minimize redundant programming. Behavior that is characteristic of larger groups of objects is coded only once within the higher-level class's definition. Therefore, legacy code can be maintained much more easily.
- Reduce the size and optimize the speed of the EXE or DLL file containing the objects.
- Increase programming flexibility. Subclasses that exhibit specialized behaviors or that may exhibit new behaviors in the future can merely add to or modify the behavior of their superclass, as required.
- Subclass existing objects. (VB6 still does not support inheritance in the classic sense of the term.) Sheridan Software Systems, Inc. (**http://www.shersoft.com**), one of the preeminent ActiveX control software manufacturers, sells a Visual Basic add-on product called *ClassAssist*, which implements inheritance and subclassing to a useful degree.

On the other hand, inheritance poses the following disadvantages to object-oriented programmers:

- The depth of the inheritance tree may create performance problems. For example, if the inheritance tree is 20 levels deep, a call to a method at the leaf-node level (the 20th level within the tree) must travel 19 levels up before execution. In addition, managing and maintaining a 20-level-deep inheritance tree becomes tedious and complex. Such a tree also greatly increases the size and decreases the speed of the EXE or DLL file containing the objects. An inheritance tree with a maximum of three to four levels is highly recommended.
- A deep inheritance tree might make it difficult to navigate and search through the objects and associated methods, variables, and so on.

Designing The Inheritance Tree

Inheritance lets you define a generic class and then create specific instances of this class for use within your applications. Therefore, you can look at inheritance as generalization and specialization. The ancestor objects define the generalization; the instances define the specific behavior. For example, an automobile represents a generic class (an ancestor object), and Saturn SL2 represents a specific instance of this generic class.

Proper design and organization of the inheritance tree are extremely critical. The design and implementation of an inheritance tree depend on your corporate environment, the nature of applications you want to build, the business requirements of these applications, and so on. Figure 1.2 shows a sample inheritance tree that should apply to most corporate environments. This inheritance tree includes ancestor, corporate, and department layers. To create the corporate inheritance tree, follow these steps:

1. Define the highest layer of ancestor objects first. These are the objects you inherit from to create the corporate and department layers. The ancestor objects are generic in nature, defining the methods and properties from which you can inherit to create specific instances. Any change you make to this layer reflects down through the inheritance tree. Building and maintaining the ancestor level of objects takes time and effort.

2. Next, define the corporate layer. This layer includes objects that are representative of your corporation as a whole. Attributes such as corporate logo, corporate mission, and so on are applicable to all the departments within the corporation. An insurance company may have a different set of objects within the corporate layer, and a financial institution may have another set. Any change you

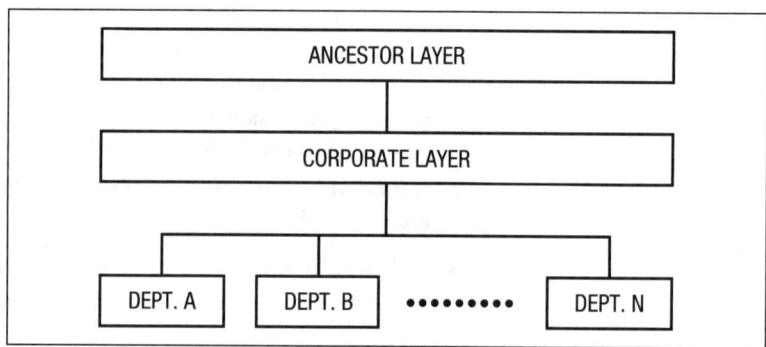

Figure 1.2
The corporate inheritance tree.

make to this layer reflects down through the department layers but does not reflect within the ancestor layer.

3. The department layer is the third layer. Each department may work on a different set of applications, and each such set may demand its own specialization. The departments within an insurance company may have a different set of objects at the department layers, and the departments within a financial institution may have another set. Any change you make to this layer reflects nowhere else within the inheritance tree, unless additional layers of objects exist underneath each department layer.

Object-Oriented Design

In his book *Object-Oriented Design With Applications*, Grady Booch defines and discusses object-oriented analysis (OOA), object-oriented design (OOD), and object-oriented programming (OOP). Building software systems is inherently complex and chaotic. Per Booch's theory, OOD brings order to this chaos. By using OOD, you can decompose a complex software system into smaller and manageable software systems—in other words, into objects. Booch defines an *object* as a tangible entity that exhibits well-defined behavior.

Of course, OOD provides its own set of advantages to object-oriented programmers. Specifically, programmers can perform the following tasks:

- Create smaller, more manageable software systems (a.k.a. objects)
- Evolve complex software systems incrementally from smaller systems
- Build a system that is a collection of objects that collaborate with each other

Note that Booch does not classify programming without inheritance as "object oriented." He calls this approach "programming with abstract data types."

Building an object-oriented application based on Booch's OOA and OOD principles calls for decomposing a complex application into objects that together exhibit the four key attributes: *encapsulation*, *abstraction*, *polymorphism*, and *inheritance*. These four attributes represent the major elements of Booch's object model. Encapsulation and abstraction together provide modularity to the system.

Booch's Definitions

The following definitions are taken from Grady Booch's *Object-Oriented Design With Applications* (Benjamin/Cummings, Menlo Park, CA, 1994):

Object-Oriented Analysis—A method of analysis that examines requirements from the perspective of the classes and objects found within the vocabulary of the problem domain. (p. 37)

Object-Oriented Design—A method of design encompassing the process of object-oriented decomposition and a notation for depicting both logical and physical, as well as static and dynamic, models of the system under design. (p. 37)

Object-Oriented Programming—A method of implementation in which you organize the programs as cooperative collections of objects, each of which represents an instance of some class, and whose classes are all members of a hierarchy of classes united via inheritance relationships. (pp. 35–36)

Two-Tier Client/Server

A two-tier client/server architecture includes one or more client machines connected to one or more servers via a network. Of course, a two-tier architecture provides its own set of advantages to object-oriented programmers. Specifically, programmers can perform the following tasks:

- Distribute the application processing between the client and server. The client handles complex input validations, sorting data, and presenting the graphical user interface. The server processes the request the client sends. For example, a database server processes the SQL requests the client sends and returns the results to the client.

- Build a system that is a collection of client and server objects that collaborate with each other.

On the other hand, a two-tier architecture has disadvantages :

- Diagnosing problems can sometimes be a nightmare. Three potential bottlenecks exist: the client, the network, and the server.

- Distribution and maintenance can also sometimes be an ordeal. A simple change within the application may require redistribution to all the client machines. Problems with specific client machines that are geographically dispersed may require the developer to travel to the client sites, thus taking time away from design and development.

Three-Tier Client/Server

A three-tier client/server architecture includes one or more client machines connected to one or more servers via a middle tier (an application server) over the network. Of course, a three-tier architecture provides its own set of advantages to object-oriented programmers.

Specifically, programmers can perform the following tasks:

- Build thin client browser-based solutions. The application remains distributed: The middle tier hosts the business logic, the client handles the presentation, and the database server processes the SQL requests.
- Make a change to the business logic of the application at the middle tier and have the clients instantly reflect this change. This makes distribution and maintenance of the application easy.

On the other hand, diagnosing problems within a three-tier architecture can still be problematic, because now there are four potential bottlenecks: the client, the network, the application server, and the database server.

Business Objects

Business objects are typically nonvisual objects that encapsulate the business logic of the application. A *nonvisual object* is an object that does not encompass a visual component or interface. Business objects handle the communication on both ends of the spectrum; they communicate with the client front end and database back end. They provide a layer of abstraction where you may, if you choose, change the client front end or database back end (or both), with the business logic essentially remaining the same. In addition, distribution and maintenance become easy. If the business logic changes as a result of the change in the requirements, the change takes place only within a single location, thus not affecting the client front end and database back end.

Business objects provide services. When the client requests a service, the appropriate business object responds. When the client requests a connection to the database, the connection business object, for example, establishes and provides such a connection. The client issues a SQL request, and the SQL business object, for example, communicates the request to the database server. Then the database server processes the request and returns the result(s) to the client via the SQL business object. The client requests an amortization schedule, and the amortization schedule business object, for example, generates and returns such a schedule.

Business objects could be JavaBeans, ActiveX DLLs, ActiveX controls, C++ objects, and so on. With VB6, you can create a number of objects, such as ActiveX DLLs, ActiveX EXEs, and so on.

An *ActiveX DLL* is an in-process component that runs within the process of an application (EXE) or another in-process component. An

ActiveX DLL includes classes the calling application can use to create instances of objects and then invoke the methods and properties of the objects. An ActiveX DLL has the .DLL extension. You'll learn more about creating ActiveX DLLs with VB6 in Chapter 7.

An *ActiveX EXE* is an application that supports COM. This means an ActiveX EXE can integrate and run ActiveX controls and ActiveX DLLs. The Windows 95, Windows 98, and Windows NT operating systems and Internet Explorer (IEXPLORE.EXE) are excellent examples of ActiveX applications. You'll learn more about COM, DCOM, and creating ActiveX EXEs with VB6 in Chapter 7.

User Interface (UI) Objects

Generally speaking, *UI objects* are visual objects that encapsulate the user interface of the application. Examples of UI objects include calendar, slider, marquee, and so on. Usually, UI objects are OCX or ActiveX controls that run and execute on the client machine. You can use VB6 to create ActiveX controls.

ActiveX controls are OLE controls redefined for the Internet. They are redefined for speed and size so that browsers download them quickly. Before using an ActiveX control, you must register the control with the Windows Registry. On Windows 95, you can register an ActiveX control with the Registration Server (REGSVR32.EXE). However, all ActiveX controls should be self-registering. An ActiveX control may have an .OCX or a .DLL extension. An OCX is not necessarily an ActiveX control. An OCX is a file that may contain one or more ActiveX controls. Generally speaking, there's no difference between an OLE control and an ActiveX control.

Technically, an ActiveX control and ActiveX DLL are both in-process components. *ActiveX control* is a term traditionally used to describe ActiveX servers that support connection points for event interfaces and, optionally, implement the visual support interfaces. The file name ends in .OCX rather than .DLL. You can embed an ActiveX control within an ActiveX container. An ActiveX control includes the interface required for communication with an ActiveX container. An ActiveX DLL does not require this type of interface and communication. *ActiveX DLL* is a term traditionally used to describe ActiveX servers that support the automation interfaces (namely, IDispatch), do not typically fire events, and do not have any visual element. The basic difference is in the ActiveX interfaces the component implements. You have to implement more interfaces for a control than for a DLL. You'll learn more about creating ActiveX controls with VB6 in Chapter 7.

Visual Basic Object Specifics

An *object* is a unit of code and data you can access, manipulate, and reuse. An object is composed of two types of entities. First, the object has procedures or members, called *methods*, that define the tasks the object can perform. Second, the object has variables, called *properties*, that you use to return or set attributes of the object.

As we discussed earlier in this chapter, an object is an instance of a class. Multiple instances of a class are created, or *instantiated*, at runtime with the same inherent methods and default property settings with which you designed the class.

Now that you understand objects a little better, let's look at some VB-specific points regarding the concept of instantiating a class:

- When you take a control or class from the toolbox and add it to a Form object, Visual Basic creates an object (an instance of that class).
- You can create an object instance of some classes with the **As New** syntax. The following statement creates a new object instance of the **Form** class:

```
Dim Form2 As New Form1
```

- You can create an object instance of public classes within COM components by using Visual Basic's **CreateObject** function. First, declare an object variable, and then use **CreateObject** to assign an object instance to the variable, as shown here:

```
Dim Dialog As Object

Set Dialog = CreateObject("EFSD.Dialog")
```

- Once an object instance of a class exists, you can modify the default settings of the class's properties.
- You can instantiate all the controls as objects, but not all the object instances of classes are controls. For example, the DAO syntax of Visual Basic's Jet database engine includes several classes, but the great majority of these DAO classes are not controls.

Collection Objects

A *collection* is an object that contains a related set of objects. An object's position within the collection can change whenever a change occurs within the Collection object. Therefore, the position of any specific object within the collection may vary. All Collection objects have a single property, **Count**, that specifies the number of items within the collection. Collection objects that you instantiate have three methods: **Add**, **Item**, and **Remove**. Visual Basic itself has several Collection objects within its object hierarchy. Visual Basic's built-in Collection objects have no methods and only one property: **Count**.

Visual Basic's Built-In Collection Objects

Visual Basic's three built-in Collection objects—**Controls**, **Forms**, and **Printers**—support the **Count** property, but they do not have the methods associated with the Collection objects you create. Let's briefly discuss Visual Basic's Collection objects:

- *Controls Collection object*—The items within this Collection object represent each control object on a Form object, including elements of control arrays. You can use the **Controls** Collection object to iterate through all the loaded control objects on a Form object.

- *Forms Collection object*—The items within this Collection object represent each loaded Form object (that is, the MDIForm object, MDI child Form objects, and non-MDIForm objects) within an application. You can use the **Forms** Collection object to iterate through all the loaded Form objects.

- *Printers Collection object*—The items within this Collection object represent all the available printers on the system. The **Printers** Collection object lets you query the available printers to specify a default printer for your application.

Creating And Using Collection Objects

You can instantiate your own Collection objects from Visual Basic's **Collection** class. Those that you create, in addition to having the **Count** property, have the **Add**, **Item**, and **Remove** methods.

Because a Collection object stores its items as **Variant** data types, it can store data of almost any type, including the **Object** data type. You can even have a Collection object that stores other Collection objects, letting you create very complex and powerful data structures. You can also use a Collection object to simulate a control array, which lets you mix various kinds of controls into the Collection object.

You can instantiate your own Collection objects from Visual Basic's Collection class by using the **As New** syntax:

```
Dim Ctls As New Collection
```

Once you create the object, the **Count** property returns the number of items within the Collection object:

```
Print Ctls.Count
```

You work with a Collection object by using its methods. You add items to the Collection object with the **Add** method and delete items from the object with the **Remove** method. For example, you could clone Visual Basic's built-in **Controls** Collection object with the following snippet:

```
' Variables:
Dim Ctl     As Variant
Dim Ctls    As New Collection

For Each Ctl In Form1.Controls
    Ctls.Add Ctl
Next Ctl

Print Ctls.Count
```

Although a Collection object does not have a **Clear** method, you can clear the contents of the object by setting the object variable containing the Collection object to **Nothing**. In addition, you can return specific items from the Collection object, either by key or by position, with the **Item** method.

A Collection object has features of both an array, because it contains a set of items, and a ListBox object, because it provides a predefined set of methods (**Add**, **Item**, and **Remove**) to process its items. However, a Collection object is more useful and flexible than an array in cases where you must add or remove items.

Overview Of A ClassModule Object

Visual Basic supplies the ClassModule (*filename*.CLS) object to enable you to create your own classes and reusable objects. You use a ClassModule object to define a class that can contain members, which you code by using **Event**, **Function**, **Sub**, and **Property** procedures.

You can have several different ClassModule objects within a single Visual Basic project.

A ClassModule object is similar to a standard (.BAS) module. However, you can call and return or set the members within a ClassModule object from any other Visual Basic project without physically loading them into the project. Depending on the types of arguments a specific method or property within a ClassModule object takes, you can also call some of them from other applications or languages that are OLE Automation client-enabled. When Visual Basic compiles a project containing a ClassModule object, it can automatically create a COM component and register this component with the Windows registration database.

A ClassModule object is a unique kind of object within the Visual Basic object hierarchy. You add a ClassModule object to a Visual Basic project by selecting Project|Add Class Module. In several respects, a ClassModule object behaves much like a standard module. You write procedures within it that are considered its members. These members can be either methods (procedures that you create with the **Function** or **Sub** statement), properties (procedures that you create with the **Property Let**, **Property Get**, or **Property Set** statement), or events (procedures that you create with VB6's new **Event** statement).

A ClassModule object defines only one class; however, you can have more than one ClassModule within a project, so you can create as many classes as your design requires. Using ClassModule objects, you can assemble classes, with their members, into a hierarchical class model. This class model can include custom collections, built with Visual Basic's Collection object.

You can use a ClassModule object in several ways within a Visual Basic project. However, there are three general kinds of applications that you most commonly use them in. First, you can use one within a normal project that runs as an executable file. Second, you can make the project that contains one into a special kind of EXE or DLL file called an *ActiveX component*. Third, you can use one as part of a Visual Basic add-in application. In this book, we use ClassModule objects primarily in the second way, as part of the class library's ActiveX component, but we also examine how to use them as part of a normal EXE file or an add-in.

ActiveX components expose the public members of their ClassModule objects to development tools, macro languages, and other applications that can function as OLE Automation clients. Visual Basic, Visual C++, Excel, Project, and Access are all examples of OLE Automation client-enabled applications that can reuse members of a ClassModule object.

The Object Browser is Microsoft's preferred utility for viewing the type or class libraries encapsulated within an ActiveX component. The Object Browser makes it very easy to view the reusable members of a class library, and it lets you determine how to call them by looking at the type libraries.

You can think of Visual Basic classes as a foreign country. At the beginning of a journey to an unknown place, many people try to get a feel for what the country is like by looking at photographs of the indigenous peoples who live there and the cultural artifacts they share. Before you start to learn how to create classes with Visual Basic and instantiate and use them as objects within your code, it's a good idea to take a look at that foreign country.

The best way to see snapshots of what Microsoft's Visual Basic OOP paradigm can accomplish is to view existing ActiveX components and the classes they contain. You can do this from Visual Basic by opening the Object Browser dialog box. We'll view a group of libraries/classes/members from the Object Browser, those constituting VB6.

Start a new project in Visual Basic and select View | Object Browser (or press F2) to display the Object Browser dialog box. Then follow these steps to view the VB6 ActiveX component and the classes and members it contains:

1. From the All Libraries list, select VB. The Object Browser fills the other lists with information about the Visual Basic ActiveX components.
2. From the Classes list, select CheckBox. The Object Browser fills the Members list with the members of Visual Basic's **CheckBox** class/object.
3. From near the bottom of the Members list, select Drag. The Object Browser appears, as shown in Figure 1.3.

At this point, you have drilled down through the hierarchy of the Object Browser to its lowest level, which is made up of the members of the class. The Members list shows three kinds of members: properties, methods, and events. You can view these members either grouped by the

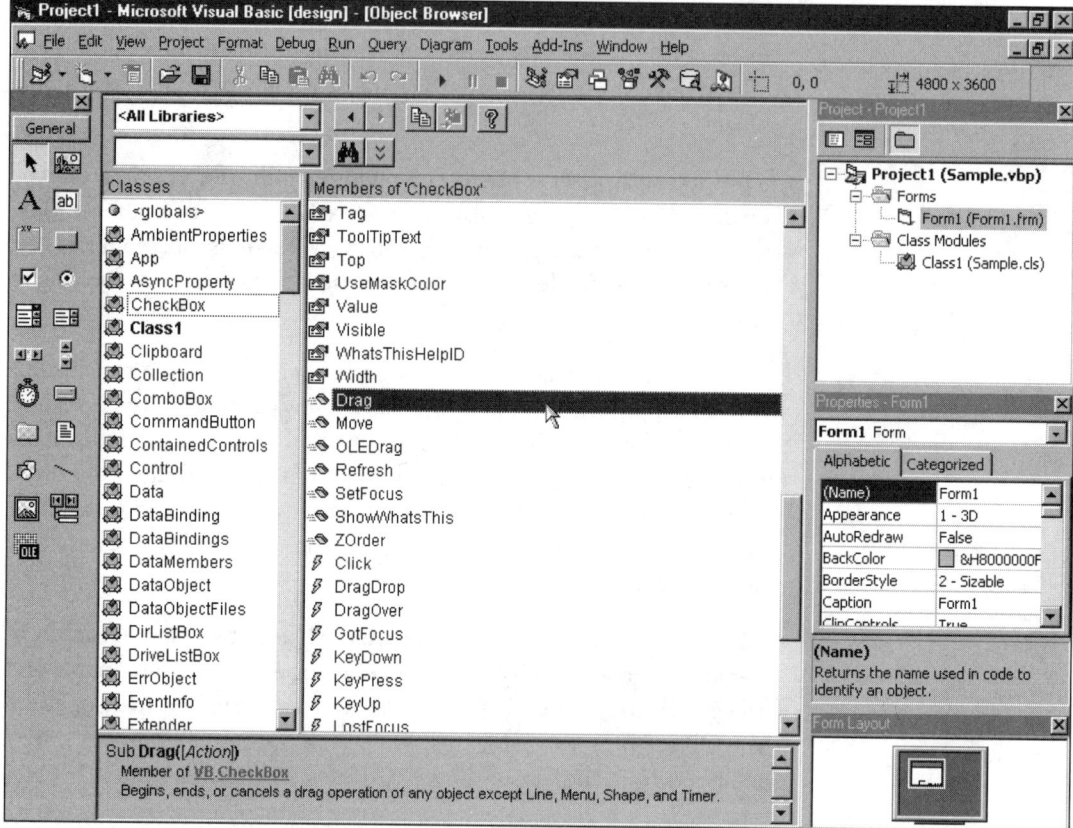

Figure 1.3
Viewing the **Drag** method of the **CheckBox** class with the Object Browser.

three categories (the default view) or sorted alphabetically. To change the order in which the Object Browser lists the members, right-click on the Members list and select or deselect the Group Members item on the pop-up menu. If the Object Browser lists the members by group, the order they appear in is properties, then methods, then events. Each group has its own icon. Select the **Drag** method from the method's group and click on the yellow question mark button within the Object Browser's toolbar to see the method's associated Help topic, which is shown in Figure 1.4.

To see the objects (that is, instantiated classes) to which you can apply this method, click on the Applies To hotspot on the Help topic. Because of polymorphism, you can apply a member to more than one object. The **Drag** method, for example, applies to more than 25 objects. To see sample code that demonstrates how to use the method, click on the Example hotspot.

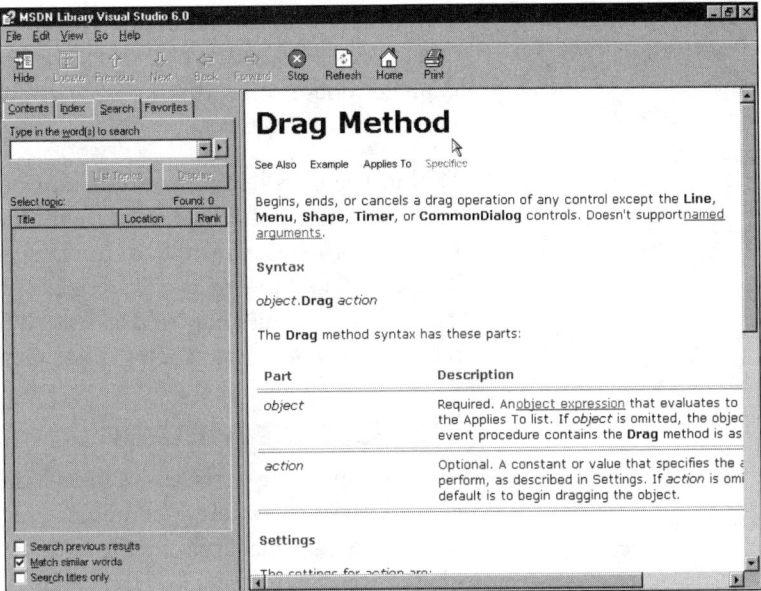

Figure 1.4
Learning more about the **Drag** method.

You'll learn more about the Object Browser in Chapter 4, and you'll read about creating a ClassModule object and adding methods to it in Chapter 3.

Polymorphism In Visual Basic Applications

If two or more classes have methods that share the same name, take the same arguments, and have the same basic purpose, but are implemented differently, the methods are said to be *polymorphic*. *Polymorphism* is the ability to hide the implementation details of a method behind a common public interface. A client application programmer can call and apply a polymorphic method to different objects without knowing anything about how the method is implemented. Polymorphism enables the object-oriented programmer to simplify the public interface to a class library by minimizing the number of different methods. For example, instead of having a **CenterForm** method, a **CenterPictureBox** method, and so on, there's just the **Center** method. Polymorphism makes the maintenance of legacy code easier and promotes reuse of the objects within a class library by client application programmers.

Polymorphism hides the complexity of the method from the client application programmer. For example, there are obviously major differences between the code you would write to center a Form object on the screen, an MDI child form on an MDIForm object, or an Image object on a PictureBox object. However, the client application programmer does not need to know anything about these differences to use the **Center** method.

Within the class library found on this book's companion CD-ROM, there are three polymorphic methods: **Center**, **Load**, and **Save**. The **Center** method is a member of the **Dialog**, **Graphic**, and **List** classes. The **Load** and **Save** methods are members of the **Graphic**, **List**, and **Text** classes. In this chapter, we focus on the **Center** and **Load** methods as they apply to the **Dialog**, **List**, and **Graphic** classes.

The Center Method

The **Center** method centers certain Visual Basic objects within the client area of their parent/container objects. "The **Center** Method's Specifications" sidebar shows the topic within the class library's Help file (EFS.HLP) that specifies the detailed functionality of the **Center** method.

The Center Method's Specifications

Syntax

```
Object.Center(Obj)
```

The **Center** method's syntax has the following object qualifier and named arguments:

- *Object*—Required. **Object** data type. An expression that evaluates to an object within the Applies To pop-up list.
- *Obj*—Required. **Object** data type. An expression that evaluates to the **Name** property of a Visual Basic object within the Applies To pop-up list. The supported objects are Form, MDIForm, ComboBox, DBCombo, DBList, ListBox, Image, and PictureBox.

Called

The **Center** method is called from any procedure within a client application; however, for a Form or MDIForm object, it's normally called from the **Load** event procedure.

Returns

The **Center** method, upon success, returns one element in a **Variant** data type. It contains a **Boolean** data type (**True**) that specifies whether the member executed successfully.

The **Center** method, upon failure, returns eight elements in a **Variant** data type. The elements contain the error codes the class library returns when a runtime or syntax error occurs during the execution of one of its members.

Object-Oriented Programming And Visual Basic

Remarks

The **Center** method can produce unexpected results when you display a large form designed at a high resolution (for example, 1024x768) on a lower-resolution monitor at runtime:

- If the design time **ScaleHeight** property of the form is greater than the height of the Screen object, Visual Basic sets the **ScaleHeight** of the form to the height of the Screen object so that the form fits. However, Visual Basic does not display any controls on the form whose **Top** property is greater than the height of the Screen object.
- If the design time **ScaleWidth** property of the form is greater than the width of the Screen object, Visual Basic sets the **ScaleWidth** of the form to the width of the Screen object so that the form fits. However, Visual Basic does not display any controls on the form whose **Left** property is greater than the width of the Screen object.
- If both the **ScaleHeight** and **ScaleWidth** properties of the form at design time are greater than the height and width of the Screen object, Visual Basic maximizes the form. However, Visual Basic does not display any controls on the form whose **Top** property is greater than the height of the Screen object or whose **Left** property is greater than the width of the Screen object.

The *Center* Method's Code: *Graphic/List* Classes

Except for the syntax-checking code, which verifies that one of the supported Visual Basic objects is passed to the method's **Obj** argument, the code for the **Center** method of the **Graphic** and **List** classes is functionally the same. Listing 1.1 shows the code for the implementation within the **Graphic** class.

Listing 1.1 The Center method's code: Graphic class.

```
Function Center(Obj As Object)

    ' Constant for literals:
    Const PROC = "Center"
    Const SYNTAX = True
    Const ONE_HALF = 0.5

    ' Variables:
    Dim OrigScaleMode    As Byte
    Dim ParWid           As Long
    Dim ParHgt           As Long
    Dim Rct              As RECT

    ' Enable error handler and do syntax checking:
    On Error GoTo ET

    If TypeName(Obj) <> "Image" And _
        TypeName(Obj) <> "PictureBox" Then
        Error.TrapSyntax 8, PROC, "Obj"
    End If
```

```
' Execute member's algorithm
' * Store original ScaleMode setting and temporarily
'   convert to twips.
' * Get client coordinates of control object's parent.
' * Compute height and width of client portion of parent
'   and convert pixels to twips (15 twips per pixel).
' * Compute X and Y coordinates of control to center.
' * Restore original ScaleMode setting.
OrigScaleMode = Obj.Container.ScaleMode
Obj.Container.ScaleMode = vbTwips
GetClientRect Obj.Container.hWnd, Rct
ParWid = (Rct.Rgt - Rct.Lft) * Screen.TwipsPerPixelY
ParHgt = (Rct.Bot - Rct.Top) * Screen.TwipsPerPixelX
Obj.Left = (ParWid - Obj.Width) * ONE_HALF
Obj.Top = (ParHgt - Obj.Height) * ONE_HALF
Obj.Container.ScaleMode = OrigScaleMode

Center = Array(True)
Exit Function

ET:

If Err = SYNTAX Then Center = frmErrCodes.Codes
If Err <> SYNTAX Then Center = CL.TrapErr(PROC)

End Function
```

The **Center** *Method's Code:* **Dialog** *Class*

The code for the **Center** method of the **Dialog** class, shown in Listing 1.2, is functionally quite different from that of the **Center** method of the **Graphic** and **List** classes.

Listing 1.2   The Center method's code: Dialog class.

```
Function Center(Obj As Object)

    ' Constants for literals:
    Const PROC = "Center"
    Const SYNTAX = True
    Const ONE_HALF = 0.5

    ' Variables:
    Dim ChildFrm    As Boolean
    Dim ParWid      As Long
    Dim ParHgt      As Long
    Dim Rct         As RECT
```

```
' Enable error handler and do syntax checking:
On Error GoTo ET

If Not CL.IsForm(Obj) And Not _
       CL.IsMDIForm(Obj) Then
           E.TrapSyntax 8, PROC, "Obj"
End If

' * If Frm argument is MDI child:
'    a) Get handle of MDIForm object and client coordinates.
'    b) Compute height and width of client portion of
'       MDIForm and convert pixels to twips.
'    c) Compute X and Y coordinates of MDI child to center.
' * If Frm argument is not MDI child, compute against
'   Screen.
' * Center Form object using Left (X) and Top (Y)
'   properties.
On Error Resume Next

If Obj.MDIChild Then

    If Err = False Then
       ChildFrm = True
       GetClientRect GetParent(Obj.hWnd), Rct
       ParWid = (Rct.Rgt - Rct.Lft) * Screen.TwipsPerPixelY
       ParHgt = (Rct.Bot - Rct.Top) * Screen.TwipsPerPixelX
       Obj.Left = (ParWid - Obj.Width) * ONE_HALF
       Obj.Top = (ParHgt - Obj.Height) * ONE_HALF
    End If

End If

If Not ChildFrm Then
    Obj.Left = (Screen.Width - Obj.Width) * ONE_HALF
    Obj.Top = (Screen.Height - Obj.Height) * ONE_HALF
End If

Center = Array(True)
Exit Function

ET:
   If Err = SYNTAX Then Center = frmErrCodes.Codes
   If Err <> SYNTAX Then Center = CL.TrapErr(PROC)

End Function
```

If you examine the code for the **Center** method within the **Graphic** and **List** classes, you'll notice how similar it is. You might wonder whether there's any advantage in consolidating all the code of the various implementations in one member within the **CL** class. It's possible to do this and then call the **Center** method of the **CL** class from the three public classes that contain the **Center** method.

In the case of the **Center** method, the number of lines of redundant code is so small that the possible reduction in size of the ActiveX component's file (DLL or EXE) is immaterial. Likewise, maintenance of the class library's code base is not made significantly easier. However, for another polymorphic method, which might apply to several different classes and be much more complex in its implementation, it might make sense to implement the details of the different algorithms within a method of the **CL** class. In that case, several instances of the polymorphic method in the public classes function essentially as wrapper procedures. The only code that the wrapper procedures include performs syntax checking, makes the call to the member of the **CL** class, and returns the result of the method to the client application.

Before you consider implementing an approach that uses wrapper methods within the public classes and a single, one-holds-all functionality class within a private class, such as **CL**, you should consider the potential disadvantages. First, there's no improvement in performance; if anything, performance degrades slightly. Second, whatever reduction in the size of the ActiveX component's file(s) you achieve is essentially immaterial, given an era when hard drives are incredibly large and cheap (and getting larger and cheaper all the time). Third, any reduction in the amount of RAM required to handle the instantiated classes of the ActiveX component is also immaterial. The Intel Pentium or Pentium Pro hardware platforms that will be typical of the desktop or workstation machine within a couple years will make almost all questions regarding available RAM obsolete. In short, when you're tempted to violate the OOP attribute of encapsulation to save a little RAM or hard drive space, think long and hard before doing so.

The Load Method

The **Load** method loads a file into certain Visual Basic objects. "The **Load** Method's Specifications" sidebar shows the topic within the class library's Help file (EFS.HLP) that specifies the detailed functionality of the **Load** method.

The Load Method's Specifications
Syntax

```
Object.Load(Obj, File, [LockFile])
```

The **Load** method's syntax has the following object qualifier and named arguments:

- *Object*—Required. **Object** data type. An expression that evaluates to an object within the Applies To pop-up list.
- *Obj*—Required. **Object** data type. An expression that evaluates to the **Name** property of a Visual Basic object in the Applies To pop-up list. The supported objects are Form, Image, PictureBox, ComboBox, ListBox, RichTextBox, and TextBox.
- *File*—Required. **String** data type. An expression that specifies the path and name of a file to load into **Obj**.
- *LockFile*—Optional. **Variant** data type whose subtype is a numeric expression that evaluates to **True**. If **LockFile** is passed, no other application can open the loaded file until it is closed by the client application.

Called

The **Load** method is called from any procedure within a client application.

Returns

The **Load** method, upon success, returns two elements within a **Variant** data type. The elements contain these subtypes:

- **0 - MBR_SUCCESS**. A **Boolean** data type (**True**) that specifies whether the member executed successfully.
- **1 - MBR_FILENBR**. An **Integer** data type that specifies the file number of the loaded file. If the **LockFile** argument is omitted, the value of this element is **vbEmpty** (that is, uninitialized).

The **Load** method, upon failure, returns eight elements within a **Variant** data type. The elements contain the error codes that the class library returns when a runtime or syntax error occurs during the execution of one of its members.

Remarks

- The **Load** method applies to the class library's Graphic object only under 32-bit Visual Basic.
- You can use the **OpenCL** method of the File object to provide the user with a common dialog box to specify the path and name of the file to pass to the **File** argument of the **Load** method.
- If you pass the **LockFile** argument, you must store the file number the **Load** method returns if you want to later replace the original file with the **Save** method.
- When you use the **Load** method with a ComboBox or ListBox object, the plain ASCII text file you load must delimit the items of the list with a carriage return character (that is, **vbCr**). If the **Save** method of the **List** class is used to create the text file, the delimiters are automatically added.
- When you use the **Load** method with a RichTextBox object, you have the option of loading a Rich Text Format (RTF) file either as rich text or as plain ASCII text.

The *Load* Method's Code: **Graphic** Class

Listing 1.3 shows the code for the implementation of the **Load** method within the **Graphic** class.

Listing 1.3   The Load method's code: Graphic class.

```
Function Load(Obj As Object, _
              File As String, _
              Optional LockWrite)

    ' Constants for literals:
    Const PROC = "Load"
    Const SYNTAX = True
    Const VALID_FILE_EXTS = "(.BMP or .ICO or .WMF)."

    ' Variables:
    Dim Msg         As String
    Dim SrcPath     As String
    Dim FileExt     As String
    Dim LockFile    As Boolean
    Dim FileNbr     As Integer

    ' Enable error handler and do syntax checking:
    On Error GoTo ET

    #If Win16 Then
        E.TrapSyntax 1, PROC, "16-bit VB"
    #End If

    If Not CL.IsForm(Obj) Then

        If TypeName(Obj) <> "Image" And _
           TypeName(Obj) <> "PictureBox" Then
            E.TrapSyntax 8, PROC, "Obj"
        End If

    End If

    CL.IsPath1 File, PROC, "File", SrcPath
    CL.IsFile File, SrcPath, PROC, "File"
    FileExt = UCase$(Right$(File, 4))

    Select Case FileExt
        Case ".BMP", ".ICO", ".WMF"
        Case Else
            E.TrapSyntax 19, PROC, "File", VALID_FILE_EXTS
    End Select
```

Object-Oriented Programming And Visual Basic

```
' Execute member's algorithm
' * If LockWrite argument is passed, turn on flag.
' * Load graphic file into object.
' * If LockFile flag is on, open file in Lock Write
'   mode.
' * NOTE: This opening of file to lock it is "kludge"
'   required by fact that VB's LoadPicture method does
'   not provide file-locking option.
' * If any runtime error occurs, substitute generic
'   error message "Can't perform requested operation" and
'   add a little information to it. This is better than
'   displaying many possible runtime errors that can
'   occur when opening/loading file.
If Not IsMissing(LockWrite) Then LockFile = True

CL.SetHourglass True
Obj.Picture = LoadPicture(File)

If LockFile Then
    FileNbr = FreeFile
    Open File For Input Lock Write As FileNbr
End If

CL.SetHourglass False
Load = Array(True, FileNbr)
Exit Function

ET:

CL.SetHourglass False

If Err = SYNTAX Then Load = frmErrCodes.Codes
If Err <> SYNTAX Then
    Err.Number = 17
    Msg = "Can't perform requested operation. "
    Msg = Msg & "Can't load file into "

    If CL.IsForm(Obj) Then
       Msg = "Form."
    Else

        If TypeName(Obj) = "Image" Then
           Msg = Msg & "Image control."
        Else
           Msg = Msg & "PictureBox control."
        End If

    End If
```

```
            Err.Description = Msg
            Err.HelpContext = 1000017
            Load = CL.TrapErr(PROC)
        End If

End Function
```

Three points should be noted concerning the code of the **Load** method of the **Graphic** class. First, the syntax-checking code checks the extension of the **File** argument to determine if the file contains a bitmap, icon, or metafile. However, the determination is made strictly on the basis of the nominal extension; if someone renames a graphics file and, in the process, changes the extension from .ICO to something besides .BMP or .WMF, the **Load** method rejects the **File** argument as invalid. Second, because the **Load** method uses Visual Basic's **LoadPicture** function, which does not provide a file-locking option, the **FreeFile** function and **Open** statement are used to obtain a file number for a dummy file that is opened as write-locked. This file number is then returned from the **Load** method to the client application. Third, several different runtime errors can occur in the process of using Visual Basic's **LoadPicture** function and **Open** statement. Rather than confuse the client application's user by displaying different runtime error messages at different times, the **Load** method substitutes the generic runtime error 17 "Can't perform requested operation" and appends the string "Can't load file into *kind* control" to the error message, where *kind* can be either a Form, Image, or PictureBox object. Chapter 6 discusses error handling within Visual Basic programs.

The **Load** *Method's Code:* **List** *Class*

Listing 1.4 shows the code for the implementation of the **Load** method in the **List** class.

Listing 1.4   The Load method's code: List class.
```
Function Load(Obj As Object, _
              File As String, _
              Optional LockWrite)

    ' Constants for literals:
    Const PROC = "Load"
    Const SYNTAX = True
    Const ADJ = 1
    Const VALID_FILE_EXT = ".TXT"
```

```vb
' Variables:
Dim Msg         As String
Dim SrcPath     As String
Dim FileText    As String
Dim LockFile    As Boolean
Dim FileNbr     As Integer
Dim Pos         As Long
Dim Item        As Long

' Enable error handler and do syntax checking:
On Error GoTo ET

If TypeName(Obj) <> "ComboBox" And _
   TypeName(Obj) <> "ListBox" Then
      E.TrapSyntax 8, PROC, "Obj"
End If

CL.IsPath1 File, PROC, "File", SrcPath
CL.IsFile File, SrcPath, PROC, "File"

If UCase$(Right$(File, 4)) <> VALID_FILE_EXT Then
   E.TrapSyntax 11, PROC, "File", VALID_FILE_EXT
End If

' Execute member's algorithm
' * If LockWrite argument is passed, turn on flag.
' * Depending on flag's setting, open file in correct
'   mode and assign file's contents to variable.
' * Assuming that text file was saved with Save method
'   (that is, for each line delimited by carriage return):
'   a) Add line to list.
'   b) Strip that line and carriage return.
'   c) Increment counter.
'   d) Repeat until end of file.
' * If LockFile flag is not on, close file.
' * If any runtime error occurs, substitute generic
'   error message "Can't perform requested operation" and
'   add a little information to it. This is better than
'   displaying many possible runtime errors that can
'   occur when opening/loading file.
CL.SetHourglass True

If Not IsMissing(LockWrite) Then LockFile = True

FileNbr = FreeFile
```

```
        If LockFile Then
            Open File For Input Lock Write As FileNbr
        Else
            Open File For Input As FileNbr
        End If

        Do Until EOF(FileNbr)
            FileText = Input$(LOF(FileNbr), FileNbr)
        Loop

        Obj.Clear
        Pos = ADJ

        Do Until Pos = False Or FileText = vbNullString
            Pos = InStr(FileText, vbCr)
            Obj.AddItem Left$(FileText, Pos - ADJ)
            FileText = Mid$(FileText, Pos + ADJ + ADJ)
            Item = Item + 1
        Loop

        If Not LockFile Then Close FileNbr

        CL.SetHourglass False
        Load = Array(True, FileNbr)
        Exit Function

ET:

        CL.SetHourglass False

        If Err = SYNTAX Then Load = frmErrCodes.Codes
        If Err <> SYNTAX Then
            Err.Number = 17
            Msg = "Can't perform requested operation. "
            Msg = Msg & "Can't load file into "

            If TypeName(Obj) = "ComboBox" Then
                Msg = Msg & "ComboBox control."
            Else
                Msg = Msg & "ListBox control."
            End If

            Err.Description = Msg
            Err.HelpContext = 1000017
            Load = CL.TrapErr(PROC)
        End If

End Function
```

Besides the points noted previously regarding the **Load** method of the **Graphic** class, you need to know something else about the **Load** method of the **List** class. The syntax-checking code checks the extension of the **File** argument to determine if the file contains ASCII text. However, the determination is made strictly on the basis of the nominal extension .TXT; if someone renames the text file and, in the process, changes the extension from .TXT to something else, the **Load** method rejects the **File** argument as invalid.

The Benefits Of Object-Oriented Programming

One of the major benefits of object-oriented programming is its potential for improving the frequency of code reuse. However, the degree to which your objects and methods are reused depends a lot on how easy the public interface is for another programmer/tester to use and call externally. Testing and debugging members internally is like a practice for an athletic team. Every coach knows the rubber doesn't hit the road until game time. Likewise, you cannot put a class library and its members to the acid test unless you test them externally.

A great book on reuse is Paul Bassett's *Framing Software Reuse: Lessons from the Real World* (which is listed in Appendix A). We strongly suggest you locate this resource. Ed Yourdon, an authority on software development, says in the book's foreword that Bassett has written the best book on reuse. In this book, Bassett cites the following statistics:

♦ The traditional reuse techniques, properly implemented by using the object-oriented development methodology, typically achieve reuse rates of anywhere from 10 to 50 percent of the code within an entire project.

♦ Component-based application frameworks, when properly designed and implemented in conjunction with object-oriented programming, can achieve reuse rates of up to 80 percent of a project's code.

♦ A study of 15 projects from 9 companies found that component-based application frameworks, on average, reduced schedules by 70 percent and development costs by 84 percent, compared to industry norms.

These statistics document the percentage of reuse achieved through the proper use of OOP methodologies and application frameworks. The claims are quite impressive. However, as you well know, statistics can be made to say or do almost anything in the hype-dominated world of computer programming and development.

The Future Of OOP And COM Components

If Microsoft maintains its dominance of the PC operating system platform arena well into the future, the next logical step is that the COM component model will soon come to dominate object-oriented development. Object-oriented analysis, design, and development are not passing fancies. In conjunction with the client/server, three-tier, and distributed objects models, object-oriented programming will be the dominant development methodology for large-scale projects for the next couple of decades, at least. You cannot find any major figure within software manufacturing or computer science, from Bill Gates to Steve Jobs to Edward Yourdon to Donald Knuth, who does not wholeheartedly believe that this is the best way to write software.

Visual Basic has changed significantly over its lifetime (about seven years). It started out as simply an easier way to write bare-bones Windows applications; however, it has now evolved to the point where its Enterprise edition can support even the largest-scale development projects that embody the following features:

- Client/server, three-tier, and distributed objects architectures
- Object-oriented analysis, design, and development
- ActiveX controls
- COM components/servers

The last feature, COM components, is the most important one of the four. If you consider, for example, what a three-tier or distributed objects architecture involves, you can visualize the separate hardware platforms running three different kinds of software models: the client's GUI, the server's data warehouse, and the middle tier's business rules.

However, what's most important to understand about this three-tier model is that each tier (including the nominal client), at a lower level of abstraction, will actually be written and programmed as a COM component. Each tier conforms to a different model and serves a different business purpose; however, in Microsoft's vision of the object-oriented future, each tier has in common with the other two the fact that it is implemented as a COM component.

There are no exceptions to this COM component-dominated model. The operating system and personal-use applications (such as the Microsoft Office suite, departmental/divisional or enterprise networks, data repositories, programming languages, and development tools) will all be written to the COM software protocol. Sure, one software entity is a server and another is a client or controller (and, in the long run, who knows what other names); however, at an easily understood and high level of abstraction, each one will function and communicate with the others in the same fundamental ways:

- By messaging (the passing in of arguments to members and the returning of values back from them)
- By polling
- By callbacks

In the near future, it will be a truism that this communication process among COM components, residing on local/distributed/remote hardware platforms, cannot really be said to have a beginning (client) or ending (server) point, or an orientation.

Developers always enjoy debating which programming language is the best. For all practical purposes, in two to three years, that debate will be strictly academic. The answer to that question will be equivalent to the answer to this question: What is the easiest way to write and develop a COM component?

Conclusion

In this chapter, we started our journey into the world of object-oriented programming and Visual Basic 6. The rest of this book will guide you through the new syntax and tools the Enterprise edition of VB6 provides to create COM components.

The only essential difference between using an out-of-process component locally or using it remotely (that is, as a Remote Automation Object) has nothing to do with Visual Basic's syntax; rather, it's strictly a function of how the two COM components (client and remote) are registered. When you have mastered the techniques that the class library found on this book's companion CD-ROM demonstrates, you'll be on the cutting edge of Visual Basic object-oriented development.

We are guessing it will probably take another year or two for project managers to fully understand and become comfortable with the several capabilities of COM components, as Visual Basic embodies them. When project managers (and IS management personnel) have reached that point, a two-tier, wage-scale model will become the norm for Visual Basic programmers. The lower tier will consist of the majority of Visual Basic programmers—those who can write decent code but lack the training and experience required to write robust, commercial-quality COM components. The upper tier will consist of a minority of Visual Basic object-oriented developers, whose value in the marketplace is commensurate with their superior skills and development methodology. Which tier will you occupy?

Chapter 2
Designing Objects

Key Topics:

♦ *The Essence Of Objects*

♦ *The Importance Of Interfaces*

♦ *The Evil Of Public Variables*

♦ *Using Properties: Encapsulating Data To Keep It Safe*

♦ *Object-Oriented Design*

This chapter continues our journey into object-oriented programming. Chapter 1 explored the basics of object-oriented programming: encapsulation, polymorphism, inheritance, and classes. Here, we'll discuss the public portions of a class and why they are important. We begin by examining the power of the object and its public interface. Then, we'll look at some more advanced object-oriented programming concepts, such as data hiding, as well as some techniques for getting the most from these concepts. Finally, we'll venture into the world of design, where you'll learn how to implement objects and build a public interface for those objects.

The power of an object lies in its capability to enforce a sort of contract between the parts of a system. Similar to a contract that fully describes, in specific language, an agreement between two people, an object's public interface fully describes, in specific language, the agreement between the object and any other object or entity in the system on how to use the object.

The public interface (properties, methods, and events) defines the way the system interacts with the object. A properly designed object controls how you or anyone else can use it. A fully specified object, with all its properties, methods, method parameters, events, and event parameters, describes the specific data paths and information-passing mechanisms between itself and other objects and the system. Visual Basic enforces the contract by checking object types, property types, return types, and parameter types.

Visual Basic helps by enforcing the letter of the law. It can make sure you match up the numbers and types of parameters; however, it cannot make sure you use the methods and properties for their intended purpose. That is up to you as a disciplined developer.

The Essence Of Objects

The most powerful concepts in object-oriented programming are *encapsulation* and *data hiding*. Without these two ideas, the rest of the object-oriented paradigm breaks down. Encapsulation lets you gather related data and processing together into a single unit—the object. Data hiding lets you "hide" implementation details of an object from the outside world by concealing the information, data structures, variables, constants, and implementation.

Encapsulation

Encapsulation literally means placement in a capsule or inside a physical barrier. Encapsulation in object-oriented programming is essentially the same thing—the placement of data and processing into a capsule with a conceptual barrier. In the real world, pharmaceutical companies put a combination of medications that work together to relieve an ailment into a medicine capsule—a literal example of encapsulation. In software, a designer or programmer puts data and processing together into a conceptual unit called an *object*.

Data Hiding

With encapsulation, related data and operations are simply grouped together. A shell is created around the encapsulated items. Encapsulation, however, does not define which data or operations are visible from the outside. Defining which data or operations to hide from the world and which to make visible is known as *data hiding*.

Imagine a small digital clock that has a display and a button for setting the time. If you examine the clock, you realize it exposes a specific public (or visible) interface to the world—its "contract." It has a case, a display, and a button. What's really amazing, however, is what the clock is hiding. If you break open the clock, you'll find many parts—a battery, wires, a computer chip, and more. The little clock hides its innermost workings from the world.

You might be wondering how this example relates to object-oriented programming. Think for a moment: What if a battery that lasts forever were developed? You could change the battery in the clock and never affect how you use the clock. Even better: What if a new computer chip with a more accurate timing mechanism were developed? You could change the chip and have a better clock—again, without changing the interface! This same principle holds true in object-oriented programming. By hiding the implementation in a class and exposing only the elements necessary to interact with the outside, you control the class's inner workings. If you come up with a better implementation for your class, the interface need not change. This way, any objects or code that use your class do not have to change, but they benefit from the improved class.

Object Vs. Class

Objects are actual things—a ball, a clock, or anything that performs work in a software system. *Classes* are abstractions of objects; they describe a group of objects. For example, the previous clock description is actually a class. The clock's properties can have different values. For example, if you have two clocks—one red and one white—you would create two instances of the class, one for each clock. You assign one clock object the color red and the other the color white. When you perform object-oriented design or program an object, you're actually describing a class. The class represents the data that describes the object.

The Essence Of Visual Basic

Visual Basic supplies the *class module* to support encapsulation. Software designers and programmers use class modules to describe and implement the "capsules" in a project. Just like the medicine capsule puts a barrier between the medicine and the outside world, the class module puts a barrier between your code and the outside world.

Class modules also provide data hiding. In our previous example, the clock hides the details of how it works from the world, but it shows a visible interface. The class module provides a mechanism for defining the *public* (or *visible*) interface of the object. The **Public** keyword preceding any variable, property, event, sub, or function makes the variable, event, sub, or function visible to anyone using the object. When you define public variables and properties, you define the visible data elements of an object. Conversely, when you define a public sub or function, you define the visible processing or actions on an object. Events, however, are another matter. The properties, subs, and functions in an object are called *incoming interfaces* to the object. That is, they are invoked from outside the object. Events, on the other hand, are called *outgoing interfaces*, because they are initiated from within an object and are handled outside the object.

These public elements define the outline of the object's "contract" with the world. This outline, along with the class module, makes up the essence of Visual Basic—objects.

The Importance Of Interfaces

We only know an object by what we see: its interface. The parts of an object that are visible limit the way we use and understand the object. In object-oriented programming, this is an important and very powerful characteristic. An object's public interface is described as a contract with the outside world, but what are the parts of the contract? Simply put, in Visual Basic, the parts of the contract are the public properties, methods, and events that describe the object. When a piece of software wants to use an object, it is limited by what the object wants the world to see. Visual Basic enforces the contract between software elements.

Visual Basic uses class modules and the power of public interfaces to implement various application types, including ActiveX controls, ActiveX components, DLLs, add-ins, and internal objects. The public properties, methods, and events exported from ActiveX applications become the public interface to the components, controls, add-ins, and so on.

Properties

Properties represent an object's data. Data that describes the object's current state or condition is represented by the object's properties. Properties describe such things as color, speed, height, weight, and relationships.

A property can be defined in Visual Basic in two primary ways: by using a public variable and by using a property declaration. Public variables give an object's users full control over a property—they can freely read the property for its value and change the value as desired. A property declared as a property procedure acts like a function or subroutine.

The Evil Of Public Variables

As previously stated, one of the ways to define a property is with a public variable. For example, when you declare a variable with the **Dim** keyword, Visual Basic declares it a public variable. However, you should declare public variables by using the **Public** keyword in the declaration. This makes the declaration explicit and easy to understand:

```
Public PropertyOne 'a public (visible) variable
Dim PropertyTwo    'a public (visible) variable
```

The **Private** keyword relegates the variable to module-level scope. A *private* (or *class*) variable is only visible in the class module or code module where you declare it:

```
Private ModuleVariable 'a private (hidden) module scope _
   variable
```

When an object uses a public variable to define a property, the object loses all control of the property. Loss of control of a property is significant, because the object no longer controls how the property is used. A good example is the clock. Suppose the clock has a color property—it comes in red, white, or blue. If you define the color property as a public variable, someone could set the color property to orange, which is an invalid value. The clock object would not complain, and the application would have an invalid clock.

Another disadvantage of public variables is readability. Using a public variable hides the fact that the variable is acting as a property. It's much clearer to declare a property by calling it a property.

The best way to deal with public variables is to avoid using them. Always use property procedures when defining properties to avoid any confusion or losing control of your object.

Using Properties: Encapsulating Data To Keep It Safe

Now that you've seen the evils of public variables, we'll take a look at how to use properties to keep control of an object. One of the best opportunities for avoiding errors in your applications comes from understanding how to define and use properties. Property procedures control everything from initialization to protecting the object from bad data.

Validation

A property procedure lets you validate the data values and data types sent to the property. The property can verify whether a value is valid; if it's not, the property can raise an appropriate error to avoid an error condition in the object. Visual Basic uses the **Let** property to provide write access to properties. The **Let** property acts like a sub, taking a single parameter that represents the new value for the property. You can write code in the sub to validate the new value before assigning it to the property. Here's an example:

```
Property Let Color(NewColor as String)
'assume theColor is a class variable
        If NewColor = "red" or
           NewColor = "white" or
           NewColor = "blue" then
        theColor = NewColor
    Else
       'raise error and don't change the color
    End if
End Property
```

For more generic style properties, such as the ones that take an object or a control, the property procedure can also validate the type of object or control sent to the property. Again, the property can raise the appropriate error when it receives an improper type.

Another form of validation is *range checking*. The property procedure lets you verify that any data sent to it is in a valid range. Here's an example:

```
Property Let Height(NewHeight As Integer)
   ' assume theHeight is a class variable
   ' defines the height of our clock
   If NewHeight >= 2 And NewHeight <= 8 Then
      theHeight = NewHeight
   Else
      ' raise error and do not set the height
   End If
End Property
```

Controlling Access

Another important aspect of property procedures is the enforcing of access restrictions. Access restrictions can include mode, verification or permission, and availability.

The *mode* is simply the data access direction. Properties can be in one of several modes: read-only, write-only, or read-write. Visual Basic lets you declare property procedures for each direction. A **Property Let** declaration defines the read procedure, and a **Property Get** declaration defines the write procedure. The access methods are discussed in detail in the next chapter.

Property procedures control *verification* (also called *permission*). Verification lets only certain entities, such as users or objects, access a property. When the property detects an invalid access attempt, it can take any desired appropriate action. Here's an example:

```
Property Let Height(NewHeight As Integer)
    ' assume theHeight is a class variable
    ' assume UserType is set when the user enters the system
    ' defines the height of our clock
        If UserType = "designer" Then
            If NewHeight >= 2 And NewHeight <= 8 Then
                theHeight = NewHeight
            Else
                ' raise error and do not set the height
            End If
        Else
            ' raise no permission to change value error
            ' do not set the height
        End If
End Property
```

Property procedures also control availability. In cases where property values rely on other properties or data, the property procedure can raise an error if it's accessed before the other property or data is available. Visual Basic uses a **Get** property to provide read access to properties. The **Get** property acts like a function, returning the value of the property. You can write code in the function to calculate or retrieve the value before returning it to the caller. Here's an example:

```
Property Get Width() As Integer
    ' Defines the width of our clock, width of our clock is
    ' simply twice the height
    If Height <> 0 Then
        Width = Height * 2
    Else
        ' assume the height is undefined
        ' raise error and do not calculate the width
    End If
End Property
```

Redirection

Redirection involves using storage methods other than a class variable to store a property's value. A property procedure can use other resources to store the property's value. Redirection hides the implementation and further enforces data hiding and encapsulation. Examples include a field in a database, a class variable, a local variable, collections, or any other storage mechanism necessary. Using redirection lets you control the internal implementation of a property. If you decide on a more efficient implementation or the database changes, you can change the property's implementation without affecting any code that uses the property. Here's an example:

```
Property Get Color() As String
    ' assume ClockRecord is a class variable of recordset
    If IsNull(ClockRecord("Color")) Then
        ClockRecord("Color") = "red"
    Else If Len(ClockRecord("Color")) = 0 Then
        ClockRecord("Color") = "red"
    End If
    Color = ClockRecord("Color")
End Property
```

Self-Initializing Properties

You can create self-initializing properties that increase the efficiency and maintainability of your code. The first time the property procedure is accessed, it can determine if the property has been previously accessed. If the property has not been previously accessed, the property procedure can initialize the property value before returning it to the user. Here's an example:

```
Property Get Color() As String
    ' assume theColor is a class variable
    If Len(theColor) = 0 Then
        theColor = "red"
    End If
    Color = theColor
End Property
```

Methods

Methods represent an object's behavior—that is, the things you can tell the object to do. Any action the object can take, or any action the object can react to, is represented by a method. Methods perform actions such as saving the object, copying the object, or deleting the object.

Visual Basic has two types of methods—functions and subroutines. *Functions* allow parameters and return values; *subroutines* allow parameters, perform some processing, and do not return values. Normally, a method causes some state change in the object—that is, it changes the values of one or more of the object's properties.

Events

Events represent the things an object does. You can write code to execute when an event occurs. Objects use events to return information such as the progress of a method or property that takes a long time to execute, notifying the system of important state changes, and other situations that may require immediate handling.

Events that return information are used to report progress during a lengthy method. This lets the system display a progress dialog box or progress bar.

An event can inform the system of important state changes. When an important property changes value, the object can raise an event to notify the calling module. This way, the calling module can display the change or take any other appropriate action.

Finishing The Contract: Getting The Details

An object's properties, methods, and events define the contract outline, but to fully define the contract, you must identify the property types, method parameters, and event parameters.

When the interface is fully specified, Visual Basic has the information it needs to enforce the contract. The Visual Basic IDE notifies you either through the editor or compiler when you violate an object's interface. This notification ensures that you use an object properly.

You have learned about the parts and importance of an object's public interface. But how do you know what you need to put in your object's public interface? More importantly, how do you find the objects in the first place? The next stop on our journey takes us into the world of object-oriented design, where you'll learn a simple but effective way to identify objects and their public interfaces.

Object-Oriented Design

Object-oriented design focuses on breaking a project or system into a cooperating group of objects. The Windows operating system lets designers implement objects in several different ways: ActiveX controls, ActiveX EXEs, ActiveX DLLs, and class modules used within standard programs. This chapter examines an effective way to get started in object-oriented design. This is not meant to be a comprehensive study of object-oriented methods and techniques, but rather a simple and powerful way to start exploring the subject.

You'll learn how to find objects within a system, identify their public properties and methods, and refine the contract by identifying the method parameters. Finally, we'll walk through an example using these techniques and examine how to apply it to larger projects.

Finding Objects

There's no simple way to find objects within a system; locating objects and designing their public interfaces and interactions are not easy tasks. There's no substitute for knowing your problem and subject. However, you do have some techniques available to help you get a handle on the system you're building. Here's a way to help you find objects within your system. It's up to you to determine if they apply to your specific problem or domain.

Describing The Problem

The first step in effective design is describing the problem you're solving. This may take the form of requirement lists, problem descriptions, or use cases—anything that gets the problem or system description on paper. For small, rather simple projects, it's beneficial to take the time to write a system description. Keep it in plain language so anyone can understand what the system is supposed to do. For larger projects, a more formal methodology, such as use cases or requirements analysis, is necessary. A *use case* defines a system from a user's point of view; it describes the steps a user performs to do his or her job. A *requirements analysis* results in a list of formal system requirements that state what the system does.

Any of these techniques is acceptable, as long as you get the description in writing. To find the objects, just analyze the descriptions. You'll also need to identify relationships between the objects and define the parameters for the methods.

A simple system description of the clock example might look something like this:

> Create a simple clock. The clock should let a person set and view the time. It should come in a variety of colors—namely, red, white, and blue. The clock should run on a battery and notify the owner when the battery is about to fail.

Finding Candidate Objects

Finding candidate objects is the next step. Begin by examining the system description for nouns. For descriptions or use cases that are several pages long, take it one paragraph or use case at a time. The nouns represent the items within the system—these are your candidate objects. Replace the pronouns (especially "it") within the sentence with the nouns they represent. Reexamine your description and find the subject of each sentence. The nouns within the subjects are the strongest object candidates.

Here's the clock system description with the nouns underlined and pronouns replaced:

> Create a simple clock. The clock should let a person set and view the time. It "The clock" should come in a variety of colors—namely, red, white, and blue. The clock should run on a battery and notify the owner when the battery is about to fail.

Here are just some of the object types you may identify:

- *Tangible objects*—Things you can touch. With your experience and domain knowledge, you can usually pick out these obvious objects.
- *Person/organization role*—Roles played by a person or organization in your problem.
- *Specification*—A model, template, or blueprint for an object. Examples include plans, house blueprints, and position descriptions.
- *Interaction*—An interaction or agreement between your entities. An example is an insurance policy, which represents an interaction between the policyholder and the insurance company.

Next, create a candidate object list. Look for duplicate nouns. If the description mentions a noun several times, it's a good candidate for an object. Use your understanding of the problem or system to pick out the nouns that play a role in the problem. These are your candidate objects.

Here's the candidate object list for the clock system description:

- clock
- person
- time
- color
- battery

Notice that "owner" is not a candidate object—it's a duplicate of "person" in this context.

Simple Tools

At this point in the process, you should start building a picture of your objects. Several good tools for creating object models are available on the market. For instance, Visual Basic comes with the Visual Modeler. The Visual Modeler lets you lay out, draw, and print classes for documentation. Refer to Chapter 4 for a detailed discussion of the Visual Modeler. It's too early now to employ a formal modeling language or tool. Instead, we'll use simple, "low-tech" tools, such as a whiteboard and sticky notes.

Take a sticky note and divide it into three parts: the object's name, properties, and methods (see Figure 2.1). Place the noun for each candidate object within the note's Name area and put the sticky note on the whiteboard. You'll use these notes to "build" your objects in later sections. You build your objects by placing the properties and methods on the note as you identify them.

As you identify objects and create a note for them, place these notes on your whiteboard. This way, it's easy to rearrange them as needed. The nice part about this method is that you're not limited by the way a tool models a solution—you have complete control and freedom. Another advantage to using the notes and whiteboard is the potential for collaboration—that is, more than one person can work on a model at a time, making for more discussion and added brainpower within the design.

Finding The Relationships

Relationships are very important to an object-oriented design. Relationships describe how objects connect and interact. The best way to find relationships is to look at the system description. Look for keywords such as "has" and "contains." For example: "A car has an engine and tires." The nouns within the sentence indicate that there are three

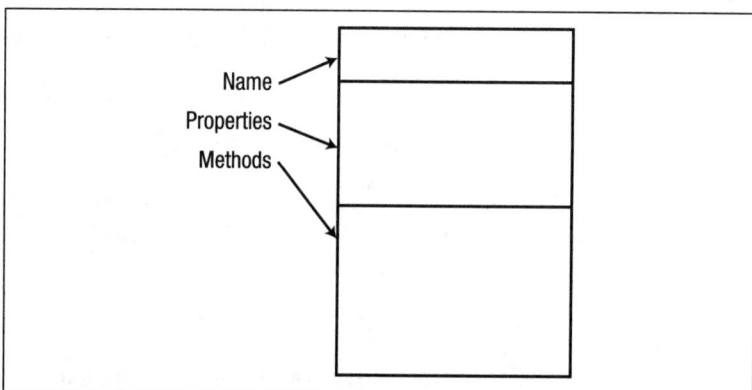

Figure 2.1
Sticky note partitioned for object-oriented design.

objects: a car, an engine, and tires. The sentence also identifies a *composite* (or "has") relationship between the car and the engine as well as the car and the tires. When you find a relationship, simply draw a line on the whiteboard between the related objects (see Figure 2.2).

Cardinality

Relationships are not always *one-to-one*, like a car to an engine. Many times, relationships are *one-to-many*, like a car to the tires, or *many-to-many*, like cars and drivers. Within a one-to-many relationship, cardinality represents the number of objects allowed within the "many" part of the relationship.

One way to detect one-to-many or many-to-many relationships is through plural nouns. If the nouns within the relationship are plural, they depict more than one object on one side of the relationship. The earlier example shows a one-to-many relationship between the car and its tires. Notice the plural form of "tires."

If you know the cardinality, write the number next to the object, as shown in Figure 2.3.

If you do not know the cardinality, write an infinity symbol next to the object. This way, you know if the relationship requires an object collection. Visual Basic does not directly support relationships. We'll discuss implementing relationships and object collections in Chapter 5.

Cutting To The Chase

You'll find that in a very short time you will be scanning system descriptions for objects and quickly creating object notes. Keep adding objects to your whiteboard. Later, if they do not fit, you can simply remove the notes.

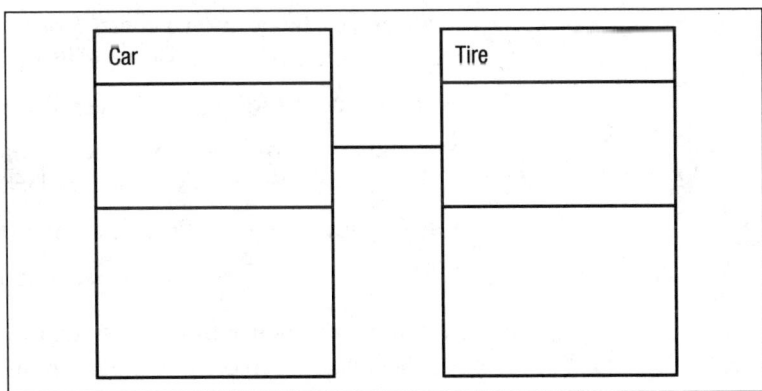

Figure 2.2
Showing relationships with object-oriented notes.

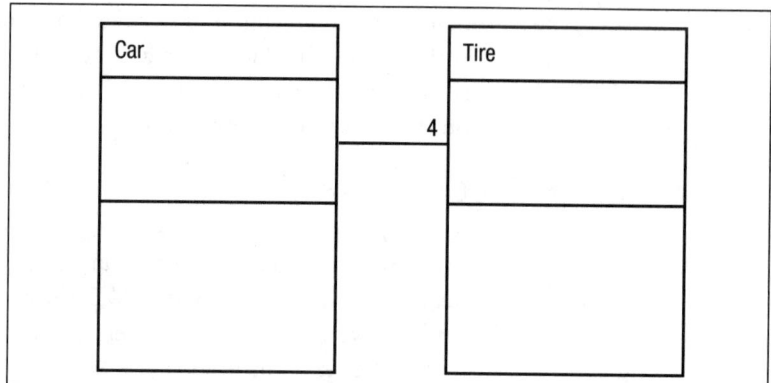

Figure 2.3
Showing relationships with cardinality.

As you identify more and more relationships, move the objects around the board and redraw the lines. This activity gives you time to think about the object model and how it all fits together. There's no substitute for thinking in object-oriented design.

When you finish identifying the objects, the next step is to identify the objects' properties and methods. In the following sections, you'll locate properties and methods and add them to your notes.

Identifying The Interface: Properties And Methods

Now that you have your objects, you need to find the outline to the contract—the public properties and methods, which define the contract with the rest of the system.

Finding The Properties

Finding properties is similar to finding objects, but first you need to know what you're looking for. There are several different types of properties, and each has its own characteristics. By knowing the types and their characteristics, it's easier to identify them:

- *Descriptive properties*—Provide detailed information about the object.
- *Naming properties*—Communicate information about an object through a commonly used name or label.
- *Referential properties*—Provide a link between two objects.
- *State properties*—Define the possible states of an object.

Remember the nouns from the system description? Revisit the ones you didn't use as objects—these are prime candidates for properties. Examine the sentences that contain the objects. Look for adjectives, nouns, and noun clauses that relate to or describe the object noun. These are the object properties. Add them to your object note on the whiteboard (see Figure 2.4).

Again, there's no substitute for thinking here. Decide whether to include a property or not. Here are some guidelines for refining the properties:

- *Existing objects*—If a property name is an existing object within your system, eliminate it as a property and draw a line to the existing object, thus identifying a relationship.

- *Objects*—Properties that have properties are objects. If you identify a property that has properties, you've discovered another object. Create a note for it, add it to your system, and draw a line to represent the relationship.

- *Identifiers*—Exclude implementation identifiers. If an object needs an "ID" property for efficient implementation, do not include it as a property. Model only the attributes visible to the outside world.

- *Invisible details*—If the property represents an internal object state or feature, eliminate it because it's not visible.

- *Mutually exclusive properties*—If two properties are mutually exclusive, a subclass may be necessary. In other words, if an object has properties that are not given values when other properties are, both sets of properties may identify distinct subclasses of the object that inherit the object's properties.

- *Common properties*—If the same properties appear within several objects, you may need to generalize the objects into a superclass. The superclass contains the common properties, and the other classes inherit the properties from the superclass.

Mode: Read-Only, Write-Only, And Read-Write Properties

Once you identify the properties, you should determine their mode. As discussed earlier, by controlling the mode, you control how the system uses an object.

If a property represents a value the object supplies, and it's one that the outside world cannot change, it is a read-only property. The battery life of the battery in the clock is a read-only property—there's no way for the outside world to set this value. However, this value is important to know so that the battery can be replaced when needed.

If a property represents a value the system can either read or set, it's a read-write property. Several properties are read-write; the clock has a

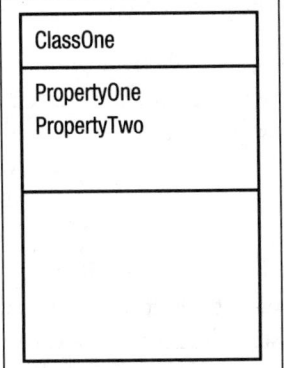

Figure 2.4
An object-oriented note with properties.

"time" property. The outside world can see the time (the read property) and can set the time (the write property).

Properties that accept values, but do not let you read their current value, are write-only properties. Write-only properties are special cases—you should use them carefully.

Finding The Methods

Finding methods is a little different than finding properties. Remember that methods represent what the object does—the actions the object can perform. This means you'll examine the system description for verbs. Find the verbs within the system description and relate them back to the nouns. The noun that performs the verb action is the object the verb relates to, and the verb is a method candidate within the object.

You can categorize methods as either computational or transitional. *Computational methods* generally perform some type of computation on information that is provided to the method and the object's properties, or provided to the object's properties only. *Transitional methods* usually result in the object changing state. You can think of these types of methods as *state transformations*.

Methods should represent real-world actions that an object performs. When you identify a verb that you believe is a method, ask the following questions:

- Does the verb cause the object to change state?
- Does the verb require computations dealing with the object's properties?

If the verb meets either of these criteria, it is a method. Add the verb to the methods section of the object note, as shown in Figure 2.5.

As you identify more methods, the object model on the whiteboard begins to flesh out.

Sometimes you need to use your knowledge of the real world, or the knowledge of a domain expert, to complete the methods. Identify all such actions and add them to the appropriate object. It's easier to remove an action that does not have any use than it is to add one later. Finding the methods is only half the object-oriented activity you'll perform in describing the actions. Methods contain the data paths or messages between objects. Visual Basic implements the messages with parameters. The second half of finding methods is to find the methods' parameters.

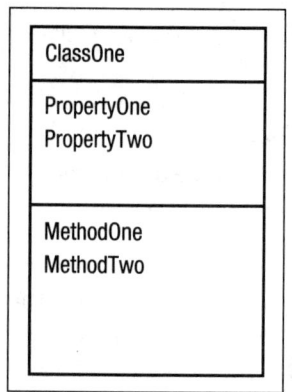

Figure 2.5
An object-oriented note with properties and methods.

The Small Print: Specifying The Contract With Parameters

You know how to find the objects, and you can find the contract outline by identifying the properties and methods. Now all you need to do is finish the contract by finding the parameters. The parameters to the methods for an object show the details of the contract. They describe the specific data and communication pathways between the objects.

Before putting parameters to methods, though, you need to know what you're looking for and how to use parameters to control the communication. There are three types of parameters:

- *Required parameters*—A method must have these parameters to do its job.
- *Optional parameters*—These parameters are not necessary for the method to perform its function, but they may control how the method performs its function.
- *Variable parameters*—These parameters let you pass any number of parameters into a method.

You must use the required parameters to call a method. The compiler checks to make sure that the parameters are present and of the correct type. The method declaration lists the required parameters first.

The compiler does not force you to use optional parameters. There are two types of optional parameters: independent and dependent. *Independent optional parameters* are used alone. They represent an optional piece of data and can either be present or not. *Dependent optional parameters* depend on other optional parameters. If one dependent parameter is present, the other dependent parameter must also be present. It's up to you to enforce dependency among the parameters. If you have dependent optional parameters, the method must check to see if all the optional parameters are passed. If they are not, the method should raise an error.

In Visual Basic, you use a **ParamArray** parameter to specify a variable number of parameters. A method with a **ParamArray** parameter accepts an arbitrary number of parameters.

Finding The Parameters

Now that you know the different types and combinations of parameters, you need to know how to identify them. Let's begin by examining the nouns around the verbs that identify the methods. Several times,

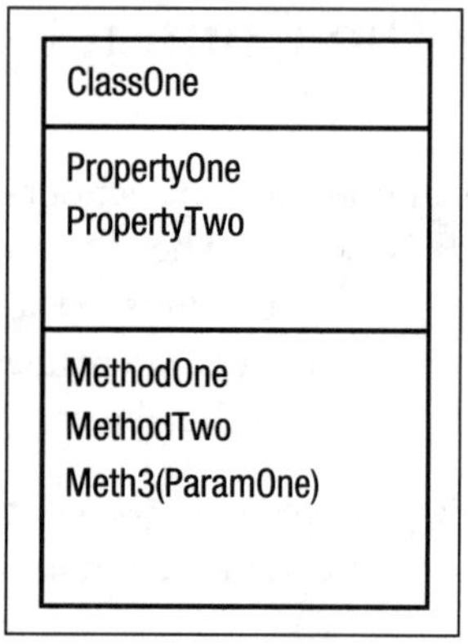

Figure 2.6
An object-oriented note with properties, methods, and parameters.

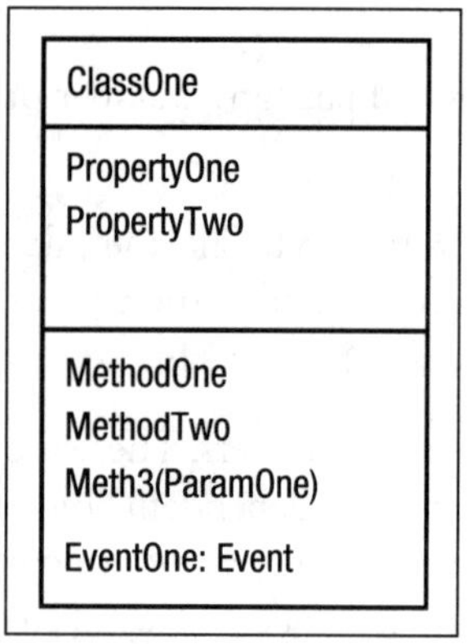

Figure 2.7
An object-oriented note with properties, methods, parameters, and events.

these nouns describe the data (or possible data) the method needs to do its job. Words such as "using" and "with" are clues that show you which nouns to link to the verb. As you identify the parameters, place them on your notes (see Figure 2.6).

Think! This is where you really begin to design. Until now, you've been identifying items and pulling information out of the system description. Now you must think about how to pass data into the object and how the object is going to respond. Use your domain knowledge and your knowledge of programming. Getting the parameters correct is the hardest part of this process, so give it some time and thought.

Finding The Events

Events are sometimes tricky to spot. *Events* are methods an object performs on the world. Events let the object notify the world that something has happened inside the object. Search for verbs or methods, such as "notify," "inform," "interrupt," or any other verb that describes the object performing an action on the world. Put these events within the methods section of your notes, as shown in Figure 2.7. Make sure to label them as events so you do not forget that fact during development.

Process Summary

Identifying events does not end the object-oriented design process, which is long and iterative. It may take you several passes through the system descriptions to get a handle on the entire problem. Only then can you begin to craft the solution. Examine the requirements and system descriptions for the system functionality and object interactions. The processes and diagrams resulting from this activity go beyond the scope of this discussion and this book. Refer to Appendix A for a list of recommended books for further study.

The next section guides you through the process of identifying objects and discovering their public interfaces. At this point, you do not design or identify an object's internal data or implementation.

Object-Oriented Design: An Example

The process described here is practical yet powerful. It lets you break down systems into their component objects and interfaces. In this section, we'll walk through an example from start to finish. In this example, you'll locate objects, identify properties and methods, and complete the contract. Lastly, we'll examine the objects within Visual Basic code. The rest of the book discusses Visual Basic code and its features in more detail and explains specific implementation methods for objects.

Designing Objects

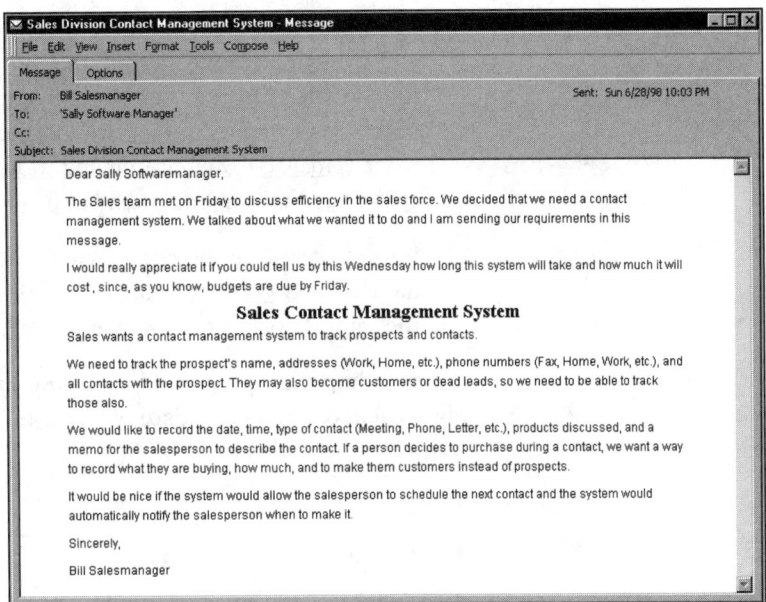

Figure 2.8
Email from the sales division.

The Problem

Here's the scenario: You are asked to design a contact management system. The sales division sends your boss an email (see Figure 2.8) describing the system. Because the boss knows you are her ace designer, she forwards it to you. Later, she drops by your office and asks you (with a "here we go again" grimace on her face) to do an object-oriented design and to present the design to her within a few days.

Because you noticed that the email provides an adequate problem statement, you grin at your boss and say, "No problem." You decide to design the system from the problem statement within the email.

Finding The Candidate Objects

You begin by pulling the system description from the email. Then, you start underlining the nouns and replacing the pronouns:

> <u>Sales</u> wants a <u>contact management system</u> to track <u>prospects</u> and <u>contacts</u>.
>
> We (<u>salespeople</u>) need to track the <u>prospect's name</u>, <u>addresses</u> (<u>Work</u>, <u>Home</u>, etc.), <u>phone numbers</u> (<u>Fax</u>, <u>Home</u>, <u>Work</u>, etc.), and all <u>contacts</u> with the <u>prospect</u>. They (<u>prospects</u>) may also become <u>customers</u> or dead <u>leads</u>, so we (<u>salespeople</u>) need to be able to track those (<u>customers</u> and <u>leads</u>) also.

We (<u>*salespeople*</u>) would like to record the <u>date</u>, <u>time</u>, <u>type</u> of <u>contact</u> (<u>Meeting</u>, <u>Phone</u>, <u>Letter</u>, etc.), <u>products</u> discussed, and a <u>memo</u> for the <u>salesperson</u> to describe the <u>contact</u>. If a <u>person</u> decides to purchase during a <u>contact</u>, we (<u>*salespeople*</u>) want a way to record what (<u>*products*</u>) they are buying, <u>how much</u>, and to make them (<u>prospects</u>) <u>customers</u> instead of <u>prospects</u>.

It would be nice if the <u>system</u> would allow the <u>salesperson</u> to schedule the next <u>contact</u> and the <u>system</u> would automatically notify the <u>salesperson</u> when to make it (<u>*contact*</u>).

After finding the nouns, you look at the subjects of the sentences and place them on your candidate object list:

- sales
- system
- prospect
- contact
- name
- address
- phone number
- work
- home
- fax
- customer
- lead
- date
- time
- type
- meeting
- phone
- letter
- product
- memo
- salesperson
- person
- how much

Now you look for obvious objects. Because this is a contact management system, it's logical to have "contact" be the first object. After examining the list, you select "prospect" and "product" as two other obvious choices. You decide not to include "system" as an object, because you're building the system. You decide not to use "name," "address," and "phone number" as objects, because the second sentence associates them with a "prospect." Using the same observation, you eliminate "date," "time," "type," and "memo." You eliminate "work," "home," and "fax" because they are types of addresses and phones. Looking at "customer" and "lead," you notice that these are really just two types of prospects. "Meeting," "phone," and "letter" are types of contacts, so you cross them out also. "Sales" and "salesperson" are references to users from the sales division—they are not part of the system. A "person" deciding to make a purchase is a customer, which you decided earlier is a prospect, so it cannot be an object. Finally, you decide "how much" is really a product's price. Below is the final candidate object list:

- ~~sales~~
- ~~system~~
- prospect
- contact
- ~~name~~
- ~~address~~
- ~~phone number~~
- ~~work~~
- ~~home~~
- ~~fax~~
- ~~customer~~
- ~~lead~~
- ~~date~~
- ~~time~~
- ~~type~~
- ~~meeting~~
- ~~phone~~
- ~~letter~~
- product

- ~~memo~~
- ~~salesperson~~
- ~~person~~
- ~~how much~~ (price)

You've identified three objects within the system: Prospect, Contact, and Product.

Now create sticky notes for each object (see Figure 2.9). These notes will help you show the relationships within the next section.

Finding The Relationships

You've quickly identified the objects. Now you need to look for relationships. In the second paragraph of the problem statement, notice the phrase "and all contacts with the prospect." This phrase means that a prospect "has" contacts. Notice that "contacts" (plural form) is used. This means that a one-to-many relationship exists between "prospect" and "contacts."

Next, look at the contact. In the third paragraph of the problem statement, you see the phrase "products discussed." This implies a one-to-many relationship between "contact" and "products."

Add the relationships to your object model, as shown in Figure 2.10.

Finding The Properties

You are on a roll now. Go back to the candidate object list and the system description to see which nouns go with which objects.

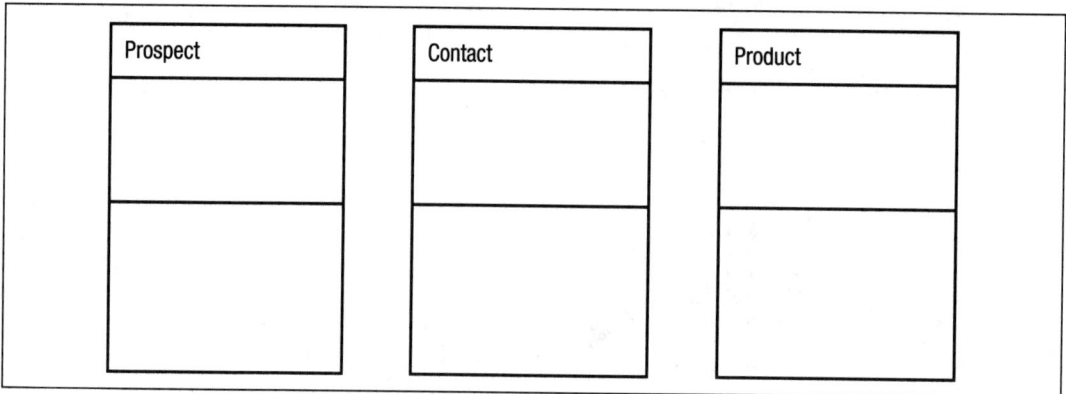

Figure 2.9
Sticky notes for the objects.

Designing Objects

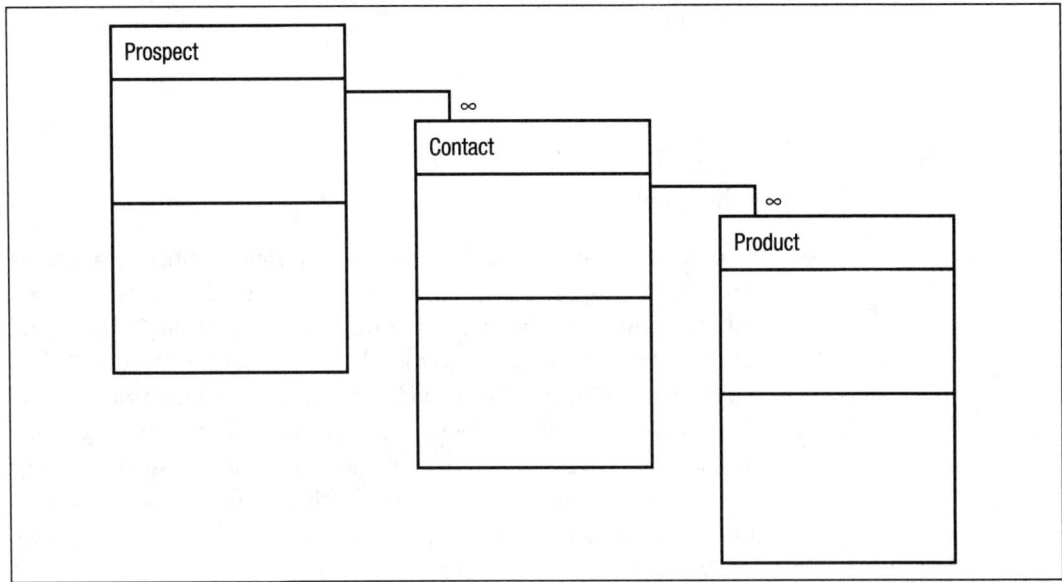

Figure 2.10
The beginning of your object model.

Candidate object list:

- sales
- system
- prospect
- contact
- name
- address
- phone number
- work
- home
- fax
- customer
- lead
- date
- time
- type
- meeting
- phone
- letter

- product
- memo
- salesperson
- person
- how much

You discover that "name," "address," and "phone number" go with the prospect. You write them on the Prospect note. Continuing on, you note the nouns that belong to a contact—"date," "time," "type," and "memo." Finally, you come across the properties for "product." The only one mentioned is "how much," which you rename "price." However, you know from your domain knowledge and common sense that a product has a name, so you write "name" on the note. Also, to account for the status change for the prospect (that is, from prospect to customer), you decide to add a "type" property to the Prospect object (see Figure 2.11).

As you review the system description, you notice that "address" and "phone number" are both used in the plural form. This implies a one-to-many relationship between address and prospect as well as phone number and prospect. Also, notice that "address" has an implied type

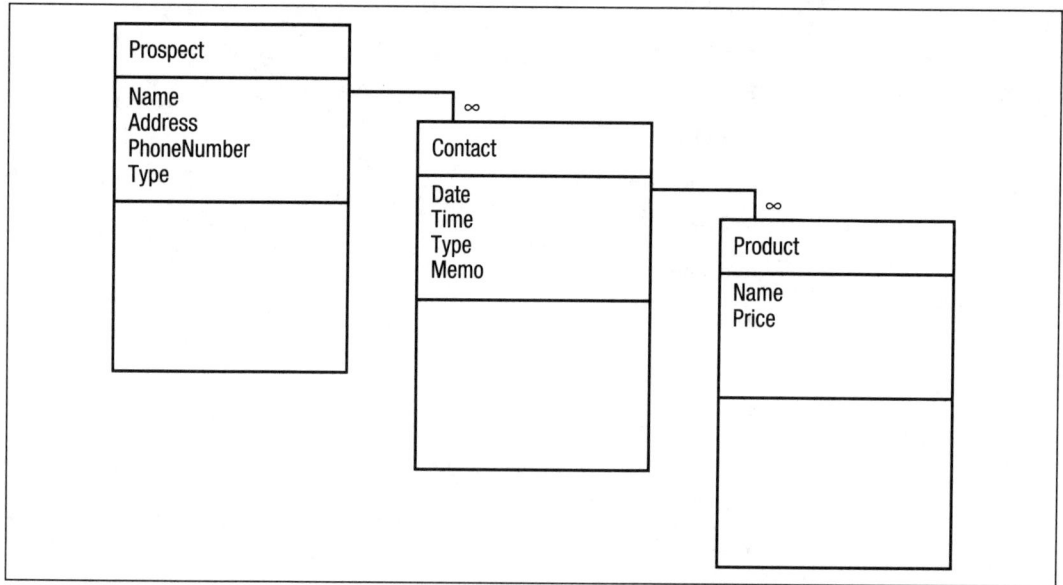

Figure 2.11
Object model with properties.

("home," "work," and so on). Therefore, it must have properties. "Phone number" is the same way. You've discovered two more objects. Add these to your model, along with their relationships (see Figure 2.12).

Once you think you've found all the properties, it's time to move on to the methods.

Finding The Methods

Your object model is coming along nicely. Now you need to find the methods. Of course, you begin by identifying the verbs within the problem statement:

> Sales <u>wants</u> a contact management system to <u>track</u> prospects and contacts.

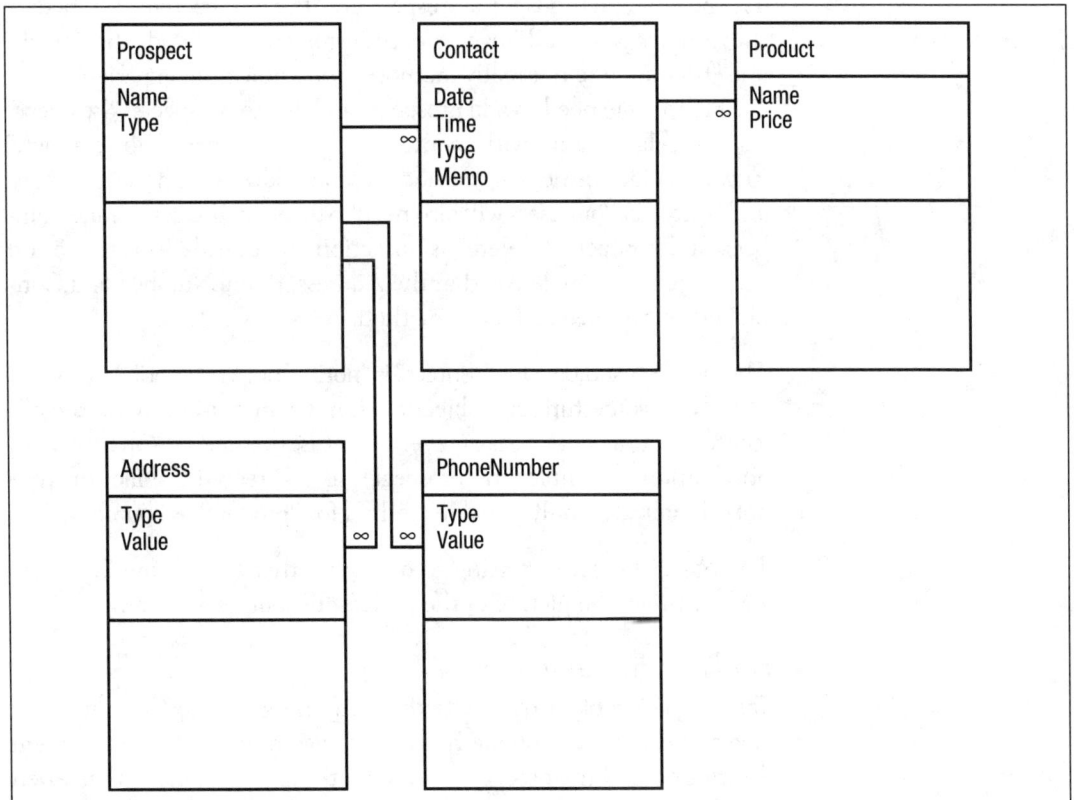

Figure 2.12
Updated object model with new objects.

We need to track the prospect's name, addresses (Work, Home, etc.), phone numbers (Fax, Home, Work, etc.), and all contacts with the prospect. Prospects may also become customers or dead leads, so we need to be able to track those also.

We would like to record the date, time, type of contact (Meeting, Phone, Letter, etc.), products discussed, and a memo for the salesperson to describe the contact. If a person decides to purchase during a contact, we want a way to record what they are buying, how much, and to make them a customer instead of a prospect.

It would be nice if the system would allow the salesperson to schedule the next contact and the system would automatically notify the salesperson when to make the contact.

The possible methods for a prospect are "track," "become," "schedule the next contact," and "make them a customer." You decide that "track" and "become" are not really methods. You know from experience that the salespeople need to add prospects and delete prospects. "Prospect" also has relationships with "address," "phone number," and "contact," so you decide to include methods to add addresses, phone numbers, and contacts. Your users will also need to delete addresses, phone numbers, and contacts. "Delete" is an action the outside world takes on each object, so you decide that the Address, PhoneNumber, and Contact objects all need a **Delete** method.

The method candidate for "contact" is "notify," but isn't "notify" an event? "Notify" is something the object does, not something you ask the object to do. You decide it is an event (that is, the salesperson receives a notification to contact the prospect), so you record the fact on your note. Finally, the only possible method for "product" is "purchase."

The object model is starting to come together (see Figure 2.13). As you continue, the picture of the project fills out even more.

Finding The Parameters

Take a quick look at the methods. Is anything missing? Yes—you decide to fully specify the methods. Once again, go back to the system description and the object model. One thing you realize is that when an address is added to the system, the next thing to do is to fill in the address type and value. Therefore, you decide to make the **AddAddress** method return an address. The same goes for the **AddPhoneNumber** and **AddContact** methods.

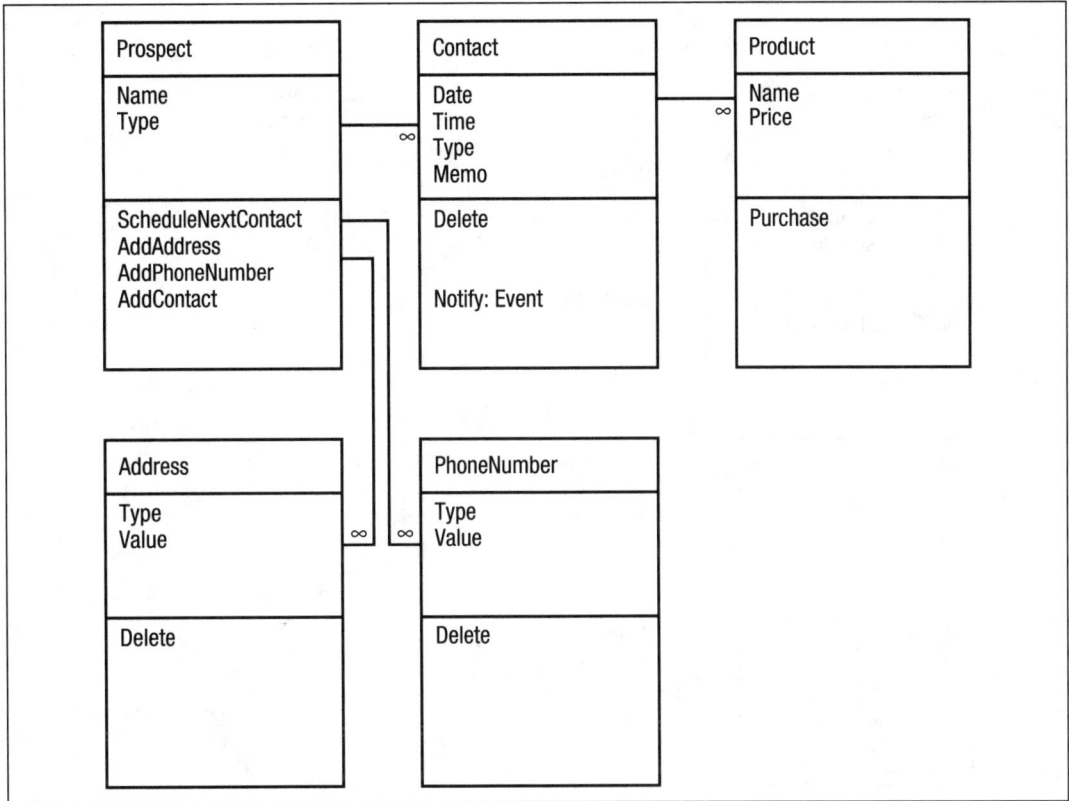

Figure 2.13
Object model with properties and methods.

The next method you examine is the Product object's **Purchase** method. The system description lumps the product purchase and the price together within the same sentence. One way to purchase a product is to assign the price property a value, then perform the **Purchase** method. Another way to model this transaction is to pass the price into the **Purchase** method as a parameter. You decide it's more efficient to send the price in during a purchase, so you add a **Price** parameter to the **Purchase** method. This also makes the product's **Price** property read-only (documented with "r/o" on your note), since you do not want anyone to change the price after a purchase (see Figure 2.14).

Finding The Events

You've already identified one event—the **Notify** event within the Contact object. Looking through the system description and the verb list, you notice the "make them a customer" phrase. You also notice the purchase action is on the "product." The Product object should notify the object that "has" the product (the parent object, which in

64 Chapter 2

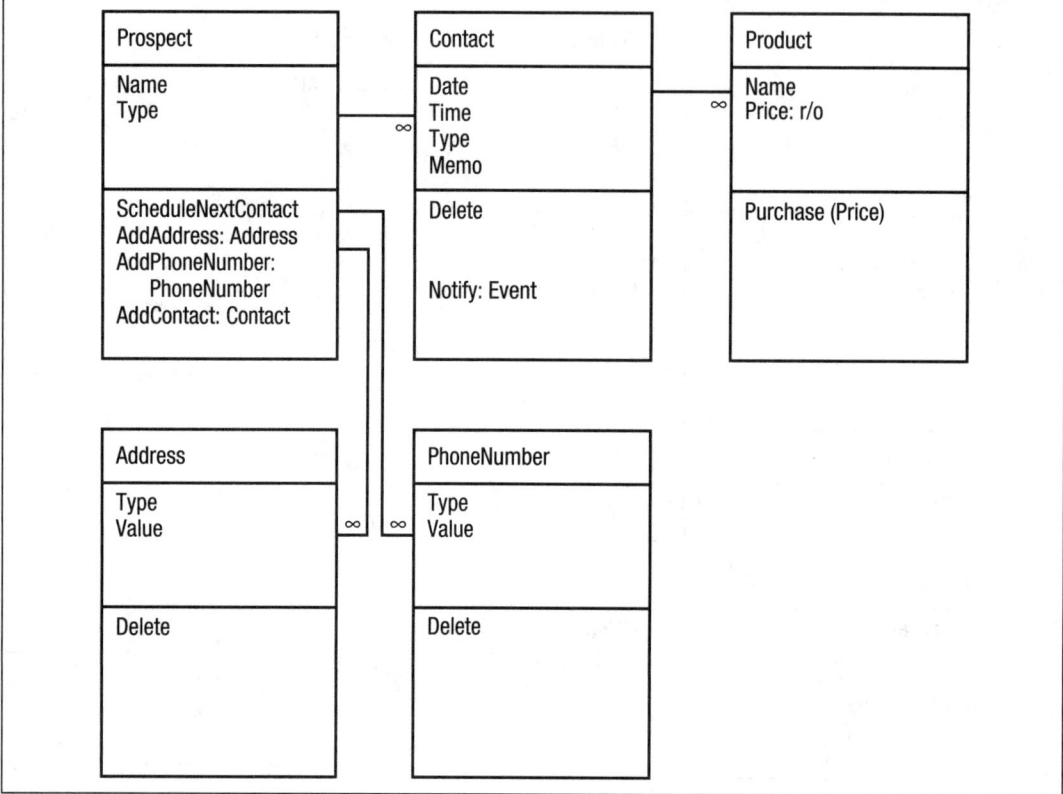

Figure 2.14
Object model with properties, methods, and parameters.

our model is the Contact object) when a product is purchased. You decide to add a **Purchased** event to the product (see Figure 2.15). You also know from the system description that the Prospect object needs to know when the prospect purchases a product. The *Product* object notifies the *Contact* object, so you decide to pass the notification to the Prospect object.

The Object Model

You complete the object model in record time, enter it into the Visual Modeler, sketch a screen design, and produce the schedule and estimate for the project. You send the complete package—the formal object model shown in Figure 2.16, the screen design laid out in Visual Basic, the schedule, and the estimate—to your boss by the end of the day.

Your quick response and the thoroughness of your design impress workers in the sales division. They add the project to their plans and present it to the executive committee a few days later. The executive committee, equally pleased by the design, approves the project for the sales

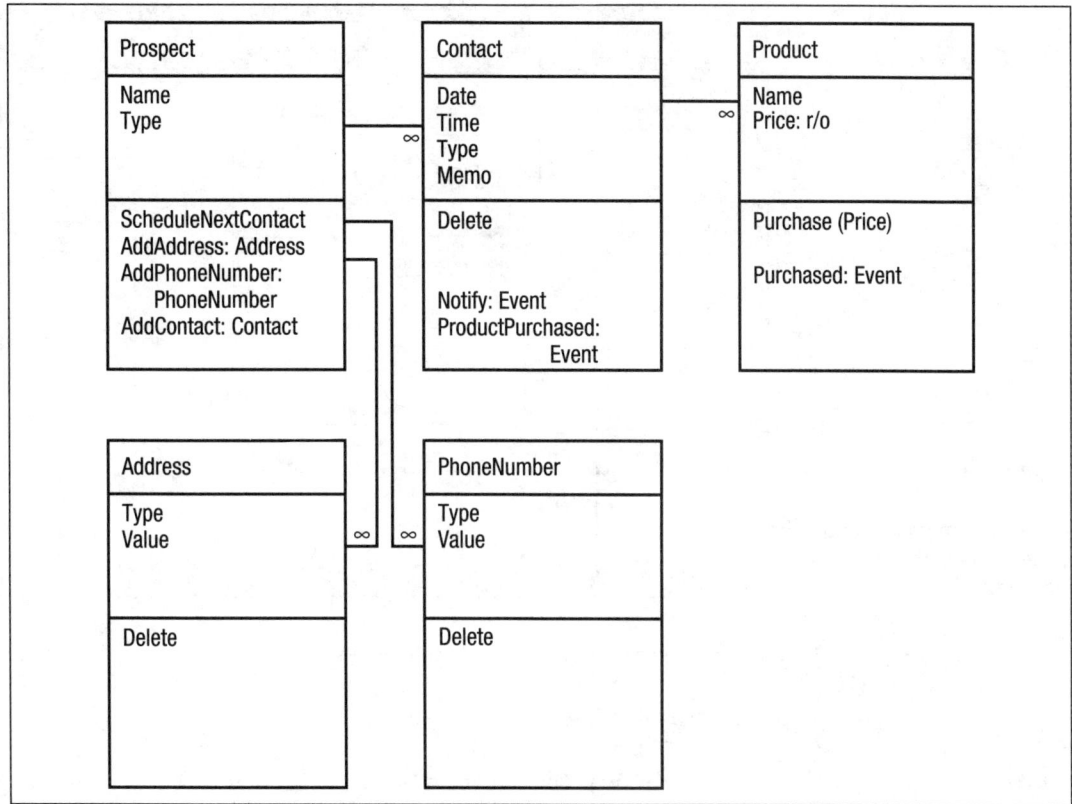

Figure 2.15
Object model with properties, methods, parameters, and events.

division. The sales division is happy, your boss is thrilled, and you move on to the next phase of the project—constructing the system.

The Visual Basic Specifications

The next phase within the process is construction. Before you begin programming, you have to get the object specifications into Visual Basic.

Listings 2.1 through 2.5 contain full specifications for the contact management system in Visual Basic. The next chapter details the specifics of the language and the class module structure.

Listing 2.1   Prospect class.

```
'Prospect Class

Option Explicit

Public Property Get Name() As String

End Property
```

66   Chapter 2

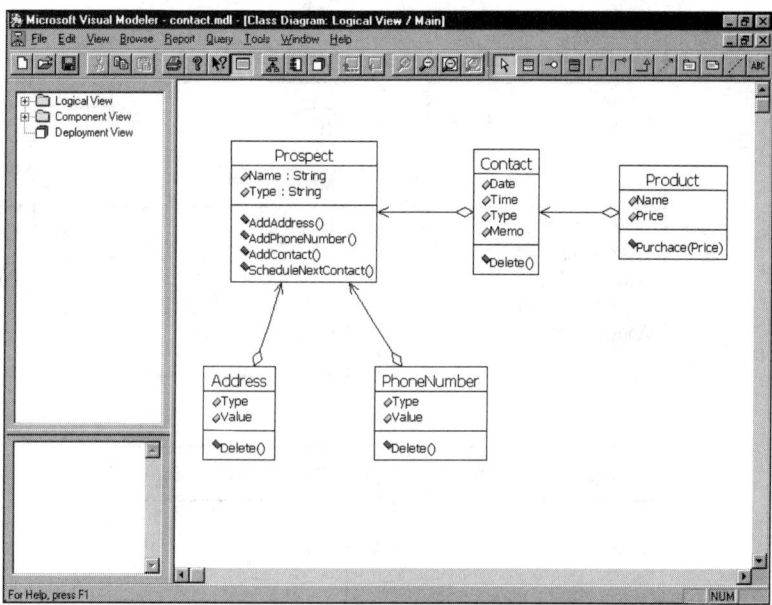

Figure 2.16
Object model with properties, methods, and parameters in the Microsoft Visual Modeler.

```
Public Property Let Name(NewName As String)

End Property

Public Property Get ProspectType() As String

End Property

Public Sub ScheduleNextContact(ContactDate As Date, _
                               ContactTime As String)

End Sub

Public Function AddAddress() As Address

End Function

Public Function AddPhoneNumber() As Phone

End Function

Public Function AddContact() As Contact

End Function
```

Listing 2.2 Contact class.

```
'Contact Class

Option Explicit

Public Event Notify()

Public Event ProductPurchased()

Public Property Get ContactDate() As Date

End Property

Public Property Get ContactTime() As String

End Property

Public Property Get ContactType() As String

End Property

Public Property Let ContactType(NewContactType As String)

End Property

Public Property Get Memo() As String

End Property

Public Property Let Memo(NewMemo As String)

End Property

Public Sub Delete()

End Sub
```

Listing 2.3 Product class.

```
'Product Class

Option Explicit

Public Event Purchased()

Public Property Get Name() As String
```

```
    End Property

    Public Property Let Name(NewName As String)

    End Property

    Public Property Get Price() As Single

    End Property

    Public Sub Purchase(Price As Single)

    End Sub
```

Listing 2.4   Address class.
```
'Address Class

Option Explicit

Public Property Get AddressType() As String

End Property

Public Property Let AddressType(NewType As String)

End Property

Public Property Get Value() As String

End Property

Public Property Let Value(NewValue As String)

End Property

Public Sub Delete()

End Sub
```

Listing 2.5   PhoneNumber class.
```
'PhoneNumber Class

Option Explicit

Public Property Get PhoneType() As String
```

```
End Property

Public Property Let PhoneType(NewType As String)

End Property

Public Property Get Value() As String

End Property

Public Property Let Value(NewValue As String)

End Property

Public Sub Delete()

End Sub
```

Scaling The Method

You may be saying at this point, "OK, this works on a small project, but what about a large one?" This may seem like a simplistic method, but it's very powerful. If you break a large project into smaller pieces, write system descriptions for each piece, then apply the method to the descriptions, it works. It's helpful to write a high-level system description that explains how all the smaller pieces fit together. Then you can apply this method to all the system descriptions, building the objects on a whiteboard.

Other Thought-Provoking Examples

To expand your thinking into object-oriented issues, look around your house and ponder the following:

- Think about how various household items are encapsulated and identify their public interfaces. For example, your television provides methods such as "changing the station," "setting the volume," and "adjusting the color." A TV's properties include volume, hue, tint, and brightness.

- Think about the complex process you start by turning the air conditioner on. How is this encapsulated by a simple interface? What is hidden?

- Identify household items that are made up of other items—for example, your stove may have an oven, microwave, and burners.
- Write a system description for your stereo. Analyze the description and develop an object model for the stereo.

After thinking about objects in this concrete way, think about the last project you worked on. Would it benefit from object-oriented design? Think about what types of objects your project would have and how they would interact.

As an additional exercise, pull out the requirements or system description documents for your current system. Analyze the description and find five classes. Place them on yellow sticky notes and put them on a whiteboard or a piece of legal-size paper. Complete the design, filling out the notes as you go.

Conclusion

In this chapter, we journeyed into the world of object-oriented design. Here are some of the highlights:

- *Encapsulation* is the essence of object-oriented design. It defines the boundary, or physical barrier, of your objects. Encapsulation lets you group related data and operations together into a "capsule."
- *Data hiding* defines which data and operations are visible outside the capsule and "hides" the important implementation.
- The *class module* is the essence of Visual Basic. As the most basic system building block, it provides encapsulation and exposes a public interface for the outside world to use.
- The basic characteristics of an object are *properties*, *methods*, and *events*. Properties and methods are "incoming interfaces" and events are "outgoing interfaces."
- A *public interface* limits and controls an object's use. The public interface defines the "contract" between the object and the outside world.
- Using public variables for properties relinquishes your control over the properties. Avoid public variables and retain control over your objects.
- *Properties* can control validation and access. Properties also provide redirection and self-initializing values.
- *Methods* represent what you can tell an object to do.

- *Events* are things the object can do.
- *Object-oriented design* is a process you use to break a problem down into its objects.
- Use simple tools, such as sticky notes and a whiteboard, during the early phases of design to increase collaboration and visualization.
- Before you can solve a problem, you must describe the problem. Create a system description (or descriptions, depending on the size of the project). Have everyone review and agree on the accuracy of your descriptions. Then perform object-oriented design on the system descriptions.

Finally, we traveled through an object-oriented design method that lets you begin your personal explorations of object-oriented methodologies. You saw a full object specification within Visual Basic. In the next chapter, we'll explore class specification and implementation details, including the parts of a class, and the Visual Basic syntax and constructs that support object-oriented programming.

Chapter 3

Object Foundations: Visual Basic Classes

Key Topics:

♦ *Class Modules*

♦ *Private Data*

♦ *Public Properties*

♦ *Public Methods And Private Procedures*

♦ *Events*

In Chapter 2, you explored the theory behind object-oriented programming, design, and defining public interfaces. In this chapter, you'll move into the real world—programming classes and objects in Visual Basic. We'll take an in-depth look at the public and private parts of a class. First, we need to agree on some terms that will define our interface. This chapter starts out with a review of object terms we've already covered and explains some new ones. Then it moves on to the nitty-gritty of objects.

If you've been programming in Visual Basic for very long, you've already used classes and objects. The basic object in Visual Basic is the Form object, and here we'll examine forms in detail. Next, we'll explore the world of user-defined objects—the ones you create and control. This journey takes us from defining a class, through properties, methods, and finally events. We get into advanced object topics in Chapter 5 and ActiveX objects and controls in Chapter 7.

Vocabulary: Defining Our Interface

Before classes can begin communicating with each other and the outside world, a public interface must be defined. The interface makes sure that classes follow the rules and, thus, facilitate communication. The following list reviews and defines the terms for objects in Visual Basic:

♦ *Class*—An abstraction of a group of items. Object classes describe a set of nonspecific items. Only when the properties have values does a class describe a specific member of the class (an object).

- *Coupling*—A measure of how dependent one class or code module is on another.
- *Data hiding*—Defines which data (properties) and code (methods) are visible or hidden. This effectively defines the class interface.
- *Encapsulation*—Placing code and data behind a barrier or within a capsule (the class). Placing code in a class module protects it from the outside world.
- *Event*—The things an object does. You write code to handle and respond to events.
- *Interface*—All the public properties and methods define an object's interface. The interface consists of all the visible parts of a class.
- *Method*—The things you can make an object do. Methods describe an object's behavior.
- *Object (or instance)*—An instance of a class, which is the realization of a class in memory.
- *Property*—Data that describes an object or an object's state.
- *Reference*—An object variable where you keep your object. In order to use an object, you must declare an object variable to hold the reference.

Class Modules

As you learned in Chapter 2, the essence of Visual Basic is the class module. Whether you're new to Visual Basic or an old pro, you've worked with classes and objects. The two most familiar types of classes in Visual Basic are forms and, introduced in Visual Basic 4, user classes.

Forms encapsulate the visual interface of your programs. You write code to perform tasks in your form and to control its visual display. Forms are extensible—that is, you can add properties, methods, and events to them.

User classes encapsulate your application's business rules. You develop user classes from analyzing a problem and designing a solution.

The Form Class

The first class we'll explore is the **Form** class. Forms are the basic building blocks of Visual Basic. Forms are objects—the windows that make up your application. A Visual Basic form has all the classic object characteristics. It encapsulates its data and behavior, and it exposes properties, methods, and events.

If you open Visual Basic and start a new project, Visual Basic creates the ever-popular **Form1** object (see Figure 3.1). Visual Basic places it in the "forms" section of the Visual Basic Integrated Development Environment (IDE) and even opens it—a canvas ready for the master's touch.

Notice the Form object's properties, conveniently displayed within the Properties window (see Figure 3.2).

Let's take a look at some of the form's properties. First, because a form is a visual object, it has many visual properties, including **Appearance**, **BackColor**, **BorderStyle**, **Height**, and **Width**. Each of these properties describes the form's physical appearance. **Appearance** controls the overall look of the form: Is it 3D, or flat like a dialog box? **BackColor** sets the background color, and **BorderStyle** controls the

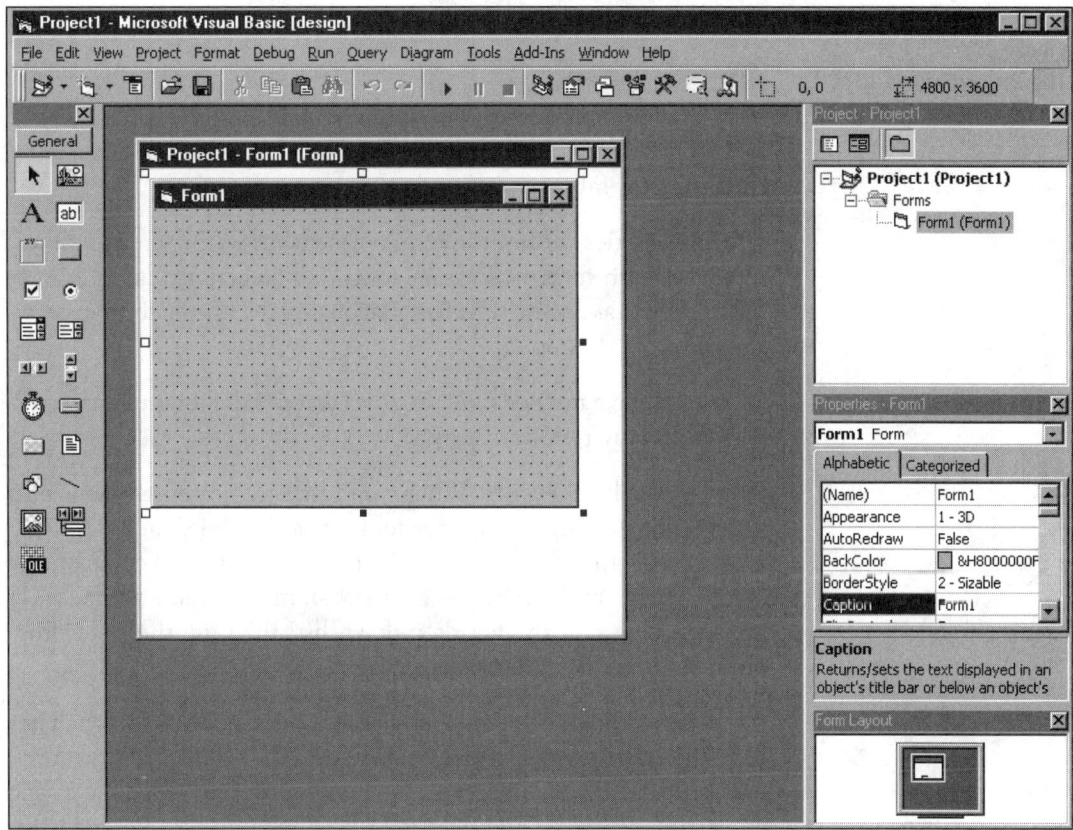

Figure 3.1
Visual Basic's default **Form1** object.

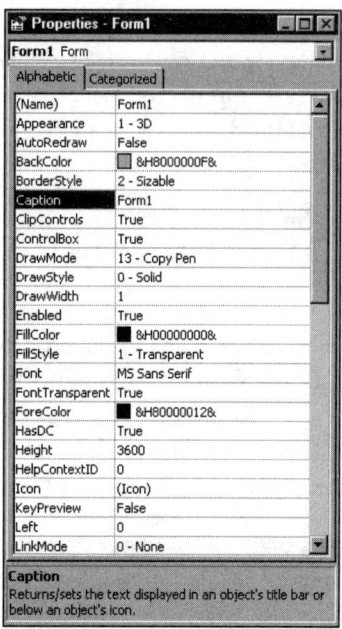

Figure 3.2
The Properties window.

look of the form's outside border. Finally, **Height** and **Width** control the form's overall size.

Other properties control the form's placement on the screen—how it interfaces with its environment, fonts, mouse activity, and a host of other items. Take some time to get acquainted with the form's properties and what they do.

Forms also have methods. Methods let you tell the form to move, display itself, or refresh its display.

Lastly, forms have events. When you resize a form on the screen, it raises an event. Other events fire for keyboard activity, mouse activity, loading the form, and destroying the form. You can get a complete list of form events in the IDE (see Figure 3.3). In the code window, select the form object in the left drop-down list; then use the right drop-down list to see the form's events.

As you can see, forms act like any other object in Visual Basic. They have the same basic parts and characteristics. You can add properties, methods, and events to forms. The next section details how to add properties, methods, and events to your own classes. Later in this chapter, we'll discuss extending forms by adding properties, methods, and events.

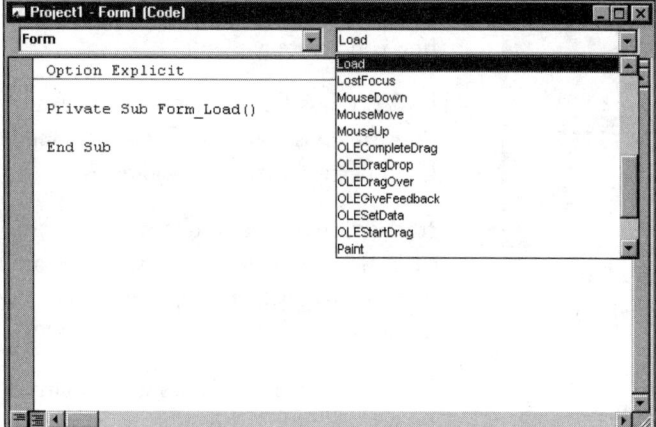

Figure 3.3
A list of form events.

Creating Your Own Classes

Because the essence of Visual Basic, as well as object-oriented programming, is creating classes, Visual Basic makes it easy. There are two ways to create classes: The first is the most direct—creating a class module. The second uses the Class Builder to fully define a class.

To create a class module, select the Project menu in the Visual Basic IDE and then select the Add Class Module menu item. Visual Basic displays the Add Class Module dialog box, as shown in Figure 3.4.

Notice the icons: Class Module, VB Class Builder, Complex Data Consumer, and Data Source. Double-click on the Class Module icon or select it and click on the Open button. Visual Basic adds the class, **Class1**, to your project window under Class Modules (see Figure 3.5).

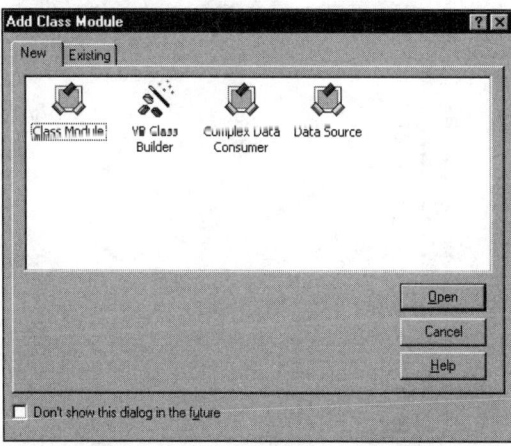

Figure 3.4
The Add Class Module dialog box.

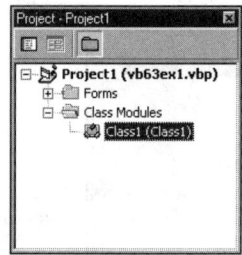

Figure 3.5
The project window.

Figure 3.6 shows the empty code window Visual Basic opens for you when you create a class.

The VB Class Builder icon in the Add Class Module dialog box invokes the Class Builder. The Class Builder lets you create a class and add properties, methods, and events.

After adding a class, you're not done yet. The default class names Visual Basic assigns to the new classes are not very descriptive. If you leave it up to Visual Basic, your project will have classes such as **Class1** and **Class2**.

Chapter 2 identifies classes with nouns. It's a good idea to name your classes with nouns, the same as those in your design. This way, it's easy to understand what the class represents and easy to track the class back to the design. To rename the class with a proper name, simply change the **Name** property in the Properties window to the correct object name. Some people like to prepend a C to identify classes—this makes for easy class identification during debugging. When you rename the class, Visual Basic updates the class name in the project and code windows. Figure 3.7 shows the class after its name is changed from **Class1** to **CExample**.

Once you rename the class, you're ready to add properties, methods, and events.

Adding Public Properties

The easiest way to add a property to the class is to define a public variable. However, as Chapter 2 explains, it's not usually a good idea to

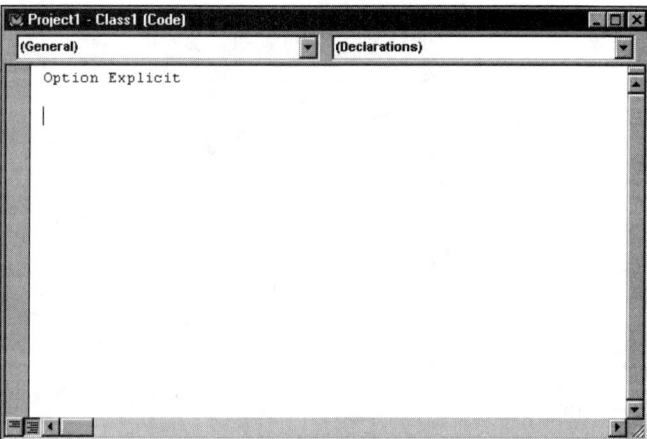

Figure 3.6
The **Class1** code window.

Object Foundations: Visual Basic Classes 79

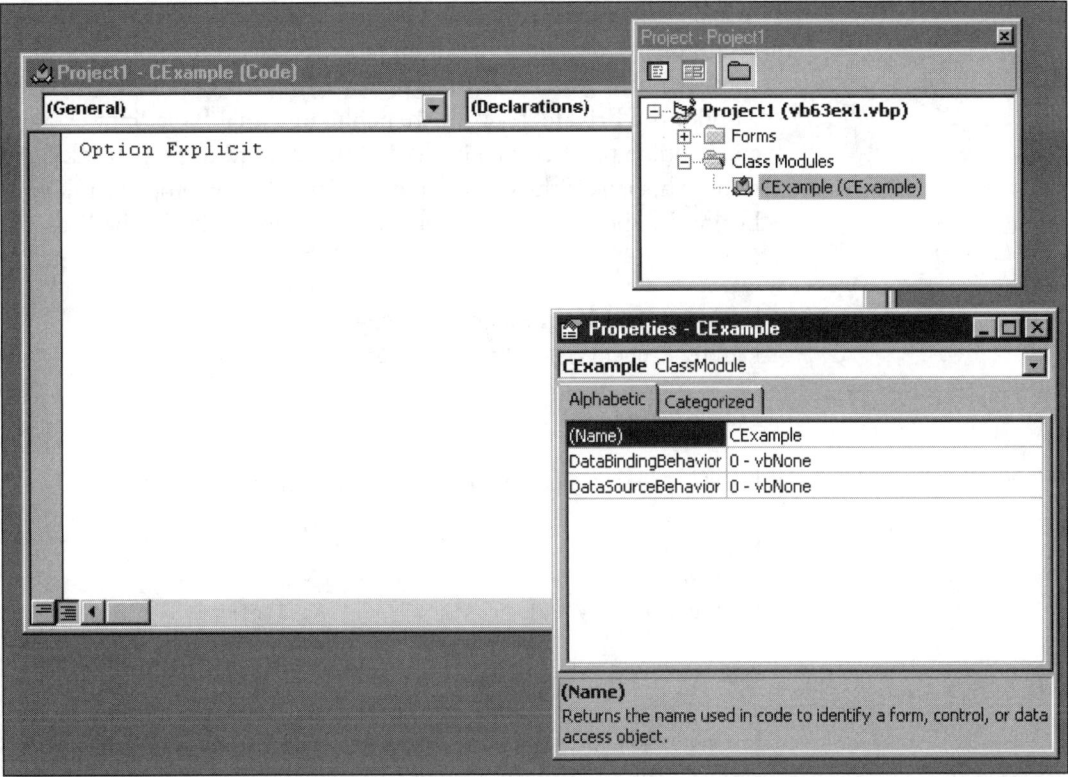

Figure 3.7
The renamed class module.

use public variables in object-oriented programming. This warning aside, Listing 3.1 shows you how to declare public variables for the **Prospect** class from Chapter 2.

Listing 3.1 Public variable properties.
```
Public Name As String
Dim ProspectType As String
```

The **Public** keyword explicitly declares **Name** as a public variable. The **Dim** keyword, however, is less obvious, because any variable declared in the class module with a **Dim** keyword is a public variable. Be careful when you declare a class-level variable. If you do not want it to be a public property, use the **Private** keyword.

The object-oriented programming way to add properties is with access methods. In older languages, such as C++, you declare a property by creating functions and procedures to access the property. These functions and procedures are called *access methods*. Usually, they are named something similar to **getPropertyOne** and **setPropertyOne**. Visual Basic provides an easy way to create access methods to define properties.

Visual Basic provides the **Let, Get,** and **Set** keywords that, when used in a property declaration, define property access methods. As when you use public variables, the **Public** keyword is optional. Properties without the **Private** keyword are public in Visual Basic. However, it's good coding practice to add the **Public** keyword to property declarations. This makes the declaration explicit that the property is public. Listing 3.2 shows the proper way to declare properties for the **Prospect** class.

Listing 3.2   Visual Basic properties.
```
Public Property Get Name() As String

End Property

Public Property Let Name(NewName As String)

End Property

Public Property Get ProspectType() As String

End Property
```

Listing 3.2 declares the same properties as the public variables declared earlier. Why go to all this trouble? To avoid public variables. Chapter 2 outlines the evils of public variables. Later in this chapter, we'll explore the properties **Let, Get,** and **Set**—and what you can do with them—in detail.

Adding Public Methods

Adding methods to your class is as easy as adding public properties. There are two types of methods in Visual Basic—subroutines (declared with the keyword **Sub**) and functions (declared with the keyword **Function**). **Sub** methods perform actions that usually cause a change in the properties (that is, a state change). **Function** methods perform actions that may cause changes in the properties, but they always return a value.

To add methods to your class, start typing the declarations. As with properties, Visual Basic makes subroutines and functions visible (or public) by default. Therefore, you can create methods by simply adding **Sub** and **Function** methods to your class. However, it's good object-oriented programming practice to explicitly declare which are public methods and which are private methods using the **Public** and **Private** keywords. Listing 3.3 shows how to declare the methods for the **Contact** class from Chapter 2.

Listing 3.3 Public methods.

```
Public Sub ScheduleNextContact(ContactDate As Date, _
                               ContactTime As String)

End Sub

Public Function AddAddress() As Address

End Function

Public Function AddPhoneNumber() As Phone

End Function

Public Function AddContact() As Contact

End Function
```

Listing 3.3 shows you how to declare Visual Basic methods, both subroutines and functions. Later in this chapter, we'll address methods, both private and public, in detail, as well as method parameters.

Adding Public Events

Adding events to classes is even easier than adding properties and methods. Visual Basic defines the **Event** keyword for events. Again, the **Public** keyword is optional, but you should use it for readability. Listing 3.4 shows how you declare the events for the **Contact** class from Chapter 2.

Listing 3.4 Public events.

```
Public Event Notify()

Public Event ProductPurchased()
```

Listing 3.4 shows you how to declare an event in a class. We'll explore events and how to raise and respond to them later in this chapter.

Figure 3.8 shows what the **Contact** class from Chapter 2 looks like in Visual Basic.

Now you know how to directly add properties, methods, and events to classes. An alternative way to accomplish these tasks is discussed next.

82 Chapter 3

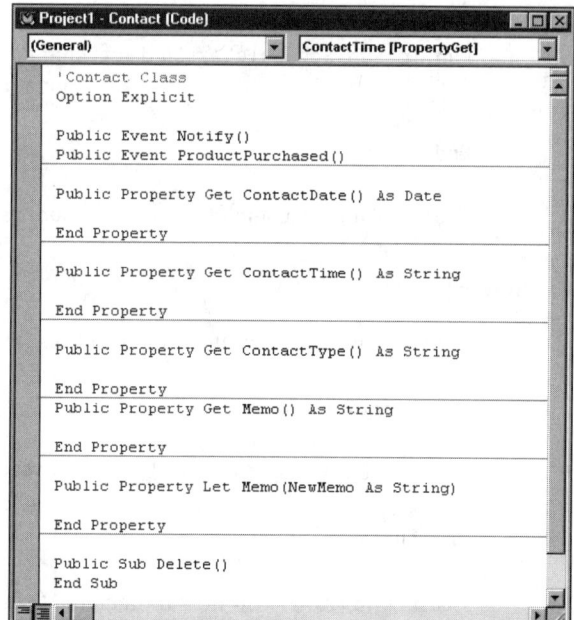

Figure 3.8
The **Contact** class with properties, methods, and events.

Building A Class With A Little Help

Visual Basic supplies another avenue for building classes—the Add Procedure dialog box. With the code window selected, open the Tools menu and click on the Add Procedure menu item. Visual Basic displays the Add Procedure dialog box, as shown in Figure 3.9.

The Add Procedure dialog box lets you add properties, method subs, method functions, and events. It also provides selections for declaring both public and private methods as well as properties. This dialog box is helpful if you're new to Visual Basic, because it inserts the proper syntax into your class.

Besides being able to add properties, methods, and events to classes, you can also add these elements to forms to customize and extend their behavior.

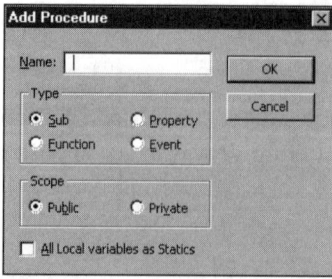

Figure 3.9
The Add Procedure dialog box.

Extending Forms

Extending forms is the best way to control how an application uses and views them. Giving forms specific properties and behavior facilitates communication between forms—especially dialog boxes. In this section, you'll create a sample dialog box by adding properties and methods to control and facilitate the use of the dialog box.

Adding Properties And Methods To A Form

Why add properties, methods, and events to forms? Don't they have enough properties, methods, and events already? It's a matter of control. If you use the default methods and properties, you relinquish control of the form to the outside world.

Returning status or values from a dialog box is a good example of why you might want to add methods or properties to a form. Figure 3.10 shows a sample dialog box with some popular controls: text boxes and command buttons. There are two text boxes (First Name and Last Name) and two command buttons (OK and Cancel).

You normally call the form's **Show** method, as shown in Listing 3.5, to display a dialog box.

Listing 3.5 Showing a dialog box.
```
Dim theDialog As new Dialog
theDialog.Show
```

Displaying a dialog box like this provides no protection. Listing 3.5, as written, has another problem—the form does not act as a dialog box. Dialog boxes in Windows are *modal*—that is, no other part of your application can receive input until you close the dialog box. The **Show** method simply displays the dialog box on the screen. The underlying application can still receive the focus and input.

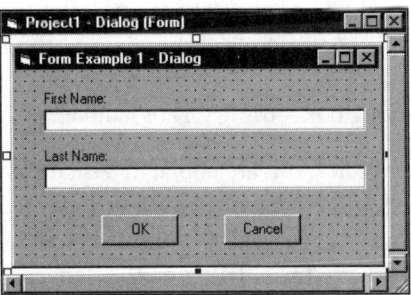

Figure 3.10
The sample dialog box.

> **NOTE**
>
> When you create an object in Visual Basic, the system creates a hidden reference to the object, called **me**. Use **me** to explicitly address the class elements. This makes it easy to read and understand what you're calling in the object.

A better implementation can protect your dialog box. For example, you could provide a **View** method that controls displaying the dialog box. Here's how: First, declare a private module variable called **mValidView** and use this variable to force a programmer, who is using the dialog box, to call the **View** method instead of the **Show** method. Second, add a **View** function method to the form, as shown in Listing 3.6.

Listing 3.6   The form's View method.

```
Public Function View() As Integer

    mValidView = True
    Me.Show vbModal
    View = mReturnStatus

End Function
```

Next, set the **mValidView** variable to **True**; then, call the **Show** method from the **View** method.

Finally, to guard against someone calling the form's **Show** method, add the code in Listing 3.7 to the form's **Activate** event handler.

Listing 3.7   The form's Activate event.

```
Private Sub Form_Activate()

    If Not mValidView Then
       Me.Hide
       MsgBox "Invalid display method for dialog.", 0, "Error"
    End If

End Sub
```

If a programmer calls your dialog box's **Show** method, the dialog box detects the improper activation, hides the form, and displays an error message. Look closely at the **View** method. Notice that it is a function. This function lets you notify the caller how the user chooses to close the dialog box—using OK or Cancel.

Controls on forms are public in Visual Basic. They appear as properties to the form. Addressing controls directly on the form is one way to put data into and get data out of the dialog box. However, addressing controls directly on a dialog box is dangerous. What if the dialog box's creator decides to change the control type or control name? You must then update any code that uses the dialog box. You cannot protect the specific data on a dialog box unless you can process or check the values sent to the controls. A better way to address this is to declare properties for your dialog box. Remember that public properties and methods form a contract between the form and the outside world. If you supply public properties for a form, it's fair to change the controls on the form. Any code that directly addresses the form's controls is violating the contract.

Our sample dialog box has two text boxes: **txtFirst** and **txtLast**. These text boxes represent a first name and last name. To control access to these text boxes, you can declare **FirstName** and **LastName** properties, as shown in Listing 3.8.

Listing 3.8 Form properties.
```
Public Property Get FirstName() As String

  FirstName = txtFirst

End Property
Public Property Let FirstName(NewFirstName As String)

  txtFirst = NewFirstName

End Property
Public Property Get LastName() As String

  LastName = txtLast

End Property
Public Property Let LastName(NewLastName As String)

  txtLast = NewLastName

End Property
```

The form properties provide access to the text boxes. You can extend the code in this example to validate the values before sending them to the text boxes. This protects the dialog box from bad data and lets you error gracefully.

Listing 3.9 shows the complete code listing for the sample dialog box.

Listing 3.9 The complete dialog box code.
```
Option Explicit

Private mValidView As Boolean
Private mReturnStatus As Integer

Public Property Get FirstName() As String

   FirstName = txtFirst

End Property
Public Property Let FirstName(NewFirstName As String)

   txtFirst = NewFirstName

End Property
Public Property Get LastName() As String

   LastName = txtLast

End Property
Public Property Let LastName(NewLastName As String)

   txtLast = NewLastName

End Property
Public Function View() As Integer

   mValidView = True
   Me.Show vbModal
   View = mReturnStatus

End Function

Private Sub cmdDone_Click(Index As Integer)

   If Index = 1 Then
       mReturnStatus = vbOK
   Else
       mReturnStatus = vbCancel
   End If
   Me.Hide

End Sub
```

```
Private Sub Form_Activate()

    If Not mValidView Then
        Me.Hide
        MsgBox "Invalid display method for dialog.", 0, "Error"
    End If

End Sub
```

Using An Extended Form

Using the dialog box is now a matter of addressing it like any other object. Listing 3.10 shows you how to call the dialog box and use the return value to determine which button the user pressed. The first call to the dialog box, using the **Show** method, produces an error message box and hides the dialog box. The **View** method not only shows the dialog box, but it forces you to show it modally and returns the dialog box's status. The dialog box's status simply reflects the button the user pressed to close the dialog box.

Listing 3.10 Using the dialog box.

```
Dim theDialog As New Dialog
    theDialog.Show 1
    theDialog.FirstName = txtFirstName
    theDialog.LastName = txtLastName
    If theDialog.View() = vbOK Then
        txtFirstName = theDialog.txtFirst
        txtLastName = theDialog.LastName
    End If
```

Lastly, if the user pressed the dialog box's OK button, the program updates its own display.

Forms act like any other object in Visual Basic. Use the power of objects and define the contract between your forms and their environment. Extend forms when your object has a visual element or when it's necessary to protect the form. When you add properties, methods, and events, you—not the outside world—control the form's use.

Coupling

No object-oriented programming book is complete unless it addresses coupling. The first section of this chapter defined *coupling* as a measure of how dependent a class module or code module is on another class or code module. *Loose coupling* is a minimal dependence, whereas *strong coupling* is a high degree of dependence, between modules.

Loosely coupled modules are preferable to strongly coupled ones. If you create loosely coupled modules, your classes stand alone as independent units. Changes in loosely coupled modules seldom affect other modules. This increases your system's stability, makes maintenance easier, and lets you deal with design changes effectively. Maintenance is easier because problems are isolated to a few loosely coupled modules without affecting large portions of the system. Design changes benefit for the same reason—system changes are isolated to a few related modules rather than having a system-wide effect.

Strongly coupled modules, on the other-hand, suffer when code and data change in the modules they depend on. This leads to confusing and hard-to-follow code (sometimes called "spaghetti" code) and unreliable systems. Strongly coupled modules suffer from their dependency. Changes, in either design or maintenance, cause a "ripple" effect through your program—that is, they cause problems or side effects in seemingly unrelated areas of your project.

Avoid using strongly coupled modules. However, if you must create strongly coupled modules, document them well and design loosely coupled modules everywhere else. Knowing how to recognize and control coupling is important in developing solid code. Knowing how Visual Basic handles data binding (that is, how modules store data and manage scope) is key to controlling coupling.

Binding

Class modules are a little different than normal Visual Basic code modules. The major differences are how they store data and manage scope.

Standard Visual Basic modules never have more than one copy of their data in memory, and the data has program scope. Having a single copy means that when you change the value of a public variable, every part of the program that uses the variable sees the new value. This is the dreaded *global variable*. Global variables suffer from the same basic evils as public variables, only worse. If you change a global variable's value, the change reverberates through your program and may cause side effects. Be very careful when using global variables—better yet, avoid them whenever possible. Having program scope means that the variable lasts for as long as your program runs. For each program scope variable, Visual Basic allocates resources to support the variable for the program's lifetime.

Class modules, on the other hand, store their data differently. Each instance of the class has its own set of data. That is, each object created from the class has its own private data set. Data in class modules only has module scope. Data declared with module scope only survives for the module's lifetime. Visual Basic allocates memory and resources to an object's data for the object's lifetime. When the object is destroyed, Visual Basic recovers the memory and resources the object used.

Class modules also differ from standard Visual Basic code modules when it comes to subroutines and functions. Subroutines and functions, declared with the **Public** keyword in a standard Visual Basic code module, have program-wide visibility. You can call the subroutines and functions from anywhere in your program. You can access public subroutines and functions in a class module only through a class variable that holds a reference to a particular instance of a class.

Avoid referencing global variables in your classes, because doing so violates the concept of encapsulation and breaks the contract of the class with the outside world. If you use a global variable in a class, the class does not contain all its data and, therefore, is not a complete class. Global data also creates strongly coupled systems. You learned in the previous section the dangers of strongly coupled modules. If you avoid using global variables, you're on your way to creating stable, maintainable, and object-oriented systems.

Keeping Data Private

One of the most important principles of object-oriented programming is *data hiding*—that is, deciding what is public and what is private. You've learned about the importance of public interfaces and defining the "contract," and you've seen how to declare public interfaces (properties, methods, and events) in Visual Basic. What about the private stuff? Data hiding's other side is deciding and defining what is hidden.

Specific data structures, control structures, and storage mechanisms are just some of the things you want to hide from the outside world. Once you decide what data is visible through properties, you must decide on and define the hidden data structures that support the internal processing and control of the class.

Designing and programming an ordered linked list is a popular exercise in computer science programs. A *linked list* is a data structure that uses a data element, with an item for a value and a pointer, to store a list of values. The value item stores the value and the pointer points (or *links*) the value item with the next item in the list. The exercise challenges students to implement the linked list by storing items in some value order. For numerical data, the order is in ascending or descending values.

There are several ways to implement a linked list. Using an array to implement a linked list is one possible way to solve the problem. It's a messy and inefficient (but easily understood) method. For a new student with little training in formal data structures, this may be the easiest way—or the only way—he knows to solve the problem.

If the student implements the linked list with an array and stores the array in a public variable or property, his implementation is in jeopardy. If he is part of a team of students implementing a system, his linked list is vulnerable. Let's say a more experienced student is on his team. When the more experienced student discovers how the linked list is implemented, she bypasses the linked list methods and accesses the array directly. Her code is more efficient and everyone is amazed by how fast her part of the project runs.

Meanwhile, the first student learns about pointers in class. He thinks, "Hey, that's a better way to implement my linked list class!" He begins to recode his class. First, he deletes the array. Then, he adds a data structure to contain the value and pointer and goes about implementing his new-and-improved linked list.

What just happened to the more experienced student's code? It's now broken. Two things occurred: The first student did not hide the internal structure effectively, and the second student took advantage of this mistake and closely coupled her code to the link list data and violated encapsulation. Had the second student not taken advantage of the linked list data structure, the new and improved linked list class would benefit everyone using it. This story highlights the power of hiding data and exposing only the data absolutely necessary to use a class.

You declare private data using the **Private** keyword in Visual Basic. Private properties look identical to public ones, except they are preceded by the **Private** keyword instead of **Public**. Other forms of hidden data are user-defined data types, enumerations, and private variables. Listing 3.11 shows how to declare private variables and properties.

Listing 3.11 Private variables and properties.

```
Private LinkedListPointers() As Long
Private LinkedListValues() As Long

Private Property Get CurrentArrayPosition() As Long
End Property
Private Property Let CurrentArrayPosition(NewPosition As _
   Long)
End Property
```

User-Defined Types

Visual Basic lets you combine several different types into user-defined types. Doing so allows you to create a "record" of data. You can use user-defined types when you want a single variable to refer to a group of related information. An obvious example, an address, is shown in Listing 3.12.

Listing 3.12 The Address user-defined type.

```
Private Type Address
    Street As String
    City As String
    State As String
    Zip As Integer
End Type
```

You declare user-defined type variables in the same way as normal variables:

```
Private theAddress As Address
```

Accessing User-Defined Types

You access user-defined types like you access members of a class:

```
Address.Street = "123 Maple Street"
```

You can also assign variables with the same user-defined types to each other:

```
Private FromStreet As Address
Private ToStreet As Address
ToStreet = FromStreet
```

User-Defined Types And Arrays

User-defined types can contain arrays, both fixed and dynamic. You can also define arrays of user-defined types, as shown in Listing 3.13.

Listing 3.13 The Address user-defined type with arrays.

```
Private Type Address
    Street(5) As String ' static array
    City As String
    State As String
    Zip As Integer
End Type
```

Or, here's another example:

```
Private Type Address
    Street() As String ' dynamic array
    City As String
    State As String
    Zip As Integer
End Type

Private Addresses() As Address
```

You access the elements of the user-defined type and arrays using the normal access rules (see Listing 3.14).

Listing 3.14 Accessing user-defined types with arrays.

```
Addresses(5).Street(1) = "123 Maple"
Addresses(5).Street(2) = "Drive"
```

Notice that the declarations are all private—you can only define private user-defined types in private modules. *Private modules* are user-defined classes in a standard Visual Basic program. You can define public user-defined types in public class modules, such as public ActiveX DLLs and ActiveX EXEs. For more information on public user-defined types and public modules, see Chapter 7.

User-defined types are a convenient way to keep track of the complex internal data of a class. By creating private user-defined types, you can manipulate complex data that is hidden by a simple, easy-to-use class interface.

Enumerations

An *enumeration* is a set of related constants. Enumerations provide an easy way to define and associate values with a group of named constants. For example, you can define a set of return values for a dialog box, as shown in Listing 3.15.

Listing 3.15 Dialog box return value enumeration.
```
Public Enum ReturnType
    DialogError
    OK
    Cancel
End Enum
```

Visual Basic stores each member of the enumeration as a long integer. Visual Basic assigns 0 to the first member and adds 1 to each successive element. In Listing 3.15, **DialogError** = 0, **OK** = 1, and **Cancel** = 2. You can assign your own specific values to an enumeration member:

```
Public Enum ReturnType
    DialogError = -1
    OK
    Cancel
End Enum
```

In this example, **DialogError** = -1, **OK** = 0, and **Cancel** = 1.

Visual Basic does not type-check enumerations. This means that if you declare an enumeration variable, you can assign it any long integer, and Visual Basic does not complain.

Enumerations can either be public or private. Using enumerations gives you more control over classes. You can use an enumeration to define named constants, which make code easy to read and understand, instead of using nondescriptive integers or long integers. For example, using the **ReturnType** enumeration, shown in Listing 3.16, for the dialog box makes the calling code easy to read and understand.

Listing 3.16 Using a class enumeration.
```
Private Sub Command1_Click()

    Dim theDialog As New Dialog
    Dim ReturnValue As ReturnType
    theDialog.Show 1
    theDialog.FirstName = txtFirstName
    theDialog.LastName = txtLastName
    ReturnValue = theDialog.View()
    If ReturnValue = OK Then
        txtFirstName = theDialog.txtFirst
        txtLastName = theDialog.LastName
```

```
    ElseIf ReturnValue = DialogError Then
        txtFirstName = "Dialog Error"

    End If

End Sub
```

Notice that the code assigns the **ReturnValue** variable the value from the **View** method on the **Dialog** form class. The code then checks **ReturnValue** and takes the appropriate action. Using enumerations makes your code easy to read, understand, and maintain.

Hiding The Details

Use the **Public** keyword sparingly, and always use the **Private** keyword when coding the details of your class. User-defined types are a convenient way to store and manage complex data and data relationships. Use them to simplify implementation and organize your class. Enumerations provide you with a powerful tool for making code readable and maintainable. Anything that makes code easy for others to understand is good object-oriented programming.

Public Properties: Property Let, Get, And Set

The emphasis of object-oriented programming is to get the interface right and then not to change it. This section describes, in detail, controlling and accessing properties. Chapter 2 introduced the concept of *mode* (the direction information flows). You learned how to control the flow of data into and out of your objects by limiting read-write access to properties. You also learned that calling mechanisms can make accessing objects easy or difficult. If you employ the proper mechanisms, your objects and programs become increasingly flexible and adaptive.

Mechanism To Define Mode

Controlling the flow of information into and out of your objects is essential in controlling how the outside world sees and uses your objects. Visual Basic provides a robust and powerful mechanism to define mode.

The **Property Let, Get,** and **Set** keywords let you define any combination of mode for properties. The **Let** keyword provides the write mode. Properties with a **Let** procedure provide the user with the means to change a property's value. The **Get** keyword provides the read mode. A **Get** property procedure lets the user access the property value. The **Set** keyword provides the write mode for objects. Visual Basic uses the **Set** keyword for assigning objects to object variables. The **Set** property procedure lets you define the properties that handle objects.

Read-Write Properties

The most common property mode is read-write. Properties that users can both access and update are called *read-write*. All three of the keywords can be used to define a read-write property, depending on the property type.

The read portion of a read-write property is defined in the **Property Get** procedure. The write portion of a read-write property is defined with either a **Property Set** procedure (for objects) or a **Property Let** procedure for all other types. You designed read-write properties in Chapter 2. Listing 3.17 shows the properties for the **Address** class.

Listing 3.17 The Address class's read-write properties.
```
Public Property Get AddressType() As String
End Property

Public Property Let AddressType(NewType As String)
End Property

Public Property Get Value() As String
End Property

Public Property Let Value(NewValue As String)
End Property
```

As you can see, read-write properties come in **Get/Let** pairs.

A **Property Get** procedure is really a function. It has a return type and must return a value. The way you return a value from a **Property Get** procedure is to assign the property name the value. For example, if you added code for the **Address** class's **Value** property, it might look something like Listing 3.18.

Listing 3.18 Code for read access to the Value property of Address.
```
Private mAddressValue
Public Property Get Value() As String
    Value = mAddressValue
End Property
```

A **Property Let** procedure is really a subroutine. It has at least one parameter—the value to assign to the property. When code assigns the property a value, Visual Basic passes the new value into **Property Let** as a parameter. If you add code for the **Value** property of the **Address** class, it might look like Listing 3.19.

Listing 3.19 Code for write access to the Value property of Address.

```
Public Property Let Value(NewValue As String)
   mAddressValue = NewValue
End Property
```

You can name the parameter anything you want. Visual Basic does not automatically store the property's value for you—you must do this yourself.

In this example, the property value is stored in a class-level variable, **mAddressValue**. However, you don't have to store property values in variables. You can "redirect" the property to use alternative storage mechanisms, such as files or a database. To do this, simply include the code to access the file or database directly in the **Property Let** and **Property Get** procedures.

Read-Only Properties

Read-only properties provide information about your object to the outside world. The outside world cannot directly change the value, but it does have access to the value. Some examples of read-only properties in the real world include the temperature on a thermometer, the time on a clock, and the gas gauge in your car. Yes, you can affect each value, but not directly. To change the temperature on the thermometer, you have to apply heat to it or remove heat from it. To change the time on a clock, you must perform an adjustment procedure or method. Lastly, to change the gas gauge readout in your car, you have to fill the tank with gas or empty it.

Read-only properties are very important; for instance, you would not want someone changing the value of your gas gauge. You may run out of gas and say, "The gauge says the tank is half full!"

You designed read-only properties in Chapter 2. Most of the **Contact** object's properties were read-only. Listing 3.20 shows the read-only properties for the **Contact** class.

Listing 3.20 The Contact class's read-only properties.
```
Public Property Get ContactDate() As Date
End Property

Public Property Get ContactTime() As String
End Property

Public Property Get ContactType() As String
End Property
```

Notice that the read-only properties for the **Contact** class do not have **Property Let** procedures. To create a read-only property, you simply delete the **Property Let** procedure from the class and leave the **Property Get** procedure.

Write-Only Properties

Some modes are less common than others, and the write-only property is one of them. A *write-only property* lets you assign a value to the property, but it does not provide a way to retrieve the value. You implement write-only properties by implementing only the **Property Let** procedure, as shown in Listing 3.21.

Listing 3.21 A write-only property.
```
Public Property Let WriteOnly(NewWriteOnlyValue As String)
End Property
```

Write-Once Properties

So far, you've learned about Visual Basic's support for properties. However, there are times when you need to further define a property's mode. One case is the write-once property.

Write-once properties let you assign a value to them, once. If you attempt to assign a value to a write-once property a second time, it may raise an error, simply ignore the new value, or respond in the appropriate manner based on your design.

One case where you may want a write-once property is when you're tracking real-world identification numbers. When you create an object, you want to assign it an ID. Once you have assigned an ID, you do not want anything to change it—in other words, it's a write-once property. Visual Basic does not support write-once properties directly; you have to write them yourself. However, it's not difficult, as you can see by the example in Listing 3.22.

Listing 3.22 A write-once property.
```
Private mID As Long
Public Property Get ID() As Long
   ID = mID
End Property
Public Property Let ID(NewID As Long)
   ' Do not allow ID=0
   If NewID = 0 Then
      ' raise error
   ElseIf mID <> 0 Then
      ' raise error, ID is already assigned
   Else
      mID = NewID
   End If
End Property
```

This example shows the power of property procedures. You protect the ID value by checking if it already has one. This way, you can take the appropriate action to ensure that the outside world uses the property correctly.

Object Properties

Properties that reference objects use the **Set** keyword instead of **Let**. Visual Basic requires a **Property Set** procedure when you're passing and handling objects. Listing 3.23 shows an example of an object property.

Listing 3.23 Property Set with objects.
```
Private mHomeAddress As Address
Public Property Set HomeAddress(NewAddress As Address)
   Set mHomeAddress = NewAddress
End Property
Public Property Get HomeAddress() As Address
   Set HomeAddress = mHomeAddress
End Property
```

First, the **Property Let** procedure is replaced with a **Property Set** procedure. Second, notice the code for the **Property Get** procedure—it has an object return type and uses the **Set** keyword to assign the property value.

Variant Properties

Perhaps the most difficult Visual Basic data type to handle with properties is **Variant**. Because **Variants** can hold any type, you must provide both **Property Set** and **Property Let** procedures. Additionally, you must make provisions for your property holding an object in your **Property Get** procedure. Listing 3.24 shows how to implement a **Variant** property.

Listing 3.24   A Variant property.
```
Private mWhatever As Variant
Public Property Get Whatever() As Variant
   ' If Whatever references an object, we
   ' must use the Set statement.
   If IsObject(mWhatever) Then
      Set Whatever = mWhatever
   Else
      Whatever = mWhatever
   End If
End Property
Public Property Let Whatever(newValue As Variant)
   mWhatever = newValue
End Property
Public Property Set Whatever(newValue As Variant)
   Set mWhatever = newValue
End Property
```

Notice that the **Property Get** procedure contains code to specifically handle an object type.

One problem with **Variant** properties is knowing what kind of value they hold. If you access the property improperly, Visual Basic raises a runtime error. For example, calling a property that holds an object, like this, causes an error:

```
Dim MyString As String
Dim AnObject to New SomeObject
MyString = AnObject.Whatever
```

A way around this is to check the type before performing the assignment:

```
If IsObject(AnObject.Whatever) Then
      ' there is a problem, the property
      ' does not hold what you expect
   Else
      If TypeName(AnObject.Whatever) = "String" Then
         MyString = AnObject.Whatever
```

```
        Else
            ' there is a problem, the property
            ' does not hold what you expect
        End If
    End If
```

This is pretty tedious, so be careful when creating **Variant** properties or working with **Variants** in general.

Accessing Properties

Now that you've defined properties, you need ways to access them. You've seen property references throughout this chapter and Chapter 2. Properties use the following syntax:

```
Object.Property
```

To assign a value to a property, use the equals (or *assignment*) operator:

```
Object.Property = Value
```

To retrieve a property's value, use the accessor operator (also an equals sign):

```
Value = Object.Property
```

Default Properties And Methods

Visual Basic objects have default properties. Controls have default properties, such as a text box's **Text** property. You can define default properties for your objects also. Defining a default property lets users bypass the **Object.Property** syntax and just use the object name. Here's an example:

```
Object.Property = Value
```

This can be shortened to:

```
Object = Value
```

The best candidate for a default property is the property you use most often. You create a default property by defining it with the Visual Basic IDE. Follow these steps:

1. Select the Tools|Procedure Attributes menu item. Visual Basic displays the Procedure Attributes dialog box (see Figure 3.11).

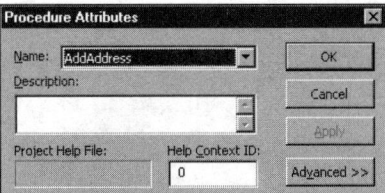

Figure 3.11
The Procedure Attributes dialog box.

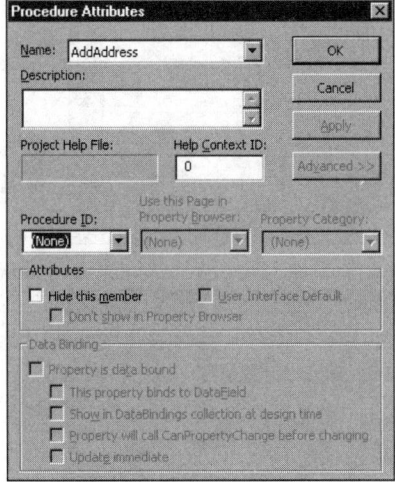

Figure 3.12
The expanded Procedure Attributes dialog box.

2. Click on the Advanced button to expand the dialog box (see Figure 3.12).

3. If a value appears in the Procedure ID drop-down list box, select (None).

4. Select the property you want to make the default in the Name drop-down list box (see Figure 3.13).

5. Select (Default) in the Procedure ID drop-down list box (see Figure 3.14).

6. Click on OK.

Be careful with default properties: If you set a default property and later decide to make the property private, it will continue to be the default property. That is to say, it will be accessible, even though it is a private property.

To remedy this problem, you must make the property public by going to the Procedure Attributes dialog box and setting the procedure ID for the property to (None). Now you can go back and make the property private.

Figure 3.13
Selecting the default property.

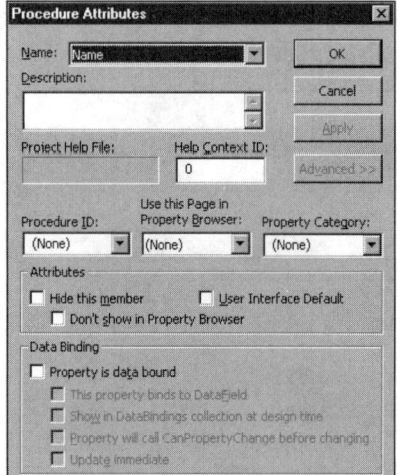

Figure 3.14
Setting the default property.

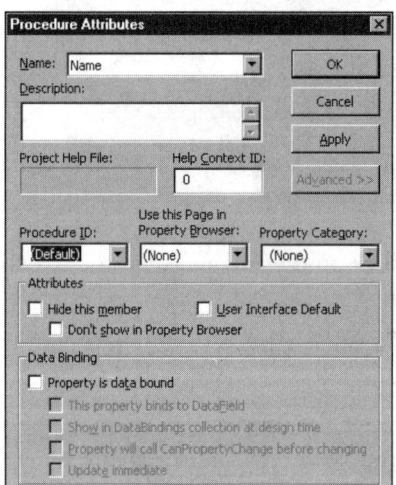

CallByName

So far, you've accessed properties through default properties or the **Object.Property** syntax. Visual Basic provides another mechanism for accessing properties and methods: **CallByName**. **CallByName** lets you call a property or method by providing the property or method name at runtime.

Here's the **CallByName** syntax:

```
Result = CallByName(Object, ProcedureName, CallType, Arguments())
```

In this statement, the following definitions apply:

- **Object**—A reference to the object that has the property or method.
- **ProcedureName**—The property or method to call.
- **CallType**—The kind of procedure to call; a Visual Basic constant that specifies a **Property Get**, **Property Let**, or **Property Set** procedure or method.
- **Arguments( )**—A list of arguments for the property or method.
- **Result**—A **Variant** containing the result or return value of the call.

CallByName is useful when you need to provide access to properties and methods that you do not know about. Usually, you can find out what properties and methods are available from an object at design time. However, there are occasions when you may want to let a user specify which properties and methods to access at runtime. **CallByName** lets you provide this without coding a long **Select Case** statement.

Another advantage of using **CallByName** is its adaptability. If you use **CallByName**, the object you're accessing can change its interface or add a property or method. Also, you can access it without changing your code.

Be careful when using **CallByName**. Although it may be appropriate in some instances, it carries with it a heavy performance penalty. Also, to guard against calling nonexistent properties or using the wrong number of arguments, you need to supply adequate error-handling code. Listing 3.25 shows how to use and handle errors for **CallByName**.

Listing 3.25   Using CallByName.
```
Private Sub Test_Click()

    Dim theDialog As New Dialog
    Dim theMethod As String
    theDialog.FirstName = txtFirstName
    theDialog.LastName = txtLastName
    On Error GoTo BadCall
    theMethod = "View"
    If CallByName(theDialog, theMethod, VbMethod) = vbOK Then
        txtFirstName = theDialog.txtFirst
        txtLastName = theDialog.LastName
    End If
    Exit Sub
```

```
BadCall:
    'Handle an invalid procedure name
    If Err = 438 Then
        MsgBox "Can't find procedure: " & theMethod, , _
            "CallByName Error"
    End If

    'Handle bad arguments
    If Err = 449 Then
        MsgBox "Argument not optional", , "CallByName Error"
    End If
    If Err = 450 Then
        MsgBox "Wrong Number of Arguments", , _
            "CallByName Error"
    End If
End Sub
```

Public Methods And Private Procedures

Another element of getting the interface right involves using methods. Public methods, with their parameters, define the full contract with the outside world. Private procedures, on the other hand, let you organize and define the internal structure and processing of your class.

Tasks such as performing internal calculations, retrieving data from storage, filling lists and controls with data, and breaking up long methods into easy-to-manage functions and subroutines are examples of candidates for private procedures. You can use traditional algorithm and data methods, such as procedural programming and functional decomposition, for programming your class.

You've seen how to identify methods. In the next section, we'll explore interfaces and passing parameters in detail. You need to understand parameters because they're the data pathways within your classes and programs.

Passing Parameters: ByVal Vs. ByRef

Visual Basic has two ways to pass parameters: "by value" and "by reference." Passing parameters "by value" means that Visual Basic passes the actual value of the parameter to the method. Passing parameters "by reference" means that Visual Basic passes a pointer to represent the parameter. The distinction (and its consequences) might not be obvious at first, but it has a big impact on controlling data inside and outside your objects.

By Value

By value is defined as passing the actual value to the parameter. If you think of a parameter as a local variable for a method or procedure, "by value" literally copies the value passed into the local variable. If you change the value in the method or procedure, you're changing a local copy of the variable, not the one owned by the calling procedure. This avoids any conflict between the method and any calling procedure.

Visual Basic uses the **ByVal** keyword to declare "by value" parameters. Place the **ByVal** keyword in front of the parameter declaration to define a "by value" parameter. Listing 3.26 shows an example.

Listing 3.26   A ByVal parameter.
```
Public Sub UpdateTime(ByVal NewTime As String)
End Sub
```

Try to declare as many parameters as possible as **ByVal**. This limits the opportunities for difficulties if you change the parameter's value and cause a problem in the calling procedure.

By Reference

As previously stated, *by reference* refers to Visual Basic passing a pointer to represent a parameter. If you call a method and use a variable to pass it a parameter, you're actually passing the address of the variable. If you change the value of the parameter in the method, you change the value in the calling procedure. This is a side effect of passing parameters by reference.

Remember the discussion of modes with respect to properties in Chapter 2? Well, parameters have modes also. A "by reference" parameter is a read-write parameter. The method that defines the parameter has full access to any variable you pass to it.

Visual Basic provides the **ByRef** keyword to declare "by reference" parameters. You place the **ByRef** keyword in front of a parameter declaration to pass a parameter "by reference." "By reference" is the default mode for parameters in Visual Basic. If you do not put a keyword in front of the parameter declaration, Visual Basic assumes **ByRef**. Listing 3.27 shows an example.

Listing 3.27 A ByRef parameter.
```
Public Sub AddTime(ByVal theTime, _
                   ByVal Seconds As String, _
                   ByRef NewTime As String)
End Sub
```

This code uses the first two parameters to calculate a new time and then passes the answer back in the **NewTime** parameter.

Avoid using "by reference" parameters. This type of parameter is seldom necessary, and its side effects are difficult to detect. Analyze the requirements of a method or procedure. If the purpose is to take in some data, transform it, and then pass the results back in the same variables, "by reference" is appropriate. Otherwise, don't use **ByRef** parameters.

So, why did Microsoft make the **ByRef** the default mode? Efficiency. A "by value" parameter literally copies the value to a local copy. This takes time, so in most cases you save a few milliseconds by passing parameters **ByRef**—an amount that you'll probably never notice. However, for large data structures, such as user-defined types, **ByRef** may be the best choice.

Don't allow the default parameter mode to cause you problems; give as much thought to passing parameters as you do to properties and methods.

Optional Parameters

All parameters might not be required. The *optional parameter* is an important feature that lets you provide an adaptive interface. An interface that can adapt to the available data is more robust than one that is rigid and requires all the data. Some parameters are always required, but for the ones that are not, Visual Basic provides the **Optional** keyword. When you define a parameter as optional (using the **Optional** keyword), Visual Basic does not require you to pass a value to it.

Optional parameters give you another way to let the user influence how processing occurs without you giving up control. By accepting selected parameters or groups of parameters, your procedure can detect which parameters are used and adapt its processing to the supplied information. For example, consider a method for retrieving an element from a linked list. The method could have an optional parameter to retrieve an element with a specific value or the current element within the list. See Listing 3.28 for an example of a linked list item with an optional parameter.

Listing 3.28 A linked list item with an optional parameter.

```
Private mCurrentItem As Long
Private mNumItems As Long
Public Function Item(Optional Index As Long) As Variant
   If Not IsMissing(Index) then
      If Index <= mNumItems And _
         Index >= 0 Then
            mCurrentItem = Index
            ' walk the list and find the desired item
         else
            ' return the current item
         end if
   Else
      ' return the current item
   End If
End Function
```

Take a look at this function, which checks for the **Index** parameter. If this function finds **Index** and it's within range, the function fulfills the request; otherwise, it simply returns the current item. To make this a fully functional method, you must do more checking. However, this example illustrates how optional parameters work.

Optional parameters can have default values. You don't have to write code to check whether the parameter is missing, because the parameter always contains a value, either the default value or the value passed to it. Listing 3.29 shows an example of an optional parameter with a default value.

Listing 3.29 An optional parameter with a default value.

```
Private mCurrentItem As Long
Public Function Item(Optional Index As Long = 0) As Variant
If Index <= mNumItems And _
   Index >= 0 Then
      mCurrentItem = Index
      ' walk the list and find the desired item
   Else
      mCurrentItem = 0
      ' return the first item
   End If
End Function
```

This implementation returns the first element within the list if you omit the index. The **Index** parameter defaults to 0.

ParamArray

There are times when you need to pass an indeterminate array of parameters to a procedure. This may be necessary when the procedure lets the user define how many parameters to pass. The **Printf** function in C uses a variable number of parameters to format a string for output. **ParamArray** lets you define similar behavior. Listing 3.30 shows the C language **Printf** function declared within Visual Basic.

Listing 3.30   A subroutine with a ParamArray parameter.

```
Function Printf(theFormat As String, _
                ParamArray Values()) As String

End Sub
```

Coding A Procedure With *ParamArray*

Treat **ParamArray** like an optional **Variant** array parameter. The example shown in Listing 3.31 implements a little of the C language **Printf** functionality.

Listing 3.31   The Printf code.

```
Function Printf(ByVal theFormat As String, _
                ParamArray Values()) As String

   Dim ResultString As String
   Dim Element As Variant
   Dim FormatLocation As Long

   If IsMissing(Values()) Then
      ' raise error
   End If

   ResultString = theFormat
   For Each Element In Values
      FormatLocation = InStr(ResultString, "%")
      ResultString = Left$(ResultString, _
      FormatLocation - 1) & _
         Element & Right$(ResultString, Len(ResultString) _
         - FormatLocation - 1)
   Next

   Printf = ResultString
End Function
```

You can check for the existence of **ParamArray**, just like any other optional parameter. Also, **ParamArray** acts like any other Visual Basic array.

Calling A Procedure With *ParamArray*

You can call a procedure with **ParamArray** like you would any other procedure. The only difference is that you can include as many parameters as you want. Listing 3.32 shows an example.

Listing 3.32   Using ParamArray.
```
Text1 = Printf("Testing %i %i %i", 1, 2, 3)
Text1 = Printf("Testing %s %s %s %s %s", "A", "B", "C", _
  "D", "E")
```

Notice that the same function call has a different number of parameters.

ParamArray Benefits

The primary benefit of using the **ParamArray** parameter is that it can accept an arbitrary number of parameters. However, the other major advantage is that you can process **ParamArray** to accept any combination of parameters, mixed types, single types, complex types, a fixed number, a maximum number, or a minimum number. The possibilities are endless—limited only by your application, design skills, and imagination.

ParamArray Limitations

In addition to its stated benefits, **ParamArray** does have some limitations:

- It must be the last parameter within the parameter list.
- You cannot use the **ByVal** or **ByRef** keywords with **ParamArray**.
- You cannot use the **Optional** keyword with **ParamArray**.
- No other parameter within the list can be optional.

Be careful when you use **ParamArray**. Because you process the **ParamArray** format inside the procedure, Visual Basic cannot check for valid syntax or types. Do anyone using the procedure a favor: Document within the procedure what parameters are valid and how the procedure processes them.

Named Parameters

Visual Basic lets you call procedures with named parameters. *Named parameters* let you pass parameters into a procedure by explicitly naming them and assigning them values. This makes your code easy to understand because it explicitly states which values you're passing to which parameters. Another benefit is that you can pass the parameters in any order. Normally, parameters must be passed to a procedure in the order you declare them within the procedure declaration. Listing 3.33 demonstrates how to call procedures with named parameters.

Listing 3.33 Using named parameters.
```
Private MyProspect As New Prospect
MyProspect.ScheduleNextContact ContactDate:=Today(), _
                               ContactTime:="3:30pm"
```

Use named parameters whenever possible. They make code easy to maintain and debug, by making information passing explicit. A good rule of thumb is to use named parameters on anything with more than one parameter.

Events

The final element of a solid interface is defining what the objects do on their own—events. *Events* provide a way for objects to notify other objects and procedures of events within the object. An object that declares and raises events is called an *event source*. In Chapter 2, you identified the **Notify** event for the **Contact** class. When the time comes for a salesperson to make a contact, the **Contact** object raises the **Notify** event. Events are important, not just because they can notify the rest of your program what is going on, but because they can also carry information.

Declaring An Event

You declare events within the declaration section of a class module. Like procedures, events can have arguments. You pass information out of your class with the arguments. Arguments follow the same rules as parameters: They can be **ByVal** or **ByRef**, and they have a type. There are some exceptions to the type of arguments you can pass within an event. You cannot pass optional arguments or **ParamArray** parameters out of an event. Named parameter association is also forbidden.

Visual Basic defines the **Event** keyword for declaring events. You place the **Event** keyword in front of the event name. All events are public. If you use the **Private** keyword within an event declaration, Visual Basic issues a compiler error. In Chapter 2, the **Contact** class's events were declared, as shown in Listing 3.34.

Listing 3.34 Events of the Contact class.
```
Public Event Notify()
Public Event ProductPurchased()
```

Take a closer look at the **Notify** event. It would be nice if it could notify the Prospect object which type of contact to make. This way, the Prospect object does not have to ask the Contact object what to do next. See Listing 3.35 for the new declaration.

Listing 3.35 The improved Notify event.
```
Public Event Notify(ByVal ContactType As String)
```

Now that you've declared the event, how do you raise it? How do you handle it? The next sections address both these questions.

Raising An Event

Once you've declared an event, you need to raise it. Visual Basic provides the **RaiseEvent** keyword for this task. Raising an event is similar to calling a procedure. The code in Listing 3.36 may appear within the **Contact** class.

Listing 3.36 Raising an event in the Contact class.
```
If Me.ContactDate = Today() then
    RaiseEvent Notify(Me.ContactType)
End If
```

Notice that this code fragment passes the **ContactType** property to the receiving procedure or object. You've raised the event, but how do you handle the event within a procedure or object?

Handling An Event

The next step in learning about events is handling them. Visual Basic defines the **WithEvents** keyword to deal with an object's events. To handle events that an object raises, declare an object variable of the object's class and use the **WithEvents** keyword. Figure 3.15 shows the **Contact** variable declaration for the **Prospect** class.

Because the **Contact** class is an event source and you're using the **WithEvents** keyword, Visual Basic includes the class-level variable

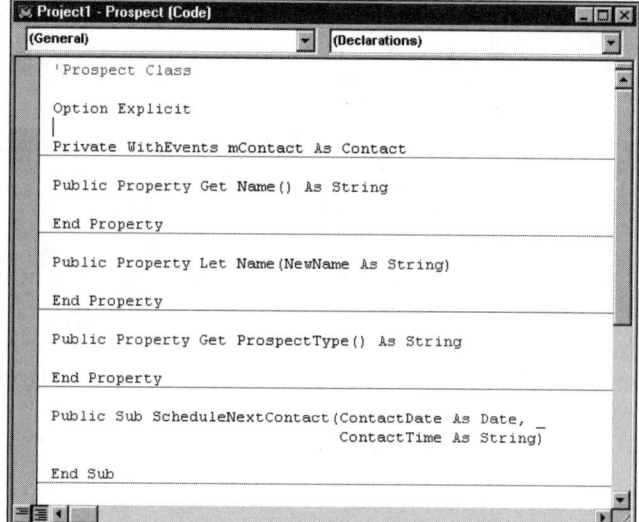

Figure 3.15
The **Prospect** class declaring a class-level variable for the **Contact** class.

name within the class members drop-down list box, as shown in Figure 3.16.

Suppose you select the **mContact** object within the class members drop-down list box. Figure 3.17 shows how Visual Basic displays this object's events.

When you select one of the events from the drop-down list box, Visual Basic adds an *event handler* to your class. Listing 3.37 shows the event handler for the **mContact** variable within the **Prospect** class.

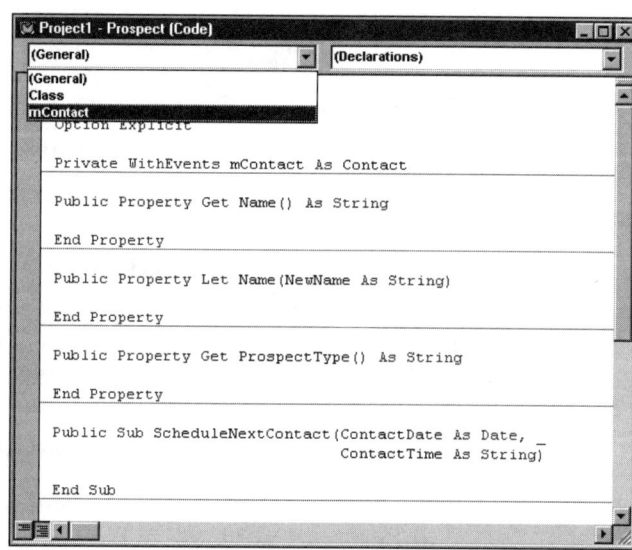

Figure 3.16
The event source within the class members drop-down list box.

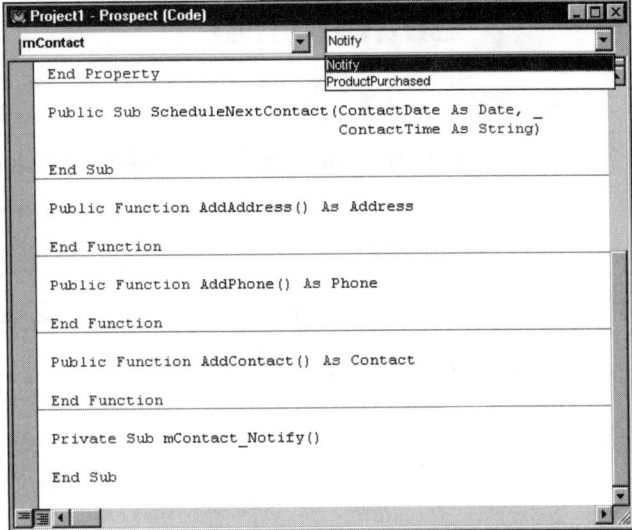

Figure 3.17
The event source's events.

Listing 3.37   An event handler.
```
Private Sub mContact_Notify(ByVal ContactType As String)
End Sub
```

You can now write code to handle the event. Notice that the information from the event is passed to the event handler, just like a parameter.

Of course, with all these cool features come some limitations on **WithEvents** variables:

- You must declare the **WithEvents** variables with a specific class type. You cannot declare them as generic **Object** types.

- You must explicitly create event source objects and assign them within the declaration. You cannot use the **New** keyword with the **WithEvents** keyword. Visual Basic will complain with a compiler error.

- You cannot create arrays of object variables with the **WithEvents** keyword. Visual Basic will complain about this with a compiler error.

- You must declare the object variable using the **WithEvents** keyword within class modules, form modules, and other modules that define a class. You cannot declare them within standard Visual Basic modules.

Conclusion

In this chapter, we explored Visual Basic's support for object-oriented programming. Topics we covered included:

- *Class modules* are the basic building blocks of Visual Basic projects.

- You've been using classes for as long as you've been programming in Visual Basic. Form modules are special class modules with an interface.

- You learned how to create your own class module, as well as how to add properties, methods, and events.

- This chapter demonstrated how to extend forms. Extending forms gives you control over how you use them.

- You learned the importance of *coupling*, which is a measure of dependency between modules. *Loosely coupled* modules depend very little on each other, whereas *strongly coupled* modules share data and depend heavily on each other.

- The way modules store data and manage scope is called *binding*. Standard modules have one copy of their data within memory, and public variables have program scope. The objects you create from the class modules have their own copy of their data, and the data is module (or class) scoped.

- Avoid using global variables. They lead to strongly coupled programs.

- Use user-defined types and enumerations to hide implementation and data.

- *Modes* help manage data flow into and out of your objects. Use the proper mode for properties: read-write, read-only, write-only, or write-once.

- Be careful to plan how you pass parameters. Parameters have modes also. Use **ByVal** for most parameters. Use **ByRef** when your procedure is required to return a value within the parameter.

- You learned how to declare, raise, and handle events. The Visual Basic IDE supports events directly. It displays *event sources* (objects that define events) and their declared events directly within the development interface.

Chapter 4
VB's Object Tools

Key Topics:

- *References Dialog Box*
- *Object Browser*
- *Package And Deployment Wizard*

VB6 comes with a number of very useful object tools and wizards that help simplify and speed up the application development process, including:

- *References dialog box*—Before you can view an ActiveX component's type library with the Object Browser, you need to set a reference to the library. You can do this via the References dialog box.

- *Object Browser*—If your Visual Basic project includes a reference to an ActiveX component's class library, you can use the Object Browser to view the reusable objects of the class library.

- *Package And Deployment Wizard*—With the Package And Deployment Wizard, you can create a set of distribution disks for VB applications, ActiveX component file(s), and dependency files.

- *Data Object Wizard*—The Data Object Wizard helps you create Class objects and the User Control objects bound to these Class objects.

- *Data Form Wizard*—The Data Form Wizard helps you create a form with objects bound to a local or remote data source.

- *ActiveX Control Interface Wizard*—The ActiveX Control Interface Wizard helps you define the interface (properties, methods, and events) and create the underlying code for the interface of the ActiveX controls you create with VB.

- *Class Builder utility*—The Class Builder utility, included within the Professional and Enterprise editions of Visual Basic, can generate much of the code you need to implement an object model. This utility creates robust object properties and collection classes; in addition, it lets you rearrange your model easily.

- *Application Wizard*—You can use the Application Wizard to build a fully functional single-document interface (SDI), multiple-document interface (MDI), or Explorer-style VB application that includes the framework and support for menus and submenus, toolbars, Internet connectivity, and more. You can edit the forms as well as view and modify the code of this application. The code that the Application Wizard generates includes comments that help you understand what the wizard has created and what you can do to add your own functionality.
- *Toolbar Wizard*—The Toolbar Wizard helps you create a new toolbar that you can integrate with your application.
- *ActiveX Document Migration Wizard*—With the ActiveX Document Migration Wizard, you can convert the forms within your current project to ActiveX documents.

Although VB6 includes a number of object tools and wizards, this chapter discusses only the most important ones: the References dialog box, the Object Browser, and the Package And Deployment Wizard. For more information on the other tools, refer to the online Help.

Given the growing popularity of OLE Automation among Windows developers over the last couple years, you now have several class libraries (that is, ActiveX components) whose public members are available for reuse within your projects.

How does a VB client application programmer find out how to reuse the objects within these class libraries? You get the necessary information to reuse the objects within ActiveX components in two ways. First, you can go to the printed documentation or online Help file for the ActiveX component, search through the information, and try to determine how to call the members of the objects. For ActiveX components created with a programming language such as an older version of Delphi, this is the only way to do it—when Delphi 2 creates an ActiveX component, it doesn't create a type library along with the ActiveX component.

Second, you can use Microsoft's Object Browser to help you find out how to reuse an ActiveX component's objects. This assumes that the ActiveX component you're interested in was developed with a programming language such as VB6, which supports the creation of type libraries that the Object Browser can read. VB's ability to automatically create a type library when it creates an ActiveX component is one of the major advantages it has over other programming languages such as Delphi 2. In this chapter, we'll take an in-depth look at how the Object Browser works.

Using The References Dialog Box

Before you can view an ActiveX component's type library with the Object Browser, you need to set a reference to it, which you can do via the References dialog box. Here are some reasons why you might want to set a reference to another class library within your VB client application:

- To view its members within the Object Browser window
- To display any Help topics related to its members
- To copy and paste the sample code into your client application to reuse one of its members
- To enable your client application to instantiate a class through early binding

To display the References dialog box, start VB6 and double-click on the Standard EXE icon. Next, select Project|References. Visual Basic reads the Windows registration database, finds all the references it might be able to use, and loads and displays the References dialog box, shown in Figure 4.1.

Depending on the speed of your PC and how many ActiveX components are registered on it, loading the References dialog box with the available references can take anywhere from 5 to 25 seconds. The References dialog box initially displays with several references selected. These preselected references are determined by Visual Basic's startup configuration. References will always be preset to four items: Visual Basic For Applications, Visual Basic Runtime Objects And Procedures, Visual Basic Objects And Procedures, and OLE Automation. When the References dialog box first displays, the last preselected reference within the list is always highlighted.

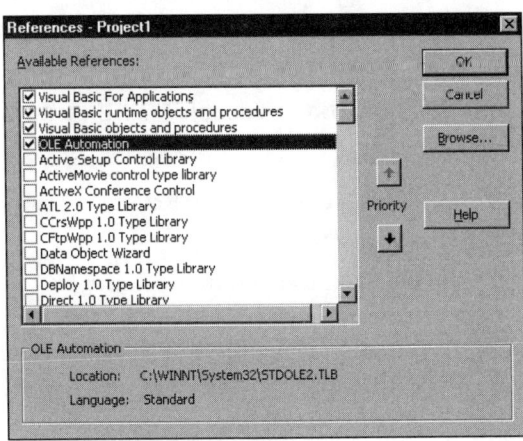

Figure 4.1
Visual Basic displaying the References dialog box.

The References dialog box has several important features:

- *Available References list box*—This section lists the references available to your project. You add a reference to your project by selecting the checkbox next to its name; likewise, you remove a reference by clearing the checkbox next to its name. You cannot remove a reference for an item that is currently being used within your project. If you're not using any objects within a referenced library, you should clear the checkbox for that reference to minimize the number of object references Visual Basic must resolve, thus reducing the time it takes your project to compile.

- *Priority buttons*—Clicking on these buttons moves a reference up and down on the list. When you refer to an object within code, Visual Basic searches each application selected within the References dialog box in the order the applications are displayed. If two applications use the same name for an object, Visual Basic uses the definition provided by the application listed higher within the Available References list box.

- *Result frame*—This frame, located at the bottom of the dialog box, displays the path of the reference selected within the Available References list box, as well as the language version.

- *Browse button*—Clicking on this button displays the Add Reference dialog box, which lets you search other directories for the file types able to be listed as a reference.

The References dialog box can list four kinds of files as references: type/class libraries (*.OLB, *.TLB), DLL files (*.DLL), executable files (*.EXE), and ActiveX controls (*.OCX).

Setting A Reference

To set a reference to a class library or ActiveX component within your project, follow these steps:

1. Start VB6 and double-click on the Standard EXE icon.

2. To display the References dialog box, select Project|References.

3. Within the Available References list, select the item to which you want to set a reference.

4. Click on the up-arrow priority button until the reference you selected moves up to the top of the Available References list box. Visual Basic will permit you to move it up to only the fourth item within the list, just below the references to Visual Basic For Applications, Visual Basic Runtime Objects And Procedures, and Visual

Basic Objects And Procedures. These three references have the highest priority and cannot be superseded.

At this point, the References dialog box should look similar to what is shown in Figure 4.2.

Using The Object Browser

The Object Browser window displays the classes and members available from class libraries as well as the modules and procedures within your Visual Basic project. Once you've set a reference within your Visual Basic project to an ActiveX component's class library, you can use the Object Browser to view the class library's reusable objects.

The Object Browser window first appeared within a Microsoft application in January 1994, when Excel 5 with Visual Basic for Applications (VBA) was released. It showed up a few months later within Project 4 with VBA. Then, in November 1995, the Object Browser made its debut within Visual Basic. A common thread runs through these applications that dictates that they have a feature like the Object Browser: They all contain programming languages that can call and reuse the objects within ActiveX components. In the cases of Excel and Project, the **CreateObject** function is available to do this. In VB6, you can use either the **CreateObject** function or the **As New** statement to instantiate a class within an ActiveX component.

Because applications that were developed as OLE Automation servers (now ActiveX components) proliferated in 1995 and 1996, the need to be able to browse these applications quickly and easily in order to reuse their objects became clear. A third-party software vendor, Apex

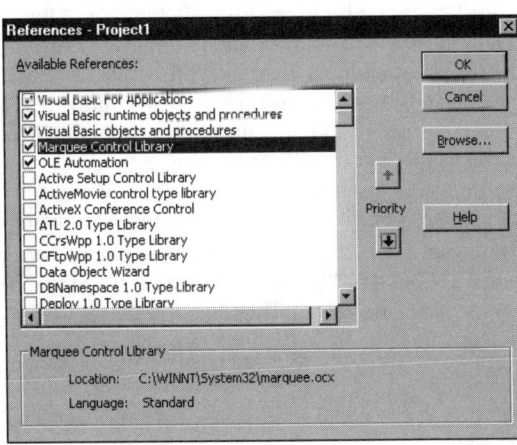

Figure 4.2
Visual Basic permits you to move the selected reference (the Marquee Control Library, in this case) up to the fourth item within the list.

Software Corporation, even released a utility called VBA Companion, which was advertised as the ultimate Object Browser for OLE Automation and VBA programming.

With the release of VB5, Microsoft upgraded its own Object Browser's functionality and flexibility with the addition of the following features:

- The Object Browser is now an MDI child window instead of a dialog box, which lets you move back and forth between your code module and the browser window without having to reopen the browser each time.
- The window and its controls are resizable.
- The window has a toolbar and supports a right-click pop-up menu to do the most common tasks quickly.
- You can sort and display the members of a class alphabetically or by type of member (that is, events, methods, and properties).
- You can do string searches and return a list of all the classes that contain the string.
- You can copy any item or text listed within the Object Browser and paste it into a code module or application.

To display the Object Browser window from VB6, select View|Object Browser or press F2. Figure 4.3 shows the window after a class library, class, and member have been selected.

Tables 4.1 and 4.2 describe the controls and pop-up menu commands that you can access from this window.

Table 4.1 The Object Browser window controls.

Control	Description
Libraries/Projects	This drop-down list in the upper-left corner of the window displays the libraries available to your project. Select from available libraries to view the classes, modules, procedures, methods, properties, and events you can use in code. When the Object Browser first appears during a Visual Basic session, the entry <All Libraries> is the selection (which actually displays the classes from Visual Basic itself). If you make another selection and then close the Object Browser, it restores your last selection the next time you display it. To add a class library to the Libraries/Projects list, use the References dialog box.
Search Text	This drop-down combo list, below the Libraries/Projects drop-down list, lets you enter a string that VB can use to search the class library. Clicking on the Search button starts the search. The Object Browser then expands its window to display a Search Results list, which contains all the classes containing that string.

(continued)

VB's Object Tools   121

Table 4.1 The Object Browser window controls *(continued)*.

Control	Description
Classes	If you choose your own Visual Basic project within the Libraries/Projects list, the Classes list, on the left side of the Object Browser window, displays modules from your project, including any classes you defined within the current project. If you choose a class library within the Libraries/Projects list, the Classes list displays the classes available within that library. If you choose Show Hidden Members from the pop-up menu, the Classes list displays any hidden members of the library.
Members	If you choose your own project within the Libraries/Project box, the Members list, to the right of the Classes list, displays the procedures, properties, methods, and events you have defined. If you choose a class library within the Libraries/Projects box, the Members list displays members for the class that's selected within the Classes list.

(continued)

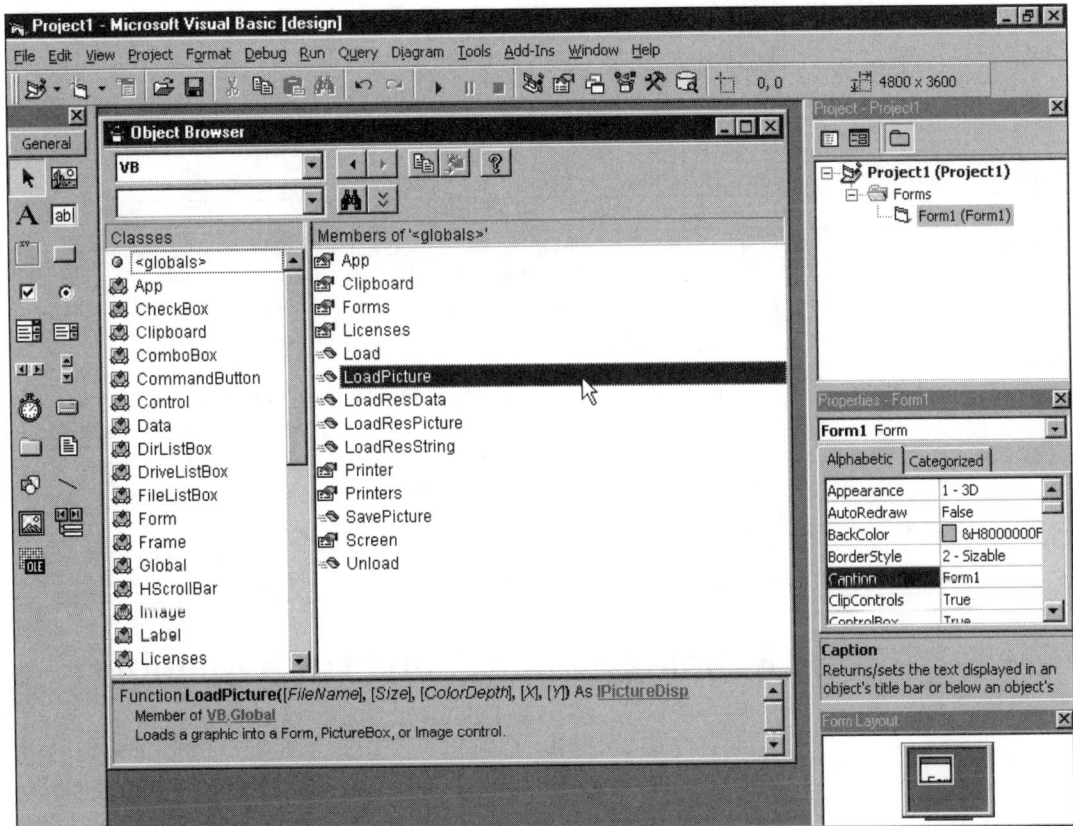

Figure 4.3
The Object Browser displaying the selected class library, class, and member.

Table 4.1 The Object Browser window controls *(continued)*.

Control	Description
Toolbar button	This button, in the upper-right side of the window, displays the online Help topic (if it has one) for the item selected within the Libraries/Projects, Classes, or Members list. If the item does not have a Help topic, it displays the Contents topic of the Help file linked to the class library.
Item Description	This scrollable, read-only edit control, at the bottom of the window, displays information about the currently selected item (its declaration and arguments, the class or library it belongs to, and a brief description of its purpose). It signifies that an argument is optional by enclosing it within brackets, or that an argument has been declared using the **ParamArray** keyword by displaying the declaration format (for example, **ParamArray Properties() As Variant**).

Table 4.2 The Object Browser window's pop-up menu commands.

Control	Description
Copy	Copies the selected item or text to the Clipboard.
View Definition	Displays the code module or procedure for the currently selected item.
Find Whole Word Only	Qualifies a search to find any whole words. This option is not selected by default.
Group Members	Sorts and displays the members of a class by kind of member (that is, events, methods, and properties). This option is not selected by default.
Show Hidden Members	Displays hidden members. This option is not selected by default.
References	Displays the References dialog box.
Properties	Displays the Member Options or Procedure Attributes dialog box, which lets you specify Help information for a member (Description, Help File, and Help Context ID). This item is enabled only for items within public classes of the current project.
Help	Displays the online Help topic (if it has one) for the item selected within the Libraries/Projects, Classes, or Members list; if the item does not have a Help topic, it displays the Contents topic of the Help file linked to the class library.
Dockable	Positions the Object Browser window in the upper-left corner of the screen or within the last position you moved it to. This option is not selected by default.
Hide	Hides the Object Browser window. This option is not selected by default. To see the Object Browser again, select View|Object Browser or press F2.

Running Sample Code For A Member

If an ActiveX component's class library has a Help file, and the Help topic for a member has sample code in it, you can display and run the sample code to see how to call the member and handle the value(s) it returns. To do so, use the Visual Basic Objects And Procedures reference as an example and follow these steps:

1. Start VB6 and double-click on the Standard EXE icon.

2. To display the Object Browser, press F2. Then, select the **VB** class and its **LoadPicture** member.

3. To display its Help topic, click on the ? button.
4. Click on the Example hotspot to display the Example code topic.
5. Select all the code; then, select Copy to place it on the Clipboard.
6. Open the code window for **Form1** and move it to the bottom of the General Declarations section.
7. Paste the sample code from the Clipboard into the code window. Visual Basic automatically assigns the sample code to the correct event procedures.
8. Select Run|Start; then, click on the Form object.
9. The **LoadPicture** method is called and executes.

Using The Package And Deployment Wizard

You can use the Package And Deployment Wizard that Microsoft distributes with VB6 to create a set of distribution disks for VB applications, ActiveX component file(s), and dependency files. The screen shown in Figure 4.4 asks you to choose the Visual Basic project file for the application you want to distribute. It doesn't matter if you've been making more than one kind of ActiveX component from the same set of source code and have more than one project file (for example, EFSD.VBP, EFSE.VBP, and so on). Select one of the project files by clicking on Browse; then, click on Package.

The Package And Deployment Wizard next prompts you to choose a packaging setup. Here, you'll choose a setup that you previously created

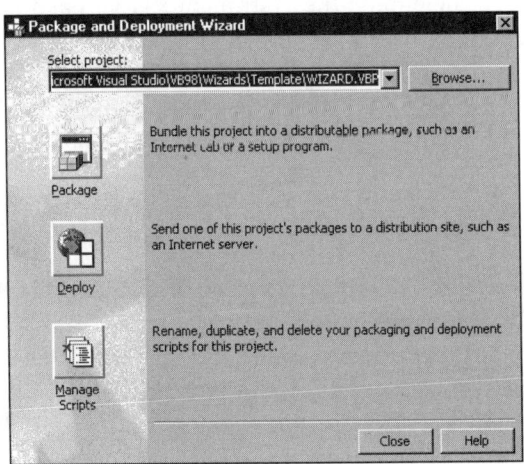

Figure 4.4
Choosing the Visual Basic project file for the application you want to distribute.

or you'll choose None to create a new one. Next, the wizard prompts you to choose one of the three distribution modes:

- *Standard Setup Package*—A package that you install with a SETUP.EXE program
- *Internet Package*— A CAB-based installation that the browser automatically downloads from the Web site
- *Dependency File*—A file list that outlines the runtime components for your application

You can distribute a VB application, ActiveX component, or dependency file under these three modes, as shown in Figure 4.5.

The following sections briefly discuss each of these modes as well as the Uninstall feature of the Package And Deployment Wizard.

Standard Setup Package

Choose Standard Setup Package and then click on Next to proceed. Specify the folder where you want the Package And Deployment Wizard to assemble the package. Next, the wizard displays a list of files that it will include within the package. Make sure this list is complete. The wizard lets you add any files that it missed. You have to know whether the Visual Basic application uses any Help files, database files, or third-party DLL files that the wizard did not list and manually add them. Next, the wizard lets you specify whether you want to create one large CAB file or multiple CAB files for your package. Because the Standard Setup Package uses floppy disks for distribution, choose the multiple CAB files option. The wizard then asks you to specify the title that the installation program should display when installing the program. Next, determine the Start menu's groups and items that will be created by

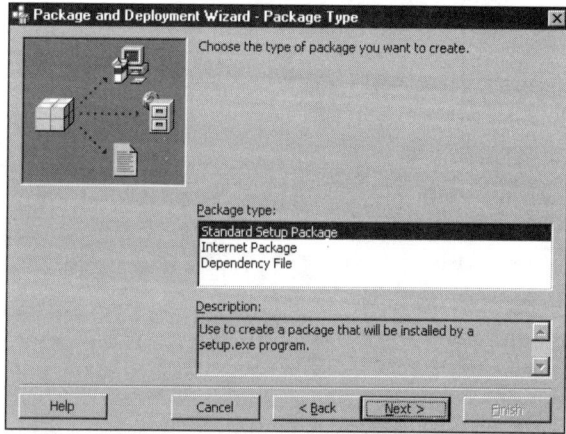

Figure 4.5
Choosing the distribution mode for your VB application, ActiveX component, or dependency file.

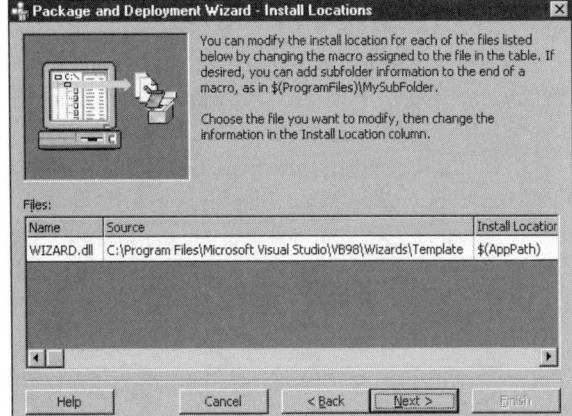

Figure 4.6
Using the Install Locations screen to modify the installation locations for the component files the application uses.

the installation process. When you reach the Install Locations screen, as shown in Figure 4.6, the wizard lets you modify the installation location(s) for the component files your application uses.

When you reach the Shared Files screen, shown in Figure 4.7, the wizard lets you specify whether some of the files your application uses can be treated as shared files.

You complete the work of the Package And Deployment Wizard by following these steps:

1. To move to the Finished dialog box, select Next.
2. To save the wizard configuration information to a script file, specify a name for the script. You can retrieve the information stored within this script file when you next use the wizard.
3. To complete the compression of the files and the creation of the distribution disks, select Finish.

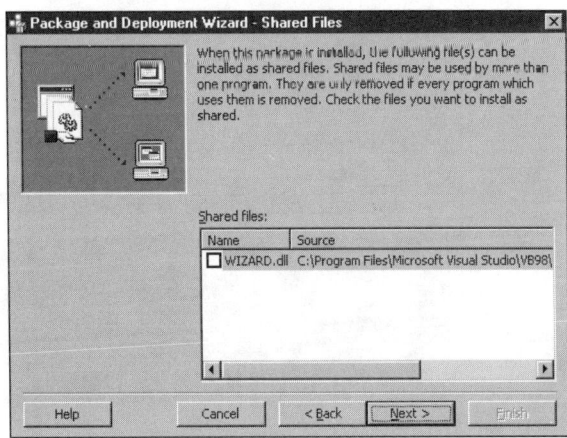

Figure 4.7
Specifying whether some of the files the application uses can be treated as shared files.

Internet Package

Choose Internet Package and then click on Next to proceed. Specify the folder where you want the Package And Deployment Wizard to assemble the package. Next, the wizard displays a list of files that it will include within the package. Make sure this list is complete. The wizard lets you add any files that it missed. You have to know whether the ActiveX components use any Help files, database files, or third-party DLL files that the wizard did not list and manually add them. When you reach the File Source screen, shown in Figure 4.8, the wizard prompts you to choose the source for each file that will be included within the package. A file can be part of the CAB file or downloaded from a Web site.

When you reach the Safety Settings screen, shown in Figure 4.9, the wizard asks you to specify the safety settings for each component. Unless

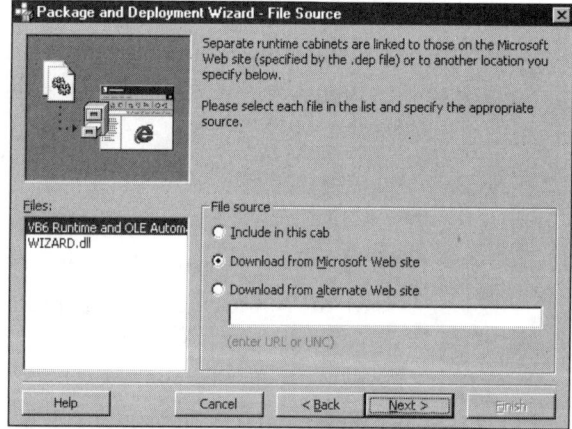

Figure 4.8
Choosing the file source.

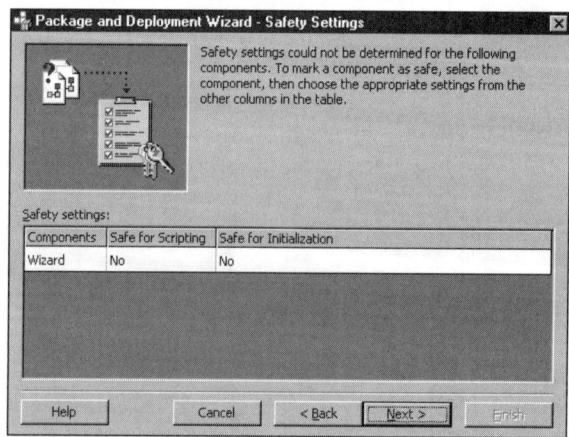

Figure 4.9
All components, by default, are marked as not being safe for scripting and initialization.

you're absolutely sure the components included within the package are safe for scripting and initialization, proceed with the default settings.

You complete the work of the Package And Deployment Wizard by following these steps:

1. To move to the Finished dialog box, select Next.
2. To save the wizard configuration information for the ActiveX component(s) to a script file, specify a name for the script. You can retrieve the information stored within this script file when you next use the wizard.
3. To complete the compression of the files and the creation of the package, select Finish.

When you actually install an ActiveX component(s) from a set of distribution disks by double-clicking on the file SETUP.EXE from Explorer or File Manager, you have no way to specify the path. The installation routine automatically performs the following tasks:

- It installs the ActiveX component and any related Help files or database files on the path for shared components. On Windows 95/98 and NT 4, this directory is \PROGRAM FILES\COMMON FILES\OLESVR.
- It installs all other DLL or EXE files on the Windows system path.

Dependency File

Choose Dependency File and then click on Next to proceed. Specify the folder where you want the Package And Deployment Wizard to assemble the package. Next, the wizard displays a list of files that it will include within the package. Make sure this list is complete. The wizard lets you add any files that it missed. You have to know whether the dependency file uses any Help files, database files, or third-party DLL files that the wizard did not list and manually add them. When you reach the CAB Information Screen, shown in Figure 4.10, the wizard prompts you to optionally package your dependency file into a CAB file. Specify the URL from which the CAB file can be retrieved.

When you reach the Install Locations screen, the wizard lets you modify the installation locations for the component files your application uses.

You complete the work of the Package And Deployment Wizard by following these steps:

1. To move to the Finished dialog box, select Next.

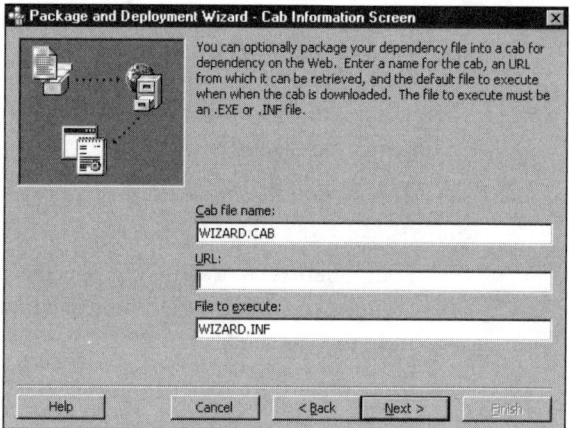

Figure 4.10
Specifying the URL for the CAB file.

2. To save the wizard configuration information to a script file, specify a name for the script. You can retrieve the information stored within this script file when you next use the wizard.

3. To complete the compression of the files and the creation of the package, select Finish.

Uninstall Feature

Visual Basic's Package And Deployment Wizard also supports the Uninstall feature—a feature required of any 32-bit application that displays the "Designed for Microsoft Windows 95" logo. If you've installed a 32-bit ActiveX component from a set of distribution disks, this Uninstall feature is the easiest and safest way to remove its files (and all its related entries within the Windows registration database) from the system.

To use the Uninstall feature, open the Windows Control Panel and double-click on the Add/Remove Programs icon. From the Add/Remove Programs dialog box, select the name of the project file under which you created the distribution disks for the ActiveX component(s) and click on Add/Remove. A series of dialog boxes leads you through the Uninstall process. At a certain point, you're asked whether you want to remove all shared components or only selected ones. With this question, the Uninstall process is reminding you that several applications can share and use ActiveX components. Don't panic. Removing all shared components means removing only those ActiveX components that were installed as part of the single installation routine to which this Uninstall process applies. The normal selection is to remove all the shared components.

Conclusion

VB6 comes with a number of very useful object tools and wizards that help simplify and speed up the application development process. These include the References dialog box, the Object Browser, the Package And Deployment Wizard, the Data Object Wizard, the Data Form Wizard, the ActiveX Control Interface Wizard, the Class Builder utility, the Application Wizard, the Toolbar Wizard, and the ActiveX Document Migration Wizard. In this chapter, you learned how to use three of these tools—the References dialog box, the Object Browser, and the Package And Deployment Wizard.

Chapter 5
Advanced Classes

Key Topics:

- *Object Lifetime*
- *Initializing Objects*
- *Object Persistence*
- *Collections*
- *Implementing Relationships Between Objects*
- *Data-Aware Classes*
- *Polymorphism*

So far, you've learned about objects, designed objects, and created classes in Visual Basic. You've also explored Visual Basic's object tools. In this chapter, we'll take a closer look at Visual Basic classes. You'll learn about an object's life and how a class becomes an object. You'll also learn how to create a self-initializing class as well as how to destroy the object when you are finished with it.

We identified relationships in Chapter 2. In this chapter, you'll learn about implementing relationships. You'll discover object collections, why they are important, and how to use them to implement relationships.

Visual Basic 6 (VB6) introduces a new concept for VB: data-aware classes. This chapter explores this new concept as well as how to implement and take advantage of it.

Finally, we'll take a closer look at polymorphism. You'll learn how Visual Basic supports it and how you can take advantage of it. But first, you'll need to learn some more terms to help in your explorations.

More Vocabulary

Once again, we must agree on a common interface to facilitate communication. This section defines the vocabulary used in this discussion of advanced classes. The following definitions introduce concepts that you'll learn more about in later parts of the chapter. For now, just read through the definitions and use this section for reference as you continue through the chapter:

- *Collection*—A way to group a set of related objects.
- *Data consumer*—A class that can be bound to an external source of data.

- *Data source*—A class that supplies data from an external source to a data consumer.
- *Initialization*—Loading a class's property and data values the first time.
- *Instantiation*—Establishing an object in memory. Instantiation creates a place for the object's code and data in memory and provides a reference to the object. After an object is instantiated, it can be initialized.
- *Persistence*—Preserving an object's state from one instantiation to another.

The Lifetime Of Objects

In Chapter 3, you learned how classes differ from standard modules, primarily in the way their data is stored. Each class, when instantiated to create an object, gets its own copy of the data defined in the class. You learned how to expose and hide the data through **Public** and **Private** properties. But how long does the data stay around? Simply put, for standard objects, as long as you have a reference to it. Later in this chapter, we'll explore reference counts and destroying objects. However, before you can destroy an object, you must create it and possibly use it.

We'll begin this examination of advanced objects with a discussion of instantiating and initializing objects. You'll learn about making your objects persistent and what it means to fully terminate an object.

Instantiating And Initializing Objects

Instantiation is defined as establishing a place in memory for an object's code and data. Visual Basic uses the **New** keyword to instantiate objects. You use the **New** keyword either in the object variable declaration or along with the **Set** keyword to create an object. Listing 5.1 shows how to use the **New** keyword, both in an object variable declaration and with the **Set** keyword.

Listing 5.1   Using the New keyword.
```
Dim anObject As New SomeObject
Dim anotherObject As SomeObject

Set anotherObject = New SomeObject
```

The first line in Listing 5.1 declares an object variable, **anObject**, and instantiates it. After Visual Basic executes the declaration, **anObject** holds a reference to an instance of **SomeObject** in memory. The second line in the listing declares another object variable, **anotherObject**. This declaration simply declares a type for **anotherObject**; no code memory or data space is actually allocated. The last line in Listing 5.1 actually instantiates **anotherObject**. Notice the **Set** keyword; Visual Basic uses the **Set** keyword to assign objects to object variables. When **Set** is combined with the **New** keyword, Visual Basic instantiates the **SomeObject** object and assigns it to the **anotherObject** object variable.

Okay, now that you've instantiated the object, what next? You need to initialize the object and assign its data elements and properties their values. One way to initialize a class is to use the class module's **Initialize** event, as shown in Figure 5.1.

When you instantiate an object, Visual Basic fires the object's **Initialize** event. You can put code in the **Initialize** event that loads the object with the correct state. However, there's a problem with the **Initialize** event: It has no context. It doesn't know what created the class or why it was created. You cannot pass the class or the event any information to let it know how to initialize.

A better way to initialize a class is to provide it with an initialization method yourself. Visual Basic does not supply default "constructor" code that initializes a class. However, as you'll learn here, you can create some powerful initialization methods for your classes. Providing your own initialization methods makes using objects a two-step process:

1. Instantiate the object with the **New** keyword.
2. Initialize the object with the initialization method.

You can initialize an object in two main ways:

♦ Set an object's properties

♦ Use an initialization method

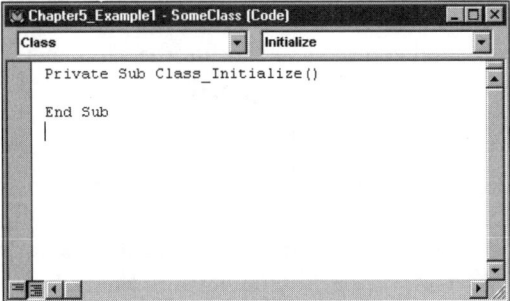

Figure 5.1
The **Class_Initialize** event.

First, you'll learn about initializing an object's properties; then, you'll learn to use an initialization method to load the properties (as well as some powerful variations on the method to provide self-initializing classes). Finally, you'll learn about initialization methods that let you initialize a class in more than one way.

Property Initialization

You learned in Chapter 2 that properties hold an object's state. Property initialization takes advantage of this by assigning the public properties after instantiation. This technique is very straightforward and easy to use. First, you instantiate an object with the **New** keyword; then, you assign the public properties their values. That's all there is to it.

This initialization technique, however, does have its disadvantages. The primary drawback is lack of control. When you allow users to initialize the class using public variables, you lose control over the object. What if they assign only some of the properties? What if several properties are required in order to complete the object? What about read-only public properties? How are they set?

As stated in Chapter 3, objects often have internal, hidden data or data structures. You must initialize these data structures and set up the object to operate properly. Assigning properties does not let you control the internal object setup.

As you can see, letting a user initialize an object by setting the properties gives up too much control and causes more problems and questions than it solves. There are ways you can control the situation, and Visual Basic will help.

Simple Initialization

The second technique is to use a simple initialization method. However, before you begin using this technique, you need to decide on a standard name for your initialization methods. To ease maintenance and coding, you can use the same method in all your classes. Here, we'll use **Init_Class** as the standard class initialization method.

A simple initialization method takes a parameter for each required property in your class. The initialization method can also assign other properties—ones not passed into the initialization method as parameters (ones for the class, if possible). The code for the simple **Init_Class** method for the **Contact** class from Chapter 2, for example, would look like Listing 5.2.

Listing 5.2 The Contact class's Init_Class method.
```
Public Sub Init_Class(ContactType As String)

    mContactType = ContactType
    mContactDate = Today()
    mContactTime = Now()

End Sub
```

The **Init_Class** in Listing 5.2 has a **ContactType** parameter. This lets you assign the type of contact when the object is created. The **Init_Class** also assigns the date and time to the internal class variables **mContactDate** and **mContactTime**; we assume the user creates a **Contact** object when a contact is made.

This simple method lets you control which properties must be provided to initialize the object. If you use an initialization method, Visual Basic helps you enforce your interface. It checks the number of parameters and forces the user to supply the information necessary to initialize the object. It also provides a way for a user to pass in read-only property values that may make sense only at initialization time.

Listing 5.2 illustrates another advantage to using an initialization method—assigning internal data. You can add code in the initialization method that determines and sets up internal data and data structures.

How do you force users to use the method instead of simply assigning values to the properties? One way is to maintain an internal "initialized" flag; you then raise an error if the user attempts to assign a property before he or she calls the class's initialization method. This is similar to how you forced the user to use the **View** method on an extended form in Chapter 3. Listing 5.3 shows you how to protect your class and force the user to use the initialization method.

Listing 5.3 Forcing the user to use the Init_Class method.
```
Private mInitialized As Boolean
Private mContactDate As Date
Private mContactTime As String
Private mContactType As String

Public Property Get ContactDate() As Date
    If Not mInitialized Then
        'raise error
        'do not return value
```

```
        Else
            ContactDate = mContactDate
        End If
End Property

Public Property Get ContactTime() As String
    If Not mInitialized Then
        'raise error
        'do not return value
    Else
        ContactTime = mContactTime
    End If
End Property

Public Property Get ContactType() As String
    If Not mInitialized Then
        'raise error
        'do not return value
    Else
        ContactType = mContactType
    End If
End Property
Public Sub Init_Class(ContactType As String)

If Not mInitialized Then
    mContactType = ContactType
    mContactDate = Today()
    mContactTime = Now()
    mInitialized = True
End If

End Sub
```

This code listing declares the class-level variable **mInitialized** to help determine if the object is initialized. If the user calls the **Init_Class** method, **mInitialized** is set to **True**. Each property checks to see if the object is initialized; if so, the property executes normally. If the **Init_Class** method is not called, however, the property raises an exception and does not return a value. This renders the class ineffective until the user initializes it properly. Notice that the **Init_Class** method also checks the **mInitialized** flag to protect itself from being invoked twice.

A simple initialization method is an improvement over assigning properties; however, it also has one big drawback. The object's user must acquire and pass the data to the method. Most of the work for setting up the class still falls on the class user. This goes against object-oriented programming, where the class is supposed to control its own processes to simplify its use.

Self-Initializing Classes

Passing parameters to initialize classes is better than letting the user assign the properties directly; however, as you've seen, it also has a downside. Another way around this problem is to create a self-initializing class. Wait a minute—didn't you just learn that the **Initialize** event is called when the class is created, and it's difficult to initialize the class in the event? That's self-initializing.

Yes, it would be great to have a truly self-initializing class that could deduce its context and set up its properties correctly. But, alas, it can't be. You can, however, create the semblance of a self-initializing class.

One way to do this is to pass a single piece of key information to the initialization method. This information lets the class retrieve, derive, or create the proper data for the properties. An example of key information is an ID for an object stored in a database. The ID lets the class retrieve its property values from the database. Another example may be a Registry key for information stored in the Windows 95/98 Registry.

Using this method, you control the full initialization of your objects. Listing 5.4 shows an **Init_Class** method that retrieves the class property values from a database.

Listing 5.4   A self-initializing class.

```
Public Sub Init_Class(ID As Long)

    Dim sSQL As String
    Dim ClassData As New ADODB.RecordSet

    sSQL = "Select Property1, Property2, " _
        & " From ClassTable " _
        & " Where ID = " & ID & ";"

    Set ClassData = GetDBConnection().Recordset(sSQL)

    If Not ClassData.EOF() Then
      Property1 = ClassData("Property1")
      Property2 = ClassData("Property2")
      mInitialized = True
    End If
End Sub
```

Listing 5.4 shows an initialization method initializing the properties from a database. This is a very powerful technique. It can be extended to include more than one key value, and the initialization method controls all aspects of the object initialization.

Another way to get the same effect is to use a write-only property. You can use a write-only property to initialize a class by placing the initialization code in the **Property Let** procedure. First, you declare a write-only ID property; then, to initialize the class, you simply assign the ID to the property (see Listing 5.5). This has one drawback: It's not obvious how to initialize the object. Using the **Init_Class** method, on the other hand, it is obvious how to initialize the object. Therefore, although the write-only property accomplishes the initialization, it's better to be explicit and use the initialization method.

Listing 5.5 A write-only initialization property.

```
Public Property Let ID(newID As Long)

    Dim sSQL As String
    dim ClassData As New ADODB.RecordSet

    sSQL = "Select Property1, Property2, " _
        & " From ClassTable " _
        & " Where ID = " & newID & ";"

    ClassData.Open sSQL, GetDBConnection()

    If Not ClassData.EOF() Then
      Property1 = ClassData("Property1")
      Property2 = ClassData("Property2")
      mInitialized = True
    End If

End Property
```

Advanced Class Initialization

Sometimes, the best way to initialize an object is not obvious. For these times, it's best to provide multiple ways to initialize the object. This can still be done with the **Init_Class** initialization method; you just have to be creative with your parameters.

In Chapter 3, you learned about dependent and independent optional parameters. You can use this information to provide multiple interfaces to **Init_Class**. *Dependent optional parameters* rely on each other to provide a complete information set for initialization. *Independent* *optional parameters* do not rely on other parameters. However, if you combine the dependent and independent ideas and define independent sets of dependent parameters, the initialization method can adapt to the required initialization. This is really easier than it sounds.

When you design a class, one of the things you must determine is how you intend to use the class. To do this, you must also determine how the class initializes and under what circumstances. For example, will the class be stored in a database? Will the class be used in a collection? Knowing the context for the class is part of the design process. You started doing this when you determined the relationships in Chapter 2. The relationships show whether an object is a candidate for a collection. The problem statement also gives clues by telling you if the system has persistent data. Persistent data and implementing relationships are covered in the "Persistence" and "Implementing Relationships" sections later in this chapter.

Knowing the context lets you design robust, effective initialization interfaces. Listing 5.6 shows an **Init_Class** method that has two interfaces. Based on what information you have or which context you initialize the class in, you'll use a different set of parameters.

Listing 5.6   Initializing a class with multiple interfaces.

```
Public Sub Init_Class(Optional ID As Long, _
                    Optional aRecordSet As Recordset)

    Dim sSQL As String
    Dim ClassData As ADODB.Recordset

    If (IsMissing(ID) And _
        IsMissing(aRecordSet)) Or _
       (Not IsMissing(ID) And _
        Not IsMissing(aRecord)) Then
        'Error. Must supply at least one parameter
        '       or cannot supply both parameters.
        Exit Sub
    End If

    If Not IsMissing(ID) Then
        sSQL = "Select Property1, Property2, "
            & " From ClassTable " _
            & " Where ID = " & ID & ";"

        Set ClassData = New ADODB.Recordset
        ClassData.Open sSQL, GetDBConnection()
```

```
      If Not ClassData.EOF() Then
        Property1 = ClassData("Property1")
        Property2 = ClassData("Property2")
        mInitialized = True
      End If

    ElseIf Not IsMissing(aRecordSet) Then
      Property1 = aRecordSet("Property1")
      Property2 = aRecordSet("Property2")
      mInitialized = True

    Else
      'Error

    End If
End Sub
```

Listing 5.6 provides two ways to initialize the object:

- The object creator may pass in an object ID, and the object will retrieve its property values from a database.
- The object creator may pass in a database recordset. The object retrieves its property values from the recordset.

Based on how you use the class, you may choose either interface. For objects that are accessed rarely or on demand, you may want to use the ID method. One example is the contact management system from Chapter 2. A possible interface for using the system might consist of a simple list box that lists all the prospects. You can query the database for the names and IDs of all the prospects in the database. Then you can load the names into the list box and the IDs into the list box's **ItemData** property. When the user clicks on a prospect, the system gets the ID from the list box and initializes the object with the ID interface. Listing 5.7 shows this implementation.

Listing 5.7 Initializing a Prospect object with the prospect's ID.

```
Private Sub lstProspects_Click()

    Set mCurrentProspect = New Prospect

    mCurrentProspect.Init_Class _
        ID:=lstProspects.ItemData(lstProspects.ListIndex)

End Sub
```

> **NOTE**
>
> The method shown in Listing 5.8 is only good for a small number of objects. It takes a long time to instantiate and initialize many objects. See "Object Collections" later in this chapter for a better way to manage object sets.

Other times, it's necessary to access a small number of objects quickly. It's inefficient for each object to access the database to initialize itself. It's faster to query the entire set of objects one time and then initialize all of them. Listing 5.8 shows how to initialize a set of objects with one query.

Listing 5.8 Initializing a set of Prospect objects with a recordset.

```
Public Sub LoadProspects()
    Dim sSQL As String
    Dim ClassData As New ADODB.Recordset

    'Get Prospects from database
    sSQL = "Select * From ProspectTable;"
    ClassData.Open sSQL, GetDBConnection()

    'Redimension the prospect list
    If Not ClassData.EOF Then
       ReDim mProspectList(ClassData.RecordCount)

       'Instantiate and initialize the list
       For i = LBound(mProspectList) To UBound(mProspectList)
          Set mProspectList(i) = New Prospect
          mProspectList(i).Init_Class _
             aRecordSet:=ClassData
          ClassData.MoveNext
       Next

    End If

End Sub
```

This code retrieves the prospects from the database and then initializes an array of Prospect objects with each record from the recordset.

You've now seen several ways to create objects. You'll learn better ways to manage objects later in this chapter. However, how do you terminate objects? Terminating objects is a little trickier than creating them. The next section explores this topic.

Terminating Objects

It's pretty easy to create a lot of objects; use them; pass them around; and put them in variables, arrays, and collections. As a matter of fact, as you get better with using objects, it may become rather difficult to keep track of them. The primary rule Visual Basic uses to know when to automatically destroy an object is: Destroy the object when all references to the object are released. The programmer makes the decision to release the last reference; however, before you do, you may want to save the object's state somewhere. This is called *persistence*.

Persistence

Persistence is defined as preserving an object's state from one instantiation to another. If you destroy an object before preserving its state, the object is gone forever.

There are many places you can save your object's state, including a file, a database, or even the Windows Registry. However, using the Registry to store objects isn't a good idea because it's limited in size and retrieval mechanisms. Saving the states of your objects involves simply storing the public properties and private, internal data, as well as data structures, to permanent storage.

One way to preserve your objects is to supply a **Save** method in your class. This method implements the chosen persistence approach for your application. Listing 5.9 shows a **Save** method storing an object's properties in a database.

Listing 5.9   Preserving an object with a Save method.

```
Public Sub Save()

    Dim sSQL As String
    Dim ClassData As ADODB.Recordset

    'Make sure the object was properly initialized
    If mInitialized Then
        sSQL = "Select Property1, Property2, " _
            & " From ClassTable " _
            & " Where ID = " & ID & ";"

        Set ClassData = New ADODB.Recordset
        ClassData.Open sSQL, GetDBConnection()

        'Update the database with the property values
        If Not ClassData.EOF() Then
            ClassData("Property1") = Property1
            ClassData("Property2") = Property2
        End If
    End If
    ClassData.Close

End Sub
```

You could also use the **Class_Terminate** event, as shown in Listing 5.10, to make your objects persistent. Before an object is destroyed, Visual Basic calls the object's **Terminate** event. You can use this event to implement your persistence approach.

Listing 5.10 Preserving an object in a Terminate event.

```
Private Sub Class_Terminate()

   Dim sSQL As String
   Dim ClassData As ADODB.Recordset

   'Make sure the object was properly initialized
   If mInitialized Then
      sSQL = "Select Property1, Property2, " _
           & " From ClassTable " _
           & " Where ID = " & ID & ";"

      Set ClassData = New ADODB.Recordset
      ClassData.Open sSQL, GetDBConnection()

      'Update the database with the property values
      If Not ClassData.EOF() Then
         ClassData("Property1") = Property1
         ClassData("Property2") = Property2
      End If
   End If
   ClassData.Close

End Sub
```

Finally, Listing 5.11 shows that you can place your object's properties in storage as they receive their values.

Listing 5.11 Preserving an object's properties when values are assigned.

```
Public Property Let Property1(NewValue As String)

   mProperty1 = NewValue
   'assume mClassData is a class level variable with
   'a recordset of the object's values
   mClassData("Property1") = NewValue

End Property
```

Objects: References And Reference Counting

You've learned how to create objects and preserve them. But how does Visual Basic decide when to destroy the objects, and more importantly, how do you control them? As you create more objects and build larger systems, it becomes easier to lose track of your objects.

Remember the simple rule Visual Basic uses: Destroy the object when all references to the object are released. To release an object, set the object variable to **Nothing**:

```
Set MyObject = Nothing
```

This rule implies that Visual Basic is keeping track of object counts for you, and it is. Visual Basic uses the Component Object Model (COM) to keep track of objects. COM uses a complex set of rules to track object references. Actually, the only thing you're sure of is when the count is 0, because the object's **Terminate** event occurs. This may seem like a problem, but you really don't want to keep track of the reference counts yourself—it's much more difficult than keeping track of the object variables in your program.

Because you can't get to the reference count in Visual Basic, you need to keep track of your objects. Here are some tips on tracking object variables:

- Don't use variables of the **Variant** or **Object** type. **Variant** and **Object** variables can hold a reference to anything. This makes it difficult to track down object references.

- Declare object variables using class types. This makes it easier to track down a variable of the specific type instead of variables of any type.

- Avoid using the **New** keyword in object variable declarations. If you declare a variable with the **New** keyword, set the variable to **Nothing**, and then reference the variable again, Visual Basic creates another instance of the object.

- Avoid the Visual Basic Collection object. The Visual Basic Collection object uses **Variants** to store values. Create Collection classes yourself, as described in "Implementing Your Own Collection" later in this chapter.

- Design your application and use your design. In Chapter 2, you learned about object-oriented design and relationships. If you use your design and your object's relationships, as described in "Implementing

Relationships" later in this chapter, you can write code to walk the design and report all the objects.

- Avoid circular references. *Circular references* occur when two or more objects reference each other, usually in a chain. For example, if you pass a parent object reference to a child object when initializing the child object, the parent references the child and the child references the parent. (See the next section, "Avoiding Circular References.")
- While debugging, avoid using the system exit (the box with the x in the top-right corner of a window) or the **End** statement. The system exit on your window and the **End** statement halt your program immediately. Visual Basic does not clean up or call any termination events. This leads to objects not being saved and leaves references to objects in memory.

Avoiding Circular References

Circular references are perhaps the most difficult situation to shut down cleanly. One way to destroy objects containing circular references is for the class to provide a shutdown method.

A *shutdown method* cleans up all the object references the object has. This way, the objects release all their references. In the example of a parent and child, the parent can't terminate because the child has a reference to it. By supplying a shutdown method on the parent, it can explicitly terminate the child. Then, when the parent reference is released, the parent object terminates. Listing 5.12 shows the **Shutdown** method for a parent object.

Listing 5.12   The Shutdown method.
```
Public sub Shutdown()

    'Set all children to nothing
    Set mChild = Nothing

End Sub
```

Here's the code for shutting down a parent object:

```
mParent.Shutdown
Set mParent = Nothing
```

Forms And Controls

Because forms and controls are visible to the user, keeping track of them is a little different than keeping track of your run-of-the-mill class. In this section, you'll learn how forms and controls differ from normal classes and how to deal with them.

Forms in Visual Basic can pass through six states during their lifetime:

- Created, but not loaded
- Loaded, but not shown
- Shown
- Unloaded
- Memory and resources completely reclaimed
- Unloaded and unreferenced while a control is still referenced

Keep in mind that not all forms pass through all these states during their lifetimes.

Created, But Not Loaded

The first and only required state for a form is "created, but not loaded." This state creates and loads the code portion of the form in memory. When you use the **New** keyword to create a form, as shown in Listing 5.13, Visual Basic does the following:

1. Creates the form in memory.
2. Executes the form's **Form_Initialize** event.

Note that:

- The form has no window.
- None of the form's controls exists.

Listing 5.13   Create a form but don't load it.
```
Dim theForm As Form1
    Set theForm = New Form1
```

When you create a form in a Visual Basic project, Visual Basic creates a hidden global variable for the form. This is why you can reference all your forms directly in code without creating an object variable first. The hidden declaration is the same as the following form declaration:

```
Dim Form1 As New Form1
```

Visual Basic hides the variable because the variable name is the same name you give your form in the property window. This way, when you change a form's name, Visual Basic can change the hidden variable's name.

The first time you access the global hidden variable, the form enters the "created, but not loaded" state.

While the form is in this state, you can call the created form's **Sub**, **Function**, and **Property** procedures that you created. If you execute any of the form's controls or built-in properties, the form advances to the next state.

Every form goes through the "created, but not loaded" state, however briefly. If you declare a form as the startup form, it passes through this state, executes the **Form_Initialize** event, and continues to the next state. By the same token, if you execute a form's **Show** method, it also passes through this state, executes its **Form_Initialize** event, and continues on to the next state.

Loaded, But Not Shown

When your form enters the "loaded, but not shown" state, Visual Basic performs the following tasks:

1. Creates the form's window.
2. Loads all the form's controls.
3. Executes the form's **Form_Load** event.
4. Adds the form to the application's **Forms** collection.

Some forms are never meant to be displayed. You may want to use a hidden form to gain access to a control but never allow your user to see it. Examples include access to the timer control to generate events in your application or access to an ActiveX control that performs some specific processing. When you access a form's built-in methods or properties (or any control on the form), Visual Basic automatically loads the form but does not show it. You can also load a form by calling the **Load** statement, as shown in Listing 5.14.

Listing 5.14 Loading a form explicitly.
```
Dim theForm As Form1
    Load theForm
```

A form will also load automatically when you call its **Show** method. Visual Basic loads the form and then immediately moves to the next state—"shown." Finally, Visual Basic will automatically load a form and move it to the next state if the form is specified as the startup object for the project.

A form returns to the "loaded, but not shown" state when you call its **Hide** method. If you show the form again, however, Visual Basic does not execute the form's **Form_Load** event. The **Form_Load** event is only called once during a form's lifetime.

Shown

When your form is visible, it's in the "shown" state. There are no special events or conditions associated with a form becoming visible. You can hide and show the form as many times as you like during the form's lifetime.

Unloaded

You can unload a form whether it's visible or not. Visible forms remain visible during the "unload" event. If you want the form to disappear, you must hide the form before unloading it. When you unload a form, Visual Basic executes the form's **QueryUnload** event. This event gives you a chance to stop the form from unloading, prompt the user for additional information, or save the form's contents.

A powerful feature of the **QueryUnload** event is its parameters. The **QueryUnload** event has both a **Cancel** parameter and an **Unload Mode** parameter. Listing 5.15 shows the **QueryUnload** event.

Listing 5.15   The Form_QueryUnload event.

```
Private Sub Form_QueryUnload(Cancel As Integer, _
                             UnloadMode As Integer)

End Sub
```

The **QueryUnload** event lets you cancel the unloading of the form by setting the **Cancel** parameter to **True**. However, the most powerful feature of this event is the **UnloadMode** parameter, which tells you why the form is unloading. Table 5.1 shows the possible reasons and their codes.

The last event Visual Basic calls when unloading a form is the **Unload** event. Setting the **Cancel** argument on the **Unload** event stops the form from unloading, and the form remains loaded.

When you unload a form, it is only in the "unloaded" state long enough to perform the **Unload** event. After executing the **Unload** event, the

Table 5.1 The QueryUnload event's UnloadMode parameter codes.

Value	Description
0	The user chose the **Close** command from the Control menu on the form.
1	The **Unload** statement is invoked from code.
2	The current Microsoft Windows operating environment session is ending.
3	The Microsoft Windows Task Manager is closing the application.
4	An MDI child form is closing because the MDI form is closing.
5	A form is closing because its owner is closing.

form can transition to either the "created, but not loaded" state or the "memory and resources completely reclaimed" state. If you keep a reference to the form, Visual Basic returns the form to the "created, but not loaded" state. The form does not have a window, its controls have been destroyed, and the static variables in the event procedures are gone. However, the object's module-level variables are still there, and it still has its resources. You can use the reference to call any custom properties or methods in the form. If you call a built-in method or control, Visual Basic reloads the form and executes the **Form_Load** event.

Be careful when you unload a form. Remember that if you use the form name without explicitly declaring it, Visual Basic creates a hidden variable for the form. Therefore, when you unload the form, the hidden variable maintains a reference to it. The next section discusses how to completely unload the form.

If you don't have a reference to the form, Visual Basic removes the form from the **Forms** collection and moves the form to the "memory and resources completely reclaimed" state.

Memory And Resources Completely Reclaimed

As is the case with normal classes, the only way to completely reclaim a form's resources and memory is to release all references to it. You do this by setting all the references to **Nothing**:

```
Set theForm = Nothing
```

When you release the last reference, Visual Basic executes the form's **Terminate** event. This event allows you to do any final cleanup for the form. If your form is not terminating correctly, you might not be releasing all the references. Remember the hidden variable. If you use a hidden variable, you must also set it to **Nothing**:

```
Set Form1 = Nothing
```

Avoid using the hidden global variable; it's better to explicitly declare form variables and then create and destroy the forms as you need them. This makes it easier to locate a missing assignment to **Nothing** during debugging.

One last note on destroying forms: If you use the **End** statement, Visual Basic destroys all your form references. However, it does not execute any of the normal unload events: **QueryUnload**, **Unload**, or **Terminate**.

Unloaded And Unreferenced While A Control Is Still Referenced

The final possible state for a form is a little strange. You either have to code it in explicitly, or it's probably a bug. In either case, you should know about it, so that when it happens, you won't be surprised.

You get into the "unloaded and unreferenced while a control is still referenced" state by setting a control or **Variant** variable that's *outside* the form to a control on the form and then unloading the form and setting the form variable to **Nothing**.

The form is unloaded; however, you still have a reference to one of its controls. This keeps the code portion of the form in memory. The module-level variables still hold their values, but all the controls are reset to their default values. If you call any of the controls, properties, or methods, Visual Basic reloads the form and executes the **Form_Load** event.

Avoid referencing controls in forms directly. Chapter 3 taught you to provide access to controls through form properties. This way, you avoid this strange state, and you gain control over your forms.

Object Collections

In the "More Vocabulary" section earlier in this chapter, a *collection* is defined as a way to group a set of related objects. The collection concept is pretty open and lets you think of and address sets of objects. The collection definition includes the following collection types:

- *Similar objects*—For example, library resources. A collection is a convenient way to group the books, newspapers, and magazines in the library.
- *Different but related objects*—For example, writing supplies. To write, you need a pencil, some paper, and an eraser.
- *The exact same type of objects*—For example, tires on a car. The tires are all distinct objects; however, they are all the same type of object. This is the most common type of collection in programming.

Depending on your program or problem, you may need any or all of these collection types.

Designing A Collection

But what does a collection do? A *collection* in object-oriented programming is an object that encapsulates the operations of a set of objects. First, you must be able to add items to the collection. By the same token, you need to be able to remove items from the collection, preferably with a key. It's also a good idea to be able to count the items in the collection. This is starting to sound like a problem statement for a Collection class.

You learned in Chapter 1 that a Collection class has items and a **Count** property. The Collection class also has **Add** and **Remove** methods. If you examine the **Items** property and the description, you'll see that an item has a key and an index. This means that **Item** is an access method with parameters for the items in the collection. Figure 5.2 shows the object definition for a general Collection class.

The Visual Basic Collection

Visual Basic provides you with a general-purpose Collection class. The Visual Basic collection has all the methods and properties shown in Figure 5.2. Listing 5.16 shows the specification for the Visual Basic collection.

Listing 5.16 Visual Basic object collection.

```
Properties
    Count As Long
Methods
    Add Item, Key, Before, After
    Item(Index)
    Remove Index
```

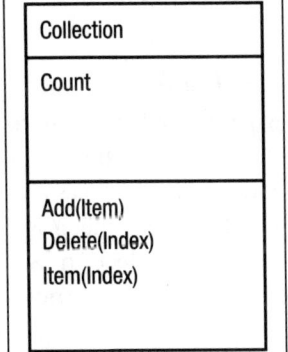

Figure 5.2
A Collection class definition.

> **NOTE**
>
> Both **Before** and **After** are mutually exclusive. You can use either **Before** or **After**, but not both.

Here are the parameter definitions for Listing 5.16:

- *Item*—A required parameter that specifies the member to add to the collection. **Item** is a **Variant**.

- *Key*—An optional parameter that designates a key value for the item. **Key** is a **String**.

- *Before*—An optional parameter that specifies a relative position in the collection at which to add the item. **Before** is a **Variant**. If you specify a number from 1 to the number of items in the collection, the new item is placed in the collection before the specified number. If the value is a **String**, the **String** must identify a current item in the collection, and the new item is put before the specified item.

- *After*—An optional parameter that specifies a relative position in the collection at which to add the item. **After** is a **Variant**. If you specify a number from 1 to the number of items in the collection, the new item is placed in the collection after the specified number. If the value is a **String**, the **String** must identify a current item in the collection, and the new item is put after the specified item.

- *Index*—A required parameter that identifies the item to return or remove. **Index** is a **Variant**. If you specify a number, the item in the numbered position is returned or removed. If the value is a **String**, the item with the key value is returned or removed.

To declare a Collection object, use the **Collection** keyword:

```
Dim Prospects As New Collection
```

Remember that **Collection** is an object, so you need to instantiate it with the **New** keyword.

The Visual Basic collection has some interesting features. First, a Visual Basic collection is ordered. This is why when you add an item to the collection, you can specify where to place it with the **Before** or **After** parameter. The Collection class uses both ordinal indexes and key values to access items in the collection. The **Index** parameter is a **Variant** for both the **Item** and **Remove** methods. The collection uses key values if **Index** is a **String**, and it uses the ordinal number if **Index** is a number.

You can use **For Each** to iterate over the items in the collection. **For Each** returns each item in the collection, one at a time, in a looping fashion. Listing 5.17 shows **For Each** in action.

Listing 5.17 For Each.
```
For Each Prospect in Prospects
    'Do some processing
Next
```

Adding Items To A Collection
Use the **Add** method to insert items into a collection. Listing 5.18 illustrates how to add an item to a collection.

Listing 5.18 Adding an item to a collection.
```
Prospects.Add aProspect, aProspect.Name
```

This adds a Contact object to the **Contact** collection using the contact's name as the key. The **Key** parameter requires a **String**, so if you use numeric values for the key, convert them to **Strings** using the **CStr** function:

```
Prospects.Add aProspect, CStr(aProspect.ID)
```

Removing Items From A Collection
Use the **Remove** method to delete items from a collection. Listing 5.19 illustrates how to remove an item from a collection.

Listing 5.19 Removing an item from a collection.
```
Prospects.Remove "Lisa"
Prospects.Remove 5
```

The first line removes the Prospect object with the key "Lisa" from the **Prospects** collection. The second line removes the fifth item from the collection.

Accessing Items In A Collection
Use the **Item** method to access items in a collection. Listing 5.20 shows how to access an item in a collection.

Listing 5.20 Accessing an item in a collection.
```
Set CurrentProspect = Prospects.Item("Lisa")
Set CurrentProspect = Prospects.Item(5)
```

The first line assigns the Prospect object with the key "Lisa" from the **Prospects** collection to **CurrentProspect**. The second line assigns the fifth item from the collection to **CurrentProspect**.

The **Index** parameter is a **Variant**. Don't make Visual Basic figure out what you mean. If you use numbers for your keys, convert them to **Strings** before using them. This way you're sure that Visual Basic uses the key values.

The **Item** method is the default method for a collection. This means you can access members like this:

```
Set CurrentProspect = Prospects("Lisa")
```

The Problems With The Visual Basic Collection Object

The Visual Basic Collection object has two major problems that make it a poor choice for creating robust applications. First, a Collection object holds **Variants**, which can be anything from objects to integers (but not user-defined types). This means you can put anything into them, and you can even mix up types in the collection.

The second problem is that there's no encapsulation. In order to create a collection of objects, you must initialize the objects correctly, decide on the key structure, and then manage the collection. If you want to reuse the same type of collection, the only way to do so is to cut and paste the code to the place you want to reuse the collection. This is inefficient and error prone. If you change the original code, you have to change it everywhere else you use the collection, which is why encapsulation is so powerful.

Because a Visual Basic Collection object can hold anything, you lose control of what the collection represents. To have a robust application, collections should be strongly typed. Because Visual Basic does not supply typed collections, you need to implement your own Collection classes that hide the implementation and enforce the type checking. The next section shows you the benefits of this as well as how to construct your own collections.

Implementing Your Own Collection

The native Visual Basic collection is pretty powerful. However, you've seen that it has a major drawback. One way around the loose type checking and loss of control is to implement your own collection. This section shows you how to encapsulate the Visual Basic collection in your own strongly typed and tightly controlled class.

Creating The Collection

The first thing you do to create a Collection class is to put the properties and methods into a class module. Because you're creating sets of objects, it's a good idea to come up with a naming convention for your Collection classes. One method is to name the class the plural form of the object it holds. I prefer to name Collection classes by appending the word "Set" to the name of the object the collection holds. This avoids difficult naming when a class's plural form is not standard; it's also easier to spot because it's a joined name. Listing 5.21 shows the beginning Collection class for the **Contact** class in the contact management system from Chapter 2.

Listing 5.21   The ContactSet Collection class.

```
Public Property Get Count() As Long
End Property
Public Sub Add(Item As Variant)
End Sub
Public Sub Remove(Index As Variant)
End Sub
Public Function Item(Index As Variant) As Variant
End Function
```

Giving The Collection A Type

The first problem to remedy is that a collection is not strongly typed. The example in Listing 5.21 suffers from this same problem. Notice that the **Add** method takes a **Variant**, and the **Item** method returns a **Variant**. This is no better than the Visual Basic Collection class.

You have to give your collection a type. You already know you're creating a **Contact** collection, so you begin by changing the **Variant** parameter in the **Add** method and the **Variant** return type for the **Item** method. Listing 5.22 shows the new methods.

Listing 5.22   Strongly typed ContactSet Collection class.

```
Public Sub Add(Item As Contact)
End Sub
Public Function Item(Index As Variant) As Contact
End Function
```

Now, the only thing you can put into and take out of your collection are Contact objects. However, you can still pass in an uninitialized Contact object. The next section discusses eliminating this problem and ensuring that you use the collection properly.

Controlling What Goes Into The Collection

Now that you have a strongly typed collection, you must ensure that only initialized objects make it into the collection. Remember the **Init_Class** method you learned about earlier in this chapter? It's the key to controlling how a user adds items to your collection.

The **Init_Class** method defines the default information necessary to initialize the class. If you change your collection's **Add** method parameters from an **Item** to the default information defined in the **Init_Class** method, you should instantiate and initialize a new object and put the initialized class into the collection. You also need to provide a key mechanism so the user can access the contacts later. (Refer back to Listing 5.2 for the **Init_Class** method for the **Contact** class.) Listing 5.23 shows the full **Add** method for **ContactSet**.

Listing 5.23   The ContactSet class's Add method.

```
Public Function Add(ContactType As String) As String
    Dim NewContact As New Contact
    Static KeyNum As Long
    Dim theKey As String

    'Initialize the new Contact object
    NewContact.Init_Class ContactType

    'Determine the key value
    KeyNum = KeyNum + 1
    theKey = "C" & Format$(KeyNum, "000000")

    'Store the new Contact object
    mContactSet.Add Item:=NewContact, _
                    Key:=theKey
    'Return the Key
    Add = theKey
End Sub
```

One thing you'll notice is the **mContactSet** variable. The **mContactSet** variable is a class-level variable that holds the Visual Basic collection you use to store your objects. This is a form of redirection, as discussed in Chapter 2.

Another thing you'll notice is the creation of a key value. You pass the key value back to the calling code so it can access the contacts it adds to the collection.

Advanced Classes

With this new **Add** method, you control how objects are put into your collection. Now you are assured that all objects going into the collection are initialized. If necessary, you can add error handling or error checking to the **Add** method to really make it bulletproof.

Accessing The Collection

You have a solid method for putting things into the collection; now we must address accessing it. Because you're encapsulating a Visual Basic Collection object, it's easy to access the collection. There are two things you provide for the collection—**Count** and **Item**—and one thing—the **Remove** method—that affects the collection. All of these delegate their functionality to the Visual Basic Collection object. Listing 5.24 provides the **ContactSet** collection code.

Listing 5.24   The ContactSet class.

```
Private mContactSet As New Collection
Public Function Add(ContactType As String) As String
    Dim NewContact As New Contact
    Static KeyNum As Long
    Dim theKey As String

    'Initialize the new Contact object
    NewContact.Init_Class ContactType

    'Determine the key value
    KeyNum = KeyNum + 1
    theKey = "C" & Format$(KeyNum, "000000")

    'Store the new Contact object
    mContactSet.Add Item:=NewContact, _
                Key:=theKey
    'Return the Key
    Add = theKey

End Sub
Public Property Get Count() As Long

    Count = mContactSet.Count

End Property
Public Function Item(Index As Variant) As Contact

    Set Item = mContactSet.Item(Index)

End Function
```

```
Public Sub Remove(Index As Variant)

    mContactSet.Remove Index

End Sub
```

One more thing: To make your collection more like a Visual Basic collection, you need to make the **Item** method the default method for the class. The procedure for making a method the default method is described in Chapter 3.

Iterating Through The Collection

One thing you lose when you create your own collection is iteration. You can't use **For Each** on the Collection class just described, at least not yet. If you're encapsulating a Visual Basic collection, you can delegate this work also.

To enable **For Each**, you must delegate to the Visual Basic Collection object's enumerator. An *enumerator* is an object that knows how to iterate through a collection. Visual Basic does not allow you to write enumerators. You can, however, use the one provided by the Visual Basic Collection object. To do this, you must add a **NewEnum** method to your collection. Listing 5.25 shows the **NewEnum** method for the **ContactSet** class.

Listing 5.25   The ContactSet class's NewEnum method.
```
Public Function NewEnum() As IUnknown
    Set NewEnum = mContactSet.[_NewEnum]
End Function
```

_NewEnum is a hidden method in the Visual Basic Collection object's type library. It's necessary to place the square brackets around it so Visual Basic will accept it.

Now that you have the enumerator delegated, you have to tell the system about it. It's also a good idea to hide the enumerator so users can't call it directly. Here are the steps you take to hide the enumerator and tell the system about it:

1. On the Tools menu, select Procedure Attributes to open the Procedure Attributes dialog box.
2. In the Name drop-down list box, select NewEnum.
3. Click on the Advanced button to show the advanced attributes.

> **NOTE**
> Visual Basic does not allow names to begin with an underscore.

> **NOTE**
> Visual Basic provides help in creating Collection classes in the Class Builder. The Class Builder is discussed briefly in Chapter 4.

4. Click on the Hide This Member checkbox to hide the **NewEnum** method in the library.
5. In the Procedure ID combo box, type in "-4" (minus four). This is the procedure ID required by **For Each**.
6. Click on OK.

Figure 5.3 shows the Procedure Attributes dialog box with the proper settings.

Implementing Relationships

In Chapter 2, you learned how to design objects and find properties, methods, events, and relationships. In Chapter 3, you learned how to implement objects, properties, methods, and events. In this chapter, you've learned more about classes. However, what about the relationships? In this section, you'll learn how to implement relationships in Visual Basic.

In Chapter 2, you identified several relationships: one-to-one, one-to-many, and many-to-many. In addition to cardinality, relationships have types. There are essentially two types of relationships: associative and composite. *Associative relationships* define a nonhierarchical relationship between equal classes. For example, a student takes a test. *Composite relationships* define hierarchical relationships. This relationship is characterized by one object containing or having other objects. For example, a car has tires.

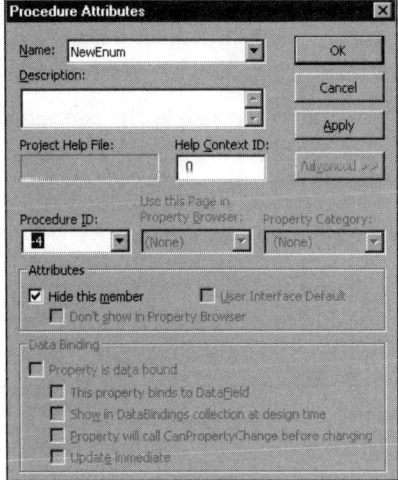

Figure 5.3
The Procedure Attributes dialog box.

One-To-One

There are two types of one-to-one relationships: associative and composite, as discussed in the previous section. To implement a composite relationship, simply create a property that encapsulates access to the contained object. Listing 5.26 shows a one-to-one composite relationship.

Listing 5.26 One-to-one composite relationship in BookClass.
```
Private mCover As New CoverClass

Public Property Get Cover() As CoverClass
    Cover = mCover
End Property
```

Depending on if the relationship needs to be visible outside the containing object, you can make the property either **Public** or **Private**.

If the relationship is public, then Listing 5.27 shows how to access the objects.

Listing 5.27 Accessing a one-to-one composite relationship.
```
Dim aBook As New BookClass
aBook.Cover.Title = "Object-Oriented Programming"
```

You can access the cover in this manner because Visual Basic evaluates from left to right. **aBook.Cover** returns the reference to **mCover** inside **BookClass**. Visual Basic then accesses the **Title** property of **CoverClass**.

Associative relationships are not usually public. However, you face two different circumstances when dealing with an association:

- *The association is an exclusive association*—The object you need to associate is only associated with one object.
- *The object you need to associate with is not exclusive*—The object you need to associate with has associations with other objects as well.

For exclusive associations, you simply define a property like a composite relationship and access it the same way.

For a nonexclusive relationship, you must either create the instance of the associated object or obtain a reference to the associated object. One way to obtain such a reference is to force whatever code initializes the object to pass a reference to the related object in the **Init_Class** method.

Another way is to create an object broker. An *object broker* keeps track of system-level objects and provides access to them. One way to create an object broker is to provide a globally available "system" object. An example of a nonexclusive relationship is with security. Suppose your system has a User object. The User object has properties such as **Username, Password,** and a set of read-only Boolean properties that represent the different privileges the user has. Most of the objects in your system need access to the user privileges. This means that a lot of the objects have a relationship with the User object.

Making the User object available with an object broker is illustrated in Listings 5.28 and 5.29.

Listing 5.28   An example of a User object.
```
Public Property Get CanPrint() As Boolean

End Property
Public Property Get CanAddContacts() As Boolean

End Property
Public Property Get CanEdit() As Boolean

End Property
Public Function Init_Class(Username As String, _
                           Password As String) As Boolean

End Function
```

Listing 5.29   An object broker: System.
```
Private mUser As New User

Public Property Get User() As CUser

   Set User = mUser

End Property
```

With this arrangement, you can now access the user's privileges from anywhere in the system. The implementation of how the system retrieves the privileges is left to the User object. The System object simply acts as a broker for access to the User object. Remember that the reference to the System object is stored in a global variable. You already know that you shouldn't use global system variables; however, this is the one exception (you'll learn why later in this section). Here's how you would check a user privilege:

```
If System.User.CanEdit Then
End If
```

This technique gives access to the User object to any code in the system, which is undesirable because not all classes have a relationship with the **User** class. Because the System object is a global variable, you need to protect its members. You can make the **User** property a function and force the user to pass in a reference to the calling object. Listing 5.30 shows how to protect the **User** property.

Listing 5.30   The protected User property.

```
Public Function User(RequestingObject As Object) As CUser

    Select Case TypeName(RequestingObject)
       Case "ValidObjectName" Or _
            "AnotherValidObjectName"
          Set User = mUser

       Case Else
          'Invalid access attempt
          'Raise Error

    End Select

End Function
```

This function uses the **TypeName** function to determine the name of the object that requests access to the property. If the object is not a valid one, the system raises an error. This implementation strictly enforces the object relationships in your system. However, because it's implementing the System object, it doesn't inhibit reusing your objects. The objects themselves are not altered, only the access to them.

Again, if you provide protection for the **System** class members, it's okay to have a single global variable. The only danger now is having someone set the **System** variable equal to **Nothing**.

One-To-Many

One-to-many relationships are generally composite relationships. You use collections to implement many-to-many relationships. You learned about collections earlier in this chapter. Now you'll learn how to use them to implement one-to-many relationships.

There are two basic ways to implement one-to-many relationships: The first relies on configuring a collection class and the second relies on coding the relationship directly.

The easiest method to implement a one-to-many relationship requires two basic steps:

1. Make the collection class's **Item** property the default property, as described in Chapter 3.
2. Add a property in the related class that returns a privately declared collection class.

By making the **Item** method the default method, you can access the items of the collection, like this:

```
Prospect.Contacts(1)
```

To access the collection class directly by using the **Count** property, simply call the property, like this:

```
Prospect.Contacts.Count
```

This behavior is consistent with the Visual Basic collection, where the **Item** method is the default method.

The second way to implement a one-to-many relationship involves coding it directly. To create a one-to-many relationship in a class, declare a class-level variable for the related class and then create an access function that models the relationship. Listing 5.31 models the "prospect has contacts" relationship from the contact management system in Chapter 2.

Listing 5.31   A one-to-many relationship interface.

```
'Prospect Class
Option Explicit

Private mContacts As New ContactSet
Public Function Contacts(Optional Index As Variant) As Object

End Function
...
```

You should note a couple of interesting things about this function. First, the **Index** parameter is present to access individual members of the collection. But why is it optional? Second, you'll notice the function returns an object instead of a contact. Both of these features let you access the resulting relationship in a more natural manner.

The **Contacts** function actually serves two purposes: First, it provides access to the **Contact** collection, **ContactSet**. Second, it provides access to the individual items in the **Contact** collection. The optional index is used to provide the access to the individual items in the **Contact** collection. If the optional index is present, the code accesses the selected item in the collection. The **Index** parameter is a **Variant**, so it can handle both ordinal values and key values, as discussed in "The Visual Basic Collection" section earlier in this chapter.

The function returns an object because it must return either a reference to the ContactSet object or a Contact object. Listing 5.32 implements the full relationship function.

Listing 5.32   The one-to-many relationship code.

```
Public Function Contacts(Optional Index As Variant) As Object

   'Check to see if the user wants the collection or an item
   If IsMissing(Index) Then
      'Return the collection
      Set Contacts = mContacts

   Else
      'Return the item chosen from the collection
      Set Contacts = mContacts.Item(Index)

   End If

End Function
```

For such a small amount of code, this function packs a lot of power. The check for the missing **Index** parameter determines which object to return. Then, the function returns the proper object. This simple redirection lets you access your relationships in a natural manner. Consider the declarations and code in Listing 5.33.

Listing 5.33   Accessing and using a one-to-many relationship.

```
Option Explicit

Dim theProspect As New Prospect

Private Sub cmdTest_Click()

   Dim theKey As String
   Dim aContact As Contact
```

```
        Debug.Print theProspect.Contacts.Count
        theKey = theProspect.Contacts.Add("Test" & _
                theProspect.Contacts.Count)
        Debug.Print theProspect.Contacts.Count
        Debug.Print theProspect.Contacts(1).ContactType
        Debug.Print theProspect.Contacts(theKey).ContactType

        For Each aContact In theProspect.Contacts
            Debug.Print aContact.ContactType
        Next

End Sub
```

Listing 5.33 is the code for a simple form that tests the prospect-contact relationship. The form has one button, and clicking on the button adds a contact to the prospect. When run in debug mode, the first **Debug.Print** statement writes the number of contacts in the system to the Immediate window. The second line adds a test contact to the prospect. It uses the word "Test" with the number of items in the collection before adding this one. The code stores the returned key value.

The next line writes the updated count to the Immediate window to show the contact was added. The next two lines access the items in the **Contact** collection with both an ordinal number and a key value.

Finally, the code demonstrates the **For Each** access. Because you set up the **ContactSet** with an enumerator, **For Each** works and writes the value of the **ContactType** property to the Immediate window for each contact in the collection.

Take a close look at the call syntax. You can access the collection with or without the **Index** parameter. This makes the code readable and understandable. If there is no **Index**, you're accessing the collection; if there is an **Index**, you're accessing the desired item.

For each one-to-many relationship in your system, you should create a relationship function for readability and flexibility.

Many-To-Many

Many-to-many relationships are special cases of the object broker and the one-to-many relationship. You should implement an object broker to facilitate the relationship and then access it in each of the related classes.

Data-Aware Classes

A driving force in client/server development is *data access*. Technologies are exploding to make it easier to access data—ODBC, DAO, RDO, ADO, OLE-DB, just to name a few. In previous versions of Visual Basic, you were forced to manipulate databases and records directly. The remedy for this was to develop database wrappers that encapsulated and protected databases while simplifying access to them. This is the equivalent to a data control in code. The data control is intended to make binding controls on a form to a record or data table easy.

VB6 introduces the concept of a *data-aware class*. It has built-in facilities to help you bind external data to controls and classes. Objects that supply data are called *data sources*. Objects that use the data are called *data consumers*.

Data-aware classes help you develop and maintain projects that use database technology to provide object persistence. This section explores the data-aware classes, how to implement them, and how to use them.

Data Source

A *data source* provides access to external data. Because the data-aware class is a custom class module, you control the binding and access. Data source objects don't have a visual interface, making them more versatile than data controls. Visual Basic provides the **DataSourceBehavior** property to enable a class to become a data-aware class. There's more to it than just setting a property, though.

BindingCollection

To bind a data source to some data consumer, you need a central method to perform the binding. A data control acts as the binding agent between a database and a control; a BindingCollection object provides this service between data sources and one or more data consumers. Remember that controls can act as data consumers.

Creating A Data Source

Visual Basic provides two ways to create a data source:

- Create a standard class module and set **DataSourceBehavior** to **vbDataSource**.
- Add a new class module to your project. In the Add Class Module dialog box, select the Data Source icon. Visual Basic will generate a class for you, complete with **TO DO** (instructions on what to do next).

Now you must give the new class the properties and methods necessary to create a data source. When you set the **DataSourceBehavior** property to **vbDataSource**, Visual Basic adds a **Class_GetDataMember** event handler to the class. This event handler returns the data for your class to the BindingCollection. The other required declaration is the database access variable. You can use any OLE-DB data provider to supply the data. Listing 5.34 shows the code for a sample data source class.

Listing 5.34   The clsDataSource class.

```
'clsDataSource Class
Option Explicit

Private WithEvents theData As ADODB.Recordset

Private Sub Class_GetDataMember(DataMember As String, _
                                Data As Object)
    Set Data = theData
End Sub

Public Sub MoveNext()
   If Not theData.EOF Then
      theData.MoveNext
   End If
End Sub
Public Sub MovePrevious()
   If Not theData.BOF Then
      theData.MovePrevious
   End If
End Sub
Public Sub Init_Class(StartID As Long)

   Dim i As Long

   Set theData = New ADODB.Recordset

   'Define the recordset structure
   With theData
      .Fields.Append "ID", adInteger
      .Fields.Append "Value", adBSTR, 50
      .Open
   End With

   'Put some data into the recordset
   With theData
      For i = StartID To StartID + 20
```

```
            .AddNew
            .Fields("ID") = i
            .Fields("Value") = "Test text #" & i
            .Update
        Next
    End With

    theData.MoveFirst

End Sub
```

The **clsDataSource** class illustrates how to set up the data source. This class uses ADO to create a recordset on the fly in the **Init_Class** method. This demonstrates the flexibility of the **Init_Class** method, because the beginning ID for the recordset is being passed in. Notice the **Class_GetDataMember** subroutine. It has two parameters: the data member name and the data itself. The **DataMember** parameter is a **String** passed in so you can select from among several data sets. You could use a **Select Case** statement to return any number of data objects in the **Data** parameter.

The last methods that the **clsDataSource** class exposes are **MoveNext** and **MovePrevious**. Because the data source encapsulates a recordset, it's a good idea to allow a user to navigate through the recordset. This class delegates the navigation to the recordset; however, it does provide protection from moving past the recordset boundaries. You could add any other properties or methods to this class, either delegating to the recordset or creating your own.

Using A Data Source

Once you've set up your data source, you're going to want to use it. One way to use your data source is to bind it to a control. For example, for the **clsDataSource** class, you could create a form with a text control, a Previous button, and a Next button, as shown in Figure 5.4.

Listing 5.35 shows the code for the data-aware class test form.

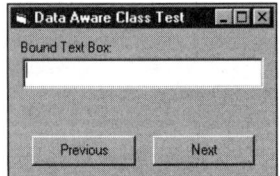

Figure 5.4
The Data Aware Class Test form.

Listing 5.35   Using a data source class.
```
Option Explicit

Private theDataSource As clsDataSource
Private theBindingCollection As BindingCollection

Private Sub Form_Load()
```

```
        Set theDataSource = New clsDataSource
        theDataSource.Init_Class 17
        Set theBindingCollection = New BindingCollection

        Set theBindingCollection.DataSource = theDataSource
        theBindingCollection.Add Object:=txtBound, _
                                 PropertyName:="Text", _
                                 DataField:="Value"
End Sub

Private Sub cmdNext_Click()
    theDataSource.MoveNext
End Sub

Private Sub cmdPrev_Click()
    theDataSource.MovePrevious
End Sub
```

The code for the form declares a variable for the data source, **theDataSource**, and a variable for the binding object, **theBindingCollection**. Next, in the **Form_Load** event, you instantiate and initialize the objects. Once you initialize the objects, you set the binding collection's **DataSource** property to the data source (**theDataSource**). Finally, you bind the text box to the data source by adding an item to the collection for the text box.

The **cmdNext** button and **cmdPrev** buttons must also be coded to call the data source's **MoveNext** and **MovePrevious** methods. This way, you can navigate through the data source.

Controls aren't the only things you can bind data sources to. The next section explores creating and binding to your own data consumers.

Data Consumer

A *data consumer* is a class you bind to external data sources. A data consumer acts like a control bound to a data source. Data-aware classes, as well as data consumers, allow you to bind a class directly to a data source, like the one we created earlier.

First, you create a new class module and set its **DataBindingBehavior** property to 1 (**vbSimpleBound**). This setting tells Visual Basic that the class will be bound to a single field in a data source. Setting **DataBindingBehavior** to 2 (**vbComplexBound**) tells Visual Basic to bind the class to a complete record in the record source.

Once you've created the class (in this example, a simple bound class), you need to create a property. Listing 5.36 shows the code for a sample data consumer class.

Listing 5.36   A data consumer class.
```
'clsSimpleConsumer
Option Explicit

Private mCurrentValue As String

Public Property Let Value(NewValue As String)

    mCurrentValue = NewValue
    Debug.Print Value

End Property
Public Property Get Value() As String

    Value = mCurrentValue

End Property
```

Because you can't see the data change in a class like you can in a control, you have to add a **Debug.Print** statement so you can see the data change in the Immediate window.

As was the case in the data source example, you now need to bind the class to the data source. Using the form from the earlier example, add a text box named **txtInternal** to display the internal (data consumer) class value (see Figure 5.5).

Listing 5.37 shows the updated form code.

Listing 5.37   The data consumer test form code.
```
Option Explicit

Private theDataSource As clsDataSource
Private aDataConsumer As clsSimpleConsumer
Private theBindingCollection As BindingCollection

Private Sub cmdNext_Click()
    theDataSource.MoveNext
    txtInternal = aDataConsumer.Value
End Sub

Private Sub cmdPrev_Click()
```

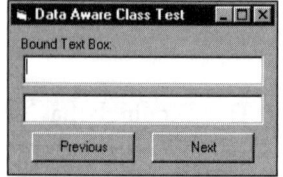

Figure 5.5
The updated Data Aware Class Test form.

```
    theDataSource.MovePrevious
    txtInternal = aDataConsumer.Value
End Sub

Private Sub Form_Load()

    Set theDataSource = New clsDataSource
    theDataSource.Init_Class 17
    Set aDataConsumer = New clsSimpleConsumer
    Set theBindingCollection = New BindingCollection

    Set theBindingCollection.DataSource = theDataSource
    theBindingCollection.Add Object:=txtBound, _
                        PropertyName:="Text", _
                        DataField:="Value"
    theBindingCollection.Add Object:=aDataConsumer, _
                        PropertyName:="Value", _
                        DataField:="Value"

End Sub
```

The additional code for the form includes the data consumer declaration and initialization. After initialization, you add the binding to the binding collection. However, instead of passing a control, you pass the object and the property name to bind the data.

You need additional code to show what's happening. When you press the Previous button or the Next button, the form writes the **Value** property to the **txtInternal** text box. When you run the program, both text boxes show the same value, because they're bound to the same data source.

Polymorphism

Chapter 1 defined *polymorphism* as two or more classes with behaviors that share the same name and the same basic purpose with different implementations. You've seen some polymorphism with the **Delete** method in Chapter 2. Here, you'll learn how Visual Basic supports polymorphism.

Most polymorphic languages support polymorphism through inheritance. Visual Basic doesn't support inheritance, so it provides other mechanisms to support polymorphism. Class modules are the first. You implement class modules with methods such as **Save** and **Delete**. These are polymorphic methods, as long as they have the same parameters.

Visual Basic also uses multiple interfaces. COM (Component Object Module) forms the infrastructure of the ActiveX specification, and objects in Visual Basic are based on ActiveX. Multiple interfaces allow you to evolve classes without breaking existing code.

Multiple Interfaces

Multiple interfaces represent a group of similar but different classes. They are similar in that they have the same interface, properties, methods, parameters, and events. They are different because of the way the properties, methods, and events may have different implementations.

Implementing multiple interfaces to objects also increases performance. When you implement interfaces, Visual Basic can *early bind* the objects. That is, it can check at compile time, instead of at runtime, whether a method or property is valid. If you pass a parameter as an object and then access a method or property, Visual Basic generates code to check whether the property or method exists at runtime. This is called *late binding*. This overhead is present for every **Object** type variable you use.

If you could tell Visual Basic what the interface—the contract—would look like and then substitute the object's implementation, Visual Basic could early bind the objects and execute faster.

Listing 5.38 shows an example of late binding.

Listing 5.38   Late binding method.
```
Public Sub Save(anObject As Object)
   'Save an object if it needs to be saved
   If anObject.isDirty Then
      anObject.Save
   End If

End Sub
```

The **anObject** parameter in the **Save** method is late bound. When this subroutine is called, Visual Basic must check at runtime to see if the **Dirty** property exists and if the object even has a **Save** method.

Implements

The **Implements** keyword lets you notify Visual Basic that a class has multiple interfaces. An *interface* is simply a class with properties and methods—in other words, any object. If you do not put any code in the properties or methods, you're in essence creating an *abstract class*. An abstract class is a class that has properties and methods, but you cannot create an object out of it. It relies on other objects to implement it. Visual Basic does not support true abstract classes; you can create objects from any class module. However, if you do not put any code in a class and then use it to define an interface, it acts as an abstract class.

Listing 5.39 defines a rudimentary interface for a persistent class. The class does not define how persistence is implemented, just the interface for a persistent class.

Listing 5.39   A persistent class interface.
```
'PersistentClass Interface
Option Explicit

Public Property Get isDirty() As Boolean

End Property

Public Property Get isLoaded() As Boolean

End Property

Public Sub Load()

End Sub

Public Sub Save()

End Sub
```

This interface is a general-purpose contract. When you use the **Implements** keyword in an object, you must implement each property and method. Therefore, to make a class persistent, you simply add the following line of code to the class:

```
Implements PersistentClass
```

Listing 5.40 shows the **Prospect** class with the **Implements** declaration.

Listing 5.40   Persistent Prospect class.
```
'Contact Class

Option Explicit
Implements PersistentClass
```

```
Private mContactDate As Date
Private mContactTime As String
Private mContactType As String
Private mMemo As String
Private mInitialized
...
```

When you use **Implements** in a class, Visual Basic adds the implemented class to the Object drop-down list in the IDE. Figure 5.6 shows the drop-down list after the **Implements** statement has been added to the **Prospect** class.

If you select the **PersistentClass** object, the methods and parameters show up in the Procedure drop-down list box, as shown in Figure 5.7.

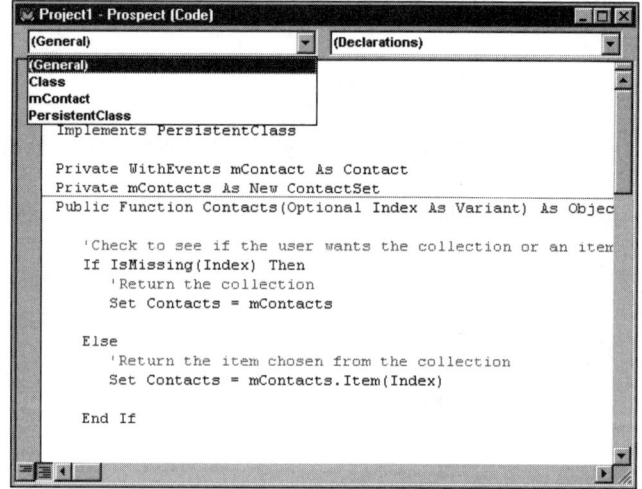

Figure 5.6
The **Prospect** class with **PersistentClass Implements**.

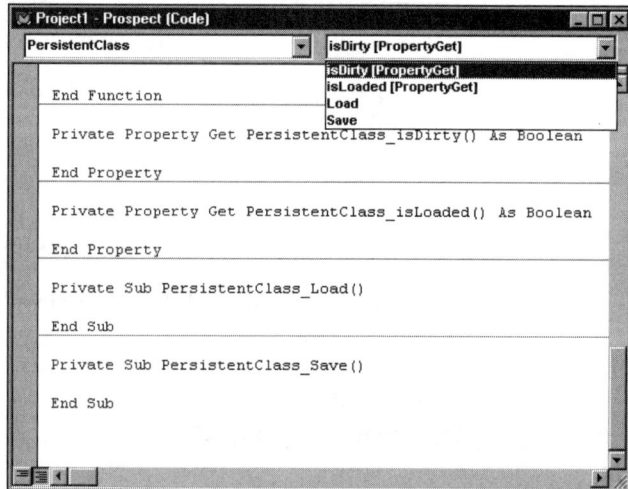

Figure 5.7
The **PersistentClass** procedures.

Once you add an interface to an object, you must implement the methods. Select each procedure from the implemented interface in the Procedure drop-down list box. This adds each procedure to your object. Listing 5.41 lists all the procedures in the **Prospect** class that you must implement from **PersistentClass**.

Listing 5.41   PersistentClass procedures in the Prospect class.

```
Private Property Get PersistentClass_isDirty() As Boolean

End Property

Private Property Get PersistentClass_isLoaded() As Boolean

End Property

Private Sub PersistentClass_Load()

End Sub

Private Sub PersistentClass_Save()

End Sub
```

You'll notice that all the procedures are private. They are private because you do not want them to become part of the public interface for the **Prospect** class. If they're part of the public interface, and then you have the same problem you had earlier, you have to call the specific method to save the object, and Visual Basic has to determine if the method exists.

Now your **Prospect** class has two interfaces: the default **Prospect** interface and the **PersistentClass** interface. You can rewrite the code from Listing 5.38 to take advantage of this, as shown in Listing 5.42.

Listing 5.42   Polymorphic Save.

```
Public Sub Save(anObject As PersistentClass)
    'Save an object if it needs to be saved
    If anObject.isDirty Then
       anObject.Save
    End If
```

Now, Visual Basic can check to make sure any parameter passed into the method implements a **PersistentClass** interface, and it can early bind the calls inside the method.

Listing 5.43 shows how you call the **Save** subroutine for both the **Prospect** class and the **Contact** class. The **Contact** class also implements the **PersistentClass** interface.

Listing 5.43   Calling the same method in two different objects.
```
Dim theProspectObject As New Prospect
Dim theContactObject As New Contact
Save theProspectObject
Save theContactObject
```

This code calls the **Save** subroutine with two different object types. The interfaces allow them to pass the compiler checks and to avoid the runtime penalty of late binding.

Conclusion

In this chapter, we explored advanced classes. Here are some of the highlights:

- Use a common method for initializing objects—it's easy to remember and gives you control of the initialization process.
- Force users to initialize objects with module-level variables and check in each public procedure.
- Use optional parameters to provide interfaces for initializing classes in different ways.
- Visual Basic destroys an object when all the references to that object are released.
- Avoid circular references to objects.
- Use collections to store sets of related objects.
- Implement your own collections for maximum protection and control.
- Create an object broker to facilitate one-to-one relationships.
- Use collections to implement containment relationships.
- Use data-aware classes to implement robust access to external data.
- Visual Basic uses multiple interfaces and the **Implements** keyword. Use this polymorphism for better control and faster execution.

Chapter 6
Object Errors: When Something Goes Wrong

Key Topics:

- *Design Of The* **Error** *Class*

- *Initialize/Terminate Events And Declarations*

- *The* **TrapRunTime** *Method*

- *The* **TrapSyntax** *Method*

- *Stepping Through The Syntax-Checking Algorithm*

- *Making The* **Error** *Class Stand Alone*

In developing the error-handling code and scheme for the class library on this book's companion CD-ROM, we had two high-level design objectives in mind. First, we wanted to meet all the requirements of a robust public interface for an ActiveX component. These requirements were discussed previously in Chapter 2. Second, we wanted the implementation to be in the form of a public ClassModule object, the **Error** class, which any client application could reuse.

More simply put, the objective of the **Error** class is to free the VB developer, either of ActiveX components or client applications, from ever having to write another error-trapping or syntax-checking routine. Because of Visual Basic's own underlying architecture, you'll always have to enable error handlers with the **On Error** statement within a client application. However, now those error handlers can call the **Error** class and let this class do the rest of the work.

Design Of The Error Class

If something goes wrong while any public member of this book's class library is executing, that member will make a call to either the **TrapRunTime** or **TrapSyntax** method within the **Error** class. The **Error** class contains the following methods:

- *LogError*—A private method that fills an array with either runtime or syntax error information to return to the client application and logs the error within the appropriate file.

- *ShowRunTime*—A private method that simulates the behavior of Visual Basic's **MsgBox** function, adds a Help button to the message box, and displays a Visual Basic runtime error message. This is a simpler version of the routine that comprises the **ShowMsg** method of the **ClientApp** class.

- *ShowSyntax*—A private method that simulates the behavior of Visual Basic's **MsgBox** function, adds a Help button to the message box, and displays a class library syntax error message.
- *SplitMsg*—A private method that splits a Visual Basic runtime error message into separate lines that do not exceed the 40-character limit of the **ShowRunTime** method.
- *TrapRunTime*—A public method that traps any Visual Basic runtime error and displays its message and associated Help topic (if it has one).
- *TrapSyntax*—A public method that traps any syntax error that occurs within the class library and displays its message and associated Help topic.

You could instantiate the **ClientApp** class and call its **ShowMsg** method to display the errors handled by the **TrapRunTime** and **TrapSyntax** methods. However, the **ShowRunTime** and **ShowSyntax** methods are called directly from within the **Error** class and, as a result, run faster because another class does not have to be instantiated. The way the **Error** class works, in its role as guardian of the class library's ActiveX component, is characterized by these specific attributes:

- Each public member of a public class within the class library contains an error handler to trap runtime errors.
- Each member implements data type mismatch and other syntax checking to the degree necessary to provide feedback to the client application programmer who is trying to call a member but is passing incorrect arguments. The class library safeguards the client application from unanticipated behavior caused by a member's execution. The golden rule, as mentioned before (and certainly worth mentioning again), is this: If there is any chance that a member could do the wrong thing (that is, something not dictated by its functional specifications), then it does nothing.
- When handling a runtime or syntax error, the **Error** class follows four general steps. First, it displays an appropriate error message (unless it's being run as an RAO). Second, it creates a set of error codes that contain comprehensive information about the error. Third, it writes this error information to a file if the client application requests that service for a runtime error or if an unexpected runtime error occurs during the execution of a member. Fourth, it returns a **Variant** containing an array of error codes.

Initialize/Terminate Events And Declarations

A ClassModule object has two events—**Initialize** and **Terminate**—that occur whenever you instantiate and uninstantiate the object. Microsoft added these syntactical elements, which are described in detail here, within VB4:

- *Initialize*—Occurs when an application creates an instance of a form, MDI form, user control, property page, or class. You write code within this event procedure to initialize any data that the instance uses.

- *Terminate*—Occurs when all the references to an instance of a form, MDI form, user control, property page, or class are removed from memory by setting all the variables that refer to the object to Nothing or when the last reference to the object falls out of scope. You write code within this event procedure to free any system resources that an object reference uses, to close any open files, and so on.

You can trigger the **Initialize** event of a ClassModule object in two ways. You can use the **CreateObject** function to create an instance of a class, as done within this code snippet:

```
' Declare a form-level object variable
Dim Error As Object

' Instantiate Error class. Two parts of programmatic ID,
' are:
' * EFSE (Project Name on General tab of Project Properties
'    dialog box.)
' * Error (Name property of ClassModule object.)
Set Error = CreateObject("EFSE.Error")
```

Or, you can use the **As New** syntax to create an instance of a class, as done in the following code snippet:

```
' Instantiate Error class to provide shared methods for
' Dialog class.
Private Error As New Error
```

Listing 6.1 shows the General Declarations section of ERROR.CLS.

Listing 6.1   General declarations within the Error class.
```
' DLL functions:
#If Win32 Then
```

```
            Private Declare Function GetSystemDirectory& _
                            Lib "KERNEL32" Alias _
                            "GetSystemDirectoryA"
                            (ByVal Buffer$, ByVal LenBuffer&)
#Else

            Private Declare Function GetSystemDirectory% _
                            Lib "KERNEL" _
                            (ByVal Buffer$, ByVal LenBuffer%)


#End If


' Class-level flags that are set within the Initialize event
' procedure and are read by different members of class:
' * If cRAOServer is True, VB instantiates the class as RAO
'   component.
' * If cEXEServer is True, VB instantiates the class as EXE
'   component.
Private cRAOServer      As Boolean
Private cEXEServer      As Boolean

' Class-level variables:
Private cKeyword        As String

' Instantiate internal classes to reuse their members:
Private CL              As New CL
```

The two class-level **Boolean** variables are assigned their values within the **Initialize** event of the **Error** class:

```
' Check for RAO (Remote Automation Object) out-of-process
' component or local out-of-process, EXE component:
If Right$(App.Title, 1) = "R" Then cRAOServer = True
If Right$(App.Title, 1) = "E" Then cEXEServer = True
```

The code within the **Initialize** event works like this: When you make the single set of Visual Basic source code that comprises the class library into the different kinds of ActiveX components, you signify the kind of component by adding a suffix (D, E, R, or 16 for DLL, EXE, RAO, or 16-bit, respectively) to the title of the project. You do this by setting the Title entry on the Make tab of the Project Properties dialog box when you make and register the ActiveX component, as shown in Figure 6.1.

Object Errors: When Something Goes Wrong 181

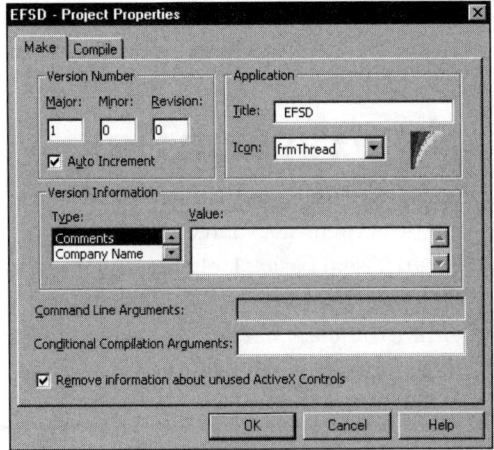

Figure 6.1
Configuring the project properties.

If you use this naming scheme for the **Title** property of the ActiveX component, the class library can tell under what kind of component it is being run and, in the case of the **Error** class, turn on either the **cRAOServer** or **cEXEServer** class-level flag. If the class library is being run as an in-process DLL component, neither of these flags is turned on within the **Error** class.

The **Terminate** event of the **Error** class has this code:

```
' Free system resources associated with objects:
Set CL = Nothing
```

You should always explicitly free the system resources associated with any module-level object variables. There is one difference, however, between how you do this for a ClassModule object and how you do it for a Form object. In the case of a Form object, you should also explicitly set the **Name** property of the Form object to **Nothing**. You cannot do this with a ClassModule object. For example, if you try to add the statement

```
Set Error = Nothing
```

to the **Terminate** event procedure, VB6 displays the syntax error message "Invalid use of property" when you try to make the ActiveX component. It's unclear what this error message is trying to say because neither the object variable **Error** nor the keyword **Nothing** are properties. VB6 permits you to make the ActiveX component without raising a syntax error, but then it crashes when you attempt to reuse the **Error** object from a client application or internally. Simply put, VB6 will not

182 Chapter 6

let you set the **Name** property of a ClassModule object to **Nothing** within its own **Terminate** event procedure.

The TrapRunTime Method

The **TrapRunTime** method handles any Visual Basic runtime error and displays its associated error message. If the error has a Help topic within Visual Basic's Help file, that topic can also be displayed. See the "**TrapRunTime** Method's Specifications" sidebar, which shows the topic within the class library's Help file (EFS.HLP) that specifies the detailed functionality of the **TrapRunTime** method.

TrapRunTime Method's Specifications
Syntax

```
Object.TrapRunTime(ErrObj, [Title], [Buttons], [Log], [IDClsLib])
```

The **TrapRunTime** method's syntax has the following object qualifier and named arguments:

- *Object*—Required. **Object** data type. An expression that evaluates to an object within the Applies To pop-up list.
- *ErrObj*—Required. **Object** data type. An expression that evaluates to VB's system-level Err object.
- *Title*—Optional. **Variant** data type whose subtype is a **String** expression that specifies the name of the procedure within which the runtime error occurred. **Title** appears within the title bar of the message box and cannot exceed 40 characters in length. If **Title** is omitted, the default setting for **Title** is **Unknown Procedure**.
- *Buttons*—Optional. **Variant** data type whose subtype is an **Integer** expression that's the sum of values that specify the number and type of command buttons, icons (if any), default command buttons, and modality of the message box. If **Buttons** is omitted, the default setting for **Buttons** is the Exclamation icon and the OK command button. See the "Settings" portion of this sidebar for the valid settings of **Buttons**.
- *Log*—Optional. **Variant** data type whose subtype is a **String** expression that specifies a valid path and ASCII text file to which an entry logging the runtime error is to be written. If the file does not yet exist, **TrapRunTime** creates it and writes the entry. If the file already exists, **TrapRunTime** opens it and appends the entry to the existing file. If **Log** is omitted, no entry is written.
- *IDClsLib*—Optional. **Variant** data type whose subtype is a **String** expression that specifies a security password. The correct password identifies the calling procedure as belonging to the class library. **IDClsLib** is only used internally; if you attempt to pass it when calling the method from a client application, a syntax error occurs.

Settings

The first group of values (0 through 5) describes the number and type of command buttons displayed within the dialog box; the second group (16, 32, 48, and 64) describes the icon style; the third group (0, 256, and 512) determines which command button is the default; and the fourth group (0 and

4096) determines the modality of the message box. When adding numbers to create a final value for **Buttons**, use only one number from each group. See the Help topic titled "Visual Basic Constants: ShowMsg/TrapRunTime Methods" for the valid settings of the **Buttons** argument.

Called

The **TrapRunTime** method is called from any procedure within a client application.

Returns

Upon success, eight elements within a **Variant** are returned. The elements contain these subtypes:

- *0 - ERR_RESULT*—An **Integer** from 1 to 7 that specifies the command button the user chooses. See the Help topic titled "Visual Basic Constants: ShowMsg/TrapRunTime Methods" for the valid settings of the **ERR_RESULT** element.
- *1 - ERR_SOURCE*—A **String** that's the name of the method or property's procedure within which the runtime error occurred. If the **Title** argument was not passed, the default of **Unknown Procedure** is returned.
- *2 - ERR_NBR*—An **Integer** that's the runtime error number.
- *3 - ERR_DESC*—A **String** that's the description of the runtime error.
- *4 - ERR_HELPFILE*—A **String** that specifies the path and name of the Help file containing the runtime error's Help topic.
- *5 - ERR_CONTEXTID*—An **Integer** that's the context ID number of the Help topic for the runtime error.
- *6 - ERR_TIME*—A **Date** that specifies the date and time of the runtime error.
- *7 - ERR_LOG*—A **Boolean** that specifies whether information about the runtime error is written to a log file. It's **True** if a valid **Log** argument is passed or **False** if the **Log** argument is not passed.

Upon failure, eight elements within a **Variant** are returned. The elements contain these subtypes:

- *0 - ERR_RESULT*—A **Boolean** (**False**) that specifies that a syntax or Visual Basic runtime error occurred while the **TrapRunTime** method itself was executing.
- *1 - ERR_SOURCE*—A **String** that is **TrapRunTime**.
- *2 - ERR_NBR*—An **Integer** that's the error number.
- *3 - ERR_DESC*—A **String** that's the description of the error.
- *4 - ERR_HELPFILE*—A **String** that specifies the path and name of the Help file containing the error's Help topic.
- *5 - ERR_CONTEXTID*—An **Integer** that's the context ID number of the Help topic for the error.
- *6 - ERR_TIME*—A **Date** that specifies the date and time of the error.
- *7 - ERR_LOG*—A **Boolean** that specifies whether information about the error was written to the file ERRLOGRT.TXT, on the same path as the class library. **False** is returned if a syntax error occurs; **True** is returned if a runtime error occurs.

Remarks

The **TrapRunTime** method does not relieve you of the need to enable an error-handling routine with the **On Error** statement within each procedure within the client application where a runtime error could occur.

The TrapRunTime Method's Code

The code for the **TrapRunTime** method and its related private members within the **Error** class is quite complex; we won't cover all its features in this chapter. Our analysis of the **TrapRunTime** method's code within this section focuses on the Visual Basic syntax that it uses, its associated methods, and a couple other noteworthy features unique to this method within the class library. The syntactical elements we tackle in this section are briefly described here:

- *Object*—An OLE Automation data type. If you want to pass a reference to a Visual Basic object to an argument within an ActiveX component's member, you must declare that argument as the data type **Object**.

- *TypeName*—A function that returns a string and provides information about a variable. This book's class library uses **TypeName** to determine what class or type of object is passed to an **Object** argument within a member.

- *Returning an array*—A function procedure can return an array of values if the values are first assigned to a **Variant**.

Parsing The Buttons Argument

We'll begin with the declaration of the **TrapRunTime** method:

```
Function TrapRunTime(ErrObj As Object, _
                    Optional Title, _
                    Optional Buttons, _
                    Optional Log, _
                    Optional IDClsLib)
```

The third argument of the **TrapRunTime** method, **Buttons**, is optional. It must be a **Variant** that contains an **Integer** or **Long** subtype. It has the same functionality as the second argument of the **ShowMsg** method of the **ClientApp** class (or Visual Basic's **MsgBox** function), and it specifies the number and kind of buttons, icons (if any), default buttons, and modality of the error message box.

Because this argument can take any combination of 15 different values (as specified within Visual Basic's Help file within the topic titled "MsgBox Function") as a valid value, it's not feasible to check the syntax of the argument with a brute force approach—too many possible permutations must be checked. The class library's **CL** class contains a method called **ParseButtons**, shown in Listing 6.2, that both the **ShowMsg** and **TrapRunTime** methods call to validate their **Buttons** arguments.

Listing 6.2 The ParseButtons method of the CL class.

```
Function ParseButtons(Buttons, _
                      Member As String)

' **********************************
' Purpose: Parses Buttons argument of different members to
'          ensure valid value for creation of message box.
'
' Called:  Internally from members of the class library.
'
' Accepts: Buttons: Variant whose subtype is Integer
'                   expression that specifies sum of
'                   values determining number and type of
'                   buttons to display, icon (if any),
'                   default button, and modality of
'                   message box.
'          Member:  String expression specifying name of
'                   member that calls this method.
'
' Returns: Upon success, 5 elements in array contained
'          within Variant variable:
'
'          Element #    Constant      Value
'                 0     PB_SUCCESS    True
'                 1     PB_BTNS       Buttons setting
'                 2     PB_ICON       Icon setting
'                 3     PB_DEF_BTN    Default button setting
'                 4     PB_SYS_MODAL  System modal setting
'
'
' **********************************

' Constants for elements within returned array:
Const PB_SUCCESS = 0
Const PB_BTNS = 1
Const PB_ICON = 2
Const PB_DEF_BTN = 3
Const PB_SYS_MODAL = 4

' Variables:
Dim RetVals(4) As Variant

If VarType(Buttons) <> vbInteger And _
   VarType(Buttons) <> vbLong Then
      E.TrapSyntax 4, Member, "Buttons", "Integer or Long"
End If
```

```vb
            ' Check system modal setting within Buttons argument and:
            ' * If it is 32-bit Windows, disallow it.
            ' * If it is 16-bit Windows, store Buttons
            '   and strip it from Buttons argument.
            If Buttons >= vbSystemModal Then
            
                #If Win32 Then
                    E.TrapSyntax 7, Member, "Buttons"
                #Else
                    RetVals(PB_SYS_MODAL) = True
                    Buttons = Buttons - vbSystemModal
                #End If
            
            End If
            
            ' Check default button setting within Buttons argument,
            ' store Buttons, and strip it from Buttons argument:
            Select Case Buttons
                Case Is >= vbDefaultButton3
                    RetVals(PB_DEF_BTN) = vbDefaultButton3
                Case Is >= vbDefaultButton2
                    RetVals(PB_DEF_BTN) = vbDefaultButton2
                Case Else
                    RetVals(PB_DEF_BTN) = vbDefaultButton1
            End Select
            Buttons = Buttons Mod 256
            
            ' Check icon setting within Buttons argument, store
            ' Buttons, and strip it from Buttons argument:
            Select Case Buttons
                Case Is >= vbInformation
                    RetVals(PB_ICON) = vbInformation
                Case Is >= vbExclamation
                    RetVals(PB_ICON) = vbExclamation
                Case Is >= vbQuestion
                    RetVals(PB_ICON) = vbQuestion
                Case Is >= vbCritical
                    RetVals(PB_ICON) = vbCritical
            End Select
            Buttons = Buttons Mod 16
            
            ' Check buttons setting within Buttons argument and, if
            ' valid, store it and return all the parameters, along
            ' with PB_SUCCESS = True to indicate success:
            If Buttons < vbOKOnly Or Buttons > vbRetryCancel Then
                E.TrapSyntax 5, Member, "Buttons"
```

```
    Else
        RetVals(PB_SUCCESS) = True
        RetVals(PB_BTNS) = Buttons
        ParseButtons = RetVals
    End If

End Function
```

The **ParseButtons** method uses an algorithm that parses the value passed into the **Buttons** argument, from the highest possible value (**vbSystemModal**, or 4096) down to the lowest possible value (**vbOKOnly** + **vbApplicationModal**, or 0). As the algorithm works its way down through the four categories of possible values (modality, default button, kind of icon, and kinds of buttons), it subtracts, or *parses out*, the values associated with the first three categories. When it gets to the bottom of the parsing algorithm, all that can be left if **Buttons** is valid is a value from **vbOKOnly** (0) to **vbRetryCancel** (5).

The other important point that the **ParseButtons** method illustrates is a type of situation that calls for conditional compilation. Not all versions of Windows support the same set of features. The **ParseButtons** method's code checks whether or not the **Buttons** argument contains **vbSystemModal** (4096). If it does and the class library is running under 32-bit Windows, Visual Basic displays a syntax error message.

Because the 32-bit version of Windows performs true multitasking, it does not permit a message box to be displayed as "system modal." Visual Basic's **MsgBox** function permits you to set **Buttons** to **vbSystemModal** under 32-bit Windows, but this approach only makes the message box application modal. Visual Basic's Help file does not document the constraint against system modality under 32-bit Windows, but API32.HLP (which comes with Visual C++) indicates that the new input model for 32-bit Windows does not permit system modal windows.

Using The *Object* And *TypeName* Syntax

The required **ErrObj** argument of the **TrapRunTime** method is declared as the OLE Automation data type **Object**. Remember, you can declare any ActiveX component's argument that takes an object reference as the type **Object**.

The **TrapRunTime** method is designed to work with just the **ErrObj** argument, which must be passed Visual Basic's built-in Err object. The **TypeName** function is used to check what kind of an object reference has been passed to the OLE Automation **Object** data type. This function returns a string corresponding to the class or type name of the object reference. VB6's class name for the Err object is **ErrObject**, and these initial lines of code within the **TrapRunTime** method check the syntax of the **ErrObj** argument:

```
If TypeName(ErrObj) <> "ErrObject" Then
    On Error GoTo ET
    TrapSyntax 8, PROC, "ErrObj"
ElseIf ErrObj.Number < 1 Or ErrObj.Number > 65534 Then
    On Error GoTo ET
    TrapSyntax 5, PROC, "Number property of Err"
End If
```

For a list of the class or type names within Visual Basic's object hierarchy, select Language Reference|Objects on the Contents tab of Visual Basic's Help file. If you're using control objects on a form, their class or type names appear within the drop-down combo box at the top of the Properties window (to the right of the **Name** property of each control object).

The Error Message's Help Topic

Once **TrapRunTime** has validated its **ErrObj** argument and its four optional arguments, the method determines the path of Visual Basic's error Help file (VEENLR3.HLP within VB5 and VB6, VB.HLP within VB4) or MSJETERR.HLP (for Jet DAO errors) for the runtime error that occurred. Listing 6.3 shows the code to accomplish this task.

Listing 6.3 The code for finding the runtime error's Help file.

```
Function TrapRunTime(ErrObj As Object, _
                    Optional Title, _
                    Optional Buttons, _
                    Optional Log, _
                    Optional IDClsLib)

    . . .

    Select Case HelpFile

        Case "MSJETERR.HLP"

            NumChars = GetSystemDirectory(WindowsPath, _
                                          Len(WindowsPath))
            HelpFile = Left$(WindowsPath, CInt(NumChars)) & _
                       "\" & HelpFile
```

```
            If Dir$(HelpFile) = NONE Then HelpFile = "NA"

            ErrHeader = "DAO error " & ErrNbr & " Ñ" & vbCr & _
                vbCr
    Case "CMDLG96.HLP"

            NumChars = GetWindowsDirectory(WindowsPath, _
                                        Len(WindowsPath))
            HelpFile = Left$(WindowsPath, CInt(NumChars)) & _
                        "\HELP\" & HelpFile

            If Dir$(HelpFile) = NONE Then HelpFile = "NA"

            ErrHeader = "CommonDialog error " & _
                ErrNbr & " Ñ" & vbCr & vbCr

    Case Else

            If Dir$(HelpFile) = NONE Then HelpFile = "NA"

            ErrHeader = "VB error " & ErrNbr & " Ñ" & vbCr & _
                vbCr

            If Right$(HelpFile, 6) = "VB.HLP" Then
                cKeyword = "errors,errors,trappable"
            Else
                cKeyword = "trappable errors"
            End If

    End Select

    . . .

End Function
```

By default, Microsoft Access installs the Help file MSJETERR.HLP on the Windows system path. If the runtime error is a Jet DAO error, the code within Listing 6.3 uses the Windows API function **GetSystemDirectory** to find the system directory. When you call it, you must first declare a fixed-length string variable (that is, **SystemPath**). **GetSystemDirectory** copies to the variable **SystemPath** the Windows system path (leaving any trailing null characters still in place in the fixed-length string) and returns the length, in characters, of the Windows system path. You then use Visual Basic's **Left$** function to parse out the path. The Jet DAO error message Help file, titled "Jet Error

Help," is not included with VB6. If the current system does not have Microsoft Access or Microsoft Office Professional installed on it, the **TrapRunTime** function will not find the Help file and will not enable the Help button on the error message box.

TrapRunTime also determines the Help topic associated with the runtime error (from the **HelpFile** and **HelpContext** property settings of the Err object). VB displays three general kinds of runtime error messages and Help topics when you use the **Raise** method of the Err object to artificially generate an error. First, it can display a specific message that matches the VBA runtime error that occurred. For example, the code within Listing 6.4 results in the error information displayed in Figure 6.2.

Listing 6.4 The code for displaying VBA error codes.

```
Private Sub Form_DblClick()

    ' Variable
    Dim Msg As String

    ' Enable error handler and artificially generate runtime
    ' error
    On Error Resume Next
    Err.Raise 3

    ' Display settings of Err object's properties and its help
    ' topic
    Msg = "Err #: " & Err & vbCr
    Msg = Msg & "Desc: " & Err.Description & vbCr
    Msg = Msg & "Help File: " & Err.HelpFile & vbCr
    Msg = Msg & "Help #: " & Err.HelpContext
    MsgBox Prompt:=Msg, _
           Buttons:=vbInformation, _
           Title:="VBA Runtime Error", _
           HelpFile:=Err.HelpFile, _
           Context:=Err.HelpContext

End Sub
```

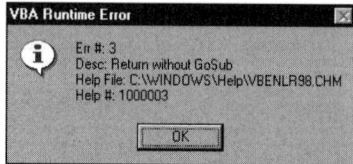

Figure 6.2
Visual Basic's display of a VBA runtime error.

Object Errors: When Something Goes Wrong

Second, Visual Basic can display the generic runtime error 95 (an application-defined or object-defined error) for non-VBA errors that are generated artificially with the **Raise** method. Application-defined or object-defined errors occur when an error is generated using the Err object's **Raise** method or the **Error** statement, but the number does not correspond to an error defined by VBA. Such errors may be defined by the host application (for example, Excel or Visual Basic), but if you want to generate them from code, you must use the **Raise** method and fill in all the relevant arguments. The **TrapRunTime** method maps a non-VBA error (generated by the **Raise** method) to its correct Help topic number, but it still displays the generic runtime error 95 message. For example, the code in Listing 6.5 results in the error information displayed in Figure 6.3.

Listing 6.5 The code for displaying artificially generated, non-VBA error codes.

```
Private Sub Form_DblClick()

    ' Variable
    Dim Msg As String

    ' Enable error handler and artificially generate runtime
    ' error
    On Error Resume Next
    Err.Raise 400

    ' Display settings of Err object's properties and its help
    ' topic
    Msg = "Err #: " & Err & vbCr
    Msg = Msg & "Desc: " & Err.Description & vbCr
    Msg = Msg & "Help File: " & Err.HelpFile & vbCr
    Msg = Msg & "Help #: " & Err.HelpContext
    MsgBox Prompt:=Msg, _
           Buttons:=vbInformation, _
           Title:="Artificially-Generated, Non-VBA Error _
        Codes", _
           HelpFile:=Err.HelpFile, _
           Context:=Err.HelpContext

End Sub
```

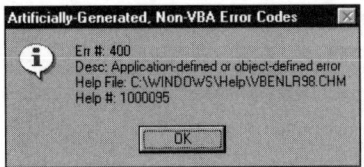

Figure 6.3
Visual Basic's display of an application-defined or object-defined error.

To see the Help topic associated with the error message, press F1.

Third, if a non-VBA runtime error actually occurs within an application (as opposed to being artificially generated), VB displays the specific error message and Help topic. For example, the code in Listing 6.6 results in the error information displayed in Figure 6.4.

Listing 6.6 The code for displaying runtime, non-VBA error codes.

```
Private Sub Form_DblClick()

    ' Variable
    Dim Msg As String

    ' Enable error handler and cause actual runtime error
    On Error Resume Next
    Show vbModal

    ' Display settings of Err object's properties and
    ' its help topic
    Msg = "Err #: " & Err & vbCr
    Msg = Msg & "Desc: " & Err.Description & vbCr
    Msg = Msg & "Help File: " & Err.HelpFile & vbCr
    Msg = Msg & "Help #: " & Err.HelpContext
    MsgBox Prompt:=Msg, _
           Buttons:=vbInformation, _
           Title:="Runtime, Non-VBA Error Codes", _
           HelpFile:=Err.HelpFile, _
           Context:=Err.HelpContext

End Sub
```

If you press F1 to see the Help topic associated with the error message, VB displays the topic shown in Figure 6.5.

We must also point out a bug within VB6 in regard to the error messages and Help topics for the three built-in ActiveX control objects. Visual Basic maps the runtime errors related to the CommonDialog, Grid, and OLE Container ActiveX controls to nonexistent Help topics. For example, if a CommonDialog ActiveX control is placed on a

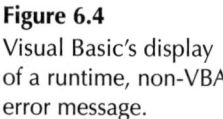

Figure 6.4
Visual Basic's display of a runtime, non-VBA error message.

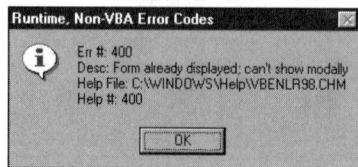

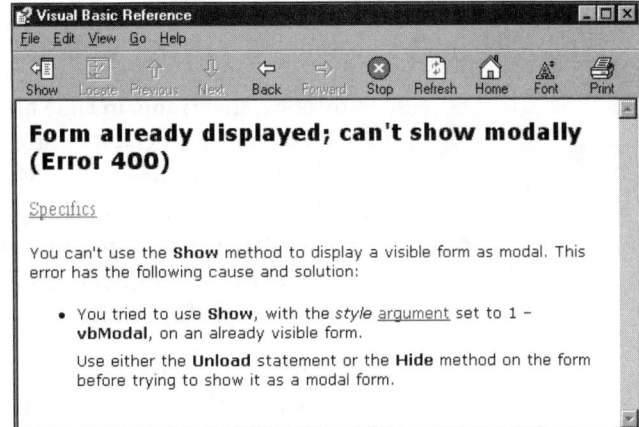

Figure 6.5
Visual Basic's display of the associated Help topic.

Form object, the code in Listing 6.7 displays the error information (if you click on Cancel from the Color dialog box).

Listing 6.7 The code to demonstrate missing Help topics for CommonDialog errors.

```
Private Sub Form_DblClick()

    ' Variable
    Dim Msg As String

    ' Enable error handler
    On Error Resume Next

    ' Set common dialog's CancelError property
    ' and display Color dialog box
    CommonDialog1.CancelError = True
    CommonDialog1.ShowColor

    ' After user chooses Cancel (which causes runtime _
    ' error 32,755), display settings of Err object's
    ' properties and its help topic
    Msg = "Err #: " & Err & vbCr
    Msg = Msg & "Desc: " & Err.Description & vbCr
    Msg = Msg & "Help File: " & Err.HelpFile & vbCr
    Msg = Msg & "Help #: " & Err.HelpContext
    MsgBox Prompt:=Msg, _
           Buttons:=vbInformation, _
           Title:="CommonDialog Error", _
           HelpFile:=Err.HelpFile, _
           Context:=Err.HelpContext

End Sub
```

If you press F1 to see the Help topic associated with the error message, either Visual Basic displays the associated topic or nothing happens.

Because of this bug, the **TrapRunTime** method remaps runtime errors for Visual Basic's built-in ActiveX control objects to different topics. In this example, **TrapRunTime** finds CMDLG96.HLP (it's located on the WINDOWS\HELP path) and remaps the error to the Help topic titled "CommonDialog Error Constants." In other cases, when no specific Help topic exists, **TrapRunTime** remaps the error to a generic Help topic titled "Trappable Errors."

Therefore, if you put a CommonDialog control on a Form object within VB6, run the code in Listing 6.8, and then click on the Help button on the error message box, **TrapRunTime** displays the associated Help topic.

Listing 6.8 The code to demonstrate the remapped Help topic for a CommonDialog error.

```
Private Sub Form_DblClick()

    ' Variable
    Dim Error As Object

    ' Instantiate Error class
    #If Win32 Then
        Set Error = CreateObject("EFSE.Error")
    #Else
        Set Error = CreateObject("EFS16.Error")
    #End If

    ' Enable error handler
    On Error Resume Next

    ' Set common dialog's CancelError property
    ' and display Color dialog box
    CommonDialog1.CancelError = True
    CommonDialog1.ShowColor

    ' After user chooses Cancel (which causes runtime _
    ' error 32,755), handle it with TrapRunTime
    ' method of Error class
    Error.TrapRunTime Err, "Form_DblClick"

End Sub
```

Object Errors: When Something Goes Wrong

Splitting The Error Message

After the **TrapRunTime** method remaps a runtime error's Help topic, if the error message (from the **Description** property of the Err object) is longer than 40 characters, the method runs the message through a private method within the **Error** class called **SplitMsg**. Because the **TrapRunTime** method uses the same routine to display an error message as the **ShowRuntime** method does, no single line within the runtime error message can be longer than 40 characters (a specification of the **Prompt** argument of **ShowMsg**). Listing 6.9 shows the code for the **SplitMsg** method.

Listing 6.9   The code for the private SplitMsg method.

```
Private Function SplitMsg(VBErrMsg As String) As String

    ' *********************************
    ' Purpose: Splits VB runtime error message into separate
    '          lines that do not exceed 40-character limit of
    '          ShowRunTime method.
    '
    ' Called:  Internally from TrapRunTime method
    '
    ' Accepts: VBErrMsg: String expression that is Description
    '                    property of Err object
    '
    ' Returns: Reformatted error message
    ' *********************************

    ' Constants for literals
    Const MAX_CHARS = 40

    ' Variables
    Dim TmpStr      As String
    Dim NewMsg      As String
    Dim Pos         As Byte
    Dim lastPos     As Byte
    Dim CharNbr     As Integer

    ' Initialize
    CharNbr = 1
    TmpStr = VBErrMsg

    ' Until entire message has been examined
    ' * Get position of next space within the message line
    '   being parsed
```

```
' * If space is more than 40 characters from start of
'   line:
'     a) If it is last space, use position of previous space
'     b) Replace space with carriage return character
'     c) Add corrected line to other corrected lines
'     d) Strip corrected line from message
'     e) Reset character counter
' * If no space is found and we've reached end of message:
'     a) Add last corrected line to other corrected lines
'     b) Set exit condition for Do Until loop
' * If space is found, but it is less than 40 characters
'   from start of line, update character counter and
'   keep looking.
Do Until CharNbr = Len(VBErrMsg)

    Pos = InStr(CharNbr, TmpStr, Chr$(vbKeySpace))

    If CharNbr > MAX_CHARS Then

        If Pos = False Then Pos = LastPos

        NewMsg = NewMsg & Left$(TmpStr, Pos - 1) & vbCr
        TmpStr = Mid$(TmpStr, Pos + 1)
        CharNbr = 1
    ElseIf Pos = False Then
        NewMsg = NewMsg & TmpStr
        CharNbr = Len(VBErrMsg)
    Else
        CharNbr = Pos + 1
    End If

    LastPos = Pos

Loop

SplitMsg = NewMsg

End Function
```

> **NOTE**
>
> The **Private** keyword, when used to declare a procedure, indicates that the procedure is accessible only to other procedures within the module where it is declared. If procedures within a standard or class module are not explicitly declared using either the **Public** or **Private** keyword, they are public, by default.

The best that can be said for the algorithm that splits the runtime error message is that it works. It's not the most elegant code, but it does the job. The most important thing to note about the **SplitMsg** method (and all the other internal methods within the **CL** and **Error** classes) is that it does not enable an error handler. Instead, an error handler is enabled within the public member (in this example, **TrapRunTime**) that calls the internal, supporting method. Because of the way Visual

Basic's own error-handling architecture works, if a runtime error occurs within a procedure that does not have an enabled error handler, Visual Basic works its way back down the stack of live procedures looking for an enabled error handler. The first enabled error handler that it finds is the one it uses to trap the error.

Not enabling error handlers in private, internal methods has three advantages:

- This approach minimizes the number of error handlers that have to be enabled throughout the ActiveX component.
- When a member fails and returns error codes to the client application, the **ERR_SOURCE** (1) element within the returned array always identifies the public member as the source of the error, not an internal member (whose name, of course, is unknown to the client application programmer and would just be confusing).
- This technique permits the **TrapSyntax** method to implement its own validation scheme in a similar and more elegant way.

Logging And Returning Error Codes

The last thing the **TrapRunTime** method does is call a private method—**LogError**—within the **Error** class to fill a **Variant** array with error codes, write them to a text file (if specified to do so), and return them to the client application. The **LogError** method performs these functions for both the **TrapRunTime** and **TrapSyntax** public methods because, although the error information itself is different, the number of elements within the array of error codes that each public method returns is the same. Listing 6.10 shows the code for the **LogError** method.

Listing 6.10 The code for the private LogError method.

```
Private Function LogError(ErrNbr As Long, _
                          Procedure As String, _
                          ErrMsg As String, _
                          HelpFile As String, _
                          Context As Long, _
                          Log As String, _
                          Button As Byte)

' *************************************
' Purpose: Fills array with either runtime or syntax error
'          information to return to the client application
'          and logs error within the appropriate file.
'
```

```
' Called:   Internally from TrapRunTime or TrapSyntax
'           members
'
' Accepts: ErrNbr:    Long expression that specifies
'                     error #
'          Procedure: String expression that specifies
'                     name of procedure within which the
'                     error occurred
'          ErrMsg:    String expression that specifies the
'                     error message
'          HelpFile:  String expression that specifies
'                     path and name of Help file
'                     containing the error's Help topic
'          Context:   Long expression that specifies Help
'                     context number assigned to the
'                     error's Help topic
'          Log:       String expression that specifies
'                     path and file to which to write the
'                     log entry. If vbNullString is
'                     passed, no entry is made.
'          Button:    Byte expression that specifies
'                     either the number of button
'                     user chose on runtime error
'                     message box or False.
'
' Returns: 8 elements within Variant
'
'          El #  Constant      Value
'          0     ERR_RESULT    Number of button or False
'          1     ERR_SOURCE    Procedure containing error
'          2     ERR_NBR       Number of error
'          3     ERR_DESC      Description of error
'          4     ERR_HELPFILE  Help file with error topic
'          5     ERR_CONTEXTID Context number of topic
'          6     ERR_TIME      Date/time error occurs
'          7     ERR_LOG       Logged to file (True/False)
' **************************************

' Constants for literals
Const NO_LOG_FILE = vbNullString

' Variables
Dim FileName    As String
Dim LogRetVal   As Boolean
Dim FileNbr     As Integer
Dim RetVals     As Variant
```

```
' * Specify the error log file
' * If error is to be logged to file:
'     a) Get next available file number and open log file
'     b) Write blank separator line and 5 entry lines
'     c) Close log file
' * Set Codes custom property within ERRCODES.FRM for
'   members to read from their error handlers. Codes are
'   stored within FRM module because, if they are stored
'   within Error class, they go out of scope (when
'   Terminate event occurs) before their values can be
'   read.
' * Return error information
If Right(HelpFile, 6) = "VB.HLP" Or _
   Right(HelpFile, 12) = "MSJETERR.HLP" Then
        FileName = Log
Else
        FileName = App.Path & "\ERRLOGST.TXT"
End If

If Log <> NO_LOG_FILE Then
    FileNbr = FreeFile
    Open FileName For Append As FileNbr
    Print #FileNbr,
    Print #FileNbr, "- Entry for " & Now & " -"
    Print #FileNbr, "Source: " & Procedure
    Print #FileNbr, "Number: " & ErrNbr
    Print #FileNbr, "Description: " & ErrMsg
    Print #FileNbr, "HelpFile: " & HelpFile
    Print #FileNbr, "HelpContext: " & Context
    Close FileNbr
    LogRetVal = True
End If

RetVals = Array(Button, Procedure, ErrNbr, ErrMsg, _
                HelpFile, Context, Now, LogRetVal)

If Right$(FileName, 12) = "ERRLOGST.TXT" Then
    frmErrCodes.Codes = RetVals
End If

LogError = RetVals

End Function
```

The first five arguments of the **LogError** method replicate and are derived from properties of the Err object. The value of the sixth argument,

Log, can either specify the path and file name to write the error information to, or be **vbNullString** (that is, a zero-length string). The value of the seventh argument, **Button**, can vary, depending on the type of error. Here are the possible combinations:

- *Syntax error* **False**—The only button the client application's programmer or user can choose from the error message box is OK, so there's no need to return a specific value for **Button**.

- *Runtime error* **vbOK** *(1) through* **vbNo** *(7)*—If the client application does not pass the optional **Buttons** argument to the **TrapRunTime** method, the **Button** argument of **LogError** is always **vbOK** (1). If the client application passes the optional **Buttons** argument, the **Button** argument for **LogError** depends on the button chosen from the error message box.

- *Runtime error* **False**—If an unexpected runtime error occurs during the execution of a member of the class library, the only button the client application's programmer or user can choose from the error message box is OK, so there's no need to return a specific value for **Button**.

For syntax errors only, the **LogError** method temporarily stores the error codes within the **Codes** custom property of the **frmErrCodes** Form object of the class library. The codes are immediately read from there by the **TrapSyntax** method and returned to the client application.

The general objective of the syntax-checking method **TrapSyntax** within the **Error** class is to mimic Visual Basic's own handling of syntax errors. A class library written as an ActiveX component is, in a very real sense, an extension to Visual Basic's integrated development environment. Therefore, when a client application programmer tries to use one of the methods of a class library, the class library's response when it's passed an invalid argument should simulate Visual Basic's response when a call to one of its methods uses incorrect syntax or an invalid argument.

If, for example, a client application programmer calls the **ShowMsg** method from the class library and passes it an invalid argument, the class library should respond in the same general way as Visual Basic itself does when you pass an invalid argument to its **MsgBox** function. The code in Listing 6.11 instantiates the class library's **ClientApp** class, calls its **ShowMsg** method, and passes an invalid value to the optional **HelpFile** argument (**HelpFile** is dependent on the **Context** argument and cannot be passed by itself). The class library handles the syntax error and responds by displaying the message box shown in Figure 6.6.

Figure 6.6
Visual Basic's display of the CommonDialog error message.

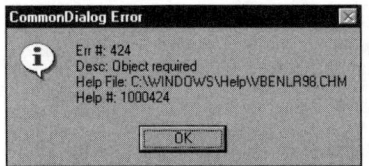

Listing 6.11 Sample syntax error handling with the class library.

```
Private Sub Form_DblClick()

    ' Declare object variable
    Dim ClientApp As Object

    ' Instantiate class
#If Win32 Then
    Set ClientApp = CreateObject("EFSE.ClientApp")
#Else
    Set ClientApp = CreateObject("EFS16.ClientApp")
#End If

    ' Call object's member using named arguments,
    ' but pass invalid value to Buttons argument
    ClientApp.ShowMsg Prompt:="Message", _
                    HelpFile:="C:\VBCLSLIB\EFS.HLP"

End Sub
```

The code in Listing 6.12 calls Visual Basic's **MsgBox** function and passes the same invalid value to the optional **HelpFile** argument (the dependent **Context** argument is not passed). Visual Basic handles the syntax error and responds by displaying the message box shown in Figure 6.7.

Listing 6.12 Sample syntax error handling with VB.

```
Private Sub Form_DblClick()

    MsgBox Prompt:="Message", _
           HelpFile:="C:\Program Files\Microsoft Visual _
    Basic\VB.HLP"

End Sub
```

You should note several things about this comparison. The message box in Figure 6.7 calls the error a *runtime error*, when what occurs is really more like a syntax error. The next thing you should notice is that neither case requires that an error handler be enabled for a client

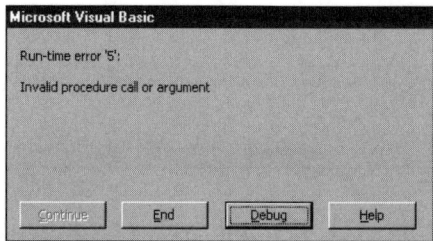

Figure 6.7
Visual Basic's display of a runtime error.

application programmer to be told a syntax error exists. In addition, both approaches let the client application programmer get further information by clicking on the Help button the message box provides. Finally, you should note that the degree to which you provide specific feedback is arbitrary. In the case of Visual Basic, everyone knows that the syntax error messages are not as focused and precise as they could be. In the case of a class library, you decide how specific you want the syntax error message to be (the syntax error messages within this book's class library provide very detailed feedback).

The TrapSyntax Method

The **TrapSyntax** method handles any syntax error that occurs within the class library and displays its message and, if the client application programmer chooses Help or presses F1, its associated Help topic. The "**TrapSyntax** Method's Specifications" sidebar shows the topic within the class library's Help file (EFS.HLP) that specifies the detailed functionality of the **TrapSyntax** method.

The TrapSyntax Method's Code

The code for the **TrapSyntax** method within the **Error** class is quite straightforward. Because we've studied the **TrapRunTime** method (and its related private methods), understanding how **TrapSyntax** works will not be too difficult. The only new syntactical element within the **TrapSyntax** method is the **ParamArray** keyword. This keyword, which is the most complex piece of syntax within VB6, allows the use of an optional argument that's a **Variant** array. The argument's **Variant** array can contain any number of elements, and each element can be any data type except a user-defined data type.

The flow of the **TrapSyntax** method's code and execution is a little more complex than that of the **TrapRunTime** method. Assuming that the method is being called from within the class library, the basic flow of **TrapSyntax** is detailed here:

TrapSyntax Method's Specifications

Syntax

```
Object.TrapSyntax(ErrNbr, Title, [IDStrs( )])
```

The **TrapSyntax** method's syntax has the following object qualifier and arguments:

- *Object*—Required. **Object** data type. An expression that evaluates to an object within the Applies To pop-up list.
- *ErrNbr*—Required. **Long** data type. A numeric expression that specifies the syntax error number.
- *Title*—Required. **String** data type. A **String** expression that specifies the name of the procedure within which the syntax error occurred. **Title** appears within the title bar of the message box and cannot exceed 40 characters in length.
- *IDStrs()*—Optional. **Variant** data type. A **ParamArray** array of expressions that customize and identify the error message. The expressions must be passed individually and there cannot be more than five expressions. When **TrapSyntax** is called internally, only **String** expressions are passed. If **TrapSyntax** is called from outside the class library, the first expression must be **True** and the other expressions must be strings; if **True** is not passed when **TrapSyntax** is called externally, an untrapped OLE Automation runtime error occurs and the error codes are not returned.

Called

The **TrapSyntax** method is called from any procedure within the class library or client application.

Returns

Upon success, eight elements within a **Variant** are returned. The elements contain these subtypes:

- *0 - ERR_RESULT*—A **Boolean** (**False**) that specifies that the public member of the class library (or a procedure within a client application) that was called failed to execute correctly.
- *1 - ERR_SOURCE*—A **String** that's the name of the method or property's procedure within which the syntax error occurred.
- *2 - ERR_NBR*—An **Integer** that's the syntax error number.
- *3 - ERR_DESC*—A **String** that's the description of the syntax error.
- *4 - ERR_HELPFILE*—A **String** that specifies the path and name of the Help file containing the syntax error's Help topic.
- *5 - ERR_CONTEXTID*—An **Integer** that's the context ID number of the Help topic for the syntax error.
- *6 - ERR_TIME*—A **Date** that specifies the date and time of the syntax error.
- *7 - ERR_LOG*—A **Boolean** that specifies whether information about the syntax error was written to an error log. **False** is always returned for syntax error messages, because the assumption is that the developer or tester of the class library will fix calls resulting in syntax errors at design time and not experience them at runtime.

Upon failure, eight elements within a **Variant** are returned. The elements contain these subtypes:

- *0 - ERR_RESULT*—A **Boolean** (**False**) that specifies that a syntax or Visual Basic runtime error occurred while the **TrapSyntax** method itself was executing.

- **1 - ERR_SOURCE**—A **String** that's **TrapSyntax**.
- **2 - ERR_NBR**—An **Integer** that's the error number.
- **3 - ERR_DESC**—A **String** that's the description of the error.
- **4 - ERR_HELPFILE**—A **String** that specifies the path and name of the Help file containing the error's Help topic.
- **5 - ERR_CONTEXTID**—An **Integer** that's the context ID number of the Help topic for the error.
- **6 - ERR_TIME**—A **Date** that specifies the date and time of the error.
- **7 - ERR_LOG**—A **Boolean** (**True**) that specifies that information about the error was written to a log file on the same path as the class library. Runtime errors are logged within ERRLOGRT.TXT and syntax errors within ERRLOGST.TXT.

Remarks

- External procedures not contained within the class library can call the **TrapSyntax** method and the error messages it supports.
- Because the **TrapSyntax** method has a **ParamArray** optional argument, it cannot take named arguments. If you try to call the member using named arguments, Visual Basic displays OLE Automation runtime error 446 ("Object doesn't support named arguments") or 448 ("Named argument not found").

- The method is passed required and optional arguments from any public member that detects a syntax error.
- The method enables its own error handler at its beginning.
- The method checks the syntax of values passed to its arguments (this is primarily to check calls from procedures within a client application and to assist in debugging the class library).
- Based on the required **ErrNbr** argument and the optional **IDStrs()** array of customizing strings, the method constructs the appropriate error message.
- The method calls the private **ShowSyntax** method to display the error message.
- The method calls the private **LogError** method to write the error information to a file (only if some runtime or syntax error occurred during its own execution) and to temporarily store the error codes (via a **Property Let** procedure within the **frmErrCodes** Form object).
- The method disables its own error handler with an **On Error GoTo 0** statement.
- The method uses VB's **Raise** method to set the **Number** property of the Err object to **True** (-1). This does two things. First, it sets **Number** to a predefined value that tells the calling member that a syntax error has occurred. Second, it reroutes code execution back to the error handler within the calling public member.

- The public member reads the value of the **Number** property of the Err object, sees that it is **True (Const SYNTAX = TRUE)**, reads the error codes that were stored within the **frmErrCodes** Form object (via a **Property Get** procedure), and then returns them to the client application.

Validating The *ParamArray IDStrs( )* Argument

Let's begin by examining the declaration of the **TrapSyntax** method, which is shown here:

```
Function TrapSyntax(ErrNbr As Long, _
                    Title As String, _
                    ParamArray IDStrs())
```

The third argument of the **TrapSyntax** method, **IDStrs()**, is a **ParamArray** optional argument that must be a **Variant** array. If passed, the subtype of the first element of the zero-based **Variant** array is normally a **String** that customizes the syntax error message. However, if **TrapSyntax** is called externally from a client application, **IDStrs()** is no longer optional; it must be passed and the subtype of the first element must be a **Boolean** that evaluates to **True**.

Whether called internally from a public member of the class library or externally from a client application, the **IDStrs()** argument can accept from one to four strings to customize a syntax error message. The customization scheme, if used, is a function of the given error message. For example, the message for syntax error 4 takes two customization strings (<*name*> argument must be <*kind*> expression). Currently, 48 different syntax error messages are contained within the class library. You can find a list of them within the class library's Help file (EFS.HLP) under the search words "error numbers". Each syntax error message's Help topic specifies its customization scheme (if any).

Listing 6.13 shows the code for validating the **Title** and **IDStrs()** arguments.

Listing 6.13 Validation code within the TrapSyntax method.

```
Function TrapSyntax(ErrNbr As Long, _
                    Title As String, _
                    ParamArray IDStrs())

   ' Constants for literals
   Const SYNTAX = True
   Const ERR_LOG = 7
   Const MAX_CHARS = 40
```

```
Const MAX_ITEMS = 5
Const FIRST_IDSTR = 0
Const NO_LOG_FILE = vbNullString
Const NO_TITLE = vbNullString
Const NO_ARG_NM = vbNullString
Const CONTEXT_BASE_NBR = 10000
Const IE_TITLE = -1001
Const IE_IDSTRS1 = -1002
Const IE_IDSTRS2 = -1003
Const IE_ERR_NBR = -1004
Const IE_EXTERNAL = -1005
Const ID = "I believe in the resurrection of the body"

' Variables
Dim Msg             As String
Dim ErrMsg          As String
Dim HelpClassLib    As String
Dim LogFile         As String
Dim External        As Boolean
Dim Str             As Integer
Dim FirstIDStr      As Integer
Dim InternalErr     As Integer
Dim Strs(1 To 5)    As String

' Enable error handler and do syntax checking
On Error GoTo ET

If Title = NO_TITLE Then
    Title = "TrapSyntax"
ElseIf VarType(Title) <> vbString Then
    InternalErr = IE_TITLE
    GoTo ET
ElseIf Len(Title) > MAX_CHARS Then
    InternalErr = IE_TITLE
    GoTo ET
End If

' If IDStrs() argument is passed, check it for:
' * Invalid upper bound
' * Invalid first element (if called externally)
' * Elements to customize message that are not strings
' Read customization strings and assign them to variables
If Not IsMissing(IDStrs) Then

    If UBound(IDStrs) > MAX_ITEMS - 1 Then
        InternalErr = IE_IDSTRS1
        GoTo ET
```

```
        ElseIf VarType(IDStrs(FIRST_IDSTR)) <> vbString Then

            If IDStrs(FIRST_IDSTR) <> True Then
                InternalErr = IE_EXTERNAL
                GoTo ET
            Else
                External = True
                FirstIDStr = 1
            End If

        End If

        For Str = FirstIDStr To UBound(IDStrs)

            If VarType(IDStrs(Str)) <> vbString Then
                InternalErr = IE_IDSTRS2
                GoTo ET
            Else

                If FirstIDStr = 1 Then
                    Strs(Str) = IDStrs(Str)
                Else
                    Strs(Str + 1) = IDStrs(Str)
                End If

            End If

        Next Str

    End If

    . . .

End Function
```

If any validation check of the **Title** and **IDStrs()** arguments fails, the relevant internal syntax error number is set and the **TrapSyntax** method is aborted. Execution is rerouted to the enabled error handler at the bottom of the method, where the internal error number is read and the internal syntax error message is displayed.

Constructing The Syntax Error Message
Now that you understand the validation check, we need to examine the code that constructs the syntax error message. Listing 6.14 shows the code to accomplish this task.

Listing 6.14 The code for constructing the message in the TrapSyntax method.

```
Function TrapSyntax(ErrNbr As Long, _
                    Title As String, _
                    ParamArray IDStrs())

    . . .

    ' Construct message related to syntax error number (Case
    ' Else below traps for invalid ErrNbr argument):
    If External Then
        ErrMsg = "Error " & ErrNbr & " —" & vbCr
    Else
        ErrMsg = "Class library error " & ErrNbr & " —" & _
                 vbCr
    End If

    Select Case ErrNbr

        Case 1
            Msg = "Member cannot run under " & Strs(1)

        Case 2
            Msg = Strs(1) & " argument is invalid." & vbCr
            Msg = Msg & "It cannot exceed " & Strs(2)
            Msg = Msg & " characters."

        Case 3
            Msg = "Prompt argument is invalid." & vbCr
            Msg = Msg & "A line exceeds 40 characters."

        Case 4
            Msg = Strs(1) & " argument must be "
            Msg = Msg & Strs(2) & " expression."

    . . .

        Case 48
            Msg = "File " & Strs(1) & " is not found." & vbCr

        Case Else
            InternalErr = IE_ERR_NBR
            GoTo ET

    End Select

End Function
```

There are a few things about this code that we need to discuss. First, if you can use either the **If...Then...Else** statement or the **Select Case** statement within a given situation, you should use **Select Case**, which runs anywhere from 30 to 40 percent faster than the **If...Then...Else** statement. The farther down within the selection levels the **True** condition is encountered, the greater the performance benefit. In addition, because of the way the **Error** class and its **TrapSyntax** method are designed, you can easily add new syntax error messages to the class library by writing additional **Case** statements and their messages above the **Case Else** statement (Case 49, Case 50, and so on). The last **Case Else** statement checks the syntax of the **ErrNbr** argument. If **ErrNbr** is not one of the existing syntax error numbers, execution is rerouted to the enabled error handler at the bottom of the method.

To understand how the customizing strings of the **IDStrs()** argument work with a specific error message, you can look at the Help topic for that error message within EFS.HLP. For example, syntax error 4 takes two customizing strings. If you look under the search words "error numbers" within EFS.HLP, you can display the Help topic for error 4.

Displaying The Message And Returning The Codes

Moving right along, the code that displays the syntax error message and stores the error codes is shown in Listing 6.15.

Listing 6.15 The code for displaying the message and return codes within the TrapSyntax method.

```
Function TrapSyntax(ErrNbr As Long, _
                   Title As String, _
                   ParamArray IDStrs())

   . . .

   ErrMsg = ErrMsg & vbCr & Msg & vbCr

   If Not cRAOServer Then
      ShowSyntax Prompt:=ErrMsg, _
                 Title:=CStr(Title), _
                 Context:=ErrNbr + CONTEXT_BASE_NBR
   End If

   HelpClassLib = App.Path & "\EFS.HLP"
   LogError ErrNbr:=ErrNbr, _
            Procedure:=CStr(Title), _
            ErrMsg:=Msg, _
            HelpFile:=HelpClassLib, _
```

```
            Context:=ErrNbr + CONTEXT_BASE_NBR, _
            Log:=NO_LOG_FILE, _
            Button:=False

    If External Then
        TrapSyntax = frmErrCodes.Codes
    Else
        On Error GoTo 0
        Err.Raise Number:=SYNTAX
    End If
    . . .

End Function
```

This code has a few points of interest. First of all, the class library does not display the syntax error message if it's running as an out-of-process ActiveX RAO component. Also, notice that the private **LogError** method is called to store the error codes. Finally, if **TrapSyntax** is called externally (that is, the **Boolean** variable **External** is **True**), the method immediately returns the error codes to the client application. However, if the method is called internally, it disables its own error handler and generates a runtime error whose **Number** property is set to **True**. This signals to the calling member of the class library that a syntax error has occurred and reroutes code execution back to the error handler within the calling member.

Stepping Through The Syntax-Checking Algorithm

As you're aware by now, the algorithm that this book's class library uses to handle syntax checking is not confined to the **TrapSyntax** method. Rather, it begins within the public member whose services are being used. At this point, the algorithm may call related internal methods within the **CL** class and then call the **TrapSyntax** method to construct and display the error message, and so on.

The best way to ensure that you understand how the class library handles syntax checking is to step through this example:

1. Open the class library's project file EFSE.VBP within 32-bit Visual Basic.

2. Select the **Error** class, select the statement **On Error GoTo 0** (toward the bottom of the **TrapSyntax** method), and then select Debug| Toggle Breakpoint (or click on the toolbar's shortcut button).

Object Errors: When Something Goes Wrong 211

3. Select the **ClientApp** class, select the statement **If Err = SYNTAX Then ShowMsg = frmErrCodes.Codes** (toward the bottom of the **ShowMsg** method), and then select Debug|Toggle Breakpoint.
4. To display the Options dialog box, select Tools|Options.
5. Display the General tab and select the Error Trapping—Break On Unhandled Errors option button. When internally testing the syntax-checking capabilities of the class library, you must select the Break On Unhandled Errors setting to simulate the behavior of the class library when it's called externally.
6. Enter the code in Listing 6.16 within the **Form_DblClick** event procedure of a code-free **Form1** object.

Listing 6.16 Tracing syntax error handling within the class library.

```
Private Sub Form_DblClick()

    ' Declare object variable
    Dim ClientApp As Object

    ' Instantiate class
    #If Win32 Then
        Set ClientApp = CreateObject("EFSE.ClientApp")
    #Else
        Set ClientApp = CreateObject("EFS16.ClientApp")
    #End If

    ' Call object's member using named arguments,
    ' but pass invalid value to Buttons argument
    ClientApp.ShowMsg Prompt:="Message", _
                    HelpFile:="C:\VBCLSLIB\EFS.HLP"

End Sub
```

Select Run|Start and double click on the Form object. The **TrapSyntax** method displays syntax error message 6; when you close the message box, code execution breaks on the statement **On Error GoTo 0**.

This is the point where the flow of the syntax-checking algorithm within the class library gets a little tricky. When you select Run|Continue, **TrapSyntax** disables its own error handler (with the **On Error GoTo 0** statement) and generates a runtime error whose **Number** property is set to **True** (with the **Err.Raise Number:=SYNTAX** statement, where **SYNTAX** is a constant whose value is -1). The reason this is done is to force code execution to reroute back to the error handler (that is, the line label **ET**) within the calling member. At that point, code execution breaks on the statement **If Err = SYNTAX Then ShowMsg = frmErrCodes.Codes**.

Now you can review the remainder of the code to see how the **ShowMsg** method completes the following tasks:

- Reads that the **Number** property of the Err object equals **True** (that is, **Err = SYNTAX**, where **SYNTAX** is a constant that equals **True**).
- Goes to the **Property Get** procedure named **Codes** within the **frmErrCodes** Form object.
- Reads the values of the error codes that were previously set by the **LogError** method.
- Returns the error codes within the **Variant** that's passed back to the client application.

Making The Error Class Stand Alone

The **Error** class is one of the most useful objects within this book's class library. If you want to pull it out of the book's class library and put it within a standalone ActiveX component, simply follow these steps:

1. Copy the members of the **CL** class used by the **Error** class and its associated Form object to the appropriate modules. Table 6.1 lists the members whose code you should copy to the Clipboard and the modules into which you should paste the code. Remember to copy the beginning and ending stubs of each member. After you copy these five members, change their declarations by prefixing them with the **Private** keyword.

2. In ERROR.CLS, remove the declaration **Private CL As New CL** from the General Declarations section, remove the existing code from the **Initialize** and **Terminate** events, and replace all instances of the string **CL** with an empty string (set the Find And Replace

Table 6.1 Members to copy from the CL class.

Member To Copy	Modules To Paste Into
IsTitle	ERROR.CLS
IsUnloadFromApp	SHOWMSG.FRM
IsWin95Shell	SHOWMSG.FRM and ERROR.CLS
ParseButtons	ERROR.CLS
ParseMsg	ERROR.CLS

dialog box to Current Module and Match Case). Visual Basic should replace four instances.

3. In SHOWMSG.FRM, remove the declaration **Private CL As New CL** from the General Declarations section, remove the statement **Set CL = Nothing** from the **Form_Unload** event, and replace all the instances of the string **CL** with an empty string (set the Find And Replace dialog box to Current Module and Match Case). Visual Basic should replace two instances.

4. Copy the Windows API function declarations listed in Table 6.2 from the General Declarations section of the **CL** class to the General Declarations sections of ERROR.CLS and SHOWMSG.FRM.

5. Copy the user-defined data type listed in Table 6.3 from the General Declarations section of the **CL** class to the General Declarations sections of ERROR.CLS and SHOWMSG.FRM.

6. Within ERROR.CLS, replace all the instances of the string **E** with an empty string (set the Find And Replace dialog box to Current Module and Match Case). Visual Basic should replace six instances.

7. Select the file STARTUP.BAS and remove the general declarations and the code within **Sub Main**, but leave the **Sub Main** procedure's stubs intact.

8. Save the files ERRCODES.FRM, ERROR.CLS, SHOWMSG.FRM, and STARTUP.BAS to the directory where you'll create the VB project that's to become the new ActiveX component.

9. Start a new Visual Basic ActiveX DLL or EXE project and remove **Class1** from it. Next, select Project|Add File and add the four files you saved to the new project.

10. Select Project | Properties and make the necessary entries to the General tab of the Project Properties dialog box (Project Type, Startup Object, and so on). Ensure that the Startup Object is **Sub Main**.

Table 6.2 Windows API function declarations to copy from the CL class.

API Function To Copy	Modules To Paste Into
FindWindow (16/32-bit)	SHOWMSG.FRM and ERROR.CLS
GetTextExtent (16-bit)	ERROR.CLS
GetTextExtentPoint32 (32-bit)	ERROR.CLS

Table 6.3 User-defined data type to copy from the CL class.

Data Type To Copy	Modules To Paste Into
SIZE (32-bit)	ERROR.CLS and SHOWMSG.FRM

11. Select File|Make Project to make and register the ActiveX component; then, save the Visual Basic project.
12. Test the **TrapRunTime** and **TrapSyntax** methods of the new ActiveX component that contains the revised **Error** class.

Conclusion

If you've religiously followed the preceding sequence of steps, you should have a standalone error-handling class in the form of an ActiveX component. You've learned the hard way the value of adhering as strictly as possible to the OOP attribute of encapsulation. Even though we only violate encapsulation within this book's class library in one general way (placing procedures called by more than one module into the private **CL** class), you can see what a hassle it is to pull together the necessary members and declarations for a standalone class. Just in case you couldn't get the standalone error class to work, you can find a copy of all the files needed to make it into an ActiveX component on the path C:\VBOOPEFS\ERRORCLS. The project name is ERRCLS.VBP. Just open it within VB6 and select File|Make ERRCLS.DLL, and you'll have a robust, commercial-quality error handler.

Chapter 7
VB's ActiveX Components

Key Topics:

♦ *ActiveX, COM, And DCOM*

♦ *ActiveX DLLs*

♦ *ActiveX EXEs*

♦ *ActiveX Controls*

Microsoft has recently added a new twist to object-oriented programming: an attempt to structure all OOP around the low-level abstraction of COM components (formerly known as *OLE Automation servers*). A COM *component* is an application that exposes programmable objects and their members for reuse by any application containing an OLE Automation-compliant programming language. Microsoft has designed Visual Basic 6 (VB6) to easily create class libraries that, at a lower level of abstraction, are COM components.

This chapter begins our journey into VB's ActiveX components. In this chapter, we discuss Microsoft's COM and DCOM technology, of which ActiveX is a significant part. We begin by examining ActiveX DLLs. Then, we travel deeper into ActiveX EXEs and learn how they differ from ActiveX DLLs. Finally, we venture into the world of ActiveX controls and look at some techniques for creating them.

ActiveX, COM, And DCOM

The Microsoft Active Platform is the foundation for designing and developing Internet and intranet business solutions by using Microsoft tools and technologies. A three-tier client/server model, the Active Platform is an extensible component-based architecture. The biggest advantages to using the Active Platform are its ease of use and reduced learning curve. To design both the client and server components of your application, you can use the same set of tools you're already familiar with. This reduces your learning curve, thus helping you deliver business solutions quickly and efficiently. The Active Platform includes three core components: Active Client (DeskTop), ActiveX, and Active Server.

Active Client

Internet Explorer is a good example of Active Client. Internet Explorer includes built-in support for ActiveX technology and client-side scripting. You can write Active scripts that execute on the client side by using scripting languages such as JScript, VBScript, and JavaScript. The scripts interact with HTML, Java applets, ActiveX controls, and so on to deliver information to the browser. The browser, in turn, displays the information to the end user.

ActiveX And ActiveX Controls

ActiveX is not a programming language. In fact, ActiveX is a suite of technologies you can use to deliver business solutions over the Internet and intranet. ActiveX technology includes developing and integrating ActiveX controls, writing ActiveX scripts, and so on.

An *ActiveX control* is a stripped-down version of an OLE control with its size and speed optimized for use over the Internet. Both ActiveX and OLE are based on Microsoft's Component Object Model (COM) technology. The basic premise of COM is that two objects can interact and communicate with each other, regardless of their language and platform, as long as they are written to conform to the COM specification. The basic premise of DCOM is that two objects can interact and communicate with each other over a network of heterogeneous systems, regardless of their language and platform, as long as they are written to conform to the DCOM specification. To learn more about COM, point your browser to **http://www.microsoft.com/default.htm**. For a list of third-party ActiveX controls, point your browser to **http://browserwatch.internet.com/activex.html**.

Active Server

IIS (Internet Information Server) is an Active Server. An Active Server supports server-side scripting, better known as *Active Server Pages (ASP)*. Check out Microsoft's Web site; you'll notice that Microsoft's server delivers client-side HTML by using ASP. Whereas an HTML file has the extension .HTML, an ASP file has the extension .ASP. To view ASP in action, visit **http://www.microsoft.com/search/default.asp**. An ASP script executes on the server, taking advantage of the server's processing power and delivering client-side HTML. Just as you can use scripting languages such as VBScript and JScript with reusable objects such as ActiveX controls and Java applets, you can use the same scripting languages with the same objects in combination with the five core server objects (Application, Session, Server, Request, and Response) and Active Server Components to build ASP.

ActiveX DLLs

Before making an ActiveX DLL file, you first need to understand what an ActiveX DLL component is. An *ActiveX DLL component* exposes OLE Automation objects and their members to OLE Automation clients for use by the clients. Like all DLL files, an ActiveX DLL is loaded in an OLE client application and uses the application's stack and process space. When a client application uses one of a ClassModule object's members, the operation remains within the client's process or memory space—hence the name *in-process component*. The terms *in-process component* and *ActiveX DLL component* are synonymous as far as VB6 is concerned. A project containing a ClassModule object that Visual Basic makes into an ActiveX DLL is, at a lower level of abstraction, really an in-process OLE Automation server.

Because an ActiveX DLL component runs as a DLL file, you don't need to create a new process or load runtime DLL files. This lets an in-process component load considerably faster than an equivalent out-of-process component (ActiveX EXE). Also, the in-process component does not incur any out-of-process call overhead when referring to the ClassModule object's members because the message is not sent between the processes. This lets an ActiveX DLL component's method run 3 to 10 times faster than it would within an ActiveX EXE component.

An ActiveX DLL component must meet several requirements:

- You can develop and run the DLL on any 32-bit Windows operating system.
- The DLL must run on the same machine as the client application that calls it.
- The DLL must contain one or more ClassModule objects.
- At least one ClassModule object's **Instancing** property must be set to either **5 - MultiUse** or **6 - GlobalMultiUse**.
- You may not use the **End** statement within an ActiveX DLL component because it causes a compile-time error.

The making of an ActiveX DLL file involves several tasks. To help you follow along, we've split these tasks into separate topics.

> **NOTE**
>
> VB4 and VB5 required that an ActiveX DLL's startup object be **Sub Main**. VB6 no longer requires this and lets you set the startup object to (None); however, this is not conventional practice and is not advisable.

Setting The Project Properties

First, open a new ActiveX DLL project within VB6. Before you set the project properties, you need to add a standard module to the project. Select Project|Add Module and add a **Sub Main** procedure to the module. You don't need to add any code to this procedure, but you should have this procedure within the project. The conventional ActiveX component programming practice is to use **Sub Main** as the component's startup object. Name this BAS module MiscExs and save the module under the file name MISCEXS.BAS.

To specify certain settings for the properties of the ClassModule object's project, select Project|Project1 Properties and then select the General tab from the Project Properties dialog box. You must set the following properties before making the project into an ActiveX DLL component:

- *Project Type*—Make sure you've selected the ActiveX DLL item.
- *Startup Object*—Make sure you've selected **Sub Main**.
- *Project Name*—This entry serves two purposes. First, it's the initial part of the programmatic ID string, which identifies the component and class, that Visual Basic writes to the Windows registration database when it creates an ActiveX DLL component. Second, it's part of the name the Object Browser dialog box displays when a reference is set to a Visual Basic ActiveX DLL component. Set the Project Name entry to **MYLIBDLL**.
- *Help File Name*—The name of the Help file associated with the ActiveX component's project. You don't need to precede this name with a fully qualified path. Because you don't have a Help file of your own, set this entry to **EFS.HLP** (the Help file of the class library found on this book's companion CD-ROM).
- *Project Help Context ID*—The context ID for the specific Help topic to be called when the user clicks on the ? button while the ActiveX component is selected within the Object Browser dialog box. This is normally the context ID associated with the Contents topic. Set the Project Help Context ID entry to zero (the number of the Contents topic of EFS.HLP).
- *Project Description*—A brief description of the ActiveX component that appears when the References dialog box (Project|References) displays the component. Set the Project Description entry to **My First Class Library - DLL**.

> **NOTE**
>
> Any ActiveX component that contains a Form object or displays a message box has an interface element. For such ActiveX components, VB disables the Unattended Execution items in the General tab of the Project Properties dialog box (that is, Thread Per Object, Thread Pool, and Number Of Threads). All of the book's ActiveX components contain interface elements.

- *Upgrade ActiveX Controls*—Enables upgrading of the ActiveX controls. Make sure you've selected this checkbox.

- *Require License Key*—Enables licensing for a project that produces ActiveX components (Automation servers, user controls, or ActiveX controls). Visual Basic creates a license file (*.VBL) when you build the ActiveX component. The VBL file must be registered on the user's machine for the components to be used. The Setup Wizard registers the VBL file. This entry is disabled for an ActiveX DLL.

- *Threading Model*—All components (single threaded or multi-threaded) that you create with Visual Basic use the apartment threading model. In this model, each thread is like an apartment. All the objects within an apartment live within that apartment; they are not aware of the other objects residing within the other apartments. This provides thread encapsulation and safety. The default option for this entry for an ActiveX DLL is Apartment Threaded; leave this entry as it is.

- *Thread Per Object*—For a component with no interface elements, this entry indicates that each instance of a class marked as **MultiUse** in the **Instancing** property will be created on a new and distinct thread. Each thread has a unique copy of all the global variables and objects and does not interfere with any other thread. This entry is disabled for an ActiveX DLL.

- *Thread Pool*—For a component with no interface elements, this entry indicates that each instance of a class marked as **MultiUse** in the **Instancing** property will be created on a thread from the thread pool. The choice of thread is determined in a round-robin fashion. Each thread has a unique copy of all global variables; however, multiple instances reside on a given thread and can interfere with each other. This entry is disabled for an ActiveX DLL.

- *Number Of Threads*—For a component with no interface elements, this entry determines the maximum number of threads Visual Basic creates for the thread pool. When VB instantiates a **MultiUse** class, it creates threads, as needed, up to the number set here. After reaching the maximum number, Visual Basic begins assigning new instances to existing threads. This entry is disabled for an ActiveX DLL.

Figure 7.1 shows a typical profile of settings for the General tab of the Project Properties dialog box for an ActiveX DLL component.

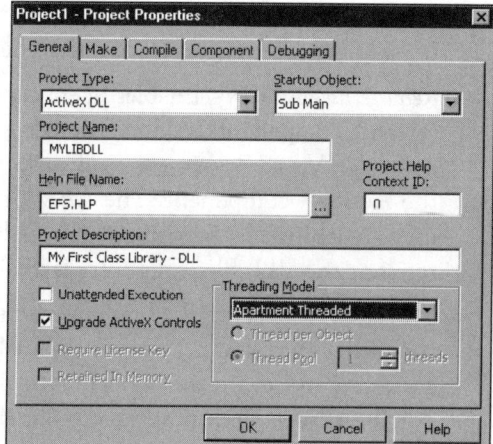

Figure 7.1
Configuring the properties for an ActiveX DLL component.

Making The ActiveX DLL

After you've set the project's properties, you can follow these steps to make the ActiveX DLL file:

1. Select File|Make MYLIBDLL.DLL to display the Make Project dialog box.

2. Within the Make Project dialog box, click on Options to display the Make tab of the Project Properties dialog box.

3. Under Version Number, make sure Auto Increment is checked.

4. For Application Title, make sure the entry is the same as the entry you made for Project Name on the General tab (that is, MYLIBDLL). These entries don't have to be the same; however, using the same name is easier and makes more sense.

5. To store these entries and close the dialog box, click on OK. Figure 7.2 shows a typical profile of settings for the Make tab of the Project Properties dialog box.

6. Within the Make Project dialog box, make sure MYLIBDLL.DLL is the file name.

7. To make the ActiveX DLL file and register the ActiveX DLL component in the Windows registration database, click on OK.

8. Select File|Save Project to save the project's files.

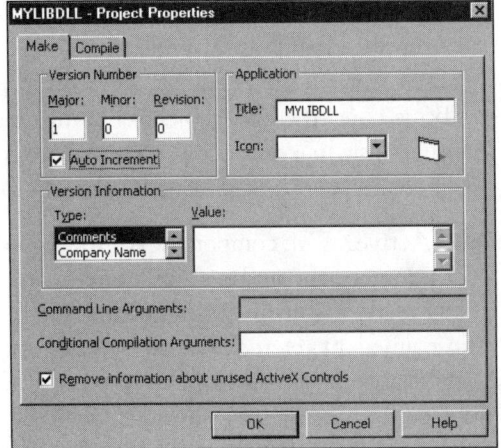

Figure 7.2
Getting ready to make the ActiveX DLL.

Examining The Possible Errors Encountered When Making An ActiveX DLL Component

Visual Basic can display the following error messages when you try to make an ActiveX DLL component:

- If you try to make an ActiveX DLL component that does not have a **ClassModule** object within the project, or if a ClassModule object exists but its **Instancing** property is not set to **5 - MultiUse** or **6 - GlobalMultiUse**, Visual Basic displays the following syntax error:

```
No creatable public class module detected. Press F1 for
more information.
```

- If an **End** statement or some other statement not supported by an ActiveX DLL component exists anywhere within the project's files, Visual Basic displays the following syntax error message:

```
Functionality not supported in DLL.
```

ActiveX EXEs

Before making an ActiveX EXE file, you need to understand what an ActiveX EXE component is. An *ActiveX EXE component* is a component whose operation does not remain within the client application's process or memory space. Out-of-process ActiveX EXE components have performance problems compared to in-process ActiveX DLL components. These performance problems manifest themselves as slow startup speed and out-of-process call overhead. The terms *out-of-process component* and *ActiveX EXE component* are synonymous as far as VB6 is concerned. A project containing a ClassModule object that Visual Basic makes into an ActiveX EXE is, at a lower level of abstraction, really an out-of-process OLE Automation server.

An ActiveX EXE component is always slower to start than an ActiveX DLL component, and every reference to a ClassModule object's method or property within an out-of-process ActiveX component is slower than an equivalent reference to an object or procedure within the calling application itself or within an in-process ActiveX component. Due to the performance penalty associated with an ActiveX EXE component, there are only a few practical reasons why you would want to use one:

- To create a class library and ActiveX component with 16-bit VB4 that runs under Windows 3.x. The 16-bit version of VB4 cannot create, and Windows 3.x cannot run, an in-process ActiveX DLL component.
- To create a Remote Automation Object (RAO) with Visual Basic Enterprise edition. An RAO must be an out-of-process component because, as the term *Remote* implies, the component runs on a different machine than the client does.
- To enable asynchronous code execution (a form of multitasking or multithreading).

Steps To Making An ActiveX EXE

The making of an ActiveX EXE file involves several tasks. To help you follow along, we've split these tasks into separate topics.

Configuring An ActiveX EXE Project

First, open a new ActiveX EXE project within VB6. Before you set the project's properties, add a standard module to the project by selecting Project|Add Module. Then, add a **Sub Main** procedure to the module. You don't need to add any code to this procedure, but you should have it within the project. The conventional ActiveX component programming practice is to use **Sub Main** as the component's startup object. Name this BAS module MiscExs and save it under the file name MISCEXS.BAS. If, as described previously within this chapter, you made the ActiveX DLL component, select Project|Add File and add the MISCEXS.CLS file from the MYLIBDLL.VBP project to this project.

Setting The Project Properties

To specify certain settings for the properties of the ClassModule object's project, select Project | Project1 Properties and then select the General tab of the Project Properties dialog box. You must set these properties before making the project into an ActiveX EXE component. Here are the settings you'll use:

- *Project Type*—Make sure you've selected the ActiveX EXE item.

- *Startup Object*—Make sure you've selected **Sub Main**. It's possible for an out-of-process ActiveX component to have a modeless form as the startup object; however, for the time being, selecting **Sub Main** helps keep things simple.

- *Project Name*—This entry serves two purposes. First, it's the initial part of the programmatic ID string, which identifies the component and class, that Visual Basic writes to the Windows registration database when it creates an ActiveX EXE component. Second, it's part of the name the Object Browser dialog box displays when a reference is set to a Visual Basic ActiveX EXE component. Set the Project Name entry to **MYLIBEXE**.

- *Help File Name*—The name of the Help file associated with the ActiveX component's project. You don't need to precede this name with a fully qualified path. Because you don't have a Help file of your own, set this entry to EFS.HLP (the Help file of the class library found on this book's companion CD-ROM).

- *Project Help Context ID*—The context ID for the specific Help topic to be called when the user clicks on the ? button while the ActiveX component is selected within the Object Browser dialog box. This is normally the context ID associated with the Contents topic. Set the Project Help Context ID entry to zero (the number of the Contents topic of EFS.HLP).

- *Project Description*—A brief description of the ActiveX component that appears when the References dialog box (Project | References) displays it. Set the Project Description entry to **My First Class Library - EXE**.

The functionality of the remaining items on the General tab (Upgrade ActiveX Controls, Require License Key, Thread Per Object, Thread Pool, and Number Of Threads) is the same as described in "Making The ActiveX DLL" earlier in this chapter. When creating an ActiveX EXE component, you should leave the Upgrade ActiveX Controls entry unchecked. The Require License Key entry is already disabled.

Choose from one of the two entries: Thread Per Object or Thread Pool. If you choose Thread Pool, specify the number of threads.

Figure 7.3 shows a typical profile of settings for the General tab of the Project Properties dialog box for an ActiveX EXE component.

Making The ActiveX EXE

After you set the project properties, you can follow these steps to make the ActiveX EXE file:

1. Select File | Make MYLIBEXE.EXE to display the Make Project dialog box.
2. Within the Make Project dialog box, click on Options to display the Make tab of the Project Properties dialog box.
3. Under Version Number, make sure Auto Increment is checked.
4. For Application Title, make sure the entry is the same as the entry you made for Project Name in the General tab (that is, MYLIBEXE). These entries don't have to be the same; however, using the same name is easier and makes more sense.
5. To store these entries and close the dialog box, click on OK.
6. Within the Make Project dialog box, make sure MYLIBEXE.EXE is the file name.
7. To make the ActiveX EXE file and register the ActiveX EXE component within the Windows registration database, click on OK.
8. To save the project's files, select File | Save Project.

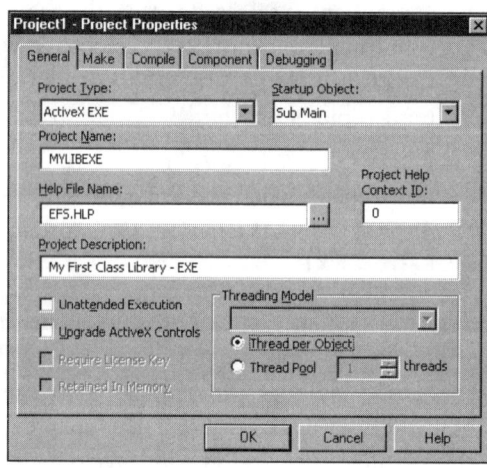

Figure 7.3
Configuring the properties for an ActiveX EXE component.

Running An ActiveX EXE In Standalone Mode

As you saw earlier in this chapter, an out-of-process ActiveX EXE component has special capabilities that an in-process ActiveX DLL component does not support. One of those capabilities (which we have not yet looked at) is that the ActiveX EXE component can run in two different modes:

- As an ActiveX component whose objects expose their members for reuse by a client application
- As a normal executable application

Note that all the Microsoft Office 7 applications had this capability. For example, you could run Excel 7 in standalone mode. Because Excel 7 was, at a lower level of abstraction, an OLE Automation server (and an ActiveX component within Excel 97), any ActiveX-compliant programming language can avail itself of the reusable objects that comprise Excel 7. The client application's programmer does this in the same way as when reusing objects written with VB6, by following the usual three-step process:

- Declaring a module-level object variable
- Instantiating the class to be reused with the **CreateObject** function and assigning the object instance to the object variable with the **Set** statement
- Calling the member of the object to reuse

One of the aesthetically elegant features of the ActiveX component architecture, as implemented within VB6, is how similar its behavior is to Microsoft's own applications. One of these similarities is that you can design an out-of-process ActiveX EXE component so that you can run it either as a component with reusable objects or as a standalone executable. Although we did not design the class library on this book's companion CD-ROM to do this, the class library does have some code within its startup object—the **Sub Main** procedure within STARTUP.BAS (see Listing 7.1)—that simulates this dual functionality and gives you a sense of how it would work on a more complex scale.

Listing 7.1 Sub Main procedure of the class library on this book's companion CD-ROM.

```
Sub Main()

    ' Simulate dual capacity of ActiveX EXE component—
    ' * If ActiveX EXE component is started in typical way,
```

```vb
'     as library of reusable objects, do nothing here in
'     Sub Main. Instead, proceed to Initialize event
'     procedure of class that is being instantiated.
'   * But if it is started as standalone EXE:
'     a) Check how it is started by calling Windows
'        API function.
'     b) If it is tested within VB's IDE, display Form1
'        (which is used to simulate client application).
'     c) If it is being used as a standalone executable
'        (for example, by double clicking it from Explorer
'        or running it with VB's Shell function), simulate
'        different kind of behavior by modelessly showing
'        mock startup Form object. Code in frmStartEXE's
'        Form_DblClick event procedure demos ability to:
'        - Reuse ActiveX component's objects internally.
'        - Or run any other kind of Visual Basic code.

' Variables:
Dim RunningInIDE As Boolean

If App.StartMode = vbSModeAutomation Then
    Exit Sub
ElseIf App.StartMode = vbSModeStandalone Then

    #If Win32 Then

        If GetModuleHandle("VB32.EXE") Or _
          GetModuleHandle("VB6.EXE") Then
            RunningInIDE = True
        End If

    #Else
        If GetModuleHandle("VB.EXE") Then RunningInIDE = True
    #End If

    If RunningInIDE Then
        Form1.Show
    Else
        frmStartEXE.Show
    End If

End If

End Sub
```

> **NOTE**
>
> An application's actual **StartMode** setting is determined by how that application is started at runtime, not by its nominal setting on the Component tab of the Project Properties dialog box when you create the executable file. Also, only an ActiveX EXE component can use the **StartMode** setting on the Component tab at design time; this setting is disabled for an ActiveX DLL component.

In Listing 7.1, the **StartMode** property of Visual Basic's App object (that is, the book's ActiveX component) returns a value at runtime that determines whether the application is started as a standalone project or as an ActiveX component. **StartMode** can have two settings:

- *vbSModeAutomation - 1*—The application is started as an ActiveX component.
- *vbSModeStandalone - 0*—The application is started as a standalone executable. It can be run from inside VB's IDE or from a command line (that is, by double-clicking on the application within Explorer, using VB's **Shell** function, selecting Start|Run from the Taskbar, and so on).

If the application is run as an ActiveX component, **Sub Main** does nothing and the code exits the procedure. If it's being run as a standalone application, the book's ActiveX component's **Sub Main** code can do one of two things:

- It can detect that the ActiveX component is being run within VB's IDE (that is, being tested internally) and, in turn, will display the simulated client application's **Form1** object. This technique only works if Start Mode on the Component tab of the Project Properties dialog box is set to Standalone.
- It can detect that the ActiveX component is being run from a command line and, in turn, will display within this simulated mockup the modeless dialog box shown in Figure 7.4.

When you double-click on the Form object shown in Figure 7.4, the code in Listing 7.2 executes.

Listing 7.2 Code in the standalone executable's startup form.
```
Private Sub Form_DblClick()

    ' Variables:
    Dim Msg     As String
    Dim Title   As String

    Title = "Demo Of Dual Capability"

    Msg = "This demo shows how an ActiveX EXE component," & _
        vbCr
    Msg = Msg & "when it's run as a standalone executable, "
    Msg = Msg & "can" & vbCr
    Msg = Msg & "call methods internally or run any other "
    Msg = Msg & "kind of " & vbCr
```

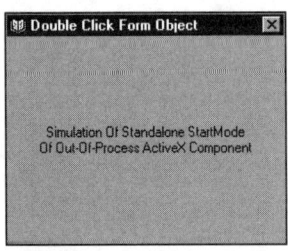

Figure 7.4
Simulation of the standalone executable's startup form.

```
    Msg = Msg & "Visual Basic code, application or program."
    Msg = Msg & vbCr & vbCr
    Msg = Msg & "The ShowMsg method displayed this message."

    ClientApp.ShowMsg Msg, vbInformation, Title

    Msg = "VB's MsgBox function displayed this message." & _
        vbCr
    Msg = Msg & vbCr
    Msg = Msg & "When you choose OK, code in the" & _
        "Form_DblClick"
    Msg = Msg & vbCr
    Msg = Msg & "event procedure of this demo form will" & _
        "unload"
    Msg = Msg & vbCr
    Msg = Msg & "the form and terminate the executable."

    MsgBox Msg, vbInformation, Title

    Unload Me

End Sub
```

The code in Listing 7.2 simply displays two message boxes. The **ShowMsg** method of the class library on this book's companion CD-ROM displays the first message box, shown in Figure 7.5. (The **ClientApp** class was instantiated within the General Declarations section of frmStartEXE so you could reuse its members.)

After you clear the first message box, Visual Basic's **MsgBox** function displays the second message box, shown in Figure 7.6. After you clear

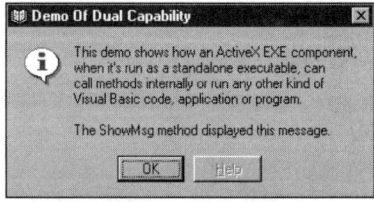

Figure 7.5
The standalone EXE displaying a message using the **ShowMsg** method.

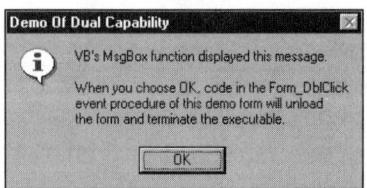

Figure 7.6
The standalone EXE displaying a message using the **MsgBox** function.

this message box, the **Unload** statement triggers the **Form_Unload** event, which uninstantiates any objects, frees system resources, and terminates the standalone executable.

This simple simulation demonstrates how easy it is to design and write an ActiveX component that can function in this dual fashion. Remember, however, that this technique works only with the out-of-process EXE version of an ActiveX component. The same code within the **Sub Main** procedure in Listing 7.1 is also compiled and made into the in-process DLL version of the class library on this book's companion CD-ROM. However, because Windows treats a dynamically linked library file differently than it does an executable file, you cannot start EFSD.DLL in standalone mode. If you try to do this, Windows displays the message box shown in Figure 7.7.

ActiveX Controls

When Microsoft released VB1, the company had high hopes for its new Windows programming language. Yet even the company's chairman, Bill Gates, admits that he was surprised by the overwhelming success of the product right from the outset. Gates, who rightly considers himself an authority on the Basic language (after all, he did help write the first Basic interpreter for a microprocessor), has been quoted several times during the 1990s as saying that the single biggest factor contributing to the early success of VB was its capability to use third-party VBX custom controls.

Extensibility is the characteristic that lets any programmer enhance the feature set of the language after a version of the language has been released. VBX custom controls were the first example of VB's extensibility architecture. Because VB is a Windows programming language,

Figure 7.7
The result of trying to start EFSD.DLL in standalone mode.

you can also extend it by calling and reusing functions within the Windows API and within third-party DLLs. After VBX custom controls, the next significant milestone in the extensibility of VB was Sheridan Software's clever VBAssist product, which enhanced the capabilities of VB's menu structure and Properties window.

Through the release of VB3, you typically had to be a C or C++ developer in order to extend the language. With the release of VB4, however, the rules of the game governing the language's extensibility were changed forever. VB4 let the VB developer extend the IDE by creating OLE Automation servers (now ActiveX components). Also, you could write these OLE servers in different ways (as class libraries, add-ins, wizards, and so on). In order for an OLE server written with VB4 to be snapped onto VB's own menu structure as an add-in, the language itself was rewritten as an OLE Automation server. Because of this change, VB4 could expose its own selected public objects and members, such as the Add-Ins menu, to VB developers at design time.

With the release of VB5 and VB6, VB's extensibility architecture has been enhanced even further. Some of the new features that fall into the category of extensions to the IDE and that we discuss in this chapter include the following:

- The ability to create ActiveX controls (formerly known as OCX *custom controls*) that you can add to VB6's toolbox or to any other ActiveX control-compliant language.

- Additions to and revisions of the VB6 add-in extensibility model. Creating add-ins with VB4 was not as easy or as flexible as it should have been. VB6 has made great progress in this area, and it includes many new add-in wizards that illustrate how you can use add-ins.

- Visual Basic Books Online. You'll never have to open VB's technical manuals again, because you can find every page within the new Visual Basic Books Online. Of course, you can search by any topic or keyword to find what you're looking for.

- Project and module templates, which are especially useful to the veteran programmer who is new to VB or to the ActiveX software paradigm.

Creating VB6 ActiveX Controls

For the last two to three years, the question most frequently asked by VB developers has been: "Will Microsoft ever make it possible to create custom controls with Visual Basic?" Well, with the arrival of VB5, that question was answered in the affirmative. In VB5, and now in

VB6, you can develop your own ActiveX controls (formerly known as *OLE/OCX custom controls* under VB4 and as *VBX custom controls* under VB3), compile them to native code, use them within your applications, and distribute them for reuse to other Windows developers.

VB6 supports several features to help you easily create ActiveX controls:

- Designing an ActiveX control is almost as easy as designing a VB Form object. You can use familiar Visual Basic commands to draw your control or create a control group using existing controls.
- You can debug ActiveX controls in process; you can step directly from the code for your test form into the code for the ActiveX control project.
- You can add data-binding to an ActiveX control. Using the Data control object, you can easily bind the individual fields within the control to the appropriate fields within a database.
- VB6 makes it easy to create professional-looking ActiveX control packages by providing wizards to help you add property pages, named constants, and events to your controls.
- You can compile your ActiveX controls directly into your application's executable or into OCX files that other ActiveX-compliant languages (Visual C++, Delphi 3, PowerBuilder 6, and so on) can use with applications such as Microsoft Office or on the Internet.

VB6 also includes a new IDE tool called a *designer*. A designer is an add-in wizard that provides a visual design window within VB6's IDE. You can use this window to design new classes visually. VB6 has built-in designers for forms, ActiveX controls, and documents. Objects you create from the classes that you designed with a designer have separate design-time and runtime behaviors and appearances, although many objects (for example, forms and controls) look very similar in the two modes.

In addition to its built-in designers, VB6 lets developers create designers for use within the VB6 IDE. These *ActiveX designers* work just like the built-in designers within VB6, making them easy to learn and use. You can use Microsoft's ActiveX Designer SDK, but unfortunately, using the ActiveX Designer SDK requires a C++ compiler, such as Visual C++. You cannot write ActiveX designers using VB6, but you can write the add-in wizard type of designer.

Probably the best systematic way to learn how to use VB6 to create an ActiveX control is to work your way through the chapter titled "Creating An ActiveX Control" within Visual Basic Books Online. Leading you through a series of procedures, the chapter shows you how to create a simple ActiveX control called *ShapeLabel*.

Instead of duplicating that material, what we want to do is examine two ActiveX controls that we built with VB6. These controls have the following features:

- They are fully functional components that you can reuse.
- They illustrate useful techniques that you can use in creating your own ActiveX controls.
- They give you a feel for how similar the underlying software architectures are for ActiveX controls and the ActiveX components/servers that this book is primarily about.

General Steps To Follow

The first thing you need to know to create an ActiveX control is the general procedure you should use. The list of steps that follows will create a simple ActiveX control that does not require a user interface and does not contain any associated control objects. Although these steps are generic, there are specific settings for the TBIcon ActiveX control (which we discuss in the next section):

1. Start VB6. From the New Project dialog box, double-click on the ActiveX Control icon. VB6 loads a project that contains a UserControl (CTL) module. The UserControl object is the basic form you use to create an ActiveX control. A new UserControl object appears, as shown in Figure 7.8.

2. Make the following entries within the General tab of the Project Properties dialog box: Project Type (ActiveX Control), Startup Object (None), Project Name (TBarIcon), and Project Description (Taskbar Icon Control). Project Description is the entry that later appears within the list of ActiveX controls in the Components dialog box.

3. Make the following entries within the Properties window: **Name** (TBIcon, the name of the class that appears when you move the mouse pointer over the ActiveX control on VB's toolbox), **InvisibleAtRuntime** (**True** for ActiveX controls that do not require a runtime GUI interface, like TBIcon), and **ToolboxBitmap** (the path to a specially sized, 16×15 pixels BMP file that appears on the ActiveX control's Toolbox icon).

4. Make any module-level declarations within the General Declarations section of the UserControl object.

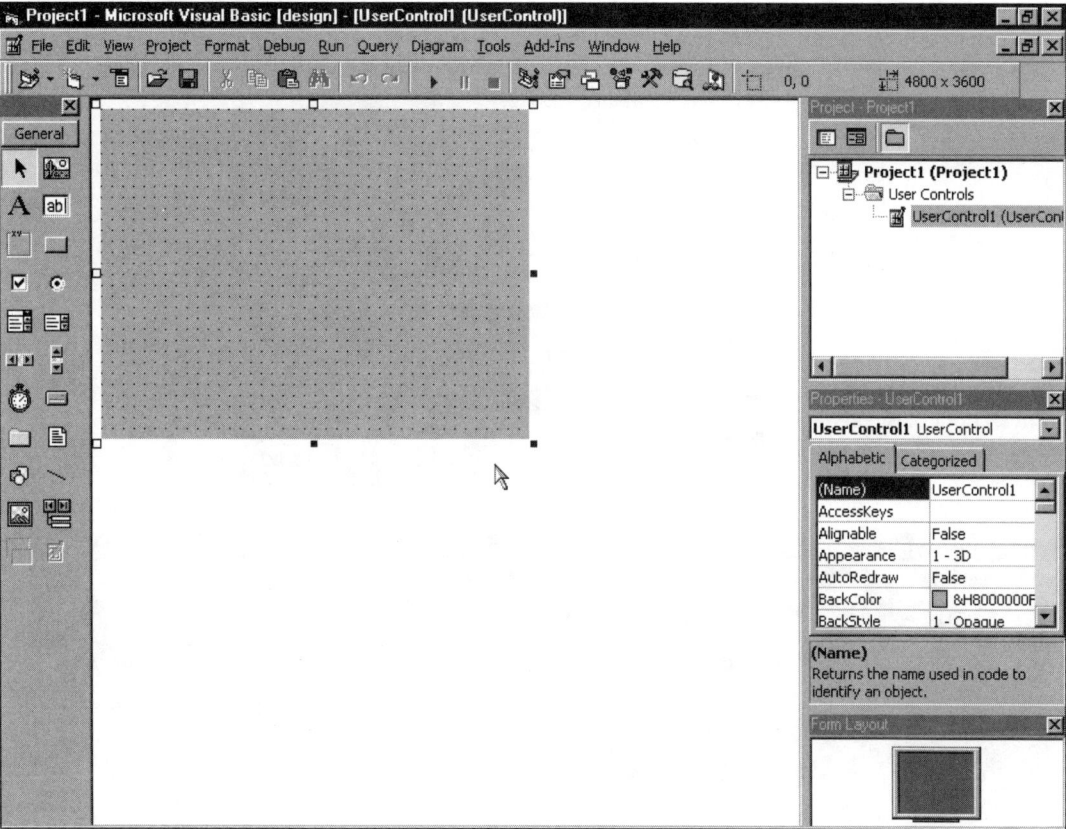

Figure 7.8
Getting ready to create an ActiveX control.

5. Declare any members (properties, methods, or events) that the UserControl object requires and write their procedures.

6. Select Project | TBarIcon Properties, click on the Compile tab, and select Compile To Native Code (Optimize For Fast Code). You need all the speed you can get for ActiveX controls.

7. Save the ActiveX control project.

8. Select File | Make TBarIcon.OCX to make and register the new ActiveX control.

At this point, you could open a new Standard EXE project and check the list of ActiveX controls (Project | Components) to ensure that your ActiveX control is registered and available for reuse. You should find it listed alphabetically by its Project Description entry on the Controls tab of the Components dialog box, as shown in Figure 7.9.

When you select the new ActiveX control and click on OK, the icon, specified by its **ToolboxBitmap** property's setting, appears within VB's toolbox, as shown in Figure 7.10.

234   Chapter 7

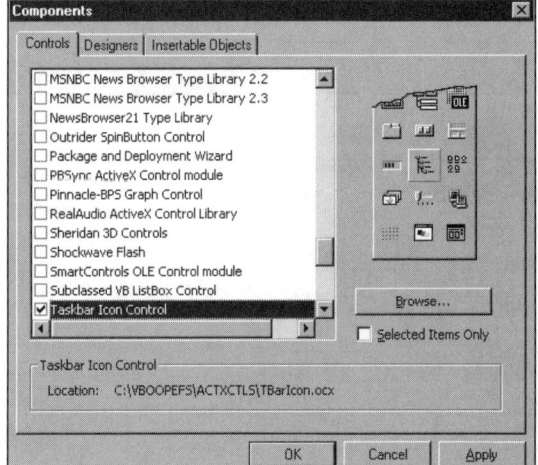

Figure 7.9
Verifying whether the ActiveX control is registered and available for reuse.

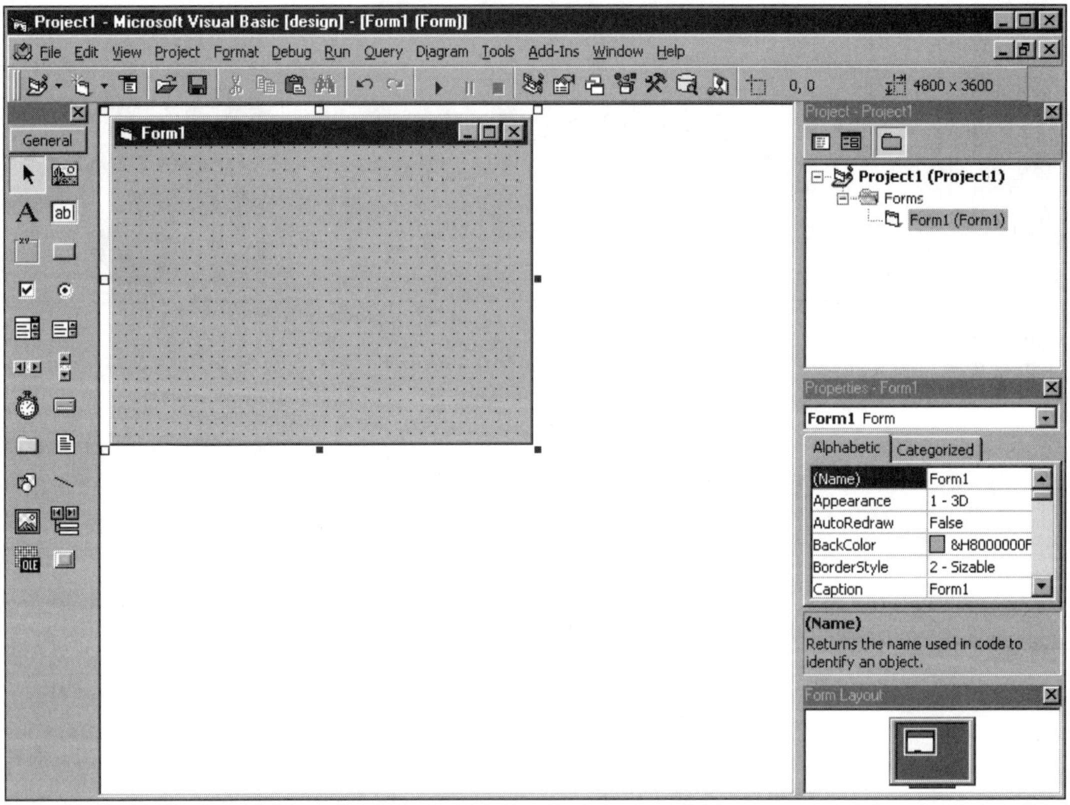

Figure 7.10
Adding the ActiveX control to VB's toolbox.

Double-click on the ActiveX control's icon to instantiate it on **Form1**. If you select the ActiveX control and its **InvisibleAtRuntime** property is set to **True**, a Properties window similar to the one shown in Figure 7.11 should appear.

At this point, if you know how to use its members, you could test the ActiveX control. For example, if you set the **Picture** property of **TBIcon1** to a specific icon and call its **Add** method with the statement

```
TBIcon1.AddIcon "New tooltip"
```

the TBIcon ActiveX control adds an icon with the specified tooltip to the right side of the Windows 95/98-style shell's Taskbar.

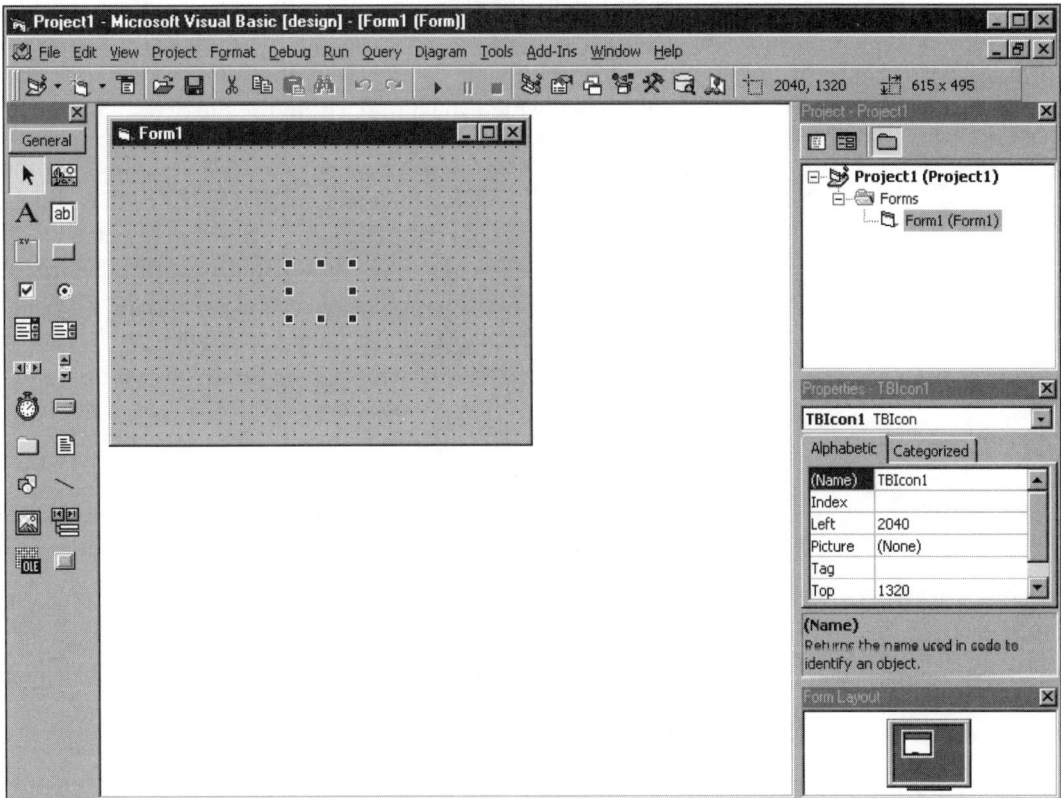

Figure 7.11
Configuring properties for the ActiveX control.

> **NOTE**
>
> To register the TBIcon ActiveX control on your machine, open the TBARICON.VBP project and select File | Make TBARICON.OCX. Accept all the current settings and save the project as TBARICON.VBP.

The Taskbar Icon ActiveX Control

Of course, as someone said a long time ago, the devil is always found in the details. Therefore, in order for you to really get a good feel for the various techniques involved in creating ActiveX controls, we need to take a closer look at the general declarations, properties, methods, and events that make up specific ActiveX controls. We'll do this first for the TBIcon ActiveX control.

What the TBIcon ActiveX control does for an application is add an icon with a specified tooltip to the right side of the Windows 95/98-style shell's Taskbar. While the application is running, you can change the tooltip, which displays the icon's name when the mouse moves over the icon. The TBIcon ActiveX control also causes the Taskbar's icon to react to left- and right-mouse button clicks and return a value to the application. This value signals the button that's been clicked. The key to this functionality is the use of the Windows API function **Shell_NotifyIcon**, which you'll find within the file SHELL32.DLL.

If you installed the files for the ActiveX controls contained on the book's companion CD-ROM when you ran SETUP.EXE, they should be on the path C:\VBOOPEFS\ACTXCTLS. What you should do now is open the VB project for the TBIcon ActiveX control (TBARICON.VBP); we'll analyze its source code within the following sections. The total amount of code, including declarations, is only about 60 lines. It consists of procedures for four methods, one property, and three events (one of which is a developer-declared event, a new syntactical element that VB6 supports).

The Taskbar Icon's General Declarations

Listing 7.3 shows the general declarations for the Taskbar icon's UserControl object.

Listing 7.3 General declarations for the TBIcon ActiveX control.

```
' User-defined data types:
Private Type ICONDATA
    TypeSize As Long
    HWnd As Long
    ID As Long
    Flags As Long
    CallBackMsg As Long
    Graphic As Long
    ToolTip As String * 64
End Type
```

```
' DLL functions:
Private Declare Function Shell_NotifyIcon& Lib "SHELL32" _
                    Alias "Shell_NotifyIconA" _
                    (ByVal Action&, Info As ICONDATA)

' Events:
Event MouseMove(Button As Integer, Shift As Integer, _
                X As Single, Y As Single)

' Module-level variables:
Private uIcon As ICONDATA
```

The code in Listing 7.3 contains two major points you need to understand. First, the Windows API function **Shell_NotifyIcon** uses the **ICONDATA** user-defined data type and only takes two arguments. The initial argument is a **Long** value or API constant that specifies the action to be taken, and the other argument is the user-defined data type. Second, you must declare the developer-declared **MouseMove** event within the General Declarations section of the module. As you'll see a little later in this section, a difference exists between the declaration of a developer-declared event and its corresponding event procedure.

The Taskbar Icon's Properties

Listing 7.4 shows the **Property** procedures for the **Picture** property of the Taskbar icon's UserControl object. Even though a UserControl object has a **Picture** property at design time, you must explicitly create a proxy **Picture** property with **Property** procedures in order for it to apply to the ActiveX control within an application.

Listing 7.4   Properties of the TBIcon ActiveX control.

```
Property Get Picture() As Picture

    ' Read by Add method of UserControl object.
    Set Picture = UserControl.Picture

End Property

Property Set Picture(ByVal Setting As Picture)

    ' Can be set in Properties window or at runtime.
    ' PropertyChanged method applies to UserControl
    ' object and notifies it that one of its properties
    ' has changed. This way it can synchronize its
    ' property window with new setting of property.
```

```
        Set UserControl.Picture = Setting
        UserControl.PropertyChanged Picture

End Property
```

You should note three points about the **Property** procedures in Listing 7.4. First, you must declare them as the object data type **Picture**. Second, you must declare the **Setting** argument of the **Property Set** procedure as **ByVal**. Third, VB6's new **PropertyChanged** method, which applies to the UserControl and UserDocument objects, changes the setting of the ActiveX control's **Picture** property within the Properties window if you change its setting at design time within an application. If you change its setting with code at runtime, the **PropertyChanged** method has no effect.

The Taskbar Icon's Methods

Listing 7.5 shows the four methods that apply to the Taskbar icon's UserControl object. Their names—**Add**, **ChangeTip**, **Delete**, and **GetBtnClicked**—clearly denote their functionality.

Listing 7.5 Methods of the TBIcon ActiveX control.

```
Sub Add(ToolTip As String)

    ' Constants for Windows API functions:
    Const NIF_MESSAGE = &H1
    Const NIF_ICON = &H2
    Const NIF_TIP = &H4
    Const NIM_ADD = &H0
    Const WM_MOUSEMOVE = &H200

    ' Size user-defined data type and
    ' assign values to its elements.
    ' ID element can be any Long value.
    uIcon.TypeSize = Len(uIcon)
    uIcon.ID = 1000
    uIcon.Flags = NIF_MESSAGE + NIF_ICON + NIF_TIP
    uIcon.HWnd = HWnd
    uIcon.CallBackMsg = WM_MOUSEMOVE
    uIcon.Graphic = Picture
    uIcon.ToolTip = ToolTip & vbNullChar

    ' Call Windows API function to add icon specified by
    ' Picture property of ActiveX control to taskbar.
    Shell_NotifyIcon NIM_ADD, uIcon

End Sub
```

VB's ActiveX Components   239

```vb
Sub ChangeTip(ToolTip As String)

    ' Constants for Windows API functions:
    Const NIF_TIP = &H4
    Const NIM_MODIFY = &H1

    ' Assign values to elements of user-defined data type:
    uIcon.Flags = NIF_TIP
    uIcon.ToolTip = ToolTip & vbNullChar

    ' Change tooltip of icon on taskbar.
    Shell_NotifyIcon NIM_MODIFY, uIcon

End Sub

Sub Delete()

    ' Constants for Windows API functions:
    Const NIM_DELETE = &H2

    ' Delete icon from taskbar.
    Shell_NotifyIcon NIM_DELETE, uIcon

End Sub

Function GetBtnClicked(X As Single) As Integer

    ' Constants for Windows API functions:
    Const WM_LBUTTONDOWN = &H201
    Const WM_RBUTTONDOWN = &H204
    Const WM_MBUTTONDOWN = &H207

    ' Variables:
    Dim Btn As Integer

    ' Convert twips to pixels.
    Btn = X \ Screen.TwipsPerPixelX

    ' Convert Windows API constant to VB intrinsic constant:
    Select Case Btn
        Case WM_LBUTTONDOWN
            Btn = vbLeftButton
        Case WM_RBUTTONDOWN
            Btn = vbRightButton
        Case WM_MBUTTONDOWN
            Btn = vbMiddleButton
```

```
            End Select
            GetBtnClicked = Btn
```

End Function

The code for the four methods in Listing 7.5 is pretty straightforward, but a couple of points do require some explanation. First, you might wonder why the **CallBackMsg** element of the user-defined data type is assigned the constant **WM_MOUSEMOVE** in the **Add** method. After the Windows API function **Shell_NotifyIcon** adds an icon to the Taskbar, either Windows 95/98 or NT 4 automatically sends back a Windows message to the TBIcon ActiveX control (identified by its **hWnd** property) that signifies the mouse event that occurred over the icon (left-click, right-click, mouse move, and so on). However, VB's architecture does not permit you to read the message directly because it does not explicitly support Windows callbacks. Instead, VB maps certain Windows messages into events. In this case, the message **WM_MOUSEMOVE** works best because it responds to all three possible kinds of mouse button clicks (left, right, and middle). Also, it maps back to an event (**MouseMove**) that VB supports and that has been declared by the developer for the ActiveX control.

Second, the purpose of the **GetBtnClicked** method isn't obvious. **GetBtnClicked** is called from the **MouseMove** event procedure of the TBIcon ActiveX control. It exists primarily to save the application programmer the trouble of writing such conversion code within the control's **MouseMove** event procedure. The actual button that gets clicked on the Taskbar's icon is mapped by VB into the **X** argument of **MouseMove** and must be converted from twips to pixels to match up with the Windows API constants (**WM_LBUTTONDOWN**, **WM_RBUTTONDOWN**, and so on). Most VB programmers do not write this kind of code on a day-to-day basis, so it's just a lot easier to provide the **GetBtnClicked** method for them and have it return the familiar intrinsic VB constants (**vbLeftButton**, **vbRightButton**, or **vbMiddleButton**). The typical code within the ActiveX control's **MouseMove** event procedure that calls the **GetBtnClicked** method is shown in Listing 7.6.

Listing 7.6   Code to call the GetBtnClicked method.
```
Private Sub TBIcon1_MouseMove(Button As Integer, _
                              Shift As Integer, _
                              X As Single, _
                              Y As Single)
```

```
    ' Variables:
    Dim Msg As String

    SetFocus

    Select Case TBIcon1.GetBtnClicked(X)
       Case vbLeftButton
          Msg = "You clicked left button on taskbar's icon."
       Case vbRightButton
          Msg = "You clicked right button on taskbar's icon."
       Case vbMiddleButton
          Msg = "You clicked middle button on taskbar's icon."
       Case Else
          Msg = vbNullString
    End Select

    If Msg <> vbNullString Then
        MsgBox Msg, vbInformation, "TBIcon ActiveX Control
Demo"
    End If

End Sub
```

The Taskbar Icon's Events

The three events of the Taskbar icon's UserControl object that contain code—**MouseMove**, **ReadProperties**, and **WriteProperties**—are shown in Listing 7.7. Of these three, only the developer-declared **MouseMove** event procedure is accessible at runtime within an application.

Listing 7.7 Event procedures of TBIcon's UserControl object.

```
Private Sub UserControl_MouseMove(Button As Integer, _
                                  Shift As Integer, _
                                  X As Single, _
                                  Y As Single)

    ' Use VB6's RaiseEvent method to trigger
    ' MouseMove event of TBIcon ActiveX control.
    RaiseEvent MouseMove(Button, Shift, X, Y)

End Sub

Private Sub UserControl_ReadProperties(PropBag As _
    PropertyBag)

    ' Variables:
    Dim Msg As String
```

```
                ' Read property's setting from storage:
                On Error Resume Next

                Set Picture = PropBag.ReadProperty("Picture", Nothing)

                If Err <> False Then
                   Msg = "VB run-time error " & Err & " -" & vbCr
                   Msg = Msg & Error(Err)
                   MsgBox Error(Err), vbExclamation, _
                      "ReadProperties Procedure"
                End If

             End Sub

             Private Sub UserControl_WriteProperties(PropBag As _
                PropertyBag)

                ' Write property's setting to storage.
                PropBag.WriteProperty "Picture", Picture, Nothing

             End Sub
```

To understand the **MouseMove** event procedure's code, you must appreciate that it's the second step within a three-step process required to create and use a developer-declared event for an ActiveX control. Let's take a moment to review these steps:

1. Within the General Declarations section of the UserControl object, use the **Event** statement to declare the developer-declared event.

2. Within the corresponding event procedure of the UserControl object, use the **RaiseEvent** method to trigger the developer-declared event within the ActiveX control at runtime.

3. At runtime within the application's ActiveX control, write a procedure in the developer-declared event (which is the only kind of event an instantiated ActiveX control supports) that reacts to the event, similar to the code in Listing 7.7.

The **ReadProperties** and **WriteProperties** event procedures definitely require some explanation. Table 7.1 lists and explains the syntactical elements they use.

Using The Taskbar Icon's ActiveX Control

Open the demo VB project that uses the TBIcon ActiveX control (DEMOTBAR.VBP) so we can examine its source code and watch how it works.

NOTE

When you open DEMOTBAR.VBP, Visual Basic displays the message "C:\VBOOPEFS\ACTXCTLS\TBARICON.OCX could not be loaded. Continue loading another project?" Click on Yes to clear the message box and then click on OK to clear the next two message boxes. You then need to delete TBIcon on the Form object. Finally, select Project | Components, check the newly registered Taskbar icon control on the Controls tab, and choose OK. You can then double-click on the TBIcon ActiveX icon on the toolbox to add it to **Form1**. This presumes, of course, that you previously registered the TBIcon ActiveX control on your PC (as a note earlier in this chapter prompted you to do).

After you've added the newly registered TBIcon ActiveX control to **Form1**, you can add an icon to the ActiveX control by setting its **Picture** property within the Properties window to some new icon. Its tooltip text is set based on the entry within the TextBox control object. Select Run | Start and note that this ActiveX control does not appear at runtime; remember, its **InvisibleAtRuntime** property was set to **True** when the control was created. Click on Add Icon and watch what happens to the right side of the Windows 95/98-style shell's Taskbar. Move the mouse over the icon on the Taskbar and watch as the tooltip is displayed. Click on the icon to see the code within the **MouseMove** event procedure of the ActiveX control display a message box like the one shown in Figure 7.12. Next, change the entry within the TextBox object and click on Change Tip or Delete Icon to call those methods of TBIcon.

The code in **Form1** of DEMOTBAR.VBP is simple. The only procedure that we'll specifically note is the **TBIcon1_MouseMove** event procedure in Listing 7.6. The procedure contains the code that takes the event procedure's **X** argument and passes it to the **GetBtnClicked** method of the ActiveX control. This method then converts the Windows pixels/constant value to a VB twips/intrinsic constant value and returns the number of the button (**vbLeftButton**, **vbRightButton**, or **vbMiddleButton**).

That's all there is to say about the TBIcon ActiveX control. At this point, you'll have to admit that it's a slick, little reusable component. Well, okay, maybe not so little—even a modest ActiveX control like this one takes up quite a bit of space on your hard drive. VB6 generates eight files with eight different extensions when it creates and registers the TBIcon ActiveX control. The 2 major files—TBARICON.OCX and TBARICON.OCA—weigh in at 16K and 17K, respectively. The other 5 files add another 13K, for a total of almost 50K.

It's also a good idea to remember exactly what kind of animal the COM/OLE software protocol considers an ActiveX control to be. When we were developing TBIcon, we looked within the Windows Registry and found the entry displayed in Figure 7.16 (shown later in this chapter) for it. It turns out that an ActiveX control is just another variation on

Figure 7.12
Clicking on the ActiveX control icon within the Taskbar displays this message box.

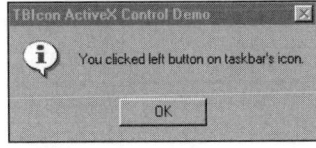

Table 7.1 VB6 syntax related to ReadProperties and WriteProperties events.

Syntax	Description
WriteProperties	An event that occurs when an ActiveX UserControl or UserDocument object is saved. The developer of the component can save the settings of its properties when the **WriteProperties** event occurs. The one argument of **WriteProperties** must be declared as a PropertyBag object.
ReadProperties	An event that occurs when loading an ActiveX UserControl or UserDocument object that has previously saved the settings of its properties. This event occurs after the control's **Initialize** event. You should always include error trapping in the **ReadProperties** event procedure to protect the control from invalid property values that may have been entered by users editing the FRM file with text editors. The one argument of **ReadProperties** must be declared as a PropertyBag object.
PropertyBag	An object that holds settings of properties that are to be saved across invocations of an ActiveX UserControl or UserDocument object. A PropertyBag object is passed into a control through the **ReadProperties** or the **WriteProperties** event, and it has **ReadProperty** and **WriteProperty** methods.
WriteProperty	A method of the PropertyBag object that saves the settings of a property of an ActiveX UserControl or UserDocument object. The **WriteProperty** method writes a string to the property bag and associates it with the String value in its first argument (that is, the name of the property). This String value is then used to read the setting when the **ReadProperty** method is called from the **ReadProperties** event procedure.
ReadProperty	A method of the PropertyBag object that returns the property setting of an ActiveX UserControl or UserDocument object that was previously saved with the **WriteProperty** method. The **ReadProperty** method returns the setting of the property associated with the String value of its argument (the name of the property). This String value must match the String value used when the property's setting was saved.

our old friend the in-process server/component, albeit one that provides a more developer-friendly interface within the form of the Properties window.

It would be a good exercise for you to consider whether and how you could implement the functionality of the TBIcon ActiveX control as a reusable object within an ActiveX DLL component. How would you design its public interface? Would it run at the same speed? Would it be harder to reuse? How much hard drive space would it require?

Next up is an example of an ActiveX control that subclasses the functionality of an existing, built-in VB control object. The ListSC ActiveX control illustrates some other interesting techniques you can use when creating ActiveX controls.

The Subclassed VB ListBox ActiveX Control

> **NOTE**
> To register the ListSC ActiveX control on your machine, you should select File | Make LSTBOXSC.OCX and accept all the current settings. Save the project as LSTBOXSC.VBP.

Open the VB project for the ListSC ActiveX control (LSTBOXSC.VBP). Within the following sections, we analyze its source code.

At this point in the book, understanding the ListSC ActiveX control's functionality and most of its procedures will be easy for you. The ListSC ActiveX control simply replicates most of the different methods of the List object in the class library found on this book's companion CD-ROM. However, the ListSC methods do not require you to pass in the **Name** property of a ListBox control object as an argument. The reason you can dispense with the object reference to a ListBox control is that the ListSC ActiveX control's UserControl object actually contains an encapsulated ListBox object. At design time, the UserControl object of ListSC appears as shown in Figure 7.13. The object with the handles is the UserControl object. It, in turn, contains a ListBox object with a **Name** property setting of **List1**.

This relationship between a UserControl object and a VB control object that it is layered on looks to be the same as the relationship between a Form object and a VB control object that it contains. However, a fundamental difference exists. If you have a ListBox object layered on a Form object, you can access a member of that ListBox object with a statement like this:

```
Form1.List1.Clear
```

As you know, this statement lets you apply the **Clear** method of the ListBox object, even from another code module within the project. However, in the case of a ListBox object layered on a UserControl object within an ActiveX control, this kind of syntax does not work. You can never directly refer to the encapsulated ListBox object by its **Name** property or directly apply any of its other properties or methods.

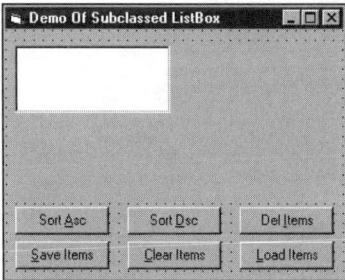

Figure 7.13
Design time display of the UserControl object of ListSC.

Instead, all references must be to the instance of the UserControl object (for example, **ListSC1**) that contains the ListBox object.

To the application programmer who is reusing the ListSC ActiveX control, it appears as if he or she is referencing a ListBox object, but the reality of what is going on inside the ActiveX control is quite different. The analysis of the ListSC ActiveX control that follows focuses on the aspects of its implementation that enable it to contain a subclassed VB ListBox object, whose members an application programmer can transparently access.

Creating Proxy Custom Members For *ListSC1*

Because the programmer who reuses the ListSC ActiveX control can never directly refer to the ListBox object it contains, any existing members of the ListBox object (that is, properties and methods) that you want to apply must be declared as custom members of the UserControl object. Listing 7.8 shows the proxy custom members for the ListSC ActiveX control.

Listing 7.8 Proxy custom members of the ListSC ActiveX control.

```
Property Get List(Index)
    List = List1.List(Index)
End Property

Property Get ListCount()
    ListCount = List1.ListCount
End Property

Property Get ListIndex()
    ListIndex = List1.ListIndex
End Property

Property Get TopIndex()
    TopIndex = List1.TopIndex
End Property

Sub AddItem(Item, _
            Optional Index)
    If IsMissing(Index) Then
        List1.AddItem Item
    Else
        List1.AddItem Item, Index
    End If
End Sub
```

```
Sub Clear()
    List1.Clear
End Sub

Sub Refresh()
    List1.Refresh
End Sub
```

When you look at the proxy custom members in Listing 7.8, keep in mind that the ListSC ActiveX control is only meant to be a demonstration version, and, as a result, the proxy custom members created for it do not constitute a complete set. Also, the four proxy properties are read-only; again, this is for demonstration purposes only.

Now, you might think that this process of creating proxy custom members for an ActiveX control to replicate the members of the built-in VB control that it contains is awkward and tedious. Couldn't Microsoft's VB6 development team come up with a simpler approach? Well, first of all, an add-in wizard that helps to automate the creation of proxy custom members is included with VB6 (the ActiveX Control Interface wizard). Second, when you're subclassing a VB control object with an ActiveX control, this proxy approach is necessary to give you the freedom to decide which intrinsic properties of the VB control you want to replicate and which ones you want to override. The next section discusses how you can override the behavior of an intrinsic property.

Overriding The Intrinsic **Sorted** Property Of A ListBox Object

The approach to subclassing that's used within the List object of the class library found on this book's companion CD-ROM does not let you completely override the behavior of the intrinsic **Sorted** property of VB's ListBox object. If **Sorted** is set to **False**, anything is possible (sort ascending, sort descending, and don't sort). However, if you set **Sorted** to **True** and you pass an object reference to that ListBox object to the **FillWithDAO** or **FillWithDataCtl** method of the List object, you can neither suspend the sort nor sort in descending order. Because **Sorted** is read-only at runtime, you're stuck with the behavior that its design-time setting of **True** dictates (that is, sort in ascending order).

The approach to subclassing a UserControl object containing a ListBox object lets you overcome the restriction discussed within the previous paragraph. The following steps are required to override the behavior of the intrinsic **Sorted** property:

1. Declare a custom **Property Let** procedure named **Sorted** for the UserControl object.
2. Within this **Property Let** procedure, specify the possible settings of the argument of the custom **Sorted** property (0 - **SORT_NONE**, 1 - **SORT_ASC**, and 2 - **SORT_DSC**).
3. If the argument is set to **SORT_NONE** (which is neither **SORT_ASC** nor **SORT_DSC**), do nothing and exit the procedure.
4. If the argument is set to **SORT_ASC** or **SORT_DSC**, run the algorithm shown in Listing 7.9.

Listing 7.9 The Sorted custom property of the ListSC ActiveX control.

```
Property Let Sorted(Setting)

' *******************************
' Sorted property is write-only at runtime. It
  demonstrates how to override a built-in property of a VB
  control object that is encapsulated inside a UserControl
  object.
' *******************************

' Constants for Windows API functions:
Const WM_SETREDRAW = &HB
' Constants for Setting argument:
Const SORT_NONE = 0
Const SORT_ASC = 1
Const SORT_DSC = 2

' Variables:
Dim Tmp       As String
Dim El        As Long
Dim Item      As Long
Dim Items()   As String

If Setting <> SORT_ASC And Setting <> SORT_DSC Then
   Exit Property
Else

   SendMessage List1.hWnd, WM_SETREDRAW, False, vbEmpty

   For Item = 0 To List1.ListCount - 1
      ReDim Preserve Items(Item)
      Items(Item) = List1.List(Item)
   Next Item
```

```
    List1.Clear

    For El = LBound(Items) To UBound(Items) - 1

        If Setting = SORT_ASC Then

            For Item = UBound(Items) To El + 1 Step -1

                If UCase$(Items(Item)) < _
                   UCase$(Items(Item - 1)) Then
                    Tmp = Items(Item)
                    Items(Item) = Items(Item - 1)
                    Items(Item - 1) = Tmp
                End If
            Next Item

        Else

            For Item = UBound(Items) To El + 1 Step -1

                If UCase$(Items(Item)) >= _
                   UCase$(Items(Item - 1)) Then
                    Tmp = Items(Item)
                    Items(Item) = Items(Item - 1)
                    Items(Item - 1) = Tmp
                End If

            Next Item
        End If
    Next El

    For Item = 0 To UBound(Items)
        List1.AddItem Items(Item)
    Next Item

    SendMessage List1.hWnd, WM_SETREDRAW, True, vbEmpty
End If

End Property
```

If **Sorted** is set to **1 - SORT_ASC** or **2 - SORT_DSC**, the procedure in Listing 7.9 follows these steps:

1. It suspends redrawing of the ListBox object to speed up the process.
2. It assigns the items in the ListBox to a dynamic String array, clears the ListBox, and sorts the elements of the String array in the specified order.

> **NOTE**
>
> When you create an ActiveX control that subclasses a VB control object, you can use the same kind of technique used with the **Sorted** property of the ListBox object on any intrinsic property of any control object that is normally read-only at runtime.

3. It uses the **AddItem** method of the ListBox (implemented as a proxy method) to reload the sorted items from the array and then redraws the ListBox. If **Sorted** is set to **0 - SORT_NONE**, nothing happens and the items remain in their current order. Note that the sort routine in Listing 7.9 works, but it's not very fast.

Sizing A Control Layered On A UserControl Object

One other technique you need to understand is how to enable an application programmer to size a VB control object that is layered on a UserControl object in an ActiveX control. In the example of the subclassed ListBox object, here's the dilemma: The UserControl object has **Height** and **Width** properties that appear in the Properties window when an application reuses the ActiveX control. The ListBox object does not have **ScaleHeight** and **ScaleWidth** properties, which are the ones you need to set when an application reuses the ActiveX control.

You might wonder why you can't just set the **Height** and **Width** properties of the ListBox object. The reason is that when an application reuses the ActiveX control, the **Height** and **Width** properties of the ListSC ActiveX control govern the dimensions of the container (or *non-client area*) of the ListBox. What you need to do is declare custom **ScaleHeight** and **ScaleWidth** properties for the ListBox (which are not intrinsic properties of a ListBox). These properties govern the dimensions of the client area of the ListBox.

Listing 7.10 shows the general declarations, property procedures, and event procedures that are needed to size the ListBox object of the ActiveX control at runtime.

Listing 7.10 Procedures to size the client area of a subclassed ListBox.

```
' General declarations:

' Module-level custom property variables:
Private uScaleHeight    As Integer
Private uScaleWidth     As Integer

Property Let ScaleHeight(ByVal Setting)

    ' Store setting of custom property and set Height
    ' of ListBox equal to ScaleHeight. Then call
    ' PropertyChanged method to notify UserControl
    ' object that property has been changed and
    ' to trigger WriteProperties event.
```

```
        uScaleHeight = Setting
        List1.Height = Setting
        PropertyChanged ScaleHeight

End Property

Property Get ScaleHeight()
    ScaleHeight = uScaleHeight
End Property

Property Let ScaleWidth(ByVal Setting)

    ' Store setting of custom property and set Width
    ' of ListBox equal to ScaleWidth. Then call
    ' PropertyChanged method to notify UserControl
    ' object that property has been changed and
    ' to trigger WriteProperties event.

    uScaleWidth = Setting
    List1.Width = Setting
    PropertyChanged ScaleWidth

End Property

Property Get ScaleWidth()
    ScaleWidth = uScaleWidth
End Property

Private Sub UserControl_WriteProperties(PropBag As PropertyBag)

    ' Write settings of properties to storage:
    PropBag.WriteProperty "ScaleHeight", ScaleHeight, 0
    PropBag.WriteProperty "ScaleWidth", ScaleWidth, 0

End Sub

Private Sub UserControl_ReadProperties(PropBag As PropertyBag)

    ' Variables:
    Dim Msg As String

    ' Read settings of properties from storage:
    On Error Resume Next
    ScaleHeight = PropBag.ReadProperty("ScaleHeight", 0)
    ScaleWidth = PropBag.ReadProperty("ScaleWidth", 0)
```

NOTE

When you open DEMOLBSC.VBP, Visual Basic displays the message "C:\VBOOPEFS\ACTXCTLS\LSTBOXSC.OCX could not be loaded. Continue loading another project?" Click on Yes to clear the message box and then click on OK to clear the next two message boxes. You then need to delete ListSC1 on the Form object. Finally, select Project | Components, check the newly registered subclassed Visual Basic ListBox control on the Controls tab, and choose OK. You can then double-click on the ListSC ActiveX icon on the toolbox to add it to **Form1**. This presumes, of course, that you previously registered the ListSC ActiveX control on your PC (as a note earlier in this chapter prompted you to do).

```
    If Err <> False Then
        Msg = "VB run-time error " & Err & " -" & vbCr
        Msg = Msg & Error(Err)
        MsgBox Error(Err), vbExclamation, _
            "ReadProperties Procedure"
    End If

End Sub
```

Using The Subclassed ListBox's ActiveX Control

Open the demo VB project that uses the ListSC ActiveX control (DEMOLBSC.VBP). Within this section, we examine some of its source code and watch how it works.

When you look at **Form1** of DEMOLBSC.VBP at design time, it appears as shown in Figure 7.14. Note that the ListSC ActiveX control on **Form1** looks the same as it does in its own LSTBOXSC.VBP project (displayed previously in Figure 7.13).

The procedures in Listing 7.10 enable the application programmer to size the client area of **ListSC1** in one of two ways:

♦ At design time within the Properties window, the application programmer can explicitly set the **ScaleHeight** and **ScaleWidth** properties to the same values as the **Height** and **Width** properties (which, remember, are really the **Height** and **Width** properties of the UserControl container object).

♦ At runtime within the **Form_Load** event procedure, the application programmer can set the **ScaleHeight** and **ScaleWidth** properties equal to the **Height** and **Width** properties with either of these two lines of code:

```
ListSC1.ScaleWidth = ListSC1.Width
ListSC1.ScaleHeight = ListSC1.Height
```

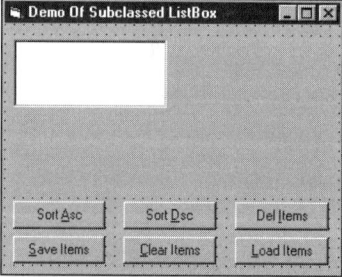

Figure 7.14
Form1 of DEMOLBSC.VBP.

DEMOLBSC.VBP takes the second approach. When you select Run | Start, the code within the **Form_Load** event procedure calls the **FillWithDAO** method of **ListSC1**. That method is passed values that tell it to fill the ActiveX control's subclassed ListBox with a field from VB's BIBLIO.MDB. When the method is done loading the ListBox, **Form1** appears, as shown in Figure 7.15.

From here on within the demonstration project, you can click on the various buttons and watch the subclassed members of the ListBox object encapsulated within the ActiveX control do their thing.

You should also remember that this demonstration version of ListSC did not implement the proxy properties and the **Sorted** custom property as writeable at design time. However, from the examples of the **ScaleHeight** and **ScaleWidth** properties here (and the **Picture** property of the TBIcon ActiveX control), you should now understand how to do this.

ActiveX Controls Vs. ActiveX Servers

To the COM/OLE software protocol, an ActiveX control is just another kind of in-process server component. There are three kinds of special features an ActiveX control component supports that an ActiveX server component cannot provide:

- An ActiveX control presents a friendlier public interface, in the form of its Properties window, to the developer who wants to reuse the control.

- You can connect an ActiveX control to a property page, which displays the control's properties in an alternate format. Each property page you connect to your control becomes a tab on the tabbed Properties dialog box. VB6 handles all the details of presenting the pages as a tabbed dialog box, and it manages the OK, Cancel, and Apply buttons. All you have to do is lay out the controls that you plan to use to set the property values. Property pages are useful when a group

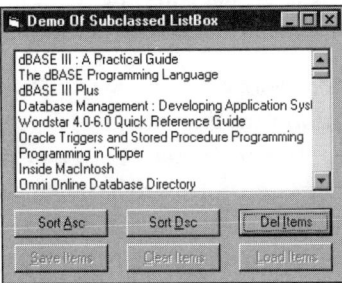

Figure 7.15
The ListBox updated with a field from BIBLIO.MDB.

> **NOTE**
>
> It used to be the case that only ActiveX controls could support developer-declared events. VB6 supports developer-declared events within ActiveX component servers.

of properties interacts in a complex fashion, as with the Toolbar ActiveX control included with Visual Basic. They are also useful for controls that are distributed internationally, because you can localize the captions for different languages.

- An ActiveX control can let you completely override the normal behavior of an intrinsic property of a VB control object (as in the example of the **Sorted** property of the ListSC ActiveX control).

Our opinion of VB6-created ActiveX controls is that they are a pretty cool addition to the toolkit of the VB OOP developer. If you or your company need a very specialized kind of functionality that no third-party vendor of ActiveX controls currently provides, you now have an easy-to-develop and easy-to-maintain solution available within VB6.

However, do not be fooled by the hype about speed. Even if you compile a VB6-written ActiveX control to native code, it will always run significantly slower than a third-party software manufacturer's ActiveX control that encapsulates the same functionality. VB6-compiled native code is definitely not as fast as C or C++, no matter what Microsoft's PR evangelists say.

You should be aware of three other issues regarding the tradeoffs between developing reusable objects as ActiveX controls versus as ActiveX servers. First, our experience with developing the ListSC ActiveX control and the List object of the ActiveX server component indicates that an ActiveX control takes significantly more time and effort to create than the same functionality in the form of an ActiveX server component. This is especially the case if you're subclassing one of VB's intrinsic control objects because of the need to replicate and test the proxy properties and methods of the control object.

Second, we find the debugging and testing process for ActiveX controls (which we do not have the space to elaborate on here) to be far more awkward and cumbersome than the process for debugging ActiveX server components. To find out what's involved in testing an ActiveX control, see the topic "Running the ShapeLabel Control at Design Time" within Visual Basic Books Online.

Third, some developers may try to tell you that an ActiveX control implementation runs dramatically faster than the same functionality encapsulated within an ActiveX server component. They will argue that an ActiveX control has to be much faster because it's actually part of the application that reuses its services. However, this is definitely not the case. The reason is related to what you see in Figure 7.16,

VB's ActiveX Components 255

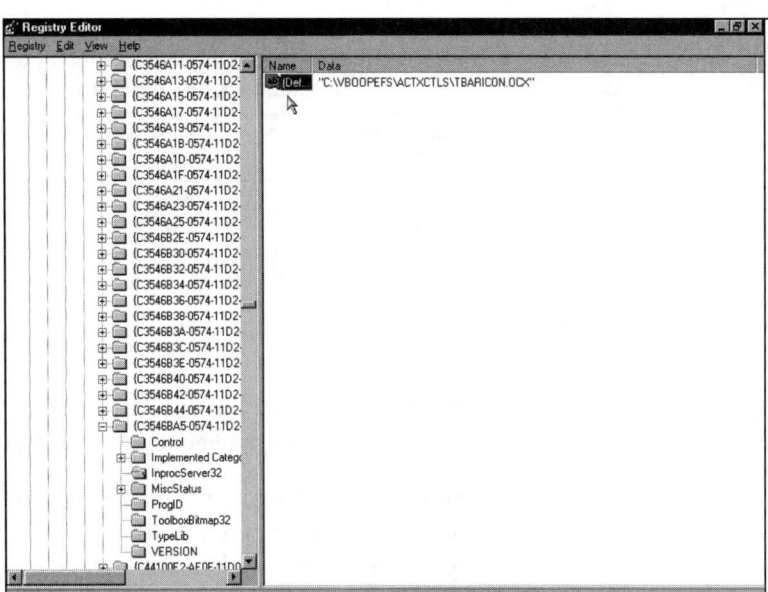

Figure 7.16
The Windows Registry entry for the TBIcon ActiveX control.

which shows the Windows Registry entry for the TBIcon ActiveX control. You must always remember that at a lower level of abstraction within the COM/OLE software architecture, an ActiveX control is just another kind of in-process ActiveX component.

To demonstrate our point about the relative performance of an ActiveX control versus an ActiveX DLL server component, we have set up two demonstration executables: DEMOCTL.EXE and DEMODLL.EXE. If you installed them when you used the setup routine of this book's companion CD-ROM, they are located in the path C:\VBOOPEFS\ACTXCTLS. Both executables reuse the same three members (**FillWithDAO**, **Sort**, and **Save**) on about 250 records from BIBLIO.MDB. However, DEMOCTL.EXE reuses them from the ListSC ActiveX control, and DEMODLL.EXE reuses them from the List object of the class library on the companion CD-ROM.

We benchmarked these two implementations. Table 7.2 lists the results. Each of the five sets of timings was done from a complete reboot of Windows NT 4 so that we could rule out any caching effects. We used the **TimeGetTime** Windows API function (which is accurate to 10 milliseconds when called under Windows NT) for the timings. In the case of the ActiveX server component, we used the in-process version and early binding to get as much speed as possible, as well as to have an apples-to-apples comparison. The results clearly show that although the ActiveX control implementation is faster overall, the

Table 7.2 Comparing an ActiveX control and an ActiveX DLL server component implementation in terms of time required to instantiate, load, and reuse.

Control Speed (Milliseconds)	DLL Server Speed (Milliseconds)	Control Faster By
3515	3665	4.3%
3524	3625	2.9%
3534	3635	2.8%
3645	3705	1.6%
3594	3635	1.1%

difference is slight. The average of the five timings indicates that the ActiveX control implementation is only 2.5 percent faster.

However, you have to remember that the server component's implementation is part of a much larger DLL file. Also, its members have quite a bit of syntax-checking code that we did not bother to put into the demonstration version of the ListSC ActiveX control. Finally, the ListSC ActiveX control would be slightly slower if we had implemented all the ListBox object's proxy members and properties. Therefore, in the end, the ActiveX control's edge over the server component is probably only about 1.5 to 2 percent.

Conclusion

In this chapter, we journeyed into the world of VB's ActiveX components. Here are some of the highlights:

- ActiveX is not a programming language. ActiveX is a suite of technologies you can use to deliver business solutions over the Internet and an intranet. ActiveX technology includes developing and integrating ActiveX controls, writing ActiveX scripts, and so on.
- An ActiveX DLL component exposes OLE Automation objects and their members to OLE Automation clients for use by the clients.
- An ActiveX EXE component is one whose operation does not remain within the client application's process or memory space.
- Designing an ActiveX control is almost as easy as designing a VB Form object. You can use familiar Visual Basic commands to draw your control or create a control group using existing controls.
- An ActiveX control's edge over the server component is probably only about 1.5 to 2 percent.

- A native-code DLL or EXE file is 80 to 85 percent larger than it would be under p-code compilation, and it takes up that much more space on your hard drive.

In the next chapter, we venture into the issues of compiling an ActiveX component, maintaining compatibility, and creating the Help file for an ActiveX component.

Chapter 8

Implementing ActiveX Components

Key Topics:

♦ *Compiling An ActiveX Component*

♦ *Maintaining Compatibility*

♦ *Creating An ActiveX Component's Help File*

♦ *Linking A Help File To An ActiveX Component*

This chapter continues the discussion of ActiveX components and outlines some guidelines for implementing them. First, we'll compare the pros and cons of using p-code versus native code. Then, we'll move on to the importance of compatibility settings and how to properly configure them. We'll finish off the chapter by addressing how you can use a wizard built into VB6 to distribute your ActiveX component, and we'll offer some tips on creating a good Help file for your ActiveX component.

Compiling An ActiveX Component

One of the exciting new features that VB6 supports is the ability to compile any kind of VB project, including ActiveX components, to either p-code or native code. The settings that let you switch between compilation modes are found on the Compile tab of the Project Properties dialog box. If you start VB6 and open EFSD.DLL, you can access these settings by selecting Project|EFSD Properties and clicking on the Compile tab.

You might not have noticed it before, but this book's ActiveX component compilation switch was set to p-code when you installed it from the CD-ROM. If you did not change the setting to native code, any time you remade and registered the book's class library while working through the examples, you were compiling the p-code version. For almost the entire development cycle of an ActiveX component, the p-code compilation setting is what you should use. Here are three reasons why:

♦ It takes significantly longer to compile to native code (200 to 300 percent longer with the book's class library).

- The native code DLL or EXE file is 80 to 85 percent larger than under p-code compilation and takes up that much more space on your hard drive.
- There's no good reason to compile to a native code version until you're ready to use VB6's Package And Deployment Wizard to create the distribution disks for the ActiveX component.

However, you definitely should set the compilation switch to native code when you make your final version. From the informal benchmarks we have run, it is clear that, although compiling to native code does not result in dramatic performance gains, you can expect to realize an average increase in speed of 15 to 30 percent. The actual increase is dependent on the specific mix of functionality and code within your ActiveX component or standard EXE project.

When you do select the Compile To Native Code option button on the Compile tab, VB enables the other possible selections related to native compilation. Table 8.1 lists these native code options and their meanings.

Table 8.1 Native code compilation options.

Setting	Description
Optimize For Fast Code	Maximizes the speed of the EXE or DLL file by instructing VB6's compiler to favor speed over size. The compiler can reduce many constructs to functionally similar sequences of machine code. In some cases, the differences offer a tradeoff of size versus speed. If you select this option, you'll have code that's larger in size but that's the fastest possible version of your project for a 486 or 586 processor.
Optimize For Small Code	Minimizes the size of the EXE or DLL file by instructing VB6's compiler to favor size over speed. The compiler can reduce many constructs to functionally similar sequences of machine code. If you select this option, you'll have code that's smaller in size but that runs slower than if the Optimize For Fast Code switch is set.
No Optimization	Compiles without optimizations. Results in an EXE or DLL file that's a compromise between the compilations achieved by the Fast Code and Small Code optimizations.
Favor Pentium Pro	Optimizes the code created to favor the Pentium Pro processor. Use this option for programs meant only for the Pentium Pro processor. Code generated with this option will still run on earlier processors, but it does not perform as well. Selecting this checkbox, in conjunction with selecting Optimize For Fast Code, results in the fastest possible version of your project for the Pentium Pro processor.

(continued)

Table 8.1 Native code compilation options (*continued*).

Setting	Description
Create Symbolic Debug Info	Generates symbolic debug information in the EXE or DLL file. An executable file created using this option can be debugged using Visual C++ or debuggers that use the CodeView style of debug information. Setting this option generates a PDB file with the symbol information for your executable.
Advanced Optimizations	Displays the Advanced Optimizations dialog box. This dialog box provides the following options: ♦ *Assume No Aliasing*—Advises the compiler that your program does not use aliasing. ♦ *Remove Array Bounds Checks*—Advises the compiler not to perform a check on the index and determines whether the index falls within the range of the array. ♦ *Remove Integer Overflow Checks*—Advises the compiler not to perform a check on integer-style data types and determines whether the value is within the range of the data type. ♦ *Remove Floating Point Error Checks*—Advises the compiler not to perform a check on floating-point data types and determines whether "divide by zero" or other invalid operations exist. ♦ *Allow Unrounded Floating Point Operations*—Advises the compiler to perform the floating-point operations more efficiently. ♦ *Remove Safe Pentium FDIV Checks*—Advises the compiler not to perform the safe Pentium FDIV check.
DLL Base Address	Sets a base address for the program, overriding the default location for a DLL file (at 0X10000000). The operating system first attempts to load a program at its specified or default address. If sufficient space isn't available, the system relocates the program. This option is only enabled for in-process DLL ActiveX components.

When you click on the Advanced Optimizations button on the Compile tab, VB6 displays the Advanced Optimizations dialog box, shown in Figure 8.1. If you're thinking of using these advanced settings, take heed of the Microsoft VB development team's warning within Visual Basic's Help file. They explicitly state that enabling these optimizations may prevent the correct execution of your program. Our advice is not to use them (too much hassle for too little payoff). If you do use them, test your ActiveX component very carefully before distributing it. If you want more information about these settings, click on Help within the Advanced Optimizations dialog box.

The bottom-line answer to the question of whether you should have VB6 compile your standard or ActiveX component project to native code is a resounding Yes. No matter what kind of VB applications you write, they will run faster when compiled to native code. However,

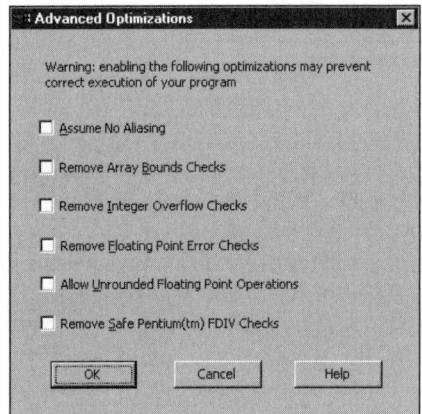

Figure 8.1
The Advanced Optimizations dialog box.

compiling to native code is nowhere close to being a panacea for all the potential performance bottlenecks within VB applications. If your application runs like a snail because it uses too many ActiveX controls, or it doesn't take advantage of the Windows API function calls when appropriate, or the poor I/O performance of the server database you're linked to is the real culprit, then compiling to native code does not solve your performance problem. However, all other factors being equal, it will speed up your VB applications by 15 to 30 percent.

Maintaining Compatibility

Within the Project tab of the Options dialog box of VB4 (Tools l Options), a Compatible OLE Component entry can be found. VB6 replaces this one entry with three possible compatibility settings. If you start VB6 and open EFSE.EXE, you can find these settings by selecting Project l EFSE Properties and clicking on the Component tab. The Project Properties dialog box will appear, as shown in Figure 8.2. VB6 uses these compatibility settings to monitor whether you're breaking the existing public interface of your ActiveX component and to warn you when you are about to do so. Table 8.2 lists the three possible compatibility settings and their meanings.

In the dialog box, the Location box setting appears directly underneath these three settings. If you use the Location box setting, it must point to the path and name of the DLL or EXE file that's your ActiveX component. You can only make the entry after you've first made/compiled an initial version of the in-process or out-of-process component. Visual Basic then uses the setting to warn you when you try to make a new version of the component that's incompatible with the previous version.

Implementing ActiveX Components

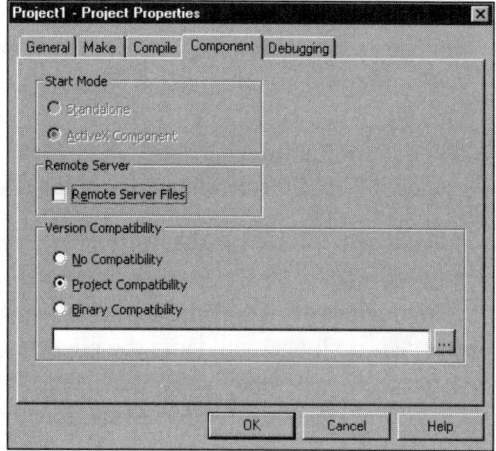

Figure 8.2
Configuring the compatibility settings.

Table 8.2   Version compatibility settings.

Setting	Description
No Compatibility	If this setting is checked, version compatibility is not enforced, and the Location box at the bottom of the tab is disabled.
Project Compatibility	If this setting is checked, the Location box is enabled. Use the Location box to search for the ActiveX component's EXE or DLL file with which the current version of the component is to be compatible when it's compiled. This setting is for an ActiveX component that has been compiled to p-code.
Binary Compatibility	If this setting is checked, the Location box is enabled. Use the Location box to search for the ActiveX component's EXE or DLL file with which the current version of the component is to be compatible when it's compiled. This setting is for an ActiveX component that has been compiled to native code.

Here's a list of some of the things you can do to an ActiveX component's project that renders it incompatible with the previously compiled version:

♦ Change the name of an existing project, class, or member.

♦ Change the declaration of a public class or member to a private one.

♦ Remove arguments or change the order of arguments within the declaration of a member.

♦ Change a custom property from read and write (that is, it has both **Property Let** and **Property Get** procedures) to read-only or write-only.

♦ Change an optional argument to a required argument within the declaration of a member.

♦ Add a required argument to the declaration of a member.

> **NOTE**
>
> For more information on creating a set of distribution disks for an ActiveX component's file(s) using VB's Package And Deployment Wizard, refer to Chapter 4.

Visual Basic uses the Version Compatibility settings to maintain the same registration number (the GUID, or *global unique identifier*) for the ActiveX component as well as within the Windows registration database when you build a new version of the ActiveX component. If you don't maintain the same registration number, the registration database gradually gets cluttered up with outdated GUIDs.

Also, if the GUID for the ActiveX component changes and you or some other developer previously hard-coded a reference to the ActiveX component within a client application (that is, *early binding*), the reference is no longer valid and the client application will no longer run correctly. This is why most Visual Basic ActiveX component developers use only the **CreateObject** function approach (that is, *late binding*) to test their components from a client application. **CreateObject** instantiates the class regardless of how many outdated GUIDs exist within the Registry. The only time **CreateObject** fails is when no valid programmatic ID string exists within the Registry at all.

Unless you're extremely disciplined in the way you design classes and their members, you will in the course of development make several changes that render the previous version of the component incompatible. Whether or not you want Visual Basic to warn you each time it detects such an incompatibility is questionable. Different Visual Basic ActiveX component developers have different philosophies about using the Version Compatibility settings; however, based on our experience, we must agree with Deborah Kurata, who says in her book *Doing Objects in Microsoft Visual Basic 4.0* that only an actual released version of the ActiveX component should be listed (under the Version Compatibility entry), not an interim build version. (See Appendix A for bibliographical information for this book.)

You can use different techniques to periodically clean up the registration database. You can manually delete outdated entries with the Registry Editor (REGEDIT.EXE). You can store clean versions of the two Registry DAT files under different names and manually replace the cluttered-up versions of the DAT files with the clean versions. Also, you can try using some of the tools that come on the Visual Basic CD-ROM, such as REGCLEAN.EXE and REGCLN16.EXE (located in \TOOLS\PSS). However, our experience has been that these tools do not clean out all the outdated entries.

Creating An ActiveX Component's Help File

One of the essential features that every ActiveX component should have is its own Windows Help file that documents the public interface of its reusable objects and members. This book is not meant to teach you how to write and compile a Windows Help file from scratch. You can find several excellent books devoted to this subject. The most complete and current book is *Developing Online Help for Windows 95* by Boggan, Farkas, and Welinske. (See Appendix A for complete bibliographical information.) However, if you have no experience writing Help files, use our book to get up to speed pretty quickly on the technical issues involved.

This section describes the design issues specific to creating a good Windows Help file for an ActiveX component. Our recommendations here reflect both our own years of experience in writing Help files (including a portion of VB4's own Help file) and Microsoft's standards for documenting its ActiveX components. Take our word for it: When it comes to ActiveX components, Microsoft writes the best Help files in the business.

The major design objectives of an ActiveX component's Help file are few in number and straightforward in concept. The following list summarizes them:

- Each public class/object needs a topic to describe the object's general purpose.

- Each public class/object's topic has three jumps that are located at the top of the topic and kept with the topic's title as you scroll through the topic: Methods, Properties, and See Also. If any of your objects have developer-declared events, you should also have a fourth jump: Events. These jumps are to topics that list all the methods and properties that apply to the object and to other topics related to the object. Including the object's topic, this results in four topics per object (five if you need one for Events). To see a sample of a four-topic set for an object, open OBJECT.RTF using Microsoft Word.

- Each public member needs a topic to document the member's purpose, syntax, where it can be called from, the values it can return, and miscellaneous remarks.

- Each public member's topic has three jumps (again located at the top of the topic and kept with the topic's title as you scroll through the topic): Example, Applies To, and See Also. The Example topic appears within a secondary Help window and contains the sample code for how to call and reuse the member. The Applies To topic lists the objects within the ActiveX component to which the member applies. The See Also jump is to other topics related to the member. Including the member's topic, this results in four topics per member. To see a sample of a four-topic set for a member, open MEMBER.RTF.

- A set of syntax error message topics should be included to document any syntax errors raised by the ActiveX component. To see how you can create these, open ERRMSGS.RTF.

Features Of The Book's Help File

While we're on the topic of Help files, let's discuss the features of the book's class library Help file. Not every class library Help file needs to have all these features (for example, the New Syntax and Glossary sections are not necessary). However, when it comes time to design and create your own Help file for a class library, you could do far worse than use the Help file that comes on this book's companion CD-ROM (EFS.HLP) as a template. The EFS.HLP file was modeled on and precisely imitates the Help file that comes with Visual Basic itself.

The Contents topic of EFS.HLP indicates the three major kinds of information contained within the book's class library Help file:

- Objects that contain functional specification topics for the public classes and public members of the class library, as well as sample code topic for each public member of the class library.
- A section pointing to all the new syntax that has been added to Visual Basic 6.
- A glossary of over 300 OOP and Windows terms.

The other features included within EFS.HLP are the help topics for the syntax error messages of the class library and a comprehensive, cross-indexed set of keywords.

All the files that comprise this book's ActiveX component's Help file (EFS.HLP) are on the book's companion CD-ROM. If you chose to install them as part of the CD-ROM's setup routine, these files should be in the path C:\VBOOPEFS\VBCLSHLP. Among these files, you'll find many graphics files that support the bitmaps EFS.HLP uses. Table 8.3 lists and describes the major files needed to compile EFS.HLP.

Table 8.3 Major files used to compile EFS.HLP.

Name	Description
CONTENTS.RTF	A contents topic (Windows 3.x style)
CLASSLIB.RTF	A main file that contains all topics for objects and their members
SYNTAX.RTF	A file that points to new VB6 syntax information
GLOSSARY.RTF	A file that contains a glossary of OOP and Windows terms
ERRMSGS.RTF	A file that contains 48 syntax error messages
OBJECT.RTF	A sample file that contains four topics used to document an object (ActiveXCtl)
MEMBER.RTF	A sample file that contains four topics used to document a member (LoadStatusBar)
EFS.HPJ	A project file that the compiler reads for settings, paths, and so on
HCP.EXE	A Windows 3.x-style Help compiler
HCP.ERR	A Help compiler's error file
*.BMP	Miscellaneous bitmap files

Once you get in the habit of documenting an ActiveX component's reusable objects and members within a Windows Help file, you'll wonder why you ever tried to do it any other way. If you organize the Help file in compliance with the files found in Table 8.3, you can easily add the necessary topics for new objects and members as you develop them. You'll also find it much easier to revise and maintain the documentation for existing objects and members. Most important, if your ActiveX component is distributed with a good Help file, other developers are much more likely to reuse your ActiveX component.

Linking A Help File To An ActiveX Component

The Object Browser's ability to display the correct Help topic for any public member of a public class is an essential feature within object-oriented programming. Without such a feature, knowing how to call members of reusable objects would be much more difficult. Within this section, we'll create the various links that tell the Object Browser which Help topic to display for any specific item within a class library. Of course, to establish these links at all, you must first write and compile the Windows Help file. In this section, you'll learn the mechanics of how to establish the links by using the book's class library.

> **NOTE**
>
> You don't have to specify the path where the ActiveX component's Help file is located. After the ActiveX component is installed on another PC, the path will probably not apply anyway. If a client application programmer tries to access the Help file from the Object Browser and the file is not located on the specified path, the Object Browser displays a dialog box, allowing the programmer to locate the Help file.

Specifying The Help File

To specify the Help file for an ActiveX component, follow these steps:

1. Start VB6 and double-click on the Standard EXE icon.
2. Select File | Open Project, find the book's EFSE.VBP project, and then click on Open.
3. To display the General tab of the Project Properties dialog box, select Project | EFSE Properties.
4. For the Help File Name entry, click on the little button with the three dots to browse for the HLP file. You can also type the path and file name (in this example, C:\VBOOPEFS\VBCLSLIB\EFS.HLP).
5. For the Project Help Context ID entry, type the context number of the Help topic to associate with the class library (in this example, type "0" for the Contents topic).
6. To store any changes you made to the General tab, click on OK.
7. Open the Object Browser, select EFSE from the Libraries/Projects list, and then click on the ? button on the toolbar to display the Help topic for the class library. If the Contents topic is displayed, the Help context ID number you assigned it is correct.

Specifying A Help Topic For A Class

If the book's ActiveX component's project is open within Visual Basic, you can follow these steps to specify a Help topic for one of its classes:

1. To display the Object Browser and select EFSE from the Libraries/Projects list, press F2.
2. Select the **ClientApp** class.
3. Right-click on the **ClientApp** item to display the Object Browser's pop-up menu; then, select Properties. Visual Basic displays the Member Options dialog box.
4. For the Description entry, type a brief statement of the purpose of the class (in this example, which is shown in Figure 8.3, a description is already entered).
5. For the Help Context ID entry, type the context number of the Help topic you want to associate with the class (in this example, type "2"). This number is specified within the project (.HPJ) file used to compile the Help file.
6. To save the changes you've made, click on OK.

Implementing ActiveX Components   269

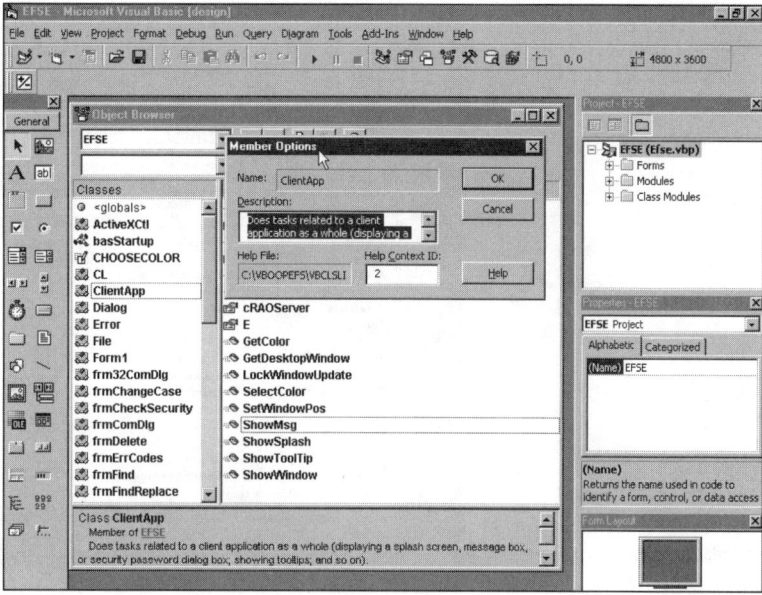

Figure 8.3
The Object Browser displaying the Member Options dialog box for the **ClientApp** class.

7. Click on the ? button on the Object Browser's toolbar to display the Help topic for the class. Also, make sure the Help context ID number you assigned it is correct.

Figure 8.3 shows the Member Options dialog box for the **ClientApp** class.

Specifying A Help Topic For A Member

If the book's ActiveX component's project is open within Visual Basic, you can follow these steps to specify a Help topic for one of its members:

1. To display the Object Browser and select EFSE from the Libraries/Projects list, press F2.

2. Select the **ClientApp** class and its **ShowMsg** member.

3. Right-click on the **ShowMsg** item to display the Object Browser's pop-up menu; then, select Properties. Visual Basic displays the Procedure Attributes dialog box.

4. For the Description entry, type a brief statement of the purpose of the member (in this example, which is shown in Figure 8.4, a description is already entered).

5. For the Help Context ID entry, type the context number of the Help topic you want to associate with the member (in this example, type "104"). This number is specified within the project (.HPJ) file used to compile the Help file.

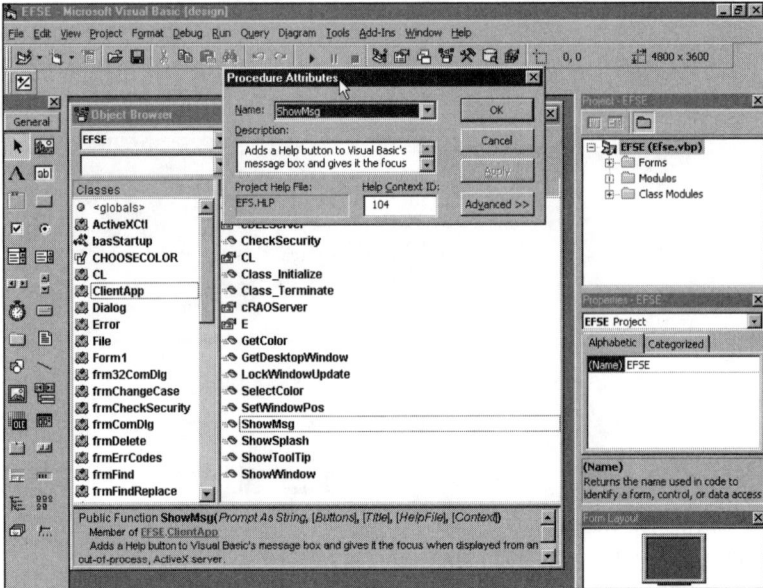

Figure 8.4
The Object Browser displaying the Procedure Attributes dialog box for the **ShowMsg** member.

6. To save the changes you've made, click on OK.
7. Click on the ? button on the Object Browser's toolbar to display the Help topic for the member. Also, make sure the Help context ID number you assigned it is correct.

Figure 8.4 shows the Procedure Attributes dialog box for the **ShowMsg** member.

Conclusion

In this chapter, we discussed some of the things you should consider when implementing ActiveX components, such as choosing the right compile option (p-code or native code). You also need to be sure to configure the compatibility settings properly, because VB6 uses these settings to monitor whether you're breaking the existing public interface of your ActiveX component and to warn you when you are about to do so. Finally, you learned some tips on creating an ActiveX component's Help file and linking a Help file to a component. Remember, if your ActiveX component is distributed with a good Help file, other developers are much more likely to reuse your ActiveX component.

Chapter 9
Object Applications: Encapsulating System Functionality

Key Topics:

- Accessing The Windows API
- Function Pointers In Visual Basic
- Encapsulating Related Functions Into A Class
- Designing A Registry/ INI Access Object
- Implementing The Registry/INI Object

So far, you've learned about objects and object-oriented design in Visual Basic. You've encountered advanced objects, ActiveX technologies, and component concepts. All these ideas are based on the object-oriented principle of *encapsulation*. You've encapsulated objects, errors, forms, controls, and components. Another important concept that encapsulation enables is *encapsulated interfaces*. Encapsulated interfaces hide and simplify interfaces to system resources, hardware, and external systems. When you hide an interface in this way, you benefit from having to implement the details of the external or system interface only once.

An example of an encapsulated interface is the Microsoft Windows printer interface. The printer interface hides the specific printer details. By defining what a printer driver must expose through the operating system, Windows makes printing to different and diverse hardware consistent.

Although Windows hides the details of printing behind the printer interface, printing is still not necessarily easy. Because Windows is a multipurpose operating system, it must make available as much information as possible to the user. This may let you access diverse hardware; however, the Windows operating system does not make it easy. Take a look at the Microsoft Windows API. The functions and procedures supplied in the Windows API let you access all the details of Windows. However, these functions and procedures are not necessarily easy to use. Encapsulated interfaces allow you to group and program Windows API calls into useful and easy-to-use objects.

Encapsulated interfaces are not limited to Windows APIs. You can create Windows device drivers and encapsulate their interfaces in objects. This lets you interface with external hardware and custom hardware.

This chapter addresses accessing Windows API calls and encapsulating Windows system services to extend your programs beyond the Visual Basic language. However, writing device drivers is a topic that's beyond the scope of this book.

Accessing The Windows API

Before you start designing and developing encapsulated interfaces for Windows APIs, you must learn how to access them from Visual Basic. The Windows API is written in the C language. You access APIs by declaring them in your Visual Basic application. This section shows how to declare and access APIs and how Visual Basic supports them.

Declaring API Functions

Before you call Windows API procedures or any other DLL procedures, you must declare them in Visual Basic. Visual Basic provides the **Declare** keyword for declaring external procedures. To access these procedures, you must specify the file or library where the procedure is located, as well as the procedure's signature.

A procedure's *signature* is simply its name, arguments, argument types, and argument mode. You'll learn more about declaring procedure signatures in the section "Passing Any Type Of Parameter" later in this chapter. Listing 9.1 shows the signature of the **Declare** statement.

Listing 9.1   The Declare statement's signature.

```
Declare Function publicname Lib "libname" [Alias "alias"] _
   [([[ByVal] variable [As type] _
   [,[ByVal] variable [As type]]…])] As Type
Declare Sub publicname Lib "libname" [Alias "alias"] _
   [([[ByVal] variable [As type] _
   [,[ByVal] variable [As type]]…])]
```

The name you call the procedure in your Visual Basic program is ***publicname***. It's also the name Visual Basic uses to identify the procedure in the API file or DLL. However, sometimes the procedure's name is not a legal Visual Basic name. For example, some procedures in the operating environment begin with an underscore. However, identifiers in Visual Basic can't begin with an underscore. This is where the

Object Applications: Encapsulating System Functionality

Alias keyword comes in. The *alias* is the true procedure name in the DLL. If the public name and the true name are the same, **Alias** is optional. Listing 9.2 shows an alias declaration for the **GetPrivateProfileString** function from the KERNEL32 library.

Listing 9.2   An Alias declaration.
```
Public Declare Function GetPrivateProfileString _
   Lib "kernel32" Alias "GetPrivateProfileStringA" _
      (ByVal lpApplicationName As String, _
       ByVal lpKeyName As Any, _
       ByVal lpDefault As String, _
       ByVal lpReturnedString As String, _
       ByVal nSize As Long, _
       ByVal lpFileName As String) As Long
```

The actual name of the **GetPrivateProfileString** function is **GetPrivateProfileStringA** in the KERNEL32 DLL. This listing also demonstrates the **Lib** clause. Visual Basic uses the **Lib** clause to specify the library in which the procedure is located. In this case, it's the KERNEL32 library.

Visual Basic has access to the entire common operating environment libraries. Table 9.1 lists these libraries.

Handling Strings

Microsoft Windows API libraries are designed to handle both Unicode and ANSI string formats. Procedures in the libraries that use string

Table 9.1   Common operating libraries.

Dynamic Link Library	Description
ADVAPI32.DLL	Advanced API services library (supports numerous APIs, including many security and Registry calls)
COMDLG32.DLL	Common dialog API library
GDI32.DLL	Graphics device interface API library
KERNEL32.DLL	Core Windows 32-bit base API support library
LZ32.DLL	32-bit compression library
MPR.DLL	Multiple provider router library
NETAPI32.DLL	32-bit network API library
SHELL32.DLL	32-bit shell API library
USER32.DLL	User interface routine library
VERSION.DLL	Version library
WINMM.DLL	Windows multimedia library
WINSPOOL.DRV	Print spooler interface (contains the print spooler API library)

> **NOTE**
>
> Only Windows NT supports Unicode. If your application is intended to run on Windows 95, you must declare your API procedures using the ANSI form.

parameters have two forms: The ANSI string form has an uppercase *A* appended to the end of the procedure name, and the Unicode version has an uppercase *W* (for wide) appended to the end of the procedure name.

To access procedures with the desired string format, declare an alias for the procedure and select the correct procedure name from the library. Listing 9.3 shows the ANSI version of the **WritePrivateProfileString** function.

Listing 9.3 An ANSI alias.
```
Public Declare Function WritePrivateProfileString _
   Lib "kernel32" Alias "WritePrivateProfileStringA" _
      (ByVal lpApplicationName As String, _
      ByVal lpKeyName As Any, _
      ByVal lpString As Any, _
      ByVal lpFileName As String) As Long
```

The real name of the ANSI version of the **WritePrivateProfileString** function is **WritePrivateProfileStringA**. This is why you add an **Alias** clause to a declaration.

Handling API Parameters

The Windows API libraries are written in the C programming language. C uses a different calling convention for parameters than Visual Basic. Because of the differences, you must know how to send parameters to API routines.

ByVal Vs. ByRef

Chapter 3 discusses **ByVal** and **ByRef** for parameters in Visual Basic. The same basic rules apply when passing parameters to library procedures. **ByVal** passes the actual value of the parameter to the procedure; **ByRef** passes a 32-bit pointer to the parameter's value.

Visual Basic passes parameters as **ByRef** by default. Although you don't need the **ByRef** keyword in a **Declare** statement, it's a good idea to include it so you know how the parameter is passed.

When you call a procedure from a DLL, you can use the **ByRef** or **ByVal** statement in the call. Listing 9.4 shows a procedure from a DLL with the **ByVal** keyword.

Listing 9.4 Using ByVal in a procedure call.
```
Status = WritePrivateProfileString (ByVal theApplication, _
                                    ByVal theKey, _
                                    ByVal theValue, _
                                    ByVal theFileName)
```

When you use a library written in C, you should keep in mind that C passes all values (except for arrays) by value. When you use a library written in any other language, be sure to check how the language passes parameters so you can declare the procedures correctly.

Strings

Passing strings to a DLL is a special case of **ByRef** versus **ByVal**. When you pass a string using **ByVal**, you're actually passing a reference to the first character in the string. When you pass a string using **ByRef**, you're passing a reference that contains a reference to the first character in the string.

All procedures in the Windows API use **LPSTR** (Long Pointer to STRing) string types for strings. **LPSTR** is the standard null-terminated C string type. Visual Basic uses the Automation-defined string type called **BSTR**. **BSTR** strings are Unicode and contain a header that specifies the length of the string. This way, the string may contain embedded null characters.

To pass a **BSTR** string to a procedure that recognizes **BSTR**, pass the parameter using **ByRef**. This passes a reference to the header portion of the **BSTR** to the procedure. Because it knows the **BSTR** format, it can read and write the string.

In general, however, you'll pass string parameters using **ByVal**. When you pass a **BSTR** string using **ByVal**, it passes a reference to the first character in the string. This is what a C procedure expects. If the procedure expects a pointer to a **LPSTR** string, pass it using **ByRef**.

If the procedure you call modifies a string parameter, make sure the string is long enough to hold the returning value. If you don't pass a string that's large enough for the return value, the procedure will write past the end of the string and corrupt the data. One way to make sure the string is long enough is to fill it with null characters. Listing 9.5 shows how to use the **String** function to fill a string.

Listing 9.5 Using the String function.
```
theValue = String$(255, vbNullChar)
GetPrivateProfileString theApplication, _
                        theKey, _
                        "", _
                        theValue, _
                        Len(theValue), _
                        theFileName
```

Arrays

Another special case when dealing with DLL procedures is passing arrays. You can pass a single array element as a parameter by simply referencing the array element. For example, you can store a list of items in a profile by storing them in an array and passing each individual item (see Listing 9.6).

Listing 9.6 Passing an array element to a DLL procedure.
```
Dim theValues(10) As String
Dim iKey As Long
'Load theValues with any string values
For iKey = LBound(theValues) To UBound(theValues)
   WritePrivateProfileString theApplication, _
                             iKey, _
                             theValues(iKey), _
                             theFileName
Next
```

When you pass an array element, Visual Basic passes it as the base type of the array. In Listing 9.6, the values are passed as **String**.

You can also pass entire arrays to a DLL procedure. The method you use depends on how the procedure is implemented. If the procedure accepts Automation data types and **SAFEARRAY** data types, you pass the array the same way as in Visual Basic, using the array name followed by empty parentheses. Consult the documentation of the DLL procedure to determine if it accepts Automation data types and **SAFEARRAY**s.

If the DLL procedure doesn't accept **SAFEARRAY**s, you can still pass entire numeric arrays. You pass the first array element by reference to the DLL procedure. Because numeric arrays are laid out sequentially in memory, the DLL procedure receives the address of the first element and has access to the remaining array elements.

Passing Any Type Of Parameter

Some Windows API parameters can accept more than one type of data for a single parameter. To handle this, Visual Basic supplies the **As Any** parameter declaration. **As Any** removes any type restrictions or type checking for the parameter. **lpKeyName** and **lpString**, the second and third parameters from Listing 9.3, show the **As Any** parameter declaration.

Use **As Any** carefully. When you remove the type checking, you add a level of risk to your application, because you increase the chance you'll pass the wrong type of data to the procedure. If you pass the wrong type of data to a library procedure, you can't be sure how it will respond. It may crash your application, return improper results, or simply hang.

One last tidbit about **As Any**: When you declare a parameter with **As Any**, Visual Basic assumes the parameter is passed using **ByRef**. To pass the parameter using **ByVal**, use the **ByVal** keyword in the call, as was done earlier in Listing 9.4.

Function Pointers

Many Windows API procedures require you to pass a function pointer as a parameter. A *function pointer* is the address of a user-defined function—one you create in Visual Basic. The function signature must conform to a specific format, as defined by the Windows API procedure. The **Enum** functions of the Windows API are examples of procedures that require a function pointer as a parameter. These function pointers are also referred to as *callback functions*.

Visual Basic provides the **AddressOf** keyword for passing the address of a user-defined function to DLL procedures. Listing 9.7 demonstrates the use of the **AddressOf** keyword and a callback function.

Listing 9.7   Passing a function pointer.
```
Status = EnumFonts(thehDC, _
                   thelpsz, _
                   AddressOf ProcessFonts, _
                   thelParam)
```

This listing enumerates the available fonts. One possible use of the **ProcessFonts** function might be to filter for a specific font; if it's found, you know the font is available.

The **AddressOf** keyword has certain rules you must follow:

- The function you pass with the **AddressOf** keyword must be in a standard Visual Basic module (BAS file). It cannot be in a form or class module.
- **AddressOf** can only be used immediately preceding the name of a user-defined function or subprocedure.
- You can't use **AddressOf** with external functions declared with the **Declare** statement or with functions from a type library.
- You can't pass function pointers to other Visual Basic procedures. Visual Basic converts them to **Long** data types. No support exists for Visual Basic to call the passed procedure.
- In break mode, Visual Basic simply returns 0 to the caller of an **AddressOf** function. This is a safety precaution Visual Basic takes because it can't call **AddressOf** in break mode.

Visual Basic passes function pointers as **Long**. This means you can pass them to parameters of the **Long** or **As Any** type.

Sometimes you need to store the pointer in a structure or variable. The **WndClass** structure, used with the Windows API, has a function pointer member. To use the structure, you must put the pointer in the structure and not pass it as a parameter. Because Visual Basic passes the function pointer as a **Long**, you can create a conversion routine to return the **Long** value of the pointer. Listing 9.8 shows a conversion function that returns the pointer value as a **Long**.

Listing 9.8   Converting a function pointer to a Long value.

```
Function FunctionPtrToLong(ByVal FunctionAddress As Long) _
            As Long
    FunctionPtrToLong = FunctionAddress
End Function
```

As is the case with any sufficiently cool technology, there are risks and limitations when using function pointers:

- *Containing errors within the callback procedure*—Don't allow errors in a callback procedure to propagate to the calling procedure. This may crash your system. Use the **On Error Resume Next** statement, or you can handle any errors before returning from the callback procedure.
- *Debugging*—In debug mode, Visual Basic ignores any breaks or steps in a callback procedure. Resets are also prohibited while in a callback procedure.

- *Passing a function with the wrong signature*—This can have unpredictable results. Passing a function with the wrong types or number of arguments can make your application fail or provide erroneous results.
- *Thunking*—This is the term Microsoft uses to describe the relocatable code mechanism in Windows. If you're in break mode and you delete a callback function and then add it back, Visual Basic may lose track of the thunk for the function. Simply avoid deleting and adding callbacks in break mode.

Creating A Registry/INI Object

The previous section discussed the mechanics of accessing the Windows API and DLL procedures. Here, you'll learn how to encapsulate related Windows API and Visual Basic functionality into reusable objects.

Some of the goals of object-oriented programming include producing reusable code, leveraging the work you do on one project to make future development faster, and making your code less error prone. Object-oriented programming does this by encapsulating similar and cooperating operations and data into reusable objects. This section discusses how to design and implement a Registry/initialization (INI) file object.

You may ask, why mess with INI files? Didn't the Registry replace them? In one sense, yes, the Registry is the preferred place to put program settings. The Registry is fast and easily managed. INI files, on the other hand, have their own advantages. INI files are easy for your users to understand: They can look at them as well as print them out. INI files provide you with a valuable resource for storing and recording information. The INI structure is flexible—you don't have to invent a structure for every program you write. However, some disadvantages of INI files are that your users can read and change them easily, the structure is flat, and large INI files are slow.

INI Files

INI files have a common structure. All INI files are based on sections, keys, and values. An INI file can contain as many sections as you need. Sections group keys together and can contain any number of keys. A key is associated with a value. Listing 9.9 shows a sample INI file.

Listing 9.9 A sample INI file.
```
[Section One]
Key One=1
Key Two=A Key
Key3=5

[Section2]
Key One=2
Key 2=3
AnotherKey=Value
```

Section names, key names, and values can be any combination of letters, characters, and spaces. Values may also be numeric.

You can use this flexibility to create any combination of data. For example, a key can be associated with more than one value. Listing 9.10 shows how to associate a list of values with a key.

Listing 9.10 An INI key with more than one value.
```
[Example]
MultiKey=1,2,3,4
```

Here, the **MultiKey** key is associated with four values.

You are limited, however. You can only store ASCII characters in an INI file, and you cannot store other forms of data, such as binary or other files.

The Registry

Windows uses the Registry for many purposes: storing keys to shared components, Windows system settings, program settings, local settings, and so on.

The Registry has a hierarchical structure, similar to a file structure. Instead of having directories, subdirectories, and files, though, the Registry has keys, subkeys, and values. The Registry has six predefined keys:

- HKEY_CLASSES_ROOT
- HKEY_CURRENT_USER
- HKEY_LOCAL_MACHINE
- HKEY_USERS
- HKEY_CURRENT_CONFIG
- HKEY_DYN_DATA

Object Applications: Encapsulating System Functionality

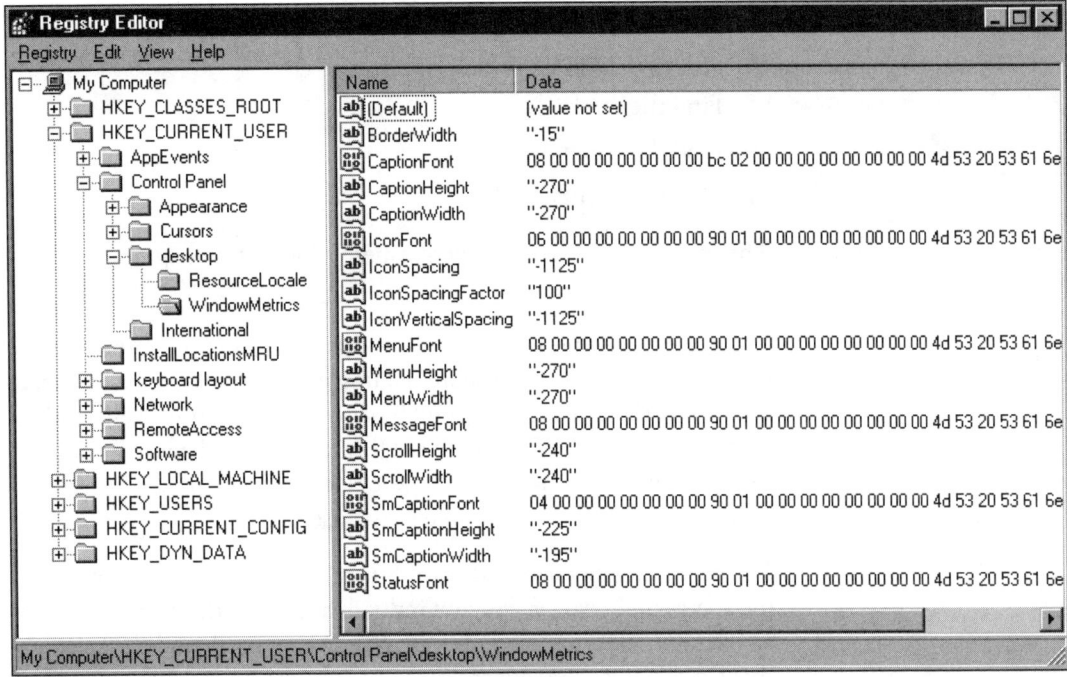

Figure 9.1
The Registry's HKEY_CURRENT_USER key.

Of these keys, the HKEY_CURRENT_USER is the one most used for application programming. Figure 9.1 shows the HKEY_CURRENT_USER key in the Registry.

Notice the directory-like structure. These are the subkeys of HKEY_CURRENT_USER. The figure shows the Control Panel\Desktop\WindowMetrics subkeys and the values associated with the WindowMetrics subkey. The Registry uses rules for writing keys that are similar to the ones used by INI files. Keys can be any combination of characters and numbers.

The Registry is a complicated and powerful resource in Windows, and further discussion is beyond the scope of this book. Read the Windows documentation if you want to gain a full understanding and appreciation of the Windows Registry.

Designing The Object

To design the Registry/INI object, you'll employ the design principles introduced in Chapter 2, which described the following steps in designing objects:

1. Describe the problem.
2. Find candidate objects.

3. Find relationships.
4. Find the properties.
5. Find the methods.
6. Find the parameters.
7. Find the events.

The following sections follow this methodology for designing the Registry/INI object.

Because of the similarities the Registry and INI files share—that is, both are hierarchical and share naming conventions—you can create one object that encapsulates and hides the complexities and details of manipulating them. This type of object lets you implement a common interface and then instantiate the object to point to the correct resource. The details are invisible to the user.

You begin by generating a description of the object. This is not a complete system, however. For any individual object, the same principles apply. Write down what you're trying to accomplish and then analyze this list to create the object.

Describe The Problem

You begin this process by creating a problem statement. The statement sets the goals and limitations of the task as well as defines the problem domain.

We begin with the problem statement. You need to access the Windows 95/98 or NT Registry or initialization (INI) files and allow users to add, retrieve, update, and delete individual values, lists of values, and multiple values at the same time. For INI files, the user should also be allowed to retrieve the available sections in the file and the available keys in a section. For the Registry, the user needs to list the subkeys of a key as well as its values.

Next, we create a design description. The Registry/INI object will enable a programmer to initialize the object once, designating the appropriate resource (a base Registry subkey or initialization file name). It will also allow a programmer to add sections, add keys, assign values to the keys, and change values assigned to keys. The object will allow the programmer to delete sections and keys. The object will also let a programmer retrieve the value assigned to a key. The Registry/INI object will let the programmer add and retrieve named lists of values.

Object Applications: Encapsulating System Functionality

Figure 9.2
The class card for the **RegIni** class.

Finally, the object will let programmers pass in a set of keys for a section and retrieve or set the keys' values.

Find Candidate Objects

First, you look for the candidate objects. However, because this is an object description, the desired product is a single object. Therefore, you just have to give the object a name. Because you're creating an object to manipulate the Registry and INI files, choose RegIni. Create a class card for the **RegIni** class, as shown in Figure 9.2.

Creating a class card for a single object seems like a little too much. However, you'll discover in Chapter 10 that having a complete class card is very helpful when using a class in a project.

Find Relationships

Because you only have one object, there are no relationships to find. Continue to the next step.

Find The Properties

The next step is to find the properties. The process says to go back to the description and examine the adjectives, nouns, and noun phrases. Here are some possible properties:

- Registry
- File name
- Section
- Key
- Value
- Subkey
- Base key

There are at least two ways to design the object. First, you could adopt the "set and act" strategy, where you require users to *set* property values and then call methods to *act* on the properties. The second approach is to use parameters on methods and use properties to represent the results of the last action the user took and to supply some status.

For the **RegIni** object, choose the second method. This translates to very few properties, because the object encapsulates a set of services. Keep the properties shown in Table 9.2.

284 Chapter 9

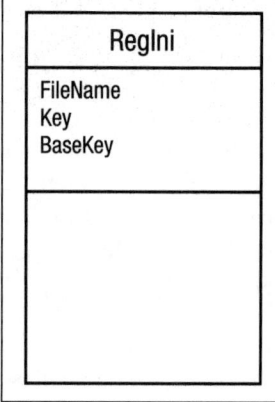

Figure 9.3
The class card for the **RegIni** class with properties.

Table 9.2   RegIni properties.

Property	Description
FileName	The INI file the object is currently accessing (read-only)
Key	The last key the object accessed (read-only)
BaseKey	The base key the object is accessing in the Registry (read-only)

At this point, you might notice that an INI section is just a key without a value. Therefore, from now on, you can simplify the terminology for the **RegIni** object. Use keys and values. Figure 9.3 shows the updated class card for the **RegIni** class.

Find The Methods

Finding the methods involves examining the description for action words (or verbs). Here are some possible methods:

- Add
- Retrieve
- Update
- Delete
- List
- Initialize
- Designate
- Assign
- Change
- Pass
- Set

This is a pretty extensive list. By following the recommendations in Chapter 2, you can narrow the list down to the methods shown in Table 9.3.

This may seem like a short list of methods for a Registry/INI object; however, as you'll soon discover, it will do quite nicely for most of your Registry and INI activities. Add these methods to the class card. Figure 9.4 shows the **RegIni** class card with both the properties and methods.

Figure 9.4
The class card for the **RegIni** class with properties and methods.

Find The Parameters

The parameters are the key to the design—they are the details. Here's where you'll do most of your thinking and discovering. Begin by looking at the nouns associated with your defined methods.

Table 9.3 RegIni methods.

Method	Description
Add	Adds a key.
Value	We decided earlier to use parameters to retrieve the values, so you need to convert the retrieve method into a value function.
SetValue	Updates a value.
Delete	Deletes a key.
List	Returns a list of values or keys.
Init_Class	Initializes the class.

The **Add** method adds a key to the object; therefore, the **Add** method needs a **Key** property. But wait, aren't the keys for the Registry and INI files different? Yes, this is true. However, because you can use any combination of characters for section names in an INI file, you can make the backslash character the delimiter between keys and subkeys. For example, Section One\Key One references the **Key One** key for the **Section One** section from Listing 9.9. This allows you to use one access scheme for both the Registry and INI files.

The **Value** method is really a property with a parameter. To access a value, the user must supply the key; therefore, the **Value** function has a **Key** parameter. Because it's a function and the Registry and INI file can hold multiple values for a key, you must provide the appropriate type for the return value. Choose a **Variant** so you can handle both strings and numbers.

SetValue updates or adds a value to a key. The **SetValue** method has both **Key** and **Value** parameters.

Delete removes a key from the object. Therefore, the only parameter you need is the **Key** to delete.

List returns a list of keys or values. For keys with multiple values or subkeys, the list returns the values or subkeys. This means **List** needs a **Key** parameter. You also need to retrieve the sections of an INI file. This means the object must return the subkeys or sections of the INI file. Therefore, make the **Key** parameter optional. When the **Key** parameter is missing, the list of sections in an INI file or the subkeys of the base key for the object are returned. (You'll read more about the base key later in this chapter.)

As mentioned in Chapter 5, an object must be instantiated and initialized. The **RegIni** object's **Init_Class** method must handle two possible initializations: one for the Registry and one for an INI file. This means you need two optional parameters: a **BaseKey** parameter for initializing

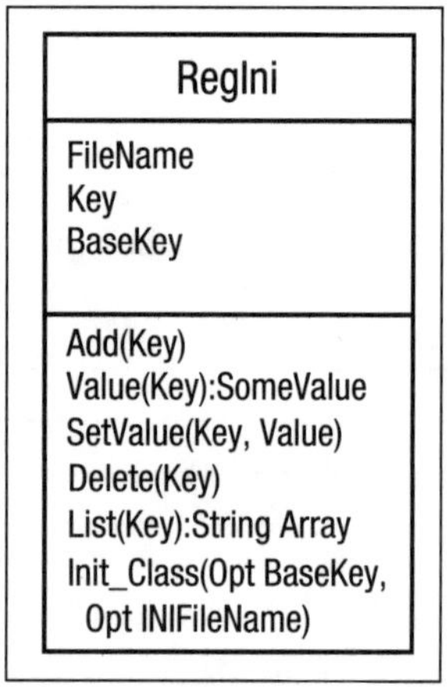

RegIni

FileName
Key
BaseKey

Add(Key)
Value(Key):SomeValue
SetValue(Key, Value)
Delete(Key)
List(Key):String Array
Init_Class(Opt BaseKey,
   Opt INIFileName)

Figure 9.5
The class card for the **RegIni** class with properties, methods, and parameters.

a Registry object and an **INIFileName** parameter for initializing an INI object.

Once again, you need to update the **RegIni** class card. Figure 9.5 shows the **RegIni** class card with the parameters.

If you happen to have too many parameters, you can translate the methods to code so you can get a feel for their complexity. Listing 9.11 shows the declarations for the **RegIni** class.

Listing 9.11   The RegIni methods.
```
Public Sub Add(Key As String)

End Sub
Public Function Value(Key As String) As Variant

End Function
Public Sub SetValue(Key As String, _
                   Value As Variant)

End Sub
Public Sub Delete(Key As String)

End Sub
Public Function List(Key As String) As String()

End Function
Public Sub Init_Class(Optional BaseKey, _
                     Optional INIFileName)

End Sub
```

Find The Events
Examining the description, you don't find any events.

Finishing The Design

The next step in the design is the Visual Basic specification. However, you need some more information first. The **RegIni** class encapsulates system-level functionality. Before moving on to the specification, you need to explore the Windows API to determine how to access the necessary system resources.

Resources For Accessing The Registry
One of the things you need to do for this object is to identify how to access the Registry. Visual Basic provides two functions for getting and

Object Applications: Encapsulating System Functionality

setting values in the Registry: **GetSetting** and **SaveSetting**. These functions are good for simple program settings; however, the **RegIni** object needs to access the Registry at a more complex level.

The Windows API defines 25 procedures for manipulating the Registry. Table 9.4 lists and briefly describes the Windows API Registry access procedures.

Not all these procedures are needed to implement the **RegIni** class. However, this list should give you a feel for the robustness and power of the Registry. The "Specification" section of this chapter details the necessary procedures for the **RegIni** class.

Table 9.4 The Windows API for manipulating the Registry.

Procedure	Description
RegCloseKey	Closes a key in the Registry.
RegConnectRegistry	Connects your application to the Registry on a remote system.
RegCreateKey	Creates a new subkey or opens an existing subkey under the specified key.
RegCreateKeyEx	A more robust and preferred way under Win32 to create a new key. It also opens an existing key if specified.
RegDeleteKey	Deletes a subkey under the specified key.
RegDeleteValue	Deletes a value under the specified key.
RegEnumKey	Lets you retrieve the subkeys under a specified key.
RegEnumKeyEx	A more robust and preferred way under Win32 to retrieve keys.
RegEnumValue	Lets you retrieve the values under a specified key.
RegFlushKey	Writes changes to keys and values to disk.
RegGetKeySecurity	Retrieves security information for keys.
RegLoadKey	Loads registration information from a file. The registration information is written to the file by the **RegSaveKey** function.
RegNotifyChangeKeyValue	The callback mechanism supplied to notify you when a Registry key or value changes.
RegOpenKey	Opens an existing key.
RegOpenKeyEx	Same as **RegOpenKey**. Preferred method for Win32.
RegQueryInfoKey	Returns information about a key.
RegQueryValue	Returns the default value for the specified key. The default value is the unnamed value.
RegQueryValueEx	Same as **RegQueryValue**.
RegReplaceKey	Replaces information with information from a file. This procedure reads the information, makes a backup of the current Registry information, and then saves the new information.
RegRestoreKey	Restores information from disk.
RegSaveKey	Saves a key and its subkeys to a disk file.
RegSaveKeySecurity	Assigns new security information for the specified key.
RegSetValue	Assigns the default value for the specified key.
RegSetValueEx	Same as **RegSetValue**.
RegUnLoadKey	Unloads the specified key and its subkeys.

Table 9.5 The Windows API for manipulating INI files.

Procedure	Description
GetPrivateProfileInt	Reads an integer from the specified section and key.
GetPrivateProfileSection	Reads data for the entire specified section.
GetPrivateProfileString	Reads a string from the specified section and key.
GetProfileInt	Reads an integer from the WIN.INI file.
GetProfileSection	Reads data for the entire specified section of the WIN.INI file.
GetProfileString	Reads a string from the specified section and key of the WIN.INI file.
WritePrivateProfileSection	Writes data for the entire specified section.
WritePrivateProfileString	Writes a string to the specified section and key.
WriteProfileSection	Writes data for the entire specified section of the WIN.INI file.
WriteProfileString	Writes a string to the specified section and key of the WIN.INI file.

Resources For Accessing INI Files

As is the case with the Registry, Windows provides access procedures for initialization files. Table 9.5 lists the INI file functions from the Windows API.

Again, not all these procedures are needed to implement or specify the **RegIni** object. The next section identifies the necessary INI procedures for the **RegIni** object.

Specification

The full specification for **RegIni** includes the properties, methods, events, and the outside (Windows API) procedures needed for the object. Listing 9.12 shows the full specification for the **RegIni** object.

Listing 9.12 The RegIni specification.

```
'RegIni Class
Option Explicit

'External Declarations
'Registry Access Procedures
Private Const REG_SZ = 1
Private Const HKEY_CURRENT_USER = &H80000001
```

Object Applications: Encapsulating System Functionality

```
Private Declare _
    Function RegCloseKey Lib "advapi32.dll" _
        (ByVal hKey As Long) As Long
Private Declare _
    Function RegCreateKey Lib "advapi32.dll" _
        Alias "RegCreateKeyA" _
            (ByVal hKey As Long, _
             ByVal lpSubKey As String, _
             phkResult As Long) As Long
Private Declare _
    Function RegDeleteKey Lib "advapi32.dll" _
        Alias "RegDeleteKeyA" _
            (ByVal hKey As Long, _
             ByVal lpSubKey As String) As Long
Private Declare _
    Function RegDeleteValue Lib "advapi32.dll" _
        Alias "RegDeleteValueA" _
            (ByVal hKey As Long, _
             ByVal lpValueName As String) As Long
Private Declare _
    Function RegEnumKey Lib "advapi32.dll" _
        Alias "RegEnumKeyA" _
            (ByVal hKey As Long, _
             ByVal dwIndex As Long, _
             ByVal lpName As String, _
             ByVal cbName As Long) As Long
Private Declare _
    Function RegEnumValue Lib "advapi32.dll" _
        Alias "RegEnumValueA" _
            (ByVal hKey As Long, _
             ByVal dwIndex As Long, _
             ByVal lpValueName As String, _
             lpcbValueName As Long, _
             ByVal lpReserved As Long, _
             lpType As Long, _
             lpData As Byte, _
             lpcbData As Long) As Long
Private Declare _
    Function RegOpenKey Lib "advapi32.dll" _
        Alias "RegOpenKeyA" _
            (ByVal hKey As Long, _
             ByVal lpSubKey As String, _
             phkResult As Long) As Long
Private Declare _
    Function RegQueryValue Lib "advapi32.dll" _
        Alias "RegQueryValueA" _
```

```
            (ByVal hKey As Long, _
            ByVal lpSubKey As String, _
            ByVal lpValue As String, _
            lpcbValue As Long) As Long
    Private Declare _
        Function RegSetValue Lib "advapi32.dll" _
            Alias "RegSctValueA" _
            (ByVal hKey As Long, _
            ByVal lpSubKey As String, _
            ByVal dwType As Long, _
            ByVal lpData As String, _
            ByVal cbData As Long) As Long

    'INI Access Procedures
    Private Declare _
        Function GetPrivateProfileInt Lib "kernel32" _
            Alias "GetPrivateProfileIntA" _
            (ByVal lpApplicationName As String, _
            ByVal lpKeyName As String, _
            ByVal nDefault As Long, _
            ByVal lpFileName As String) As Long
    Private Declare _
        Function GetPrivateProfileSection Lib "kernel32" _
            Alias "GetPrivateProfileSectionA" _
            (ByVal lpAppName As String, _
            ByVal lpReturnedString As String, _
            ByVal nSize As Long, _
            ByVal lpFileName As String) As Long
    Private Declare _
        Function GetPrivateProfileString Lib "kernel32" _
            Alias "GetPrivateProfileStringA" _
            (ByVal lpApplicationName As String, _
            ByVal lpKeyName As Any, _
            ByVal lpDefault As String, _
            ByVal lpReturnedString As String, _
            ByVal nSize As Long, _
            ByVal lpFileName As String) As Long
    Private Declare _
        Function WritePrivateProfileSection Lib "kernel32" _
            Alias "WritePrivateProfileSectionA" _
            (ByVal lpAppName As String, _
            ByVal lpString As String, _
            ByVal lpFileName As String) As Long
    Private Declare _
        Function WritePrivateProfileString Lib "kernel32" _
            Alias "WritePrivateProfileStringA" _
```

```
                (ByVal lpApplicationName As String, _
                 ByVal lpKeyName As Any, _
                 ByVal lpString As Any, _
                 ByVal lpFileName As String) As Long

Public Property Get Filename() As String
'The INI file the object is currently accessing. (Read-only)

End Property
Public Property Get Key()
'The last key the object accessed. (Read-only)

End Property
Public Property Get BaseKey()
'The base key the object is accessing in the Registry.
'(Read-only)

End Property
Public Sub Add(Key As String)
'Key format "key\key\key"

End Sub
Public Function Value(Key As String) As Variant
'Key format "key\key\key"

End Function
Public Sub SetValue(Key As String, _
                    Value As Variant)
'Key format "key\key\key"

End Sub
Public Sub Delete(Key As String)
'Key format "key\key\key"

End Sub
Public Function List(Key As String) As String()
'Key format "key\key\key"

End Function
Public Sub Init_Class(Optional BaseKey, _
                      Optional INIFileName)
'BaseKey format "key\key\key"

End Sub
```

Listing 9.12 also contains the next stage of development: code-level design. Notice the use of comments to clearly show how you intend to handle keys. This is important information to capture as you move to coding the object.

Coding

Once the public interfaces are defined, it's time to move to development and coding. You've been thinking about how to implement the various parts of the object; now, it's time to do it.

Initialization

Chapter 5 described object initialization in detail. The **RegIni** class uses a multiple interface for initialization. The **Init_Class** method has two optional parameters. To initialize the class, the user must supply one and only one of the parameters. If the class is initialized with no parameters or both parameters, an error is raised.

You also want to force programmers to call the **Init_Class** method. (Chapter 5 shows how to protect the class and force programmers to call the **Init_Class** method.) Listing 9.13 shows the complete **Init_Class** method.

Listing 9.13   The Init_Class method for the RegIni class.

```
Public Sub Init_Class(Optional BaseKey, _
                      Optional INIFileName)
'BaseKey format "key\key\key"

    Dim BaseKeySupplied As Boolean
    Dim INIFileNameSupplied As Boolean
    Static Initialized As Boolean

    If Not Initialized Then
        mObjectType = Uninitialized
        BaseKeySupplied = Not IsMissing(BaseKey)
        INIFileNameSupplied = Not (IsMissing(INIFileName))

        If Not BaseKeySupplied And Not INIFileNameSupplied Then
            'No parameter supplied, raise an error
            Err.Raise Number:=vbObjectError + 513, _
                    Source:="RegIni Class", _
                    Description:= _
                      "No parameter supplied on initialization"
        End If
```

```
        If BaseKeySupplied And INIFileNameSupplied Then
            'Both parameters supplied, raise an error
            Err.Raise Number:=vbObjectError + 514, _
                    Source:="RegIni Class", _
                    Description:= _
                        "Too many parameters supplied " & _
                                "on initialization. " & _
                                "Only one is allowed."
            Exit Sub
        End If

        If BaseKeySupplied Then
            If BaseKey = "" Then
                'Invalid Base Key
                Err.Raise Number:=vbObjectError + 515, _
                        Source:="RegIni Class", _
                        Description:="Invalid Base Key"
                Exit Sub
            End If
            'Set the type of object
            mObjectType = Registry
            mBaseKey = BaseKey

        Else
            'To get this far, INIFileName must be supplied
            If INIFileName = "" Then
                'Invalid INIFileName
                Err.Raise Number:=vbObjectError + 516, _
                        Source:="RegIni Class", _
                        Description:="Invalid INIFileName"
                Exit Sub
            End If
            'Set the type of object
            mObjectType = INI
            mFilename = INIFileName
        End If

    End If
End Sub
```

To support the **Init_Class** method, you need to make the following class-level declarations:

```
Private Enum ClassType
    Uninitialized
    Registry
    INI
```

```
End Enum
Private mBaseKey As String
Private mFilename As String
Private mObjectType As ClassType
```

The initialization method checks for a valid initialization. It verifies whether the correct parameter combination is passed. If the initialization is valid, the **Init_Class** method sets the appropriate private state variables.

Notice the **mObjectType** variable and the **ClassType** enumeration. This variable is used in the rest of the methods and properties to determine whether the class is initialized and which resource (the Registry or INI file) the object encapsulates. The declaration order of the **ClassType** enumeration is important. Visual Basic initializes variables to 0, which is the corresponding value for the **Uninitialized** value of the enumeration. If **mObjectType** isn't set, the default value is **Uninitialized**. Listing 9.14 shows how the class uses **mObjectType** to force programmers to use the object properly.

Listing 9.14   The FileName and BaseKey properties for the RegIni class.

```
Private Const ObjectNotInitializedError = vbObjectError + 550

Public Property Get Filename() As String
'The INI file the object is currently accessing. (Read-only)

    If mObjectType = INI Then
       Filename = mFilename

    Else
       Err.Raise Number:=ObjectNotInitializedError, _
                 Source:="RegIni Class", _
                 Description:="Object not initialized " & _
                 "or not initialized properly."
    End If

End Property

Public Property Get BaseKey()
'The base key the object is accessing in the Registry.
' (Read-only)
    If mObjectType = Registry Then
       BaseKey = mBaseKey
```

Object Applications: Encapsulating System Functionality

```
      Else
         Err.Raise Number:=ObjectNotInitializedError, _
                   Source:="RegIni Class", _
                   Description:="Object not initialized " & _
                   "or not initialized properly."
      End If

End Property
```

If either of these properties is referenced before the object is initialized, or if the wrong one is referenced out of context, the property raises an error. These types of errors are programming errors and must be handled by the programmer.

Once you've handled initialization and forced programmers to use **Init_Class**, you must implement the rest of the class. The next sections address some of the more advanced aspects of the **RegIni** class.

Handling Keys

One of the small details decided on earlier was how to handle keys. The key format looks like this:

`Key\SubKeyOne\SubKeyTwo`

For an INI file, you need to break the string apart into a section and a key. We decided to use the key as it was, taking the last subkey as the key, and everything else as the section. This means, in the previous example, that the section equals **Key\SubKeyOne** and the key equals **SubKeyTwo**. One way to process the keys is to write a procedure that breaks a key into the section and the key. Listing 9.15 shows a procedure, **ProcessINIKey**, that does this processing.

Listing 9.15 The ProcessINIKey private subprocedure.

```
Private Sub ProcessINIKey(ByVal theKey As String, _
                         Section As String, _
                         Key As String)
   Dim aDelimiter As Long

   aDelimiter = InStr(theKey, theDelimiter)
   Section = ""
   While aDelimiter <> 0
      Section = Section & Left$(theKey, aDelimiter)
      theKey = Right$(theKey, Len(theKey) - aDelimiter)
      aDelimiter = InStr(theKey, theDelimiter)
   Wend
   Key = theKey
```

```
    On Error Resume Next
    Section = Left$(Section, Len(Section) - 1)
End Sub
```

The **ProcessINIKey** uses a class-level constant, **theDelimiter**, to hold the backslash character you're looking for. This way, if you decide to change the format of your keys, it's easy to do so.

Writing Values To The Registry Or INI File: *SetValue*

The most basic method you must perform is to write values to the Registry or INI file. The **RegIni** class has a method for writing to the resource: **SetValue**.

The **SetValue** method must first determine which resource—the Registry or the INI file—the object encapsulates. After it determines the resource, it can call the appropriate Windows API procedure. Listing 9.16 shows the **SetValue** method for the **RegIni** class.

Listing 9.16   The SetValue method.

```
Public Sub SetValue(Key As String, _
                    Value As String)
'Key format "key\key\key"
Dim theSection As String
Dim theKey As String

    If mObjectType = INI Then
        ProcessINIKey Key, theSection, theKey
        WritePrivateProfileString theSection, _
                            theKey, _
                            Value, _
                            Filename

    ElseIf mObjectType = Registry Then
        RegSetValue HKEY_CURRENT_USER, _
                    BaseKey & "\" & Key, _
                    REG_SZ, _
                    Value, _
                    Len(Value) + 1

    Else
        Err.Raise Number:=ObjectNotInitializedError, _
                    Source:="RegIni Class", _
                    Description:="Object not initialized " & _
                    "or not initialized properly."

    End If

End Sub
```

Object Applications: Encapsulating System Functionality

The first **If** statement checks for an INI resource. If the object is an INI object, the method calls **ProcessINIKey** to determine the section and key to write the data. Once it determines the section and key, it calls the **WritePrivateProfileString** Windows API procedure to actually write the value to the file.

The next section determines whether the object is a Registry object. If it is a Registry object, the **RegSetValue** Windows API procedure is called to write the value to the Registry. Notice the second parameter in this call—here's where you specify the base key and the key passed in by the user. This is what allows you to restrict the object's use. This arrangement protects the rest of the Registry from poorly formed keys.

The third section, the **Else** clause, is your standard error for an uninitialized class—again, forcing the programmer to initialize the class before use. This guarantees that **INIFileName** or **BaseKey** has a value.

Removing A Key From An INI File

One of the more tricky things to figure out about INI files is how to remove keys from them. For the Registry, the Windows API defines the **RegDeleteKey** procedure; however, the Windows API doesn't provide any procedures for deleting keys from an INI file.

It can be done, though. **WritePrivateProfileString** lets you accomplish this task by passing a null value for the **lpString** parameter. Listing 9.17 shows the **Delete** method of the **RegIni** class, which deletes a key in an INI file.

Listing 9.17   The Delete method.

```
Public Sub Delete(Key As String)
'Deletes a key/section from the INI file or Registry
'Key format "key\key\key"
'
'   To remove a section from an INI file, omit the final key
'       and leave the final slash: "key\key\".

Dim theSection As String
Dim theKey As String

    If mObjectType = INI Then
        ProcessINIKey Key, theSection, theKey
        If Len(Trim$(theKey)) <> 0 Then
            WritePrivateProfileString theSection, _
                                      theKey, _
                                      vbNullString, _
                                      Filename
```

```
            Else
                'No key specified, delete section
                WritePrivateProfileSection theSection, _
                                           vbNullString, _
                                           Filename
            End If

        ElseIf mObjectType = Registry Then
            RegDeleteKey HKEY_CURRENT_USER, _
                         BaseKey & "\" & Key

        Else
            Err.Raise Number:=ObjectNotInitializedError, _
                      Source:="RegIni Class", _
                      Description:="Object not initialized " & _
                      "or not initialized properly."

        End If

End Sub
```

This listing shows how to delete keys from the Registry and an INI file. However, the **RegIni** class only has one **Delete** function. Notice that the INI section of the code detects whether you want to delete an entire INI section. If you do not specify a key, Visual Basic will interpret it as deleting a section. If you pass in a key value like this

```
Key\SubKey\
```

the code will delete the section from the INI. Document this behavior in the procedure header.

Further Exercises

The earlier listings show how you can encapsulate the Registry and INI Windows API procedures to create an easy-to-use class. The full code for the entire object is left to you, the reader, to complete. We strongly urge you to take on this task; it will further both your understanding of object-oriented programming and the Windows API.

Using The RegIni Class

Once you've coded the **RegIni** class, it greatly simplifies accessing INI files and the Registry. By simply instantiating and initializing an object, you can access and manipulate the INI files and the Registry effortlessly. Listing 9.18 shows some sample code that adds and deletes information from both the Registry and an INI file.

Listing 9.18 Using the RegIni class on a simple form.

```
Dim anINIObject As New RegIni
Dim aRegistryObject As New RegIni
Private Sub cmdAdd_Click()

    anINIObject.Init_Class INIFileName:=App.Path & "\test.ini"
    anINIObject.SetValue "INITest\SectionOne\KeyOne", _
                         "Test String"
    anINIObject.SetValue "INITest\SectionOne\KeyTwo", _
                         "20"
    anINIObject.SetValue "INITest\SectionOne\KeyThree", _
                         "30"
    anINIObject.SetValue "Test\SectionOne\KeyA", _
                         "A Test String"
    anINIObject.SetValue "Test\SectionOne\KeyB", _
                         "1,2,1,2,1,3"

    aRegistryObject.Init_Class BaseKey:="RegINI\Test"
    aRegistryObject.SetValue "SubKeyA", "Test Registry Value"
    aRegistryObject.SetValue "SubKeyB", "10"
    aRegistryObject.SetValue "SubKey3", "C"

End Sub

Private Sub cmdDelete_Click()

    anINIObject.Delete "INITest\SectionOne\KeyTwo"
    anINIObject.Delete "Test\SectionOne\"

    aRegistryObject.Delete "SubKeyA"

End Sub
```

This code is for a simple form with two command button controls. The first command button (Add) is for adding information to the Registry and an INI file; the second command button (Delete) deletes some of the information added via the first command button.

If you click on the Delete command button before clicking on the Add command button, you get an error. The object initialization calls are in the Add command button code; therefore, the **RegIni** object throws an error when you attempt to delete keys without first initializing the object.

Figure 9.6 shows the Registry after the Add command button is clicked.

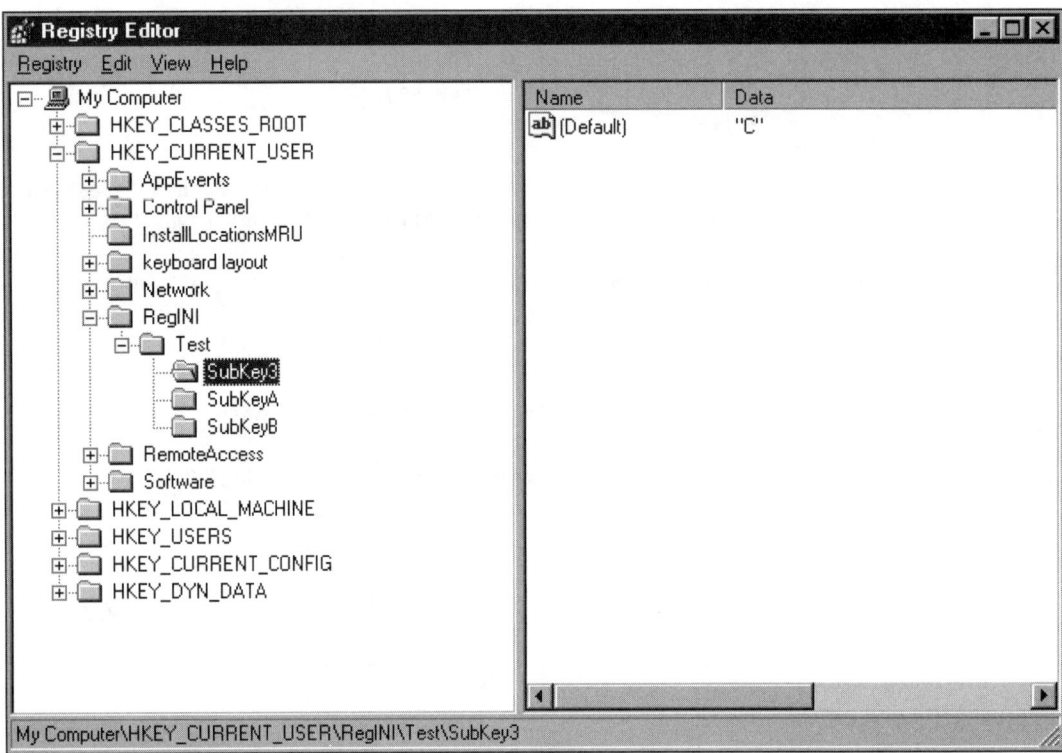

Figure 9.6
Custom values in the Registry.

The Registry now holds the custom values specified in the **cmdAdd_Click** procedure.

Figure 9.7 shows the contents of the TEST.INI file created with the **cmdAdd_Click** procedure.

Figure 9.7
TEST.INI: a private INI file.

Object Applications: Encapsulating System Functionality   301

Notice the section names in the INI file. They contain the slashes and represent the same key structure as the Registry. **RegIni** effectively hides the internal implementation and lets you access the INI file just like the Registry.

Figure 9.8 shows the Registry after the Delete command button is pressed.

Notice that SubKeyA and its value are deleted from the Registry with a single, simple line of code:

```
aRegistryObject.Delete "SubKeyA"
```

Finally, Figure 9.9 shows TEST.INI after the Delete command button is pressed.

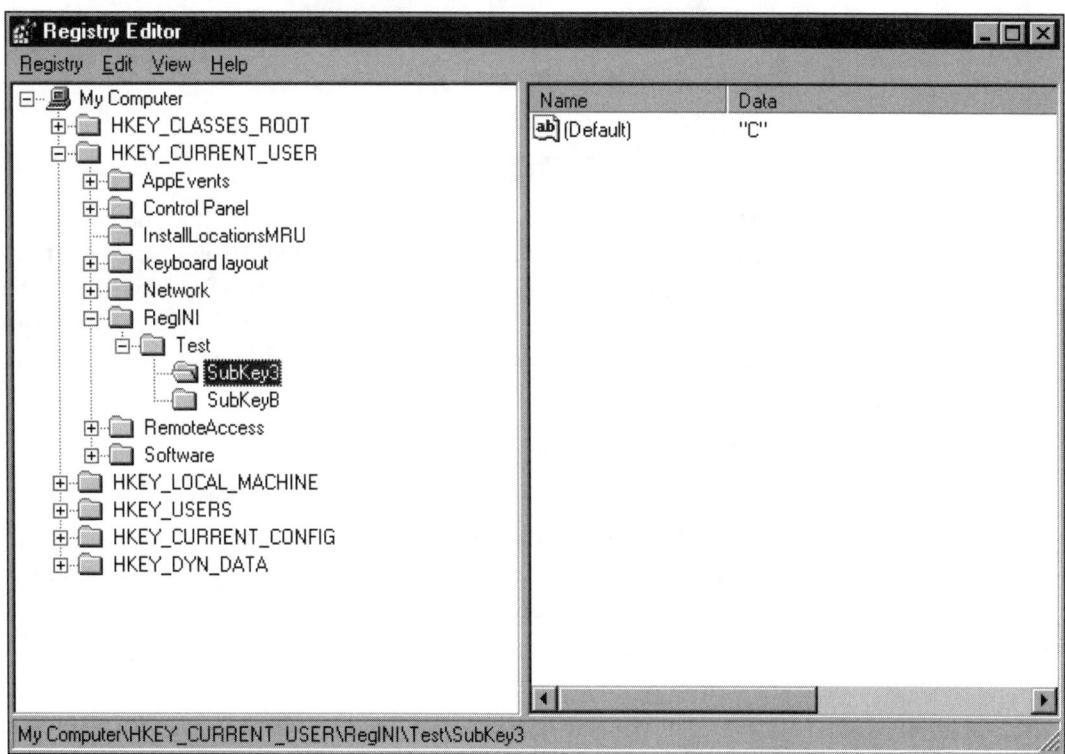

Figure 9.8
The updated Registry after **Delete** is called in the **RegIni** object.

Figure 9.9
Updated TEST.INI after **Delete** is called in the **RegIni** object.

Not only is the key **KeyTwo** gone from section **INITest\SectionOne**, but the entire section **Test\SectionOne** is gone, again with just one line of code:

```
anINIObject.Delete "Test\SectionOne\"
```

Conclusion

This chapter introduced you to the Windows API and the power that lies within its procedures. You also explored encapsulated interfaces and creating your own classes to simplify using the Windows API. The API contains many areas that may be helpful in your everyday development tasks—file access and management, directory manipulation, and multitasking, just to name a few.

Let's review some highlights of this chapter:

- Visual Basic can access the Windows API directly.
- Use the **Declare** statement to declare Windows API procedures in your Visual Basic applications to gain access to Windows internals and system services.
- Use the **Alias** clause of the **Declare** statement to access procedures with invalid Visual Basic names.
- Use **ByVal** and **ByRef** to control passing parameters to DLLs.
- Be careful when passing **String** and **Array** data types to DLLs.
- Use **AddressOf** to pass function pointers to DLLs.
- Make sure the function signature of the function you pass to a DLL matches the signature the DLL expects.

- Encapsulate Windows APIs and services in class modules.
- Design your class modules and think about how you'll use them in the future.
- Document your design and implementation decisions so you (and others) can use your classes over and over.

You also learned:

- How to access the Windows Registry
- How to access initialization files
- How to add and delete keys and sections

Chapter 10
Reusable Application Frameworks

Key Topics:

- Defining And Describing Frameworks
- Horizontal And Vertical Frameworks
- Designing Frameworks
- Generic Programming
- Implementing Frameworks
- Visual Basic Templates
- The Future Of Software Engineering
- Creating Quality Software
- Code Inspections
- Creating Self-Testing Objects
- Leveraging Your Efforts

This book emphasizes the power and versatility of object-oriented methods: analysis, design, and programming. The future of software engineering is firmly rooted in object-oriented techniques and languages such as Visual Basic. The ultimate power of objects lies in their reusability. Reusing code leverages all aspects of the development process. Fully tested objects eliminate design time when they're reused, as well as development time and test time. When you reuse an object, you use this leverage to create more robust applications faster.

Frameworks represent another level of reuse. Frameworks, unlike single reusable objects, are partial solutions to problems. You must provide the specific details to completely develop or customize the solution. Frameworks provide a very powerful class of software component that leverages design and allows the design to be customized for a specific application.

This chapter addresses frameworks and framework-based development. It examines frameworks in detail as well as shows you how to design and develop one, how Visual Basic supports frameworks, and how frameworks fit into the future of software engineering.

Frameworks

A *framework*, in its most basic form, is a solution skeleton. Frameworks consist of cooperating objects that represent a partial solution to a problem. For example, most companies use the same well-known basic accounting principles. However, they do not all use them in the same way. Each company defines its own accounting process, such as flow of information, accountability procedures, and departmental responsibilities.

A framework implements the basic accounting practices and then allows you to integrate them into the final solution, using only those portions that apply to your situation or solution.

Frameworks can also represent a shell for an entire application. For instance, if your Windows applications all use a common interface style or "look and feel," you can develop the interface as a framework and reuse it each time you start a program. This way, you don't have to recode or re-create the interface. Frameworks also work at a code level. If you code basic cut/copy/paste menu items over and over again, put the code into your framework and simply reuse it.

Lastly, a framework can also be a shell for a single or cooperating group of subroutines. These subroutines usually provide solutions to general programming problems or interface behaviors that are easier to cut and paste than to develop entire classes to handle.

The two categories of frameworks are horizontal and vertical. The horizontal framework is the more general, and the vertical is more specific.

Horizontal Frameworks

Horizontal frameworks operate over a broad range of problems. The application shell example represents a horizontal framework. Horizontal frameworks provide solutions to more general problems, such as handling queues and other data structures, general interface behavior, and common functionality.

A horizontal framework is usually a true skeleton—code that you use, add to, and modify in order to create your program. Visual Basic 6 contains wizards that represent frameworks to help you start your programs. Figure 10.1 shows the New Project dialog box.

When you create a new application using the New Project dialog box, Visual Basic sets up the correct structures for the type of application

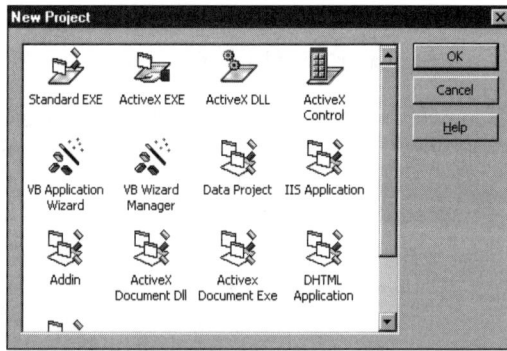

Figure 10.1
The New Project dialog box.

Reusable Application Frameworks **307**

you want to create. Notice the VB Application Wizard icon. This wizard leads you through a process that ultimately produces an application framework for you to use to begin an application. The VB Application Wizard lets you specify application elements such as your application's interface type, menus, toolbar, standard forms, and so on. Figure 10.2 shows the VB Application Wizard's Standard Forms screen.

This screen lets you select from a standard group of forms that are common in Windows applications. When you finish with the wizard, Visual Basic generates the options you select. Figure 10.3 shows the results of selecting all the standard forms.

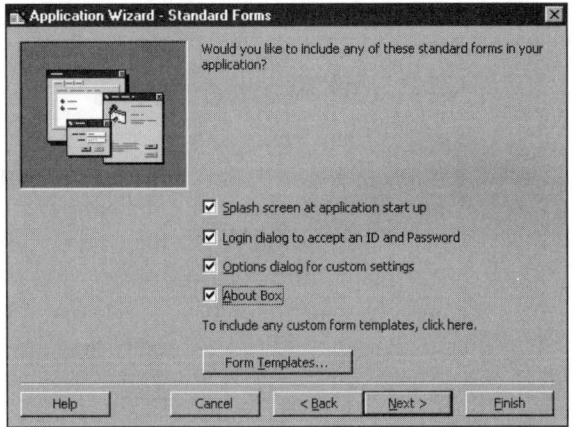

Figure 10.2
The VB Application Wizard's Standard Forms screen.

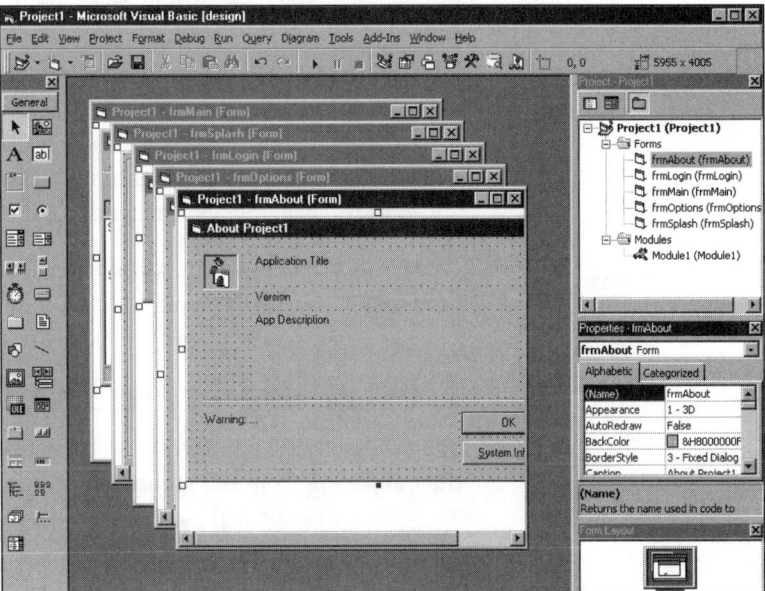

Figure 10.3
Visual Basic framework with standard forms.

The framework actually runs. If you run the application, you're first prompted for a username and password. After clicking on the OK button, you see the application's splash screen and then the main window. If you start clicking on the buttons, the application nicely informs you that you need to add code to implement the functionality. It does, however, implement some of the menu functions. Select the File|Open menu, and the application shows the common File Open dialog box. Wow—all that code from simply running a wizard.

Visual Basic categorizes its frameworks. These categories are all horizontal in nature. They represent general application forms: basic applications, ActiveX controls, ActiveX DLLs, IIS applications for the Internet, DHTML applications, and so on.

Vertical Frameworks

Vertical frameworks address more specific domains. The accounting framework mentioned earlier is an example of a vertical framework. Vertical frameworks provide skeleton solutions to specific domain problems. These frameworks may take the form of reusable objects encapsulated into ActiveX servers and COM objects that you integrate into specific solutions. They may also take the form of skeleton code that you add to and modify to realize your solution.

Microsoft Outlook is an example of a vertical framework. It addresses the information and contact management domain. Microsoft Outlook provides a complete solution; however, it also provides ActiveX interfaces for automation. You can automate Outlook in Visual Basic and leverage the functions, storage, and services that Outlook provides. To automate Outlook, add it to your project's references by selecting the Project|References menu item and checking the appropriate item in the References dialog box. Figure 10.4 shows the Outlook object model added in the References dialog box.

Once you add the reference, you can use the Object Browser to run Outlook.

Designing Frameworks

You can approach framework design in two basic ways: You can design the framework from the ground up or derive it from existing code.

Designing a framework from the ground up is very similar to the design process for objects. First, you describe your framework in the form of a problem description (or, in this case, a *framework* description). Then

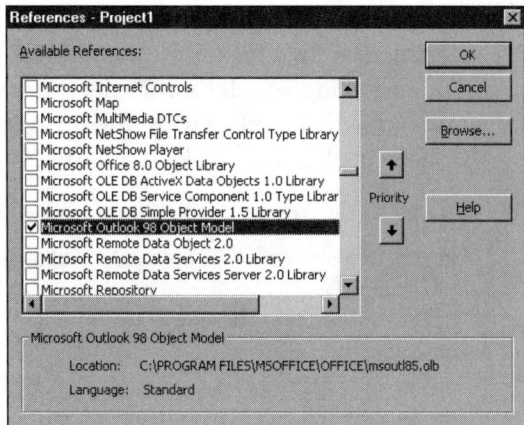

Figure 10.4
The References dialog box.

you perform "object analysis" to extract the objects, properties, methods, and method parameters. Because your problem statement describes a framework, the statement will be very general. For example, the Visual Basic Collection class is a form of framework item. It handles objects of different types. A description of the collection could be as follows:

> An ordered collection of objects that lets the user add, delete, and iterate through the Collection objects. The collection will store and return items based on a key, as well as let the user insert items anywhere in the collection.

This is a pretty general description of a Collection class. It handles multiple types; once coded, it can be used over and over again. As a matter of fact, this type of framework item is so powerful that Microsoft included it with Visual Basic. In Chapter 5, you learned how to create your own collections and how to use them to implement relationships in objects. In the next sections, you'll learn about generic programming and how to turn object relationships into a framework.

Generic Classes

One very important concept when considering frameworks is *generic programming*. Generic programming involves creating operations that make groups of objects or classes work together. This means that the operations must know about the objects' properties and methods and manipulate them to achieve some purpose or state change.

Generic programming also addresses when a class or subroutine operates on an unspecified type. For frameworks and Visual Basic, this may mean that the class or subroutine operates on a **Variant** type. However, it's always better to strongly type classes and procedures; therefore, using **Variant** types is not always the best approach.

You've already seen one candidate for generic programming—the Collection class. In Chapter 5, you designed your own Collection class. The first thing you did was create a generic form of the Collection class—one that worked with **Variant** types. The general form of the Collection class looked like the code in Listing 10.1.

Listing 10.1   The generic Collection class.
```
Public Property Get Count() As Long
End Property
Public Sub Add(Item As Variant)
End Sub
Public Sub Remove(Index As Variant)
End Sub
Public Function Item(Index As Variant) As Variant
End Function
```

Notice that the generic Collection class handles only **Variant** types. This represents a framework. In Chapter 5, the next thing you did was to strongly type the collection. When you did this, you customized the generic version to suit your application. In Chapter 5, you created the **ContactSet** Collection class to use with the design example from Chapter 2. Listing 10.2 shows the **ContactSet** class as generated from the generic Collection framework.

Listing 10.2   The ContactSet class.
```
Private mContactSet As New Collection
Public Function Add(ContactType As String) As String
    Dim NewContact As New Contact
    Static KeyNum As Long
    Dim theKey As String

    'Initialize the new Contact object
    NewContact.Init_Class ContactType

'Determine the key value
    KeyNum = KeyNum + 1
    theKey = "C" & Format$(KeyNum, "000000")

    'Store the new Contact object
    mContactSet.Add Item:=NewContact, _
                Key:=theKey
    'Return the Key
    Add = theKey

End Sub
```

```
Public Property Get Count() As Long

    Count = mContactSet.Count

End Property
Public Function Item(Index As Variant) As Contact

    Set Item = mContactSet.Item(Index)

End Function
Public Sub Remove(Index As Variant)

mContactSet.Remove Index

End Sub
```

Generic Procedures

Another aspect of generic programming addresses *generic procedures*. Generic procedures provide operations that operate on groups of objects to make the objects work together. Chapter 5 once again supplies the example. That chapter demonstrates how to implement a one-to-many relationship: It uses a function that returns an object. The power of the one-to-many relationship function is that it can return two types of objects: either the Collection object that represents the relationship, or an item of the base class. To turn this into a framework for one-to-many relationships, you must change the function's name to something generic and store it in a place where you can find it. Listing 10.3 shows the generic one-to-many relationship function.

Listing 10.3   The generic one-to-many relationship function.
```
Private mOne_to_Many As New Collection
Public Function One_to_Many(Optional Index As Variant) _
                 As Object

    'Check to see if the user wants the collection or an item
    If IsMissing(Index) Then
       'Return the collection
       Set One_to_Many = mOne_to_Many

    Else
       'Return the item chosen from the collection
       Set One_to_Many = mOne_to_Many.Item(Index)

    End If

End Function
```

312 Chapter 10

This generic code can be cut and pasted into any class; then, **One_to_Many** can be replaced with the name of the relationship. This code includes the declaration for the local collection variable. This ensures that you do not forget to include it when you paste the function into your code. Listing 10.4 shows the code once it has been added to the parent class.

Listing 10.4   The one-to-many relationship for a specific relationship.

```
Private mContacts As mContactSet
Public Function Contacts(Optional Index As Variant) As Object

   'Check to see if the user wants the collection or an item
   If IsMissing(Index) Then
      'Return the collection
      Set Contacts = mContacts

   Else
      'Return the item chosen from the collection
      Set Contacts = mContacts.Item(Index)

   End If

End Function
```

Generic procedures also address visual components. When you need a group of visual components or controls to operate in a cooperative manner, you can design generic code.

One example is a jump box. *Jump boxes* are those list boxes that have two arrows between them that allow you to select an item in one box, press an arrow button, and "jump" the item from one box to the other (see Figure 10.5). This is a very powerful and easy-to-understand metaphor (and it's a good piece of code to have in your arsenal). However, making the items "jump" from one list box to the other is actually a

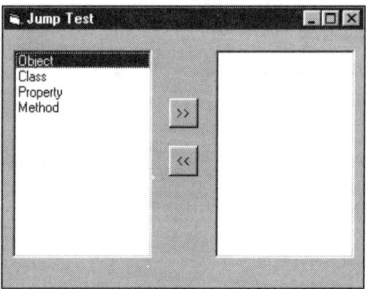

Figure 10.5
Jump boxes.

minor part of the design. Many more aspects of this little set of cooperating controls must be considered in order to produce a generic solution.

The first thing you need to decide is how many functions are needed to create this functionality. One approach is to develop code for each button's **Click** event. The code for each button controls the jump in the desired direction. This means two copies of the code are needed. Okay, now we're moving. If both **Click** events do the same thing (only in different directions), you can generalize this code into one function. Listing 10.5 shows the **JumpList** procedure's signature.

Listing 10.5   The JumpList signature.
```
Public Sub JumpList(FromList As ListBox, _
                    ToList As ListBox)
End Sub
```

Notice that the parameter types are list boxes. This is an example of generic programming. This generic procedure does not care which list box it operates on; therefore, you can call it any time you want this behavior. To use the procedure, call the **JumpList** procedure with the proper list box names for the direction of the jump. Listing 10.6 shows the call for jumping from the left list box to the right, as well as from the right to the left.

Listing 10.6   Using JumpList.
```
Private Sub cmdLeft_Click()
   JumpList FromList:=List2, _
            ToList:=List1

End Sub

Private Sub cmdRight_Click()
   JumpList FromList:=List1, _
            ToList:=List2
End Sub
```

You can make this procedure even more generic. By making the parameter types **Control**, you can create jump box behavior between any number and combination of controls, including grids and trees. Listing 10.7 shows the full generic form with an extended implementation that modifies the jump possibilities.

Listing 10.7 Generic JumpList.

```
Private Sub JumpList(FromList As Control, _
                    ToList As Control, _
                    Optional Move, _
                    Optional Parent)


    Dim i As Integer
    Dim j As Integer
    Dim Found As Integer
    Dim DoMove As Boolean
    Dim ThisNode As Node

    If Not IsMissing(Move) Then
        DoMove = Move
    Else
        DoMove = True
    End If

    If TypeOf FromList Is ListBox Then
        For i = 0 To FromList.ListCount - 1
            If FromList.Selected(i) Then
                Found = False
                For j = 0 To ToList.ListCount - 1
                    If FromList.List(i) = ToList.List(j) Then
                        Found = True
                    End If
                Next
                If Not Found Then
                    ToList.AddItem FromList.List(i)
                End If
            End If
        Next
        If DoMove Then
            RemoveSelected FromList
        End If
    End If
    If TypeOf FromList Is TreeView Then
        '...
    End If

End Sub
```

The generic **JumpList** must check for the correct control types, implement the appropriate behaviors, and be very robust. This makes the procedure generic and extensible. If you need jump behavior for other list control types, simply add the control type to the **JumpList** procedure and implement the code for moving the list items.

Fill In The Blank

In the earlier examples, you created framework elements that actually compile. Although this is sometimes desired, one of the aims of using a framework is to force the programmer to customize its elements. This introduces *fill-in-the-blank software*. A fill-in-the-blank framework is one in which the elements you want the programmer to provide are coded with noncompiling tags. The noncompiling tags represent the parts of the framework you want to force the programmer to supply. Listing 10.8 demonstrates the generic Collection class with noncompiling tags.

Listing 10.8   The generic fill-in-the-blank Collection class.

```
Private <Module Collection Name> As New Collection
Public Function Add(<Init_Class parameters>) As String
   Dim New<TypeName> As New <TypeName>
   Static KeyNum As Long
   Dim theKey As String

   'Initialize the new <TypeName> object
   New<TypeName>.Init_Class <Init_Class parameters>

'Determine the key value
   KeyNum = KeyNum + 1
   theKey = "C" & Format$(KeyNum, "000000")

   'Store the new Contact object
   <Module Collection Name>.Add Item:=New<TypeName>, _
                Key:=theKey
   'Return the Key
   Add = theKey

End Sub
Public Property Get Count() As Long

   Count = <Module Collection Name>.Count

End Property
Public Function Item(Index As Variant) As <TypeName>

   Set Item = <Module Collection Name>.Item(Index)
```

```
End Function
Public Sub Remove(Index As Variant)

<Module Collection Name>.Remove Index

End Sub
```

Because the generic fill-in-the-blank Collection class code will not compile, the compiler will "help" the programmer fill in the framework. This technique ensures that programmers do their work by filling in the framework instead of using it in its generic form. To complete the example, Listing 10.9 shows the fill-in-the-blank form for the one-to-many relationship function.

Listing 10.9 The generic fill-in-the-blank form for the one-to-many relationship function.

```
Private <Module Variable Name> As <Collection Set Type>
Public Function <Relationship Name> _
              (Optional Index As Variant) As Object

   'Check to see if the user wants the collection or an item
   If IsMissing(Index) Then
      'Return the collection
      Set <Relationship Name> = <Module Variable Name>

   Else
      'Return the item chosen from the collection
      Set <Relationship Name> = _
            <Module Variable Name>.Item(Index)

   End If

End Function
```

Designing Horizontal Frameworks

The Windows API—with its collection of file, window, security, MAPI (and so on) DLLs and servers—represents a horizontal framework. Because horizontal frameworks are applicable to many domains, they're not so much designed as they are *discovered*. When you discover that you've done the same thing in many applications (and that the task has generic functionality), encapsulate this functionality in a DLL or EXE and then reuse it when you need it.

One example is a set of container classes. If you discover you're always using stacks and queues, implement them using generic programming techniques and encapsulate them into a DLL. Now, the next time you need a stack object, you can simply link to the horizontal framework (the DLL).

Designing Vertical Frameworks

Vertical frameworks are also discovered instead of designed. You extract domain processing and program the knowledge into the framework, then implement generic interfaces to it. We don't recommend that you go out and design a framework; it takes a long time, and if you haven't implemented the processing in an application before, you may be including useless items and wasting time.

However, if you're constantly implementing the same set of business rules and you've fully tested code that implements them, it may be time to consider a framework. The first step in designing a framework is to determine how much functionality to put in. Make sure that all the classes and their functionality are related—that way, when you use the framework, it does not take up more resources than it needs.

An example of a vertical framework is an accounts payable system. Most companies, if they're attempting to make money or at least collect money, have a concept of accounts payable. Accounts payable accounting is a well-known and time-honored process. If you write accounts payable software often or must integrate the functionality into your systems often, then creating a framework is a good idea.

Remember, a framework only provides the base or common functionality. You use the framework as the basis to develop a custom solution. Most companies have their own twist or flavor of accounts payable; however, almost all of them use basic accounts payable functionality. Therefore, look at the accounts payable systems you've put together in the past, determine what functionality is common across all the designs, design the framework interface, and then implement the framework as a group of cooperating classes.

Level Of Effort

How much effort you put into the framework and how well you promote it in your organization determines what you get out of the framework. Frameworks are not easy undertakings—they require a sufficient investment in talent and time. If you can find a commercial framework that provides the functionality you need, buy it and use it instead of writing one. After all, we're going for reuse here, and nothing is better to reuse than other people's code.

Implementing Frameworks

Now that you've learned about what frameworks are and a little about what it takes to design them, let's look at how Visual Basic supports them. Visual Basic lets you implement frameworks in several ways—cutting and pasting, templates, wizards, and ActiveX components.

The cut-and-paste method is the most dangerous. If you create code-level templates, make sure you test them thoroughly and only change the parts that you designed to change. One of the most dangerous (and perhaps counterproductive) things you can do is to cut and paste bugs into your code. Therefore, be extremely careful with this type of framework. There is one advantage to cut-and-paste frameworks, however—they're easy to understand. Now that this warning is out of the way, the rest of this section moves on to discuss templates, wizards, and ActiveX components in more detail.

Templates

The first approach Visual Basic supports for implementing frameworks is via templates. Visual Basic provides for the following templates: Forms, MDI Forms, Modules, Class Modules, User Controls, Property Pages, and Projects.

File Templates

Forms, MDI Forms, Modules, Class Modules, User Controls, and Property Pages represent file templates you can add to your project. To access the available file-based templates, right-click in the Project window of the Visual Basic IDE, select the Add menu item, and then select the template type to add to your project. Figure 10.6 shows the Add menu.

When you select a template type to add, Visual Basic shows the appropriate dialog box. For example, if you select the Form menu item, Visual Basic displays the Add Form dialog box, shown in Figure 10.7.

The Add Form dialog box allows you to select a form style. Figure 10.7 shows nine different standard forms and the VB Data Form Wizard. This wizard helps you set up a data-based form.

You can even add your own templates to Visual Basic. File-based templates can be any code you develop. The earlier examples in this chapter discuss file-based frameworks (that is, frameworks in which you cut

Reusable Application Frameworks 319

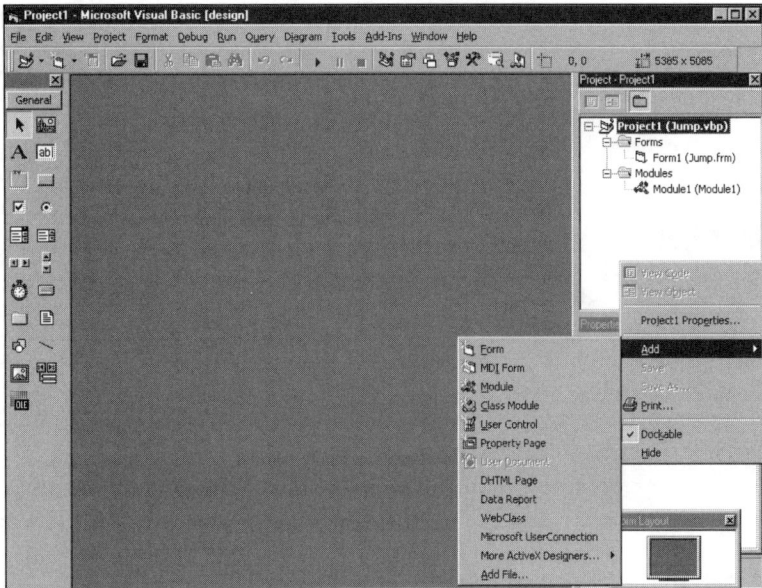

Figure 10.6
Visual Basic's template Add menu.

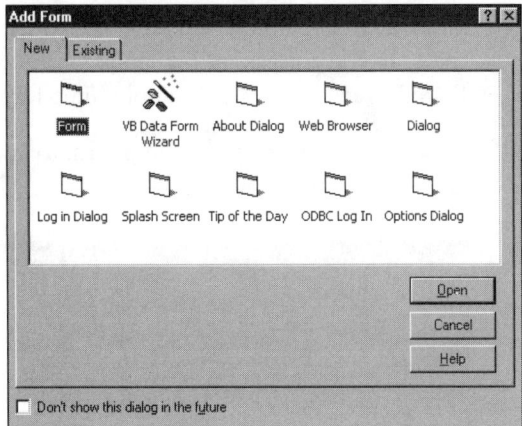

Figure 10.7
The Add Form dialog box.

and paste code, objects, forms, and so on into your projects). Templates give you a convenient way to make the frameworks readily available. Before you add your own forms or classes to Visual Basic's templates, you must find where Visual Basic keeps its templates. To find out, click on the Tools|Options menu item and then click on the Environment tab. Figure 10.8 shows the Options dialog box's Environment tab.

The Environment tab lets you specify which template types you want to see. Select the desired templates by checking the appropriate template types in the Show Templates For section of the tab.

320 Chapter 10

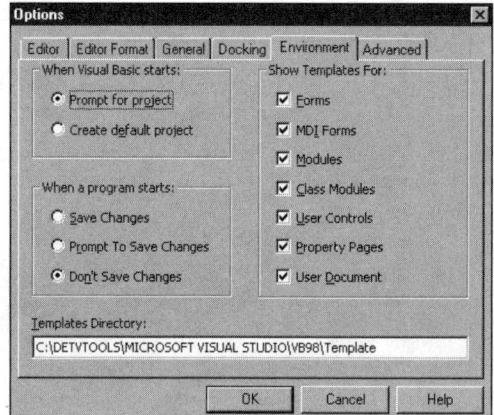

Figure 10.8
The Options dialog box's Environment tab.

Your template directory is shown in the Templates Directory text box. You're free to change your template's directory by typing in a new location in the text box. You're not really typing in the template's directory—what the template's directory points to is the base of the template's directories. There's a template directory for each type of file you can add. You add a template by simply copying the appropriate file(s) to the corresponding template directory. Figure 10.9 shows the Forms directory with the sample Jump form.

Now, if you want to add a Jump form to your application, simply open the Add Form dialog box and double-click on the Jump icon. Visual

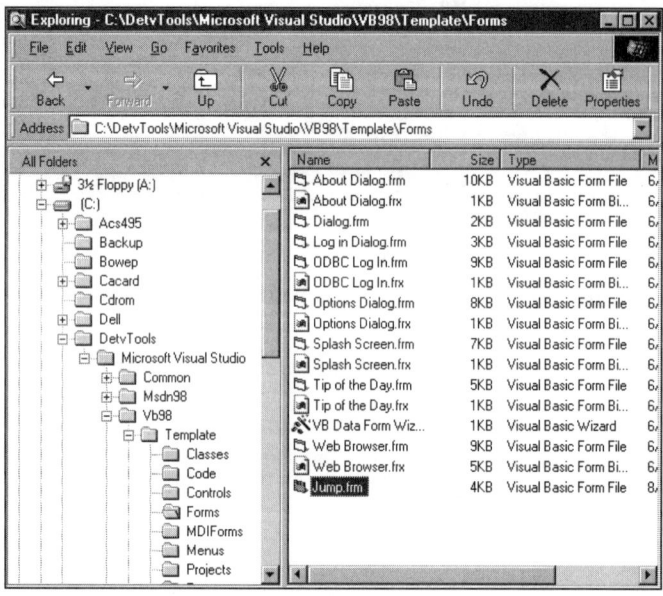

Figure 10.9
The Forms template directory with the Jump form.

Reusable Application Frameworks   **321**

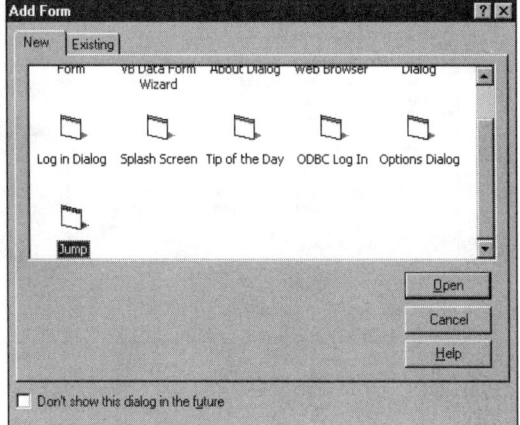

Figure 10.10
The Add Form dialog box with the Jump form available.

Basic will add a Jump form to your project. Figure 10.10 shows the Add Form dialog box with the Jump form available.

This same principle works for the other file-based templates. Simply copy a class module to the Template\Classes directory, a user control to the Template\Userctls directory, and so on. This means that if you want to add the **RegIni** class from Chapter 9, you simply copy the RegIni.CLS file to the Template\Classes directory. Figure 10.11 shows the Add Class Module dialog box with the **RegIni** class available for use.

Project Templates

Visual Basic also lets you add project types to the New Project dialog box. To show the New Project dialog box, select the File|New Project menu item. This dialog box lets you select the type of project for Visual Basic to create. Adding your own project type to the Project templates

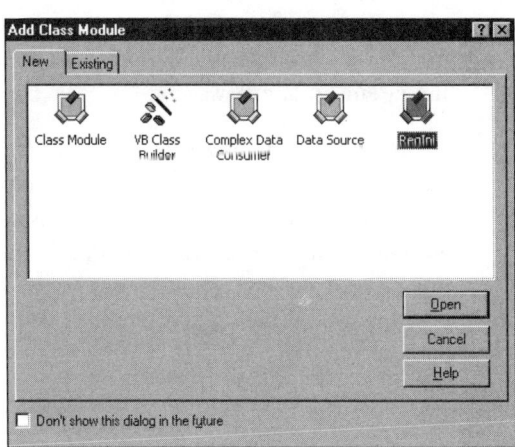

Figure 10.11
The Add Class Module dialog box with **RegIni** available.

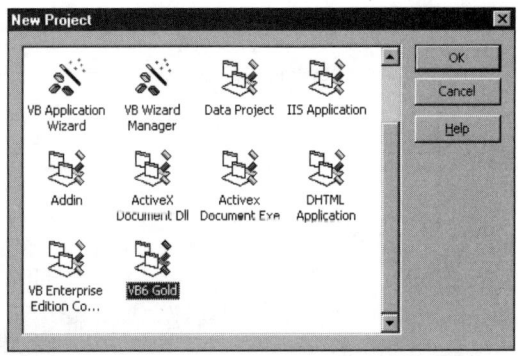

Figure 10.12
The New Project dialog box with the custom VB6 Gold project available.

is as easy as adding a file. You simply copy the project VBP file and all related files to the Template\Projects directory. Figure 10.12 shows a sample project that includes the **RegIni** class and the Jump form as the VB6 Gold project type.

Using project templates lets you define standard project components for yourself and your company. This saves a lot of work when you are starting up a new project, because you don't have to add in all the standard menu items, screen items, toolbars, and so on.

ActiveX Components

Visual Basic supports frameworks through simple cut-and-paste operations, templates, and components. Chapters 7 and 8 showed you how to create and implement ActiveX components in Visual Basic. ActiveX components, EXEs, and DLLs form the basis for horizontal and vertical frameworks.

When you discover and implement a vertical or horizontal framework, you can encapsulate it in ActiveX components. ActiveX components are the backbone of the Windows architecture and are the most portable items in Windows.

In Chapter 9, you designed the **RegIni** class. You created a single class card (and we pointed out that this may be overkill). Well, if you create class cards for single classes and the classes are in a horizontal or vertical framework, they serve as documentation for the class. This way, if anyone wants to know how a class works or needs to maintain it, he or she can see just what you originally intended.

The Future Of Software Engineering

Where do we go from here? Object-oriented programming is only one link in the chain of software engineering and development. In Chapter 1, we challenged you to decide which tier of software developers you wanted to occupy. We hope that by reading this book and taking the time to learn the techniques contained within, you've chosen to enter the upper tier.

Learning a few programming and technology concepts is not enough. There are many aspects to becoming a top-tier developer and software engineer. Design, as you have seen, plays a major role in good development, and thinking, above all else, will separate you from the lower tier. This section discusses briefly where the future of software engineering is going, with respect to Visual Basic and in general.

Speed

The demand for programming speed is increasing, and time to market is decreasing. This reality sends software engineers in search of the best tools for software development. This book shows the power and versatility of Visual Basic and ActiveX. Design carefully and encapsulate—these simple principles will serve you better than any specific methodology.

Encapsulation, when properly used, will pay you back more than any other programming technique. If you discover, create, or buy a horizontal framework, you'll recoup the investment in time to market. If you're in a more specialized field, look for a vertical framework that addresses your problems. Any time or money spent in the short term will pay big dividends in the long run.

Quality

Because we're developing so fast, we must do something to ensure quality. Here are four techniques to ensure we're writing quality software: frameworks, patterns, code inspections, and unit tests. Frameworks, because they're already tested, provide high quality. High-quality frameworks are worth their weight in gold (bad analogy because components don't actually weigh anything, but you get the idea).

Patterns

The emerging field of patterns holds the promise of repeatable and adaptable designs. *Patterns* are generalized solutions to common problems. They represent a proven, common approach to a problem. Patterns allow designers to apply general solutions to specific circumstances. A full discussion of patterns is beyond this book's scope; however, for the classic definitions of 23 patterns and how to apply them, we encourage you to read *Design Patterns: Elements of Reusable Object-Oriented Software* by Erich Gamma, Richard Helm, Ralph Johnson, and John Vlissides (see Appendix A for full bibliographical information).

Code Inspections

Using *code inspections* is a simple way to ensure quality. Code inspections can be as simple as having another developer review and comment on your code or as formal as having a corporate policy that outlines how to run inspections and how often to hold them. Inspections serve a dual purpose. First, and most obvious, they improve code quality, readability, and maintainability. Second, they cross-train and educate your peers. When you put a mix of programmers in a room to inspect code, they ultimately share experience, techniques, and ideas. A powerful way to increase both quality and communication is to create a code-inspection process.

Self-Testing Objects

Unit testing is particularly important in ensuring quality. Repeatable unit testing that's executed constantly is exponentially more powerful. As you create and implement objects, add a **SelfTest** method to the object. The **SelfTest** method calls and "exercises" the class's properties and methods. Set up different scenarios and test cases to check boundary conditions, data ranges, or whatever is appropriate for the object. Check the expected results in the method and print any problems to the Immediate window. Listing 10.10 shows a **SelfTest** item for the **RegIni** class.

Listing 10.10   The SelfTest method for RegIni.

```
Public Sub SelfTest()

    'Self-tests the object
    If mObjectType = INI Then
        'Store some values in the INI and
        'Verify the data

        Me.SetValue "INITest\SectionOne\KeyOne", _
                    "Test String"
        If Me.Value("INITest\SectionOne\KeyOne") <> _
            "Test String" Then
```

```
        Debug.Print "Error in Regini SelfTest, 1"
    End If

    Me.SetValue "INITest\SectionOne\KeyTwo", "20"
    If Me.Value("INITest\SectionOne\KeyTwo") <> _
        "20" Then
        Debug.Print "Error in Regini SelfTest, 2"
    End If

    Me.SetValue "INITest\SectionOne\KeyThree", "30"
    If Me.Value("INITest\SectionOne\KeyThree") <> _
        "30" Then
        Debug.Print "Error in Regini SelfTest, 3"
    End If

    Me.SetValue "Test\SectionOne\KeyB", "1,2,1,2,1,3"
    If Me.Value("Test\SectionOne\KeyB") <> _
        "1,2,1,2,1,3" Then
        Debug.Print "Error in Regini SelfTest, 5"
    End If


    Me.Delete "INITest\SectionOne\KeyTwo"
    If Me.Value("INITest\SectionOne\KeyTwo") <> _
        "" Then
        Debug.Print "Error in Regini SelfTest, 6"
    End If

    Me.Delete "Test\SectionOne\"
    If Me.Value("INITest\SectionOne\KeyOne") <> _
        "" Then
        Debug.Print "Error in Regini SelfTest, 7"
    End If

ElseIf mObjectType = Registry Then
    Me.SetValue "TestKeyA", "Test Registry Value"
    If Me.Value("TestKeyA") <> _
        "Test Registry Value" Then
        Debug.Print "Error in Regini SelfTest, 8"
    End If

    Me.SetValue "TestKeyB", "10"
    If Me.Value("TestKeyB") <> "10" Then
        Debug.Print "Error in Regini SelfTest, 9"
    End If

    Me.SetValue "TestKey3", "C"
    If Me.Value("TestKey3") <> "C" Then
```

```
            Debug.Print "Error in Regini SelfTest, 10"
        End If

        Me.Delete "TestKeyA"
        If Me.Value("TestKeyA") <> "" Then
            Debug.Print "Error in Regini SelfTest, 11"
        End If

    Else
        Err.Raise Number:=ObjectNotInitializedError, _
                  Source:="RegIni Class", _
                  Description:="Object not initialized " & _
                  "or not initialized properly."

    End If

End Sub
```

Create a menu item that instantiates and initializes the object and then executes the **SelfTest** method. I usually use the Help menu and add a Test item (see Figure 10.13). In the menu's **Click** event, call your **SelfTest** procedures. Keep adding all your **SelfTest**s to the Help|Test **Click** event. This way, you're building a set of regression tests that you execute often. Another way to call these procedures is to put them in the **Sub_Main** procedure. This has the advantage that every time you run your program, the tests are run. However, this may not be ideal when you're trying to debug.

Conclusion

This entire chapter is devoted to leverage. Frameworks, the concept of reuse, and patterns are all based on leveraging past experiences, code, and effort. Only by understanding leverage and harnessing its power will you be able to achieve full effectiveness and attain admittance into the top tier of programmers.

Today's software engineer must leverage all aspects of the development process—analysis, design, development, and testing. Working with previously developed code, components, and patterns provides the leverage. Review the following list as you go through your everyday development activities and ask yourself: Am I leveraging my efforts?

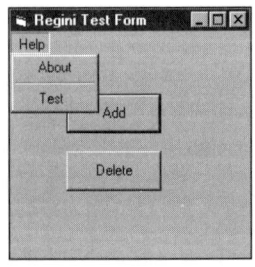

Figure 10.13
Help|Test menu.

- A *framework* is a solution skeleton.
- A framework can be simple cut-and-pasted code, templates, an entire application shell, or cooperating components.

- *Horizontal frameworks* address more general solutions.
- *Vertical frameworks* address domain-specific solutions.
- *Generic programming* lets your code address a broad range of solution domains.
- Develop working code first and then derive framework code from the working, tested code.
- Use fill-in-the-blank frameworks when you want to give guidance while forcing programmers to supply the details.
- Be careful with cut-and-paste reuse. You might be cutting and pasting bugs.
- Create and use file templates for forms, MDI forms, modules, class modules, user controls, and property pages.
- Create and use project templates to ensure a consistent look and feel and to share common program elements across your programming spectrum and organization.
- Encapsulate horizontal and vertical frameworks (that is, cooperating objects or generic objects) into ActiveX components.
- Use component-level reuse for high-quality, high-leverage programming.
- Use patterns to speed design.
- Use code inspections to ensure quality, maintainable code.
- Create self-testing objects and test them often.
- Leverage all aspects of the development process.
- Strive to be a top-tier programmer.
- Think.
- Have fun!

Appendix A
Resources For The Visual Basic Developer

Key Topics:

- *Online Documentation*
- *TechNet*
- *The Internet*
- *Newsgroups*
- *Books*

With the ever-changing nature of software development, no one book or medium can be enough to help you develop mission-critical, robust applications. Different situations may require you to look beyond any one resource. This appendix provides you with a broad range of resources, including information about development strategy and vision, information on various Web sites, some useful books and magazines, connection with peers and industry experts via user groups, events and seminars, certifications, and more.

Online Documentation

This excellent resource should be your first stop when you are looking for help. Visual Basic's online documentation provides you with syntax, structure, and code examples to assist you in developing your applications. When you install Visual Basic, you need to install the online documentation.

TechNet

The TechNet is a very useful resource for case studies and troubleshooting techniques. It also provides you with lots of tips and tricks. The TechNet not only covers Visual Basic, but a vast range of other topics, including Microsoft BackOffice products. You can subscribe to the Microsoft TechNet or research the TechNet on the Web at **http://www.microsoft.com/ithome**.

The Internet

The Web is today's medium of information exchange. Whether you want to know more about design concepts or programming with Visual Basic 6 (VB6), your best bet to finding the most reliable information is the Web. More often than not, you'll find that the Web helps you keep up to date with the latest and greatest information.

Also, given the rapid pace at which companies launch software these days, you may need to keep surfing the Net for more information about the software you use. The Internet's most explosive growth has happened within the software arena, with companies making beta software available for free to their customers. Moreover, you can now get all the upgrade patches, notes, work-arounds over bugs, and more right from the Web. You can also discuss your development issues within the various forums and Help desks the vendors create.

Just as you browse your newspaper every day, you should browse the Web daily. The following list contains sites that may interest you—some from established corporations that help you deliver solutions with Visual Basic, and others from Visual Basic pundits:

- *http://www.cobb.com/ivb/index.htm*—This site is within the domain of the Cobb Group's Web site. It provides a wealth of information on Visual Basic. The Cobb Group also publishes the *Inside Visual Basic for Windows* magazine. You can review this magazine online.

- *http://www.devx.com/home/devxhome.asp*—This site, which hosts the Development Exchange, is a good place for Visual Basic, Java, C++, and database developers. In addition to articles, this site hosts product and book reviews, as well as *Visual Basic Programming Journal*, a discussion area for developers, and more.

- *http://www.inquiry.com*—This site provides an excellent search facility for information, tips, and articles on many products. Also, this site has an "Ask the Pro" section that lets you review frequently asked questions and post new ones. The site provides you with expert advice on ActiveX, VBScript, Visual Basic, and more. You can search the *DBMS* magazine online, too.

- *http://www.mvps.org/vb*—This site hosts a number of Visual Basic utilities, tricks, and tips, and also demonstrates different techniques for manipulating the Windows API from Visual Basic. Besides being useful, each utility includes source code—a great learning tool.

- *http://www.pinpub.com*—This site hosts the *Visual Basic Developer* magazine. In addition to the archives of the magazine, this site provides online subscription and some helpful tips.
- *http://www.pparadise.com*—The Programmer's Paradise is an excellent one-stop shop for several third-party tools.
- *http://www.xtras.com*—This site provides catalogs and brochures for several Visual Basic tools. VBxtras is an excellent resource for Visual Basic add-ons, tools, and services. Here you'll find reviews of over 180 products, including pricing and ordering information, Visual Basic news, and other services.

Microsoft Information Center

The Microsoft Web site at **http://www.microsoft.com** is probably the most popular and extensive resource for developers. The domains within the Microsoft Web site that will interest you include:

- *Microsoft Developer Network (MSDN)*—MSDN is the essential resource for programmers, bringing together everything you need to be successful, including tools, technologies, education, information, and technical events. MSDN provides access to the timely, comprehensive resources you need to stay ahead of the curve via MSDN online, the MSDN online membership, and MSDN subscriptions.

  You can go live with the MSDN site at **http://www.microsoft.com/msdn**. If you would like to be in touch with the latest and greatest from Microsoft, MSDN is the place to be.

  MSDN CD-based subscriptions are annual membership programs that have three subscription levels designed to ensure that developers remain up to date with the latest programming technology and information from Microsoft.

- *Microsoft Events*—Microsoft holds a number of events and seminars, almost all of which are free. You can learn about these events at **http://www.microsoft.com/events**. Also, you can sign up for a mailing list that keeps you posted about the forthcoming events and seminars within your area.

- *Microsoft Online Support*—The Microsoft site at **http://support.microsoft.com** covers in-depth answers to specific product problems. At this site, you can choose a product and specific keyword(s) to narrow your search. For example, you can choose "Microsoft Visual Basic" and enter the keyword "installation" to find all the tips about installing Microsoft Visual Basic.

- *Microsoft Products*—Microsoft continues to roll out new products and upgrades very frequently. The best place to obtain the extensive list of all the current products from this software giant is **http://www.microsoft.com/products/default.asp**.

- *Microsoft Search Page*—You can search the entire Microsoft site with the Microsoft Search Page at **http://www.microsoft.com/search/default.asp**.

- *Microsoft Site Builder Network*—Visit the Site Builder Network (**http://www.microsoft.com/sitebuilder/**) to obtain information about Internet products from Microsoft. The site includes a Webzine, technical articles, and a download area with lots of goodies available (these include trial and beta versions of Microsoft products for the Internet).

  You can become a member of the Site Builder Network and get access to third-party downloads, promotional opportunities, and special offers. Including the guest membership, four membership levels are available:

  - *Guest level*—At the guest level, you get access to a select group of free Web tools to download as well as news-oriented emails to keep you up to date on all the latest products and technology announcements from the Site Builder Network. Guest membership is free.

  - *Level 1*—You can become a Level 1 member of the Site Builder Network by adding the Microsoft Explorer logo to your Web site. Level 1 membership is free.

  - *Level 2*—You can become a Level 2 member of the Site Builder Network by adding ActiveX controls to your Web site. Level 2 membership is free.

  - *Level 3*—To qualify for the Level 3 membership of the Site Builder Network, you should have deployed at least three separate commercial sites with ActiveX content. Level 3 membership costs $2,500 per year.

- *Microsoft Training And Certification*—Microsoft provides a number of certifications, including the popular MCP (Microsoft Certified Professional). You can learn more about these certifications at **http://www.microsoft.com/train_cert/ie40.htm**. This site also explains how and where you can get training on the different Microsoft tools.

Newsgroups

Apart from the Web, Internet newsgroups offer a great way to get answers to your questions and problems. When you post a question within the relevant newsgroup, you're almost guaranteed to receive an answer or pointer to an answer within hours. However, the key is finding the relevant newsgroup. To assist you with this task, here's a list of Visual Basic newsgroups:

- *Add-Ons And Microsoft Visual SourceSafe For Windows*—**microsoft.public.vb.addins**
- *Bug Reports*—**microsoft.public.vb.bugs**
- *Controls*—**microsoft.public.vb.controls**
- *Controls: Data Aware*—**microsoft.public.vb.controls.databound**
- *Controls: Internet Aware*—**microsoft.public.vb.controls.Internet**
- *Crystal Reports For Visual Basic*—**microsoft.public.vb.crystal**
- *Database*—**microsoft.public.vb.database**
- *Database Connection With DAO*—**microsoft.public.vb.database.dao**
- *Database Connection Via ODBC*—**microsoft.public.vb.database.odbc**
- *Database Connection With RDO*—**microsoft.public.vb.database.rdo**
- *DOS*—**microsoft.public.vb.dos**
- *Enterprise Version*—**microsoft.public.vb.enterprise**
- *General Visual Basic Discussion*—**microsoft.public.vb.general.discussion**
- *Installation Issues*—**microsoft.public.vb.installation**
- *OLE*—**microsoft.public.vb.ole**
- *OLE Automation*—**microsoft.public.vb.ole.automation**
- *OLE CDK*—**microsoft.public.vb.ole.cdk**
- *OLE Servers*—**microsoft.public.vb.ole.servers**
- *Setup Wizard*—**microsoft.public.vb.setupwiz**
- *Syntax For Visual Basic*—**microsoft.public.vb.syntax**
- *Third Party Tools For Visual Basic*—**microsoft.public.vb.3rdparty**
- *Visual Modeler*—**microsoft.public.vb.visual_modeler**
- *Win API*—**microsoft.public.vb.winapi**
- *Win API: Graphics*—**microsoft.public.vb.winapi.graphics**
- *Win API: Network*—**microsoft.public.vb.winapi.networks**

Books

Besides electronic resources, many books are helpful to the VB6 developer. Consult the following list for some interesting titles that deal with Visual Basic, object-oriented design, and Web application development:

- Aitken, Peter. *Visual Basic 6 Programming Blue Book.* The Coriolis Group, Scottsdale, AZ, 1998. 1-57610-281-5. This book describes how to create ActiveX controls quickly and easily. It includes highly practical tutorials that give plenty of hands-on examples and clear explanations. This book clarifies the inner workings of database design and teaches you about the tools for developing database applications.

- Bassett, Paul. *Framing Software Reuse: Lessons from the Real World.* Yourdon Press (Prentice-Hall), Upper Saddle River, NJ, 1996. 0-13327-859-X. Written by the inventor of the Bassett Frame Technology, this book provides a step-by-step guide of frame engineering principles and discusses how you can dramatically improve IS cost-effectiveness through reuse technologies. It explains the basic concepts, especially the central role of reuse within software engineering, and presents the software assembly commands of frame technology. This book will help you understand the design principles for software construction tools and the connection between frames and advanced mathematical ideas, such as context-sensitivity.

- Boggan, Scott, David Farkas, and Joe Welinske. *Developing Online Help for Windows 95.* International Thomson Publishing, Stamford, CT, 1996. 1-85032-211-2. This book provides valuable resources and practical guidance for developing Help for Windows 95 products. It demonstrates some specific techniques backed by clearly explained concepts and principles. To help you create your own Help files, the CD-ROM contains samples of compiled WinHelp files with source text files, Word for Windows Help template with macros, and bitmap clip art.

- Booch, Grady. *Object-Oriented Design With Applications.* Benjamin/Cummings, Menlo Park, CA, 1994. 0-80535-340-2. This book provides a very good insight into the implementation of object-oriented design in real-world scenarios. Reading this book will give you a better understanding of how to effectively analyze and design applications in the real world with object-oriented technology.

  - ———. *Object Solutions: Managing the Object-Oriented Project.* Addison-Wesley, Needham, MA, 1995. 0-80530-594-7. This book guides developers and managers with practical suggestions for applying object technology, whether for first-time developers or seasoned object-oriented veterans. Drawing on his worldwide experience in object-oriented technology, Booch demonstrates the sound principles of object-oriented software engineering that can make systems development more timely and effective. In addition, Booch draws from his extensive hands-on experience to present the reader with pragmatic advice, including recommended practices and rules of thumb that are the hallmarks of successful projects.

- Chandak, Ramesh and Purshottam Chandak. *Web Programming with Microsoft Tools 6-In-1*. Que Education & Training, Indianapolis, IN, 1997. 0-78971-215-6. In this book, you learn how to find the best Microsoft tool for any job. It presents the strengths and weaknesses of the different Microsoft products, covers how to incorporate them for easy Web programming, and provides hands-on examples of the important functions you want to learn. This book covers Visual J++, Internet Information Server, Visual Basic, Internet Explorer Technology, FrontPage, and Visual InterDev.

- Firesmith, Donald G. *Object-Oriented Requirements Analysis and Logical Design: A Software Engineering Approach*. John Wiley & Sons, New York, NY, 1996. 0-47157-807-X. This book describes advanced object-oriented design techniques, from object-oriented models to logical design.

- Gamma, Erich, Richard Helm, Ralph Johnson, and John Vlissides. *Design Patterns: Elements of Reusable Object-Oriented Software*. Addison-Wesley, Needham, MA, 1995. 0-20163-361-2. Based on the idea that there are a finite number of design problems in computer programming, this book identifies some common program-design problems—such as adapting the interface of one object to that of another object or notifying an object of a change in another object's state—and explains the best ways to solve them. The idea is that you can use the sophisticated design ideas to solve problems that you often waste time solving over and over again in your own programming.

- Holzner, Steven. *Visual Basic 6 Black Book*. The Coriolis Group, Scottsdale, AZ, 1998. 1-57610-283-1. Written by a veteran author for the programming community, this comprehensive, extremely accessible book has nearly 800 examples and covers about a thousand tasks in all areas of VB computing.

- Jacobson, Ivar. *Object-Oriented Software Engineering: A Use Case Driven Approach*. Addison-Wesley, Needham, MA, 1994. 0-20154-435-0. This excellent book on object-oriented requirements gathering, documentation, and design produces system descriptions that lend themselves easily to object-oriented analysis and design.

- Kurata, Deborah. *Doing Objects in Microsoft Visual Basic 5.0*. Ziff Davis Press, Medford, MA, 1997. 1-56276-444-6. This book offers you a step-by-step tutorial on designing and building an object-oriented application, including reviewing requirements, project planning, and scheduling. This book teaches you to develop your own classes with properties, methods, events, global constants, and multiple interfaces.

- Lalani, Suleiman, Kris Jamsa, and Ramesh Chandak. *ActiveX Programmer's Library*. Jamsa Press, Las Vegas, NV, 1997. 1-88413-352-5. This book teaches you how to fully master ActiveX through programming examples within Visual Basic, Visual C++, VBScript, and Visual J++. Easy-to-understand source code lets you quickly master ActiveX while creating state-of-the-art Web sites along the way. The companion CD-ROM contains source code for each object the book presents. You can quickly cut and paste the book's examples to your own Web site.

- MacDonald, Michael D. *MCSD Microsoft Visual Basic 5 Exam Cram*. The Coriolis Group, Scottsdale, AZ, 1998. 1-57610-236-X. This book serves as a complement to study guides for MCSD Exam #70-165: Developing Applications with Visual Basic 5. It includes practice quizzes at the end of each chapter that help you zero in on areas where you need more work. This book is a ready reference for Visual Basic programming techniques.

- McConnell, Steve. *Code Complete: A Practical Handbook of Software Construction*. Microsoft Press, Redmond, WA, 1993. 1-55615-484-4. A modern-day classic on software engineering, *Code Complete* focuses on specific practices you can use to improve your code and your ability to debug it—and ultimately deliver better, more efficient programs in less time. With all the advice this book offers, you'll certainly improve your ability to write elegant, self-documenting, maintainable software. McConnell does not focus on the idiosyncrasies of any single language, but rather on the general issues developers face: naming subroutines and variables in meaningful ways, designing control structures, finding and correcting errors within code, and more.

- ———. *Rapid Development: Taming Wild Software Schedules*. Microsoft Press, Redmond, WA, 1996. 1-55615-900-5. Written for team leaders, managers, and programmers alike, *Rapid Development* is an excellent book on scheduling software development effectively and quickly. McConnell convincingly outlines potential hazards within the development process and possible steps to avoid them. The chapter on classic mistakes will fill some with an overwhelming sense of déjà vu. The first two-thirds of the book is filled with clear-headed takes on topics ranging from scheduling to productivity tools, interspersed with examples, supporting data, and insightful anecdotes. The last section of the book discusses *best practices*, which are suggestions for more efficient development. Each is explicitly described and analyzed for potential effectiveness.

- Microsoft Corporation. *Microsoft Office 95 Data Access Reference*. Microsoft Press, Redmond, WA, 1995. 1-55615-942-0. This book introduces Visual Basic for Application language, which you can use with Microsoft Access 95 and Microsoft Office 95 to create powerful applications. The book also explains the famous Leszynski naming conventions.

- Microsoft Corporation. *Microsoft Office 97 Visual Basic Programmer's Guide*. Microsoft Press, Redmond, WA, 1997. 1-57231-340-4. This book teaches you to develop powerful applications with Microsoft Office 97; helps you create concise, efficient and powerful code with Visual Basic for Applications; and serves as a guide to Visual Basic naming conventions recommended by Microsoft.

- Petroutsos, Evangelos. *ActiveX Development with Visual Basic 5*. The Coriolis Group, Scottsdale, AZ, 1997. 1-56604-648-3. This book provides professional guidance to programming Internet/intranet applications featuring a wide selection of complete sample programs for putting ActiveX controls to use immediately within a variety of practical projects. This book includes a collection of excellent applets and controls and shows you how to implement them as ActiveX controls. It also shows you how to use Visual Basic 5 to develop ActiveX controls.

- Rumbaugh, James and Michael Blaha, et al. *Object-Oriented Modeling and Design*. Prentice Hall, Needham, MA, 1991. 0-13629-841-9. Notable mainly for its clear and thorough exploration of the *object modeling technique* (OMT)—a generic way of representing objects and their relationships—this book is good as a primer and great as a knowledge booster for those already familiar with object-oriented programming concepts. This book teaches you how to approach problems by breaking them down into interrelated pieces and then implementing the pieces. In addition to its documentation of OMT, this book does a first-rate job of explaining basic and advanced object-oriented programming concepts. This book concludes with a sort of recipe section, detailing architectures for the different types of programs within OMT.

- Wirfs-Brock, Rebecca, Brian Wilkerson, and Lauren Wiener. *Designing Object-Oriented Software*. Prentice Hall, Needham, MA, 1990. 0-13629-825-7. This older book, a good read for a well-rounded look into object-oriented methods, brings a unique perspective to object-oriented techniques. It provides a step-by-step guide to implementing object-oriented methods with the help of a couple good examples.

Appendix B
Third-Party Tools

Key Topics:

- *ActiveReports*
- *Crystal Reports*
- *DevPartner*
- *ERwin*
- *HOW*
- *InstallShield 5.1 Professional Edition*
- *Microsoft Windows CE Toolkit For Visual Basic*
- *Rational Rose*
- *RoboHelp*
- *Sheridan Software Tools*
- *System Architect*
- *Track Record*
- *Visio Professional 5.0*
- *Vision Builder 3.0*
- *Visual Components*

The best part about Visual Basic is the vast number of third-party tools and resources you can use to plug into your applications. These tools can help you develop sophisticated applications quickly and efficiently. This appendix provides you with information on some of the best third-party tools and add-ons available in the marketplace.

ActiveReports

Data Dynamics, Ltd.
2600 Tiller Lane
Columbus, OH 43231
U.S.A.
Phone: 614-895-3142
Fax: 614-899-2943
Internet: **http://www.datadynamics.com**

ActiveReports is a neat reporting tool that combines the power and ease of use of Microsoft Visual Basic with advanced ActiveX technology.

ActiveReports is fully integrated in the Visual Basic programming environment. It includes a report wizard that steps you through creating simple reports without writing any code. The wizard is integrated into the Visual Basic environment as an add-in module.

ActiveReports provides a fully open architecture that lets you use VB code, ActiveX, and OLE objects in your reports. You can insert any control or OLE object, such as a graph or document, into the report. You can also bind the OLE objects to BLOB fields in your database.

Crystal Reports

Seagate Software
920 Disc Drive
Scotts Valley, CA 95067
U.S.A.
Phone: 408-438-6550
Fax: 408-438-7612
Internet: **http://www.seagatesoftware.com**

Since its first inclusion within Visual Basic 3, Seagate Software's Crystal Reports has been the reporting tool of choice for Visual Basic developers. Here are some of the reasons for its popularity:

- Crystal Reports accesses more than 30 data sources.
- Crystal Reports has powerful data analysis capabilities and report type options, and it produces presentation-quality output with ease.
- Crystal Reports' modular design lets you integrate royalty-free reporting into database applications.

Here are some of the new features found in version 6.0 of Crystal Reports:

- *Additional runtime preview window functions*—The new features with version 6.0 include an automatically generated group tree summary of your report, printer setup button, a variable zoom control, a refresh button, and search capabilities. You can customize all these features for your reports.
- *User-defined functions can be added to your reports*—Crystal Reports lets you write custom formulas within Visual Basic or any programming language that supports the Component Object Model (COM). You can perform customized calculations within your reports by writing your own reusable user-defined functions.
- *Automation server interface to the Crystal Reports engine*—You can now integrate the functionality of the Crystal Reports engine with any of the controls or class libraries included within Crystal Reports. In addition to the ActiveX control (OCX) and Visual Basic custom control (VBX), Crystal Reports now contains a powerful Automation server interface for simple, object-oriented access to the entire Crystal Reports engine.

You can now quickly create, view, and modify presentation-quality reports from directly within the Visual Basic design environment, making it easier than ever to integrate reporting into your applications.

- *Event support*—By handling report and window events, you can customize how your application responds to user actions. For example, when a user clicks on a report element, your application can present additional report details, launch another report, or execute application code.

- *Reporting from application data*—With the new Active Data Driver, you can design report files without specifying an actual data source. At runtime, you can change the data source to a Recordset or Rowset object through Microsoft's DAO, RDO, and ADO, or through the Visual Basic Data control, for truly flexible and portable reports. This lets you bind your reports to any runtime data source, including grid data or memory blocks.

  The Crystal Data Object (CDO), a new ActiveX data source, lets you define fields and records at runtime, based on data that exists only at runtime. Through CDO, any type of data can become a virtual database and can be reported with Crystal Reports.

  You can now design reports from almost any data source, including PC databases, SQL databases, ODBC-compliant data sources, multidimensional (OLAP) data, Web server activity logs, as well as special Microsoft data sources such as Exchange, Outlook, NT event logs, Internet Information Server logs, and application data sources.

- *Reporting can be taken to the Web*—With the Internet/intranet becoming an extremely important medium of communication, almost every application is required to deploy reports over the Web. Web reporting also makes cross-platform distribution of reports a reality.

  Crystal Reports 6.0 is ready for all of this. Deploying your reports to the Web is extremely easy. Just link the reports to your Web server, install the Crystal Web Report Server components, and your reports are Web ready.

Crystal Reports 6.0 features *Smart Viewers*, which are lightweight ActiveX- and Java-compatible components that allow you to view your reports within a browser.

Even if you're deploying large reports to your intranet, the thin-wire architecture of Crystal Reports ensures superior response times and reduces Web traffic: Users can pull reports to the browser a page at a time, as desired.

DevPartner

Compuware NuMega Lab
9 Townsend West
Nashua, NH 03063
U.S.A.
Phone: 800-468-6342
Fax: 603-578-8401
Internet: **http://www.numega.com**

NuMega's DevPartner provides support for Microsoft Visual Basic within the development environment. DevPartner speeds development by automatically detecting, diagnosing, and facilitating the resolution of software errors and performance problems. DevPartner supports both individual and team development.

DevPartner is a suite of powerful and easy-to-use "SmartDebugging" tools that enable you to quickly detect, diagnose, and repair application or component errors and performance problems.

DevPartner for Visual Basic includes the tools discussed in the following sections. Each tool addresses a particular portion of the development cycle:

- *CodeReview*—Spots programming errors before they show up within an executable program
- *FailSafe*—Addresses the detection and analysis of errors within deployed applications
- *SmartCheck*—Detects, identifies, and resolves tough runtime errors
- *TrueTime*—Improves application and/or component performance

NuMega CodeReview

CodeReview is a source code analysis tool for Visual Basic. It rigorously examines Visual Basic source code for hundreds of potential problems within components, logic, and Visual Basic itself.

NuMega FailSafe

FailSafe captures and reports the critical information required to solve errors that occur within deployed Visual Basic applications. FailSafe records where each error happened, exactly what the user was doing, and the state of the program and system when the error occurred. This information is then automatically transmitted back to the developer or help desk for resolution.

NuMega SmartCheck

SmartCheck solves runtime errors within compiled Visual Basic programs, including third-party components, by automating the process of tough runtime error detection and diagnosis.

NuMega TrueTime

TrueTime, Visual Basic edition, is an automatic performance analysis and optimization tool that lets you build performance and usability by accurately pinpointing performance problems anywhere within an application or its components.

ERwin

Platinum Technology
1815 South Meyers Road
Oakbrook Terrace, IL 60181
U.S.A.
Phone: 800-442-6861
Fax: 630-691-0718
Internet: **http://www.platinum.com**

ERwin is a powerful, easy-to-use database design tool. It helps you with the design, generation, and maintenance of database applications.

From a logical model of your information requirements and business rules that define your database, to a physical model optimized for the specific characteristics of your target database, ERwin helps you visually determine the proper structure, key elements, and optimized design of your database.

ERwin models provide a blueprint that helps you understand, analyze, and communicate the structure of your database. Also, ERwin implements your design, creating a database or data warehouse optimized for your business.

ERwin makes it incredibly easy to design a database. You simply point and click to create a graphical E-R (Entity-Relationship) model of all your data requirements as well as capture business rules within a logical model that displays all entities, attributes, relationships, and key groups. Also, you can extend ERwin using its unique user-defined properties to capture any additional information important to your business directly within the model.

ERwin is more than just a design tool. Sophisticated modeling capabilities within ERwin help you design a better database. For example, attribute manipulation lets you drag and drop attributes from one entity to another, making changes and normalizing on the fly. On-diagram editing lets you change models in place without opening dialog boxes. Relationship navigation lets you move quickly across large models to pinpoint an entity's parent or children. Also, model validation reports let you easily check your design.

An ERwin design is optimized for the physical characteristics of your target database. ERwin automatically keeps your logical and physical designs synchronized and easily transforms logical constructs, such as many-to-many relationships, into physical implementations.

ERwin establishes a live, native connection between your database design and your database that allows both forward and reverse engineering. Using this connection, ERwin automatically generates tables, views, indexes, referential integrity rules (primary key and foreign key), defaults, and domain/column constraints.

ERwin includes a set of optimized referential integrity trigger templates and a rich macro language that lets you customize your own triggers and stored procedures.

ERwin also includes Complete-Compare, a new technology from Logic Works that changes the way modeling tools and databases interact. When you make any change to either the model or database, Complete-Compare provides a comprehensive comparison of all the differences. Complete-Compare highlights any discrepancies, so you can migrate changes from model to database or from database to model. ERwin also automatically generates **ALTER** command scripts to update any database while preserving existing data. Complete-Compare keeps the model synchronized with the database at all times.

You can edit, view, and print ERwin data models in a variety of ways. ERwin comes with RPTwin, an easy-to-use, graphical, banded report writer, and a built-in report browser with predefined and custom reporting options, providing complete control over the appearance and content of your reports. In addition, a unique template interface lets you apply design standards to all of your models and display preferences for them.

HOW

Riverton Software
One Kendall Square
Building 200
Cambridge, MA 02139
U.S.A.
Phone: 617-588-0500
Fax: 617-588-0412
Internet: **http://www.riverton.com**

HOW is a component-modeling tool and deployment framework for building business applications. With HOW, you can extend the traditional role of modeling to include development and deployment.

HOW's philosophy is based on the fact that Computer Aided Software Engineering (CASE) tools need to do more than just data modeling. With the corporate industry moving toward n-tier distributed applications, there's a need for collaboration on large-scale distributed applications. These applications also require help being partitioned into clean architectural layers. Riverton's HOW 2.0 is positioned to help you with all these issues.

HOW 2.0 adds support for Visual Basic and Java to the product's existing support for PowerBuilder. As you model your applications in HOW's business analysis and component design tools, HOW displays a built-in understanding of each target platform. When you generate components or component-based applications to your target platform, they take advantage of the distributed computing capabilities of the platform you choose.

HOW 2.0 enhances OpenFrame, HOW's business component deployment framework, to support a number of distributed computing technologies and middleware products, such as DCOM, Microsoft Transaction Server (MTS), and Jaguar CTS. As a result, you can host HOW-generated components within these transaction server products, allowing you to leverage the performance and scalability benefits that distributed component architectures deliver.

HOW ships with a detailed tutorial that does an excellent job of exposing new users to the depth and breadth of the tool.

InstallShield 5.1 Professional Edition

InstallShield Software Corporation
900 National Parkway, Suite 125
Schaumburg, IL 60173
U.S.A.
Phone: 847-240-9111
Fax: 847-240-9120
Internet: **http://www.installshield.com**

Gone are the days when installing a program was as simple as creating a new directory and copying the files from a disk. In order to install a program, you now have to place some files in a couple of different shared-component directories, create a new program directory, update the reference count for DLLs, add and change Registry settings, and more. At the same time, you need to make sure you provide the user with a simple way to get rid of all this mess when he or she tries to uninstall your program.

InstallShield 5.1 Professional edition provides you with a great way of handling such heavy-duty installations. The installation development environment contains everything you need to create a professional installation.

InstallShield provides a project wizard that will get you started with an installation framework within minutes. InstallShield also includes a Visual Basic project wizard that can create Visual Basic installation in three simple steps.

InstallShield has a color script editor that visually organizes the elements of installation scripts with color-coded syntax elements. The Function Wizard guides function use and automatically inserts syntactically correct function statements.

InstallShield provides ready-to-use templates for installing ODBC, DAO, RDO, MFC, OLE DB, ADO, VB5, NT services, and DirectX.

You can visually organize all the files to be contained in the installation using an easy drag-and-drop feature. Another feature of InstallShield is its multitiered file layout system, which provides maximum flexibility for grouping files.

The MediaBuild Wizard handles everything needed to create builds for various media on the fly. The automated media builder (ISBUILD.EXE) and InstallShield script compiler (COMPILE.EXE) allow you to include installation-build functionality in your batch file build process.

InstallShield, which lets you choose the target platforms at build time, allows you to create a single installation for Windows 3.1, Windows 95, and Windows NT.

InstallShield also provides you with good documentation of the product. The product, though complex, allows you a great deal of flexibility.

Microsoft Windows CE Toolkit For Visual Basic

Microsoft Corporation
One Microsoft Way
Redmond, WA 98052
U.S.A.
Phone: 425-882-8080
Fax: 425-936-7329
Internet: **http://www.microsoft.com**

Here's a product that can help you capitalize on your Visual Basic expertise. The Microsoft Windows CE operating system is a 32-bit, multithreaded operating system for the handheld PC and other mobile and embedded devices. With its cross-processor support, plus industry backing for a number of future non-PC devices, Windows CE provides a wealth of development opportunities. With the rapidly expanding market for this new platform, the need for quality Visual Basic-based applications and solutions continues to grow.

This product lets you apply your current knowledge of the Visual Basic programming model, environment, and language to building Windows CE-based solutions and applications. The Windows CE Toolkit for Visual Basic 5 is an add-in to the Visual Basic 5 product. Although Microsoft has not yet declared its intentions, it will probably release Windows CE Toolkit for Visual Basic 6 around the same time as it releases Visual Basic 6.

The Windows CE Toolkit puts a leading-edge emulator on your PC that gives you the look and function of a Windows CE-based device. You can develop, test, and debug your programs on your desktop—no device is needed. When you can work directly with a Windows CE-based device, programs are transferred to the device automatically through a standard connection. You can also monitor and debug your applications remotely, right from your PC.

What's more, Windows CE cross-processor support means you can code your Windows CE-based solutions once and then use them on a variety of processors.

The Toolkit provides Windows CE versions of the most commonly used ActiveX controls, as well as new ActiveX controls that provide Windows CE-specific functionality.

The auto-download features of the Windows CE Toolkit let you automatically download and register your builds from your PC to target Windows CE-based devices for testing and debugging.

The Toolkit provides you with a jump-start and gets you up to speed quickly with sample projects and applications designed specifically for Windows CE.

You can monitor and debug programs running on your Windows CE-based device right from your desktop-development environment using remote tools such as Spy, Process Viewer, and Registry Editor.

All in all, Windows CE is a platform with great potential, and the Windows CE Toolkit for Visual Basic is a great tool that helps you leverage your current Visual Basic skills and exploit this potential.

Rational Rose

Rational Software Corporation
18880 Homestead Road
Cupertino, CA 95014
U.S.A.
Phone: 800-728-1212
Fax: 408-863-4120
Internet: **http://www.rational.com**

Rational Rose is one of the hottest products on the market and is getting rave reviews from the industry. Rational Rose/VB is a great visual tool for object-oriented analysis and design. Rational's approach to visual modeling is based on Unified Modeling Language (UML).

Microsoft supports this approach, and Visual Basic 6 now includes Visual Modeler, a subset of Rose. Rose is the centerpiece of the Rational Toolkit, which aims to provide you with integrated processes to support the full application life cycle using object-oriented methodologies.

Rose facilitates object-oriented analysis and design, requirements description, database and component design, and iterative code generation. Rose provides other tools for requirements tracking and test automation, as well as tools that help integrate and report on all the steps of the process.

Rose supports UML for providing a standard way of describing objects, systems, and requirements, eliminating the notation wars that hampered the advancement of object-oriented methods. You can use UML for use-case diagrams and high-level descriptions. You can then link these use-case diagrams with full use-case descriptions created with Microsoft Word or any other text editor.

Component-based development has emerged as the most effective design process thus far. Rose users can now model their components and interfaces even more effectively through component modeling. Rose allows you to define class diagrams. You can then define methods and properties for each class. Rose allows you to define the parameters for method calls, the data or object type of properties, and whether the method or property is public. You can also create sequence and collaboration diagrams to show the interaction of objects derived from your classes.

Rose allows you to move easily from analysis to design to implementation and back to analysis again—it supports all phases of a project's life cycle. Rose supports a dynamic change management process with forward engineering, reverse engineering, and model-updating features that allow you to alter your implementation, assess your changes, and automatically incorporate them in your design. Rose's support for round-trip engineering ensures that the iterative development cycle is controlled and productive.

The Visual Differencing tool is a graphical comparison and merge utility within Rose that shows the differences between two models or controlled units. Using this utility, you can merge elements of one model into another model, automatically or interactively. The merge facility is especially useful during parallel development, where a model (or parts of a model) is changed by several developers, generating several model versions. These changes eventually need to be incorporated into a single model.

Rose can help with the generation of code skeletons in Visual Basic based on the properties and methods you described for your classes. Rose generates Interface Definition Language (IDL) for CORBA applications and Data Definition Language (DDL) for database applications. Using the IDL Code Generator, you can produce IDL source code from the information contained in a model. The code generated for each selected model element is a function of that element's specification, the model's properties, and the model's project properties. These properties provide the language-specific information required to map your model into IDL.

The gap between object technology and relational databases is closed by providing a mapping interface to relational databases via generation of persistent classes to Structured Query Language (SQL) and DDL.

Rose supports teams of analysts, architects, and engineers by enabling each to operate in a private workspace that contains an individual view of the entire model. Multiple engineers can work on complex problems concurrently; changes are made available to others by checking them into a configuration management and version control (CMVC) system. Protected workspace means that one person's changes won't affect the whole model until the time comes to share these alterations with the rest of the project.

Rose integrates with major CMVC tools, including Rational ClearCase and Microsoft SourceSafe, and is open to other CMVC systems, as well.

Rose allows the generation of a data dictionary from a model using Microsoft Word OLE Automation objects. You can specify the report type: a Logical View report with class specification or a Component View report with component specification. Furthermore, you can customize a report to set the attribute and operation syntax (UML, language syntax, and more). Rose also provides for other report options, such as inclusion of documentation fields.

RoboHelp

Blue Sky Software
7777 Fay Avenue
La Jolla, CA 92037
U.S.A.
Phone: 800-793-0364
Fax: 619-551-2486
Internet: **http://www.blue-sky.com**

RoboHelp lets you focus on creating the content and look of your online help without requiring you to learn the details of the complex Windows help compiler.

When you install RoboHelp, the installation program automatically finds the location of Word 97 and augments it with the RoboHelp toolbar and menu choices. To start a new help project or edit an existing one, you launch RoboHelp, which in turn launches Word. The RoboHelp toolbar is embedded within the other Word toolbars, and a RoboHelp Explorer window opens separately from Word. To present views of your help project, the RoboHelp Explorer window uses a pane-and-tree interface similar to the Windows Explorer interface.

Using the RoboHelp Explorer along with the RoboHelp toolbar icons makes it easy to quickly create a complete online help system. If you're already familiar with Word, RoboHelp is easy to use because you can simply use Word formatting commands on your text. Other toolbar buttons display dialog boxes to organize topics within a hierarchy; add contents, links, and jumps; and insert buttons and graphics.

RoboHelp lets you create help systems for all Windows versions, including Windows 95/98, Windows 3.x, and Windows NT versions 3.51 and 4.0. If you're creating a Windows 95/98 help system, RoboHelp supports the latest features such as "What's This?" help, 256-color graphics, and transparent bitmaps. If you create a Windows 3.1 help system, you can later convert it to Windows 95/98. You can also save the help project and run the final compile from the RoboHelp toolbar.

Under the hood, RoboHelp uses the standard Windows help compilers HCW.EXE and HC31.EXE. RoboHelp manages all the separate files and format codes that go into the final help file compilation. You can create a full help system for a moderate-sized Visual Basic application in about half a day, without having to know any of the formatting codes or how to run the help compiler. Using the screen capture and image editor utilities provided with RoboHelp, you can easily add screenshots and graphics to help make the content more understandable.

Other RoboHelp features let you create sophisticated help systems that interact with users in several useful ways. For example, you can add to your help system several different button types that provide links to other topics, execute help macros, and even open an Internet browser and download a file.

The Internet link capability adds a nice touch to a help system. Instead of just showing your company's Web site as part of the help system text, you can add a button or hyperlink that automatically opens the user's Web browser and navigates to the specified URL. Using Internet links requires you to distribute additional runtime DLLs, so if you're considering this option, figure out in advance how to package these with your help system. RoboHelp supports WAV and AVI files as well, so you can add a movie to your help project to show a user a feature of your application.

RoboHelp documentation is well written and well organized. You get detailed printed manuals and a well-designed online help system.

Sheridan Software Tools

Sheridan Software Systems, Inc.
35 Pinelawn Road, Suite 206E
Melville, NY 11747
U.S.A.
Phone: 516-753-0985
Fax: 516-753-3661
Internet: **http://www.shersoft.com**

Sheridan offers two kinds of add-on products for Visual Basic:

- ActiveX components
- Productivity tools

In addition to these components, discussed next, Sheridan offers several other tools that help you develop your applications rapidly.

ActiveX Components

These products give you extensive collections of custom controls for creating state-of-the-art Visual Basic applications quickly and easily.

ActiveListBar

This is a great add-on for Web and client/server developers. ActiveListBar lets you create Web pages and traditional applications that emulate the sliding group metaphor used within Office 97's Outlook bar.

ActiveThreed

This component gives your applications the look and feel of the Internet, with active control features such as a multipane splitter, transparent backgrounds, and style buttons with active borders.

ActiveToolBars

This component lets you create menu bars and toolbars quickly and easily with its unique WYSIWYG designer.

ActiveTreeView

This is an ideal drop-in replacement and a perfect superset of the tree view control within Visual Basic.

Productivity Tools

These tools help you with Visual Basic development.

ClassAssist

ClassAssist is a great product from Sheridan that will change the way you use classes within Visual Basic. It adds features and capabilities that make Visual Basic classes more "OOP like," more powerful, and easier to use.

With ClassAssist, creating reusable classes that inherit functionality from other classes is as simple as pointing and clicking. Also, overriding inherited properties or methods is just as easy. The ClassAssist main window shows the relationships between the classes you have created in a clear, easy-to-read tree view.

Its integrated check-in/check-out facilities and multiuser capabilities make it perfect for creating and managing class hierarchies in teams of two or more developers.

ClassAssist lets you create specialized OCX controls for use within your Visual Basic projects by inheriting functionality from any of the nine ClassAssist base controls provided with the product. Simply derive a new class from one of those provided, and you can override properties and methods to implement the behavior and appearance you need—and you do it all using Visual Basic code.

Whether you're developing alone or as part of a team, ClassAssist is the ideal tool for both the novice and the experienced Visual Basic developer who wants to create libraries of reusable classes to maximize productivity.

sp_Assist

sp_Assist is a multiuser development tool for SQL Server that's used to manage the coding process of SQL database objects, including stored procedures, triggers, tables, indexes, keys, defaults, and rules. sp_Assist provides a multiuser SQL coding environment, code generation of both SQL and Visual Basic code, encapsulation of all the SQL keywords, executable statements, system stored procedures, database administration tools, and more.

sp_Assist also provides an enhanced development environment by storing all your SQL Server source code in a multiuser, indexed, searchable database. This approach lets you share the same source code, even if you are not connected to a SQL Server. The object-locking feature at the object or procedure level resolves possible conflicts when you're developing within a multiuser environment, and designated user levels let you determine which user can access which function.

VBAssist

VBAssist attaches itself, both visually and functionally, to Visual Basic. VBAssist builds on the strengths of Visual Basic to maximize your development process. The product utilizes the CommandBar object for seamless integration with the rest of the Visual Basic design IDE.

Because they are in-process servers, most VBAssist tools use the shared memory area of the operating system to load, thus ensuring faster loading of VBAssist. VBAssist does exactly what a productivity tool should do—speeds development, makes processes easier (especially the repetitive tasks), and gives you features not available within Visual Basic itself.

The end result is that you can bring better projects to fruition sooner.

System Architect

Popkin Software & Systems, Inc.
11 Park Place
New York, NY 10007
U.S.A.
Phone: 212-571-3434
Fax: 212-571-3436
Internet: **http://www.popkin.com**

Popkin's System Architect (SA) has been strongly linked with Microsoft and Windows. It was the first CASE tool to be designed for Windows and the first modeling product to offer support for Visual Basic. Most recently, SA has announced support for complete integration with the Microsoft Repository.

With the current release of System Architect version 4, Popkin introduces two new products in the SA family: SA/Data Architect and SA/

Object Architect. Both of these offer what their names imply. The core functions of the former are included in System Architect, whereas those of the latter remain optional for System Architect users.

With the next release of System Architect, Popkin will replace the existing encyclopedia structure with the Microsoft Repository, which is extensible. Attributes are optional and can be associated with edit rules that enforce data integrity (text, numeric, range, Boolean, date, time, or user defined).

You can access and change all defined metadata, including the names and properties of standard methods' symbols and definitions. For example, you can specify the format, thickness, curvature, angles, and colors of lines, as well as the color and size of symbols. You can also customize a method. If the method you're using specifies a crow's foot symbol and you would prefer to use a double arrowhead, you can specify it as such. Finally, you can add your own rules to a method.

System Architect supports team development. Owners may be assigned to each data item, and a variable-locking strategy exists with locks applicable at the diagram, project, or dictionary level. Read-only access is permitted when a diagram is locked, whereas details of who has placed the lock are available if a second developer wants to work with a diagram. Check-in/check-out facilities enable team development as well as version control. There's also an import/export facility to PVCS.

You can use the Microsoft Repository for sharing model information across vendors. Users who have developed a class model in another tool (for example, Rational Rose or Microsoft Visual Modeler) can import it into System Architect (or SA/Object Architect) via the Microsoft Repository and load it into a UML, OMT, or Booch class diagram. And, of course, the reverse option is also available. System Architect supports a number of structured analysis and design methodologies.

System Architect also includes support for automatic leveling of data flow diagrams (DFDs), together with the automatic generation of decomposition diagrams to show their hierarchical structure. Another automated feature is the conversion of control flows in Ward & Mellor DFDs to conditions and actions in the relevant state transition diagrams.

A major feature is the introduction of much more extensive integrity checking. The product has always included such things as checking for vertical balancing (from the perspective of either the parent symbol or child diagram), but now Popkin has added wider verification of model integrity through rules checking.

Schema generation is an optional feature of System Architect. It generates DDL for table creation and maintenance (either via a file or ODBC connection), primary and foreign keys, both unique and nonunique indexes, rules, constraints, defaults, messages, triggers, functions, stored procedures, database comments, user-defined data types, physical storage parameters, database statements (tablespace, segment, and create), C typedefs, and COBOL copy books.

Reverse data engineering is another option for System Architect. Both physical and logical data models can be created from an existing database schema, from which you can then modify the system, create GUI dialog boxes (through SA's built-in Screen Painter), and generate documentation. Perhaps the most interesting facet of this module is its relaxed syntax engine, which is tolerant of improper language variants and new language extensions.

Finally, System Architect includes its own reporting facilities that provide a graphical interface for building customized reports for any model. This is specifically designed to enable model analysis, change control, relationship reports, impact analysis, and so forth. There are more than 125 standard reports particular to each supported methodology.

Track Record

Compuware NuMega Lab
9 Townsend West
Nashua, NH 03063
U.S.A.
Phone: 800-468-6342
Fax: 603-578-8401
Internet: **http://www.numega.com**

Track Record 4.0 is a great tool for tracking bugs, features, and virtually all other project details.

Track Record tracks bugs from first report through reproduction, fixing, and testing—but it doesn't stop there. Track Record puts you in control of the entire development cycle, preventing important details from falling through the cracks.

Track Record lets you track feature requests, releases, and bug reports by priority and developer. Furthermore, Track Record is fully configurable—you can completely customize your database to keep virtually all the information you need at your fingertips. You can even track bugs across several projects at once—automatically.

Track Record supports team development. With dynamic reports that always reflect the most current information within your database, Track Record automatically keeps everyone up to date. Best of all, Track Record offers seamless integration with popular version control software, including Microsoft Visual SourceSafe, PVCS, and MKS Source Integrity. From within Track Record, you can check files in and out, keep a history of files and version numbers associated with each bug report or feature, synchronize Track Record releases with labels within your version control system, and more.

Totally customizable reports let you organize information based on any criteria. Reports are always current.

Track Record offers new Web browser support. If you have a browser (and, of course, the appropriate access privileges), you can enter bugs within your Track Record database, update items, view outlines, and track just about any information.

NuMega also provides AutoAlert, an add-on utility for Track Record. Now you can be automatically notified via email whenever new information is entered into your Track Record database. You can use AutoAlert to:

- Notify programmers about bugs to fix via email
- Alert your customers about the status change on their specific issues
- Update managers when your Quality Assurance (QA) department finds "showstopper" bugs

Best of all, people do not need to own Track Record to benefit from these great new capabilities. AutoAlert uses Track Record query technology to generate email. You determine which queries generate email messages, so you control which types of changes trigger notification.

Visio Professional 5.0

Visio Corporation
520 Pike Street, Suite 1800
Seattle, WA 98101
U.S.A.
Phone: 206-521-4500
Fax: 206-521-4501
Internet: http://www.visio.com

You may wonder why Visio, a drawing program, is included in this list of third-party tools for Visual Basic. Surprisingly, Visio 5.0 enables you to do a lot more than just draw a flow chart. Visio Professional 5.0 includes a wide variety of special templates and stencils. The different templates support various conventions and methodologies, including Yourdan and Coad, Jacobsen (use-cases), Gane-Sarson, and several others. You can now use Visio Professional to design software with Universal Modeling Language (UML) and import and export design information to and from the Microsoft Repository.

The Microsoft software universe is gravitating toward using the Microsoft Repository for design information. The Repository is included with the Visual Modeler, which now supports UML.

Visio Professional 5.0 now lets you draw database designs. It comes with stencils for entities and relationships. Visio also allows for reverse engineering and can create a database diagram from the database.

You can also use Visual Basic for Applications (VBA) with Visio. The VBA environment is pretty similar to the one available within Microsoft Excel.

Visio has definitely developed into an extremely useful product—it's more than just a drawing tool.

Vision Builder 3.0

Vision Software Tools, Inc.
2101 Webster Street, 8th Floor
Oakland, CA 94612
U.S.A.
Phone: 800-984-7638
Fax: 510-238-4100
Internet: **http://www.vision-soft.com**

Vision Builder is a rules-based application generator that lets you visually model client/server applications—including the database, user interface, and business layer components—and then generate a Visual Basic application. Vision Builder is capable of generating client-side applications and Component Object Model (COM) objects for use under Microsoft Transaction Server, as well as stored procedures and triggers in the target database.

Vision Builder represents a truly different development paradigm. Although it generates Visual Basic code, you don't have to use Visual Basic for anything except the final touches and compilation. Vision Builder creates both the appearance and logic of the application, all by itself.

Vision Builder accomplishes this feat by providing a rich set of tools for specification of data entries, relationships, user-interface elements, and business rules. The specifications are stored in a Microsoft Access database repository.

Vision Builder is also capable of reverse engineering the data model from an existing RDMBS. You can then model your application with Vision Builder.

Object business rules can be defined to specify the derivation or source, validation, and presentation (including caption, formatting, display control type, and status message). You can specify rules for referential integrity and constraints and can include trigger code. Rules are specified using a stripped-down syntax, and you can use external COM objects within these rules.

You can create user-interface elements in a graphical diagram with the interface behavior defined by Vision Builder's intelligent understanding of the data underlying the forms and controls, the business rules associated with the objects, and by the archetype, or *template*, upon which the form or component is based. *Archetypes* are key elements of Vision Builder, because they constitute the bridge between the rules-based application specifications and the implemented code. In essence, they are the fill-in-the-blank templates, and they include macros for complex code creation.

Vision Builder also includes an archetype metalanguage that you can use to create archetypes or modify existing ones.

Visual Components

Visual Components, Inc.
12980 Metcalf South Creek Building, Suite 300
Overland Park, KS 66213
U.S.A.
Phone: 913-851-2200
Fax: 913-851-1390
Internet: **http://www.visualcomp.com**

Visual Components Studio from Visual Components is a suite of the ActiveX components discussed in the following sections.

dbComplete 1.5

dbComplete is a suite of powerful ActiveX components designed to enable the building of complex database applications with greater functionality in less time. The suite contains nine controls, including an outline data grid, an intelligent data source control, and a control library of six ActiveX components for data entry, editing, and presentation (such as a data-aware checkbox, option group, masked text, calendar, combo box, picture combo box, and more).

The VcGrid control is dbComplete's most unique component. At its simplest, this control displays table data in rows and columns, much like other data-aware grid controls do. It also lets you build complex multitable joins, defining master-detail relationships almost effortlessly. At design time, the control's Grid Designer tool helps you define master-detail relationships. A tree view display on the left shows the hierarchical design as you build it. If you click on a component within the tree view, the right side of the designer provides tools you can use to define the component. You can specify the tables, fields, join conditions, sort order, and even customized SQL **WHERE** clause information to define the item.

VcGrid displays data in a hierarchical way, much like a tree view control or Windows Explorer. You can click on the master record to expand it and view the detail entries. If the detail has its own nested detail, you can click on it again to view the lower level of detail. You can configure the VcGrid to insert, update, and delete records, all with no extra coding on your part.

First Impression 5.0

First Impression brings data to life with a powerful charting engine. This product features more than 35 unique chart types, including two-dimensional and three-dimensional options, as well as a chart wizard and chart designer to ease the building of charts. The component's extensive programming interface offers a great deal of charting and graphical customization and control for the developer.

Formula One 5.0

Formula One, another ActiveX component, offers you Excel-compatible spreadsheet functionality and an efficient alternative to desktop spreadsheet applications. Additionally, you can use Formula One as a database access and reporting tool, or you can construct and execute prepared SQL statements. Formula One is safe for scripting to Internet Explorer.

VisualSpeller 2.1

VisualSpeller provides you with seamless spellchecking functionality in reusable component form. VisualSpeller gives you immediate access to a standard American English dictionary with more than 100,000 entries. This component is extremely easy to plug into your application.

Glossary

accelerator key—A keyboard shortcut for an on-screen control. Pressing Alt plus the accelerator key gives the focus to the control and activates one or more of its events. The activated events vary with the type of control.

Active Data Object (ADO)—An object-oriented data access interface similar to Remote Data Object (RDO). ADO "flattens" the object model used by Data Access Object (DAO) and RDO, meaning that it contains fewer objects and more properties, methods (and arguments), and events.

Active Server Pages (ASPs)—A method for creating programs that run on a Web server (first available on Microsoft Internet Information Server 3). ASPs contain a mixture of HTML code and scripting code. ASPs use the ActiveX scripting engine to support both VBScript and JScript code. (You can use only one type of script per page.)

ActiveX Control Viewer—A key element in Internet Explorer 4.x, the ActiveX Control Viewer is a folder that makes it easy to manage the ActiveX controls you download and use. The ActiveX Control Viewer presents an icon of each control. You use the icon to retrieve information about the control or to uninstall the control.

agent—A form of intelligent software that carries out a well-defined task, such as seeking out information on the Internet or automating your tasks within an application. Some agents watch users' behavior and learn to anticipate their needs.

applet—A small Java program embedded in a Web page.

argument—A variable that a subroutine or function must have in order to execute.

array—A collection of items tied together because they're similar in some way. You can refer to these items by the name of the array and the index number. This is similar to a table and its rows, where the table is an array and the row numbers are indexes.

attribute—A unique characteristic of an object.

bitmap—A graphic file format.

class—A group of objects that have the same attributes, behaviors, or structure.

compiled code—A code that runs by itself, without the need for any interpreter.

Component Object Model (COM)—A specification developed by Microsoft for building software components that can be assembled into programs or that add functionality to existing programs running on Microsoft Windows platforms.

Computer-Aided Software Engineering (CASE)—A working environment that consists of programs and other development tools that help managers, systems analysts, and programmers to automate the design and implementation of programs and procedures for business, engineering, and scientific computer systems.

control—A user interface component, such as a command button, tree view, or list box.

control assembly—An ActiveX control formed by grouping existing controls.

Data Access Object (DAO)—An object-oriented interface that exposes the Microsoft Jet database engine (used by Microsoft Access) and allows you to directly connect to Access tables—as well as other databases—through Open Database Connectivity (ODBC). DAO is best suited for either single-system applications or for small, local deployments.

data control—Provides access to data stored in databases using any one of three types of recordset objects.

Distributed Component Object Model (DCOM)—Microsoft's specification for building components that can communicate over Windows-based networks. DCOM permits distributing different components for a single application across two or more networked computers, running an application distributed across a network so that the distribution of the components is not apparent to the user, and remotely displaying an application.

dockability—A feature in Visual Basic that enables you to determine whether you can drag a window, such as the toolbox, and reposition it in the Integrated Development Environment (IDE).

dynamic array—An array whose size is undeclared and is set at runtime.

Dynamic HTML—A set of innovative additions to Hypertext Markup Language (HTML) that allows page authors and developers to dynamically change the style and attributes of elements on an HTML page, as well as insert, delete, and modify elements and their text after a page has been loaded.

dynamic Web page—A Web page that has a fixed form but variable content, thus allowing it to be tailored to a visitor's search criteria.

e-commerce—Stands for *electronic commerce* over the Internet. Using e-commerce, you can do business over the Internet (for example, you can pay your phone bill, order flowers, and more via the Internet).

encapsulation—The ability to implement details of a class whose contents don't need to be known by the programmer using that class.

event—An occurrence—such as a click, a double-click, or a value change—that causes an object to respond.

event handler—A procedure activated by a specific event.

focus—The ability of an object to take input (such as keystrokes or mouse-clicks). The application or the user determines which object has the focus, and only one object can have the focus at any given time. A highlighted caption or title bar indicates the object that currently has the focus.

function—A procedure that returns a value.

Global Unique Identifier (GUID)—A 128-bit integer that Component Object Model (COM) assigns to an object. You can see a GUID every time you look at the class identifier (CLSID) for an object embedded in an HTML document or a layout.

global variable—A variable that is available to the application at all times and can be accessed by all the subroutines and functions within the application.

Graphic Interchange Format (GIF)—A graphics file format developed by CompuServe and used for transmitting raster images on the

Internet. An image can contain up to 256 colors, including a transparent color. The size of the file depends on the number of colors actually used.

Hypertext Markup Language (HTML)—The language used for creating documents on the Internet. HTML uses tags (indicated by surrounding angle brackets) to mark the structural parts of a document.

image map—Links a part of an image to a URL. Creating point-and-click maps is a typical application of this feature.

index—An item's position in an array. In a zero-based array, the top position is zero and the bottom position is one less than the number of items in the array.

inheritance—The feature of object-oriented programming that endows an instance of a class with the same properties as all the other instances of the same class.

Integrated Development Environment (IDE)—Visual Basic's development environment that integrates layout, design, editing, and a number of other functions.

interleaving—The combining of video and audio signals into one signal.

interpreted code—Code that needs an interpreter at runtime in order to execute.

Java—An object-oriented programming language developed by Sun Microsystems, Inc. Although similar to C++, Java is smaller, more portable, and easier to use, because it's more robust and manages memory on its own. Java is designed to be secure and platform independent (meaning that it can run on any platform).

Java applet—A Java class that's loaded and run by an already-running Java application, such as a Web browser or an applet viewer. Java applets can be downloaded and run by any Web browser capable of interpreting Java, such as Internet Explorer, Netscape Navigator, and HotJava. Applets can be activated automatically when a user views a page, or they may require some action on the part of the user, such as clicking on an icon in the Web page.

Joint Photographic Experts Group (JPEG)—An image format widely used for displaying images on the Web. JPEG file formats are generally used for complex images, such as photographs.

JScript—Microsoft's version of JavaScript, which is built into the Microsoft Internet Explorer Web browser. JScript is a powerful scripting language targeted specifically for the Internet. It's implemented as a fast, portable, lightweight interpreter for use with Internet Explorer and other applications that use Microsoft ActiveX controls, Automation servers, and Java applets.

Lightweight Directory Access Protocol (LDAP)—A protocol for clients to query and manage information in a directory service over a TCP connection (port 389). The LDAP protocol was designed by the University of Michigan to provide access to the X.500 directory while not incurring the resource requirements of the Directory Access Protocol (DAP). This makes LDAP very suitable for use on the Internet.

local area network (LAN)—A group of computers and other devices dispersed over a relatively limited area and connected by a communications link that enables any device to interact with any other device on the network.

message queue—An ordered list of messages awaiting transmission. They are taken care of on a first in, first out (FIFO) basis.

method—A behavior built into a control. A *method* is a procedure that a control knows how to follow automatically.

module—A set of declarations (such as **DIM** statements that define variables) followed by procedures. Each code window displays a module.

network architecture—The underlying structure of a computer network—including hardware, functional layers, interfaces, and protocols—used to establish communication and ensure the reliable transfer of information. Network architectures are designed to provide both philosophical and physical standards for the complexities of establishing communications links and transferring information without conflict.

object—An instance of a class. An *object* has properties, events, and methods.

object-oriented programming—A kind of programming that focuses on objects that perform procedures as well as on procedures that operate on objects (rather than on sequences of programming steps).

OLE—A technology for transferring and sharing information among applications. When an object (such as an image file created with a paint program) is linked to a compound document (such as a spreadsheet or a word processing document), the document contains only a reference to the object. Any changes made to the contents of a linked object will be seen in the compound document.

OLE DB—A set of interfaces designed by Microsoft for data access (based on its component database architecture) that provides universal data integration over an enterprise's network—from mainframe to desktop—regardless of the data type.

Open Database Connectivity (ODBC)—A widely accepted application programming interface (API) for database access. ODBC is based on the Call-Level Interface (CLI) specifications from X/Open and ISO/IEC for database APIs. ODBC uses Structured Query Language (SQL) as its database access language.

parameter—A value given to a variable, either at the beginning of an operation or before an expression is evaluated by a program. Until the operation is completed, a parameter is effectively treated as a constant value by the program. A *parameter* can be text, a number, or an argument name assigned to a value that's passed from one routine to another.

polymorphism—The ability to redefine a routine in a derived class (that is, a class that inherited its data structures and routines from another class). Polymorphism allows the programmer to define a base class that includes routines that perform standard operations on groups of related objects, without regard to the exact type of each object. The programmer then redefines the routines in the derived class for each type, taking into account the characteristics of the object.

procedure—A function or a subroutine.

property—An attribute of an object. You can set values to determine the characteristics of the object or aspects of the object's behavior.

property sheet—A window that lists the properties of an object and allows you to change them.

push technology—A technology that sends news to computers as events occur. This technology is called "push" to distinguish it from the standard method of information retrieval from the Web in which users "pull" the information they need when they need it.

query—The process of extracting data from a database and presenting it for use.

Rapid Application Development (RAD)—A method of building a computer system in which the system is programmed and implemented in segments (rather than waiting until the entire project is completed for implementation).

record—A data structure that's a collection of fields (elements), each with its own name and type. Unlike an array, whose elements all represent the same type of information and are accessed using an index, a record's elements represent different types of information and are accessed by name. A record can be accessed as a collective unit of elements, or the elements can be accessed individually.

Registry—The Windows 95/98 central repository of information for how you've configured the software and hardware on your computer.

relational database—A database or database management system that stores information in tables (rows and columns of data) and conducts searches by using data in specified columns of one table to find additional data in another table. In a relational database, the rows of a table represent records (collections of information about separate items) and the columns represent fields (particular attributes of a record).

Remote Data Object (RDO)—An object-oriented data access interface to Open Database Connectivity (ODBC) that's combined with the easy-to-use style of Data Access Object (DAO). RDO provides an interface that exposes virtually all of ODBC's low-level power and flexibility. RDO is limited, though, in that it doesn't access Jet databases very well. Also, it can only access relational databases through existing ODBC drivers. However, RDO is the interface of choice for a large number of developers who use Structured Query Language (SQL) Server, Oracle, or some other large relational database. RDO provides the objects, properties, and methods needed to access the more complex aspects of stored procedures and complex result sets.

repository—A database that contains information models in conjunction with the executable software that manages the database.

reverse engineering—A method for analyzing a product in which the finished item is studied to determine its makeup or component parts, typically for the purpose of creating a copy or a competitive product.

schema—A description of a database to a database management system (DBMS) in the language provided by the DBMS. A *schema* defines aspects of the database, such as attributes (fields), domains, and parameters of the attributes.

script—A program or piece of code written in a scripting language.

scripting language—A language, such as Visual Basic Scripting Edition (also known as VBScript), designed to operate inside another environment (for example, a Hypertext Markup Language [HTML] document). Code written in a scripting language is interpreted.

security—The protection of a computer system and its data from harm or loss.

setting box—The rectangular area at the top of a properties sheet into which you enter values for a control's properties.

sizing handles—Little squares that appear on the boundaries of a control at design time.

subclassing—The act of customizing a control to produce a new one. For example, you can subclass a text box to accept only text values.

subroutine—A procedure that does not return a value.

tag—An angle-bracketed element in Hypertext Markup Language (HTML) that marks the structures in a document.

technology—The application of science and engineering to the development of machines and procedures in order to enhance or improve human conditions (or at least to improve human efficiency in some respect).

transaction—A discrete activity within a computer system (such as an entry of a customer order or an update of an inventory item). Transactions are usually associated with database management, order entry, and other online systems.

Uniform Resource Locator (URL)—The address of a document or any other resource on the Internet.

UserDocument object—The base object of an ActiveX document. The *UserDocument object* resembles a standard ActiveX Document.

variable—A named storage location capable of containing data that can be modified during program execution.

view—The display of data or an image from a given perspective or location.

visual programming—A method of programming that uses a programming environment or language in which basic program components can be selected through menu choices, buttons, icons, and other predetermined methods.

wizard—An interactive Help utility within an application that guides the user through each step of a particular task (for example, starting up a word processing document using the proper format for a business letter).

Index

A

Abstract classes, 173
Abstraction
  and classes, 73
  and object-oriented programming, 4, 7, 11
Access methods, creating, 79-80
Accessor operators, 100
Activate event, 84
Active Client, 215, 216
Active Platform. *See* Microsoft Active Platform.
Active Server, 215, 216-217
Active Server Pages. *See* ASP.
ActiveListBar, 352
ActiveReports, 339
ActiveThreed, 352
ActiveToolBars, 353
ActiveTreeView, 353
ActiveX, 215-217, 256-257
ActiveX components, 215-257
  ClassModule objects as, 18-19
  compiling, 259-262
  creating Help files for, 265-267
  as frameworks, 322
  implementing, 259-270
  linking Help files to, 267-270
  maintaining compatibility of, 262-264
  and Object Browser, 19-21, 119-122
  optimizing code for, 260-262
  Package And Deployment Wizard for, 123-128
  reusing objects within, 116
  running sample code in, 122-123
  setting references to, 118-119
  Sheridan Software Tools custom controls for, 352-353
ActiveX Control Interface Wizard, 115
ActiveX controls, 14-15, 216, 229-256
  creating, 232-235
  installation time for, 255-256
  ListBox example, 245-253
  as references, 118
  Taskbar Icon example, 236-244
  in VB6, 230-232
  versus ActiveX servers, 253-256
ActiveX designers, 231
ActiveX DLL components, 217
ActiveX DLLs, 13-15, 92, 217-221
  ActiveX EXEs versus, 222
  as references, 118
ActiveX Document Migration Wizard, 116
ActiveX EXE components, 221-222
ActiveX EXEs, 13-14, 92, 221-229
  ActiveX DLLs versus, 222
  making, 222-224
  as references, 118
  running standalone, 225-229

ActiveX servers
    ActiveX controls versus, 253-256
    installation time for, 255-256
Add Class Module dialog box, 77-78
Add Form dialog box, 318-319
Add method
    in Collection objects, 16-17, 151, 153, 155, 156, 157
    in **RegIni** class, 285
    of TBIcon ActiveX control, 238
Add Procedure dialog box, 82
AddAddress method, in contact management system example, 62-63
AddContact method, in contact management system example, 62-63
AddPhoneNumber method, in contact management system example, 62-63
Address class
    in contact management system example, 68
    read-write properties of, 95-96
Address user-defined type, 91-92
AddressOf keyword, 277-278
Advanced class initialization, 138-141
Advanced Optimizations dialog box, 261-262
After parameter, in Collection objects, 151, 152
Alias keyword, 273
Aliases, of procedures, 272-273
Ancestor layers, in inheritance trees, 10-11
ANSI strings, in Windows API, 273-274
Apartment threading model, for ActiveX components, 219
Apex Software Corporation, VBA Companion by, 119-120
API functions, declaring, 272-274
API parameters, handling, 274-279
Appearance property, for **Form1** object, 75-76
Application servers, in three-tier client/server architecture, 12-15
Application Wizard, 116, 307-308
    Standard Forms screen for, 307
Applications, Package And Deployment Wizard for, 123-128

Arrays
    in function returns, 184
    as linked lists, 90
    as parameters, 276
    user-defined types and, 91-92
As Any parameter declaration, 277
As New statement, and ActiveX components, 119
As New syntax, 15, 179
    and Collection objects, 17
ASP, 216-217
Assignment operators, 100
Associative relationships, 159
    one-to-one, 160-161
Automation data types, 276
Availability, controlling of, 43
Available References list box, in References dialog box, 118

B

BackColor property, for **Form1** object, 75-76
.BAS modules, ClassModule objects as, 18
Base classes. *See* Superclasses.
BaseKey parameter, in **RegIni** class, 285-286
BaseKey property, in **Init_Class** method, 294-295
Bassett, Paul, 33
Before parameter, in Collection objects, 151, 152
BIBLIO.MDB file, 253
Binding, 88-89, 264
    in ActiveX controls, 231
    of data consumers, 169-171
    of data sources, 166-169
    early and late, 172
BindingCollection objects, 166-167, 168-169
Booch, Grady, object-oriented programming principles by, 11-12
Boolean variables, in **Error** class, 180
BorderStyle property, for **Form1** object, 75-76
Browse button, in References dialog box, 118
BSTR string types, 275

Business objects, 13-14
Buttons argument, in **TrapRunTime** method, 184-187
"By reference" parameter passing, 104-106
"By value" parameter passing, 104-105
ByRef keyword, 105-106, 114
   and **As Any** parameter declaration, 277
   ByVal keyword versus, 274-276
   and events, 110
   and **ParamArray** property, 109
ByVal keyword, 105, 114
   and **As Any** parameter declaration, 277
   ByRef keyword versus, 274-276
   and events, 110
   and **ParamArray** property, 109

C

C language, Windows API and, 274-275
Callback functions, 277
   debugging, 278-279
CallByName, 102-104
Cancel parameter, in **QueryUnload** event, 148-149
Candidate objects, in OOD, 47
Cardinality, of relationships, 49
Center method, 21-26
   code for, 23-25
   specifications for, 22-23
cEXEServer flag, 181
ChangeTip method, of TBIcon ActiveX control, 238, 239
CheckBox class, of Object Browser, 19-21
Child objects, shutdown method for, 145
Children. *See* Subclasses.
Circular references, 145
CL class
   and **Error** class, 212-214
   including **Center** method in, 26
   ParseButtons method in, 184-187
   syntax checking and error handling in, 210-212
Class Builder, 77-78, 115, 159

Class libraries
   of ClassModule objects, 5-6
   as references, 118
   setting references to, 118-119
   syntax checking and error handling in, 210-212
Class Module icon, 77-78
Class modules, 74-89, 114
   creating, 77-78
   data storage and scope management by, 88-89
   and polymorphism, 171
   as templates, 318-321
   in Visual Basic, 39-40, 70
Class names, default, 77-78
Class1 class module, 77-78
ClassAssist, 9, 353
Classes
   and abstraction, 7
   building, 82
   creating, 77-82
   data-aware, 131, 166-171
   defined, 4-5, 73
   and encapsulation, 4-7
   generic, 10-11, 309-311
   hierarchies of, 5
   in inheritance-tree design, 10-11
   initializing multiple-interface, 139-140
   naming, 78
   and polymorphism, 7-8
   self-initializing, 137-138
   specifying Help topics for, 268-269
   using **Center** method, 23-26
   versus objects, 39
   in Visual Basic, 15, 73-114, 131-176
Class_GetDataMember event handler, 167-168
ClassModule objects, 5-7
   Initialize and **Terminate** events in, 179-182
   in Visual Basic, 17-21
Class_Terminate event, preserving objects with, 143
ClassType enumeration, in **Init_Class** method, 294

Clear method, in Collection objects, 17
Client areas, within ListBox objects, 250-252
ClientApp class
    ShowMsg method of, 178
    and specifying Help topics, 268-269
    and syntax checking and syntax error handling, 200-201
Clients, in client/server architecture, 12-15
Client/server architecture, 12-15
    data access in, 166
CLS files, 7. *See also* ClassModule objects.
clsDataSource class, 167-169
cmdAdd_Click procedure, 300
cmdNext button, 169
cmdPrev button, 169
Code inspections, in software engineering, 324
Collection classes, 17, 151-154
    accessing user-defined, 157-158
    controlling user-defined, 156-157
    creating user-defined, 155
    fill-in-the-blank, 315-316
    frameworks as, 309
    generic, 310
    iterating through user-defined, 158-159
    user-defined types for, 155
Collection keyword, 152
Collection objects, 16-17. *See also* Object collections.
    problems with, 154
    and tracking object references, 144
Collection types, 150-151
    user-defined, 155
Collections. *See also* Object collections.
    accessing items in, 153-154
    adding items to, 153
    defined, 131, 150-151
    designing, 151
    implementing user-defined, 154-159
    removing items from, 153
    in Visual Basic, 151-154
COM, 216
    tracking object references with, 144

COM components, 215
    future of, 34-35
    and object-oriented approach, 1-3
    in VB6, 35-36
Common operating libraries, 273
CommonDialog error message, 201
Compatibility, of ActiveX components, 262-264
Compatibility settings, 263
Compatible OLE Component entry, of VB Options dialog box, 262-263
Compile To Native Code option, optimization options under, 260-261
Component Object Model. *See* COM.
Composite relationships, 48-49, 159
    Many-to-many, 165
    one-to-many, 162-165
    one-to-one, 160-162
Computational methods, 52
Constants, in enumerations, 92-94
Contact class
    in contact management system example, 67, 110-111, 112
    declaring methods for, 80-82
    read-only properties of, 96-97
    simple initialization method for, 134-137
Contact management system
    Collections in, 152-154
    generic Collection classes for, 310-311
    implementing collections for, 155-159
    implementing relationships in, 159-165
    initializing Prospect objects in, 140-141
    OOD for, 54-69
    simple initialization method for, 134-137
ContactSet class, for contact management system example, 310-311
Controls Collection object, 16
Controls on forms, 87, 146-150
    public, 84-85
Corporate layers, in inheritance trees, 10-11
Count property
    in Collection objects, 16-17, 151
    in one-to-many relationships, 163

in user-defined collections, 157
Coupling, 87-88, 114
  defined, 74
cRAOServer flag, 181
"Created, but not loaded" state, 146-147
CreateObject function, 15, 119, 179, 264
Crystal Reports, 340-341

D

Data
  within class modules, 88-89
  controlling access to, 42-43
  and properties, 40
Data access, in client/server development, 166
Data Aware Class Test form, 168
  updated, 170
Data consumers, 166, 169-171
  defined, 131
Data control, 166
Data Form Wizard, 115
Data hiding, 4, 38-39, 70, 89-94, 114
  defined, 74
  encapsulation and, 5-7, 38
  and redirection, 43-44
Data Object Wizard, 115
Data sources, 166-169
  defined, 132
Data-aware classes, 131, 166-171
Database servers, 13
DataBindingBehavior property, in data consumers, 169-171
DataMember parameter, 168
DataSource property, 169
DataSourceBehavior property, 166-167
dbComplete 1.5, 360
DCOM technology, 215, 216
Debugging
  of callback functions, 278-279
  of data consumer classes, 170
  of one-to-many relationships, 165
Declare statement, signature of, 272

Default class names, 77-78
Default methods, 100-104
Default parameter passing, 106
  and optional parameters, 107
Default properties, 100-102
Delete method
  in contact management system example, 62-63
  in **RegIni** class, 285, 297-298, 301-302
  of TBIcon ActiveX control, 238, 239
Delphi 2, ActiveX components and, 116
DEMOCTL.EXE file, 255
DEMODLL.EXE file, 255
DEMOLBSC.VBP file, 252-253
DEMOTBAR.VBP file, 243
Department layers, in inheritance trees, 10-11
Dependency File, of Package And Deployment Wizard, 124, 127-128
Dependent optional parameters, 53, 138-139
Derived classes. *See* Subclasses.
Descriptive properties, 50
Design Patterns: Elements of Reusable Object-Oriented Software (Gamma, Helm, Johnson & Vlissides), 324
Designers, in VB6, 231
Developing Online Help for Windows 95 (Boggan, Farkas & Welinske), 265
DevPartner, 342-343
Dialog boxes
  for extending forms, 83-87
  as objects, 87
  protection of, 83-87
Dialog class, and **Center** method, 24-26
Different but related objects, 151
Dim keyword, 40, 79
DLL files, 14-15, 217
  making, 220-221
  as references, 118
  setting project properties of, 218-220
DLL procedures, passing arrays to, 276
Doing Objects in Microsoft Visual Basic 4.0 (Kurata), 264
Drag method, of Object Browser, 19-21
Dynamic arrays, user-defined types and, 91-92

E

Early binding, 172, 264
EFSD.DLL, running standalone, 229
EFSE.EXE file, 262
EFS.HLP file, 266-267
EFS.HLP setting, 218, 223
Encapsulated interfaces, 271-272
Encapsulation, 70, 323
   with Collection objects, 154
   defined, 74
   and OOA and OOD, 11
   in OOP, 4, 5-7, 8, 38, 39-40, 89
   with properties, 41-44
   and redirection, 43-44
   of user-defined collections, 154-159
   of Windows API interfaces, 271-303
End statement
   and ActiveX DLLs, 217, 221
   terminating forms with, 150
   and tracking object references, 145
Enum functions, 277
Enumerations, 92-94, 114
Enumerators, in iteration methods, 158-159
Equals operator, 100
ErrObj argument, of **TrapRunTime**
   method, 187-188
Error class, 177-214
   in class library syntax checking, 210-212
   design of, 177-178
   error handling by, 178
   General Declarations of, 179-180
   and **Initialize** event, 179-182
   as standing alone, 212-214
   and **Terminate** event, 179-182
   TrapRunTime method of, 182-202
   TrapSyntax method of, 202-210
Error codes. *See also* Non-VBA error codes, VBA
   error codes.
   logging, 197-202
   returning, 197-202, 209-210
Error handling
   commercial-quality, 212-214
   by **Error** class, 178
ERROR.CLS file, 212-214
Errors, 177-214
   CallByName and, 103-104
   runtime, 201-202
   when making ActiveX component, 221
ERwin, 343-344
Event handlers, 112-113
Event keyword, 110-111
Event procedures
   and abstraction, 7
   for ClassModule objects, 5, 17-18
Event sources, 111, 114
Events, 70, 71
   adding to classes, 82
   in contact management system example, 63-64
   defined, 44, 74
   for **Form1** object, 76-77
   handling, 111-113
   in interfaces, 110-113
   in OOD, 54
   raising, 111
   of **RegIni** class, 286, 288-292
   of TBIcon ActiveX control, 241-242
Exact same type of objects, 151
Exclusive association, 160
EXE files. *See also* ActiveX EXEs.
   making, 222-224
   setting project properties of, 223-224
Extending forms, 83-87
Extensibility, of Visual Basic, 229-230

F

File argument, for **Load** method, 27
File templates, 318-321
FileName property, in **Init_Class**
   method, 294-295
Fill-in-the-blank software, 315-316
First Impression 5.0, 360
FirstName property, 85-86
Fixed arrays, user-defined types and, 91-92
For Each method
   in Collection objects, 152-153

in one-to-many relationships, 165
in user-defined collections, 158-159
Form class, 15, 74-77
Form properties, 85
Form1 object, 75-77
Form_Initialize event, 146-147
Form_Load event, 147-148, 149
   in data sources, 169
   within ListBox objects, 252-253
   and "unloaded and unreferenced while a control is still referenced" state, 150
Form_QueryUnload event, 148-149
Forms, 146-150
   adding properties and methods to, 83-87
   creating, 146-147
   extending, 83-87
   fill-in-the-blank, 316
   loading, 147-148
   reclaiming memory for, 149-150
   showing, 148
   as templates, 318-321
   unloading, 148-149, 150
Forms collection, adding new forms to, 147-148
Forms Collection object, 16
Formula One 5.0, 360
Frameworks, 305-327
   ActiveX components as, 322
   defined, 305
   designing, 308-318
   fill-in-the-blank software as, 315-316
   in future of software engineering, 323-326
   generic classes in, 309-311
   generic procedures as, 311-318
   horizontal, 306-308, 316-317
   implementing, 318-322
   templates as, 318-322
   versatility of, 305-306
   vertical, 308, 317
Framing Software Reuse: Lessons from the Real World (Bassett), 33
FreeFile function, and **Load** method, 30
Function keyword, 80
Function pointers, 277-279

Function procedures
   and abstraction, 7
   for ClassModule objects, 5-6, 17-18
   in newly created forms, 147
Functions
   adding to classes, 82
   within class modules, 89
   as methods, 44, 80
   passing with wrong signatures, 279

G

Gates, Bill, 229
General Declarations section
   of **Error** class, 179-180
   of TBIcon ActiveX control, 236-237
Generic classes, 10-11, 309-311
Generic procedures, 311-315
Generic programming, 309-310
Get property, 43-44, 80. *See also* **Property Get** procedures.
GetBtnClicked method, of TBIcon ActiveX control, 238, 239-240, 240-241
GetPrivateProfileString function, 273
Global unique identifiers. *See* GUIDs.
Global variables, problems with, 88, 114
Graphic class
   and **Center** method, 23-26
   and **Load** method, 28-30, 33
GUIDs, for ActiveX components, 264

H

Height property
   for **Form1** object, 75-76
   within ListBox objects, 250-252, 252
Help file
   for ActiveX components, 122-123, 265-270
   for runtime errors, 188-194
Help topics, 188-194
   missing, 193-194
   and non-VBA error codes, 191-193

remapped, 194
and VBA error codes, 190-191
HelpContext property, 190
HelpFile argument, 200-201
HelpFile property, 190
Hide method, and newly created forms, 148
Hiding. *See* Data hiding.
Horizontal frameworks, 306-308
HOW, 345
HTML, 216
Hypertext Markup Language. *See* HTML.

I

IDStrs() argument, of **ParamArray**
keyword, 205-207, 209
IIS, 216
Implements keyword, 172-174, 176
Incoming interfaces, 39
Independent optional parameters, 53, 138-139
Index parameter, 107
in Collection objects, 151, 152, 154
in one-to-many relationships, 163-164, 165
Information hiding, 4. *See also* Data hiding.
Inheritance
and OOA and OOD, 11
in OOP, 4, 5, 8-11
and polymorphism, 171
Inheritance trees
designing of, 10-11
disadvantages of deep, 9
INI files, 279-302
sample, 280
INIFileName parameter, in **RegIni** class, 286
Init_Class method
for advanced class initialization, 138-141
for classes with multiple interfaces, 139-140
in data sources, 167-168
for **RegIni** class, 285-286, 292-294
for self-initialization, 137-138
simple, 134-137
for user-defined collections, 156

Initialization, 133-141
advanced, 138-141
of classes with multiple interfaces, 139-140
defined, 132
forcing user, 135-137
in **RegIni** class, 292-295
self-, 137-138
simple, 134-137
Initialize event, 133.
See also **Form_Initialize** event.
in ClassModule objects, 179-182
In-process components, 217. *See also* ActiveX DLL components.
Installation time, for ActiveX controls and servers, 255-256
InstallShield 5.1 Professional Edition, 346-347
Instances, defined, 74
Instantiation, 132
of Collection objects, 16-17
in Visual Basic, 15, 132-134
Interactions, as objects, 47
Interfaces. *See also* Incoming interfaces, Outgoing interfaces, Public interfaces.
accessing properties in, 100-104
class modules in, 74-89
data hiding in, 89-94
defined, 74, 172-173
encapsulated, 271-272
events in, 110-113
initializing classes with multiple, 139-140
methods in, 104-110
modes in, 94-100
in Visual Basic, 40-45, 73-74
Internet, 330-331
Internet Explorer, as Active Client, 216
Internet Information Server. *See* IIS.
Internet Package, of Package And Deployment Wizard, 124, 126-127
InvisibleAtRuntime setting, for TBIcon ActiveX control, 232, 235
Item method
in Collection objects, 16-17, 151, 152, 153-154, 155

in one-to-many relationships, 163
in user-defined collections, 157-158
Items property, in Collection objects, 151
Iteration, through user-defined collections, 158-159

J

Java applets, 216
JavaScript, 216
Jet DAO error message Help file, 189-190
JScript, 216
Jump boxes, generic code for, 312-315
Jump forms, 320-321
JumpList procedure, 313-315

K

Key parameter
in Collection objects, 151, 152, 153
in **RegIni** class, 285
Key values, in user-defined collections, 156
Keys. *See also* License keys.
for INI files, 280
and **Init_Class** method, 295-296
for Registry, 280-281
Kurata, Deborah, 264

L

LastName property, 85-86
Late binding, 172, 264
Let property, 41-42, 80.
See also **Property Let** procedures.
Leverage, in software engineering, 326
Libraries. *See also* Class libraries.
common operating, 273
License files, 219
License keys, 219
Lifetime, of objects, 132-150
Linked lists, 89-90, 107

List class
and **Center** method, 23-26
and **Load** method, 30-33
List method, in **RegIni** class, 285
ListBox objects, 245-253
ListSC ActiveX control, 245-253
proxy custom members for, 246-247
Sorted property of, 247-250
UserControl objects and, 245-246, 250-252
using, 252-253
Load method, 22, 26-33. *See also* **Form_Load** event.
code for, 28-30, 30-32
and newly created forms, 147
specifications for, 27
"Loaded, but not shown" state, 146, 147-148
LoadPicture function
in ActiveX components, 122-123
and **Load** method, 30
LockFile argument, for **Load** method, 27
LogError method, 197-200, 210
in **Error** class, 177
Logging error codes, 197-202
Long data type, 278
Loose coupling, 87-88, 114
LPSTR string types, 275
LSTBOXSC.OCX file, 245
LSTBOXSC.VBP file, 245, 252-253

M

Many-to-many relationships, 49
implementing, 165
MDI, Application Wizard for building, 116
MDI forms, as templates, 318-321
me reference, 84
"Memory and resources completely reclaimed" state, 146, 149-150
Messages
defined, 3-4
between modules, 5-6

Methods, 44, 70, 70
  access, 79-80
  adding to classes, 82
  adding to forms, 83-87
  CallByName access of, 102-104
  in contact management system example, 61-62
  default, 100-104
  defined, 3, 15, 44, 74
  for **Form1** object, 76
  in OOD, 50-52
  in OOP, 3-4
  and polymorphism, 5, 7-8
  public, 80-81
  of **RegIni** class, 284, 285-286, 288-292
  of TBIcon ActiveX control, 238-241
Microsoft Access, Help files with, 189-190
Microsoft Active Platform, 215
Microsoft Corporation
  object-oriented programming development and implementation by, 1-3, 34-35
  VB philosophy of, 229-230
Microsoft Information Center, 331-332
Microsoft Office 7 applications, standalone mode of, 225
Microsoft Outlook, as vertical framework, 308
Microsoft Windows CE Toolkit for Visual Basic, 347-348
Middle tier.
  See Three-tier client/server architecture.
MISCEXS.BAS file, 218, 222
MISCEXS.CLS file, 222
mObjectType variable, in **Init_Class** method, 294
Modal dialog boxes, 83
Modes, 114
  defining, 94-100
  as properties, 51-52
  of properties, 42, 94-95
Modularization
  in OOA and OOD, 11-12
  in Simula, 2
Modules, 5
  coupling of, 87-88
  as templates, 318-321

MouseDown method, polymorphism of, 8
MouseMove event, of TBIcon ActiveX control, 237, 240, 241-242
MoveNext method, in data sources, 168-169
MovePrevious method, in data sources, 168-169
MsgBox function
  and **ShowRunTime** method, 177
  with standalone EXE, 228-229
MSJETERR.HLP file, 189
MultiKey key, for INI files, 280
Multiple inheritance, 9
Multiple interfaces
  initializing classes with, 139-140
  and polymorphism, 172
Multiple-document interface. *See* MDI.
MultiUse class, 219
mValidView variable, 84, 86-87
MYLIBDLL setting, 218
MYLIBDLL.DLL file, as ActiveX DLL, 220-221
MYLIBEXE setting, 223
MYLIBEXE.EXE file, as ActiveX EXE, 224

N

Name property, 78
  in **Terminate** event, 181-182
Named parameters, 110
Naming properties, 50
Native code, compiling ActiveX components in, 259-262
Networks, in client/server architecture, 12
New keyword, 134
  and Collection objects, 152
  and form initialization, 146
  instantiation with, 132-134
  and tracking object references, 144
New Project dialog box, 306-307, 321-322
NewEnum method, for contact management system example, 158-159
Newsgroups, 333
Non-client areas, within ListBox objects, 250
Nonexclusive association, 160-161

Non-VBA error codes, displaying, 191-193
Nonvisual objects, 13
Nothing keyword
  as Collection object, 17
  reclaiming memory and resources with, 149-150
  releasing objects with, 144
  in **Terminate** event, 181-182
  and tracking object references, 144
Notify event, in contact management system example, 63-64, 110-111
NuMega CodeReview, 342
NuMega FailSafe, 342
NuMega SmartCheck, 343
NuMega TrueTime, 343

O

Obj argument, for **Load** method, 27
Object argument, for **Load** method, 27
Object brokers
  implementing, 161-162
  in many-to-many relationships, 165
Object Browser, 115, 116, 119-123
  Help files in, 267-270
  References dialog box and, 117-119
  viewing Visual Basic classes with, 19-21
  window controls in, 120-122
Object collections, 150-159
Object data type, 184
  in Collection objects, 16-17
  ErrObj argument as, 187-188
  and **Load** method, 27
  and tracking object references, 144
Object hierarchy, type names in, 188
Object models, in contact management system example, 64-65
Object properties, 98
Object-oriented analysis. See OOA.
Object-oriented approach, COM components in, 1-2
Object-oriented design. See OOD.
Object-Oriented Design With Applications (Booch), principles articulated in, 11-12

Object-oriented programming. See OOP.
Objects, 38-40.
  See also Business objects, UI objects.
  abstraction of, 7, 73
  circular references to, 145
  in collections, 16-17, 131, 150-159
  in contact management system example, 54-58
  in data-aware classes, 166-171
  defined, 3, 11, 15, 74, 74
  designing of, 37-71
  encapsulation of, 5-7, 38
  finding properties and methods for, 50-52
  forms as, 74
  initialization of, 132, 133-141
  lifetime of, 132-150
  persistence of, 142-143
  public interfaces of, 5-6, 37-38, 39-40, 40-45
  references to, 144-145
  in **RegIni** class, 283
  relationships among, 48-50, 159-165
  self-testing, 324-326
  tangible, 47
  techniques for finding, 46-50
  terminating, 141-145
  versus classes, 39
  in Visual Basic, 15
  visualization of, 48
OCX custom controls, 230.
  See also ActiveX controls.
OCX files, 14-15
OLE Automation clients, and ClassModule objects, 18-19
OLE Automation servers, 2, 230.
  See also COM components.
OLE/OCX custom controls, 231.
  See also ActiveX controls.
On Error Resume Next statement, 278
One-to-many relationships, 49
  fill-in-the-blank, 316
  generic, 311-312
  implementing composite, 162-165
One-to-one relationships, 49
  implementing composite, 160-162

Online documentation, 329
OOA, 12
   principles of, 11-12
OOD, 11-15, 37-71
   and client/server architecture, 12-15
   defined, 12, 71
   examples of, 54-70
   finding objects in, 46-50
   interfaces in, 50-52
   parameters in, 53-54
   principles of, 11-12, 45-46
OOP, 12. *See also* Abstraction, Data hiding, Encapsulation, Inheritance, Modularization, Polymorphism.
   benefits of, 33
   future of, 34-35
   history and development of, 2-3
   Microsoft implementation of, 1-2
   and Visual Basic, 1-36
Optimization, of ActiveX component code, 260-262
Options dialog box, 320
Optional keyword, 106-107, and **ParamArray** property, 109
Optional parameters, 53, 106-107
   and events, 110
Outgoing interfaces, 39
Out-of-process components, 221-222. *See also* ActiveX EXE components.

P

Package And Deployment Wizard, 115, 116, 123-128, 264
   compiling ActiveX components for, 260
ParamArray keyword
   IDStrs() argument of, 205-207, 209
   Title argument of, 205-207
   in **TrapSyntax** method, 202, 203
ParamArray parameter, 53, 108-109
   and events, 110
Parameters
   arrays of, 108-109

   in contact management system example, 62-63
   default passing of, 106, 107
   named, 110
   in OOD, 53-54
   optional, 106-107
   passing of, 104-106
   of **RegIni** class, 284-286
   in Windows API, 274-279
Parent classes. *See* Superclasses.
Parent objects, shutdown method for, 145
ParseButtons method, in **CL** class, 184-187
Patterns, in software engineering, 323-324
P-code, compiling ActiveX components in, 259-262
Permission, 43. *See also* Verification.
Persistence, 142-143
   defined, 132, 142
Persistent class interface, 173
PersistentClass object, with **Prospect** class, 174-176
PhoneNumber class, in contact management system example, 68-69
Picture property, of TBIcon ActiveX control, 237-238
Polymorphic Save, 175-176
Polymorphism
   with **Delete** method, 62-63
   and OOA and OOD, 11
   in OOP, 4, 5, 7-8
   in Visual Basic applications, 21-33, 131, 171-176
Printer interface, in Windows, 271
Printers Collection object, 16
Printf function, 108
Priority buttons, in References dialog box, 118
Private keyword, 41, 79, 80, 90-92, 94, 196
   and events, 111
Private modules, 92
Private procedures, public methods and, 104-110
Private properties, 90-92
   and default, 101
Private variables, 90-92
Privileges, implementing, 161-162

Procedure Attributes dialog box
   default properties and, 100-102
   for iteration through collections, 159
Procedures
   aliases, 272-273
   generic, 311-315
   naming of, 272-273
   of **RegIni** class, 288-292
   signatures of, 272
ProcessFonts function, 277
ProcessINIKey subprocedure, in **Init_Class** method, 295-296
Product class, in contact management system example, 67-68
Program scope, 88
Programming paradigms, history and development of, 2-3
Project Properties dialog box, 262-263
Project templates, 318, 321-322
Properties, 3-4, 70, 70. See also Public properties
   accessing, 100-104
   adding to classes, 82
   adding to forms, 83-87
   CallByName access of, 102-104
   in contact management system example, 58-61
   controlling access with, 42-43
   controlling availability with, 43
   default, 100-102
   defined, 3, 15, 40, 74
   encapsulation with, 41-44
   modes as, 51-52
   object, 98
   in OOD, 50-52
   preserving, 143
   private, 90-92
   and public variables, 40-41
   range checking with, 42
   read-only, 96-97
   read-write, 95-96
   and redirection, 43-44
   of **RegIni** class, 283-284, 288-292
   self-initializing, 44
   of TBIcon ActiveX control, 237-238
   validation with, 41-42
   Variant, 98-100
   verification with, 43
   write-once, 97-98
   write-only, 97
Properties window, for **Form1** object, 75-76
Property declarations, and public variables, 40
Property Get procedures, 42-43, 43-44, 94-100. See also **Get** property.
   for ClassModule objects, 5-6, 18
Property initialization, 134
Property Let procedures, 41-42, 94-100. See also **Let** property.
   for ClassModule objects, 5, 18
   and self-initialization, 138
Property pages, as templates, 318-321
Property procedures
   and abstraction, 7
   for ClassModule objects, 17-18
   in newly created forms, 147
Property Set procedures, 94-100. See also **Set** property.
   for ClassModule objects, 5, 18
PropertyChanged method, and TBIcon ActiveX control, 238
Prospect class, 80
   in contact management system example, 65-66, 112
   persistent class interface for, 173-176
Proxy custom members, for ListSC ActiveX control, 246-247
Public classes and objects, documentation of, 265-266
Public interfaces, 70, 73-74
   of objects, 5-6, 37-38, 39-40
   persistent, 173-176
Public keyword, 39, 40-41, 79, 80, 89, 94, 196
Public methods, 80-81
   and private procedures, 104-110
Public properties
   adding to classes, 78-80
   of events, 110-111
Public variable properties, 79

Public variables, disadvantages of, 40-41
Purchase method, in contact management system example, 63
Purchased event, in contact management system example, 64

Q

Quality, in software engineering, 323-326
QueryUnload event, 148-149, 150

R

Raise method, displaying VBA error codes and, 191
RaiseEvent keyword, 111
Range checking, 42
RAO, and ActiveX EXEs, 222
Rational Rose, 348-350
Readability, of public variables, 41
Read-only mode, 42
 as property, 51-52
Read-only properties, 96-97
ReadProperties event, of TBIcon ActiveX control, 241-242, 244
Read-write mode, 42
 as property, 51-52
Read-write properties, 95-96
Recordsets, initializing objects with, 141
Redirection, 43-44
 in user-defined collections, 156
Reference count, in Visual Basic, 144
References, 117-119
 circular, 145
 counting, 144-145
 defined, 74
 setting, 118-119
References dialog box, 115, 116, 117-119, 309
Referential properties, 50
RegDeleteKey procedure, and **RegIni** class
 class card for, 283
 Delete method in, 297-298

 events of, 286, 288-292
 handling keys in, 295-296, 297-298
 initialization in, 292-295
 methods of, 284, 285-286, 288-292
 objects of, 283
 parameters of, 284-286
 procedures of, 288-292
 properties of, 283-284, 288-292
 relationships in, 283
 SelfTest method for, 324-326
 SetValue method in, 296-297
 specification for, 288-292
 and templates, 321-322
 using, 298-302
Registration numbers, for ActiveX components, 264
Registry, 280-281
 accessing, 286-288
Registry Editor, 264
Registry/INI objects, 279-302
 designing, 281-288
RegSetValue procedure, and **RegIni** class, 297
Relationships
 in contact management system example, 58
 implementing, 159-165
 among objects, 48-50
 in **RegIni** class, 283
Reliability of systems, coupling and, 88
Remote Automation Object. *See* RAO.
Remove method
 in Collection objects, 16-17, 151, 152, 153
 in user-defined collections, 157-158
Required parameters, 53
Requirements analysis, 46
Result frame, in References dialog box, 118
Returning error codes, 197-202, 209-210
ReturnType enumeration, 93-94
ReturnValue variable, 93-94
Reuse of software, 33
RoboHelp, 350-352
Roles, as objects, 47
Runtime errors, 201-202

S

SAFEARRAY data type, 276
Safety Settings screen, in Package And Deployment Wizard for Internet, 126-127
Sample code, in ActiveX components, 122-123
Save method, 22
   late binding in, 172
   polymorphic, 175-176
   preserving objects with, 142
ScaleHeight property
   of **Center** method, 23
   within ListBox objects, 250-252, 252-253
ScaleWidth property
   of **Center** method, 23
   within ListBox objects, 250-252, 252-253
Scope, within class modules, 88-89
SDI, Application Wizard for building, 116
Select Case statement, 168
Self-initializing classes, 137-138
Self-initializing properties, 44
SelfTest method, for **RegIni** class, 324-326
Self-testing objects, in software engineering, 324-326
Servers, in client/server architecture, 12-15
Set property, 80.
   See also **Property Set** procedures.
New keyword and, 132-133
SetValue method, in **RegIni** class, 285, 296-297
ShapeLabel control, 231-232
Shell_NotifyIcon function, and TBIcon ActiveX control, 236, 237
Sheridan Software Systems, Inc., 352-354
   inheritance implementation by, 9
Show method, 83-84, 87
   and newly created forms, 147
ShowMsg method
   of **ClientApp** class, 178
   ParseButtons method in, 184-187
   and specifying Help topics, 269-270
   with standalone EXE, 228-229
Shown state, 146, 148
ShowRunTime method, in **Error** class, 177-178
ShowSyntax method, in **Error** class, 178
Shutdown method, 145
Signatures
   passing functions with wrong, 279
   of procedures, 272
Similar objects, 151
Simple forms, and **RegIni** class, 299-302
Simple initialization, 134-137
Simula language, 2
Simulation languages, 2
Single inheritance, 9
Single-document interface. *See* SDI.
Sizing, within ListBox objects, 250-252
Software, reuse of, 33
Software engineering, 323-326
Software objects. *See* Objects, OOP.
Sorted property, of ListSC ActiveX control, 247-250
"Spaghetti" code, 88
sp_Assist, 353-354
Specifications
   of contact management system example, 65-69
   as objects, 47
Speed, in software engineering, 323
SplitMsg method, 195-197
   in **Error** class, 178
Splitting error messages, 195-197
SQL business objects, 13
Standard forms, in Visual Basic framework, 307-308
Standard modules, ClassModule objects as, 18
Standard Setup Package, of Package And Deployment Wizard, 124-125
StartMode property, applications settings of, 227
State properties, 50
State transformations, 52
Sticky notes, 71
   in OOD, 48-50, 58
String data type
   arrays and, 276
   in Collection objects, 152-153, 154
String function, 275-276

Strings
  ByRef and ByVal passing of, 275-276
  in Windows API, 273-274
Strong coupling, 87-88, 114
Sub keyword, 80
Sub Main procedure
  in class library, 225-227
  in .DLL files, 218
  in .EXE files, 222, 223
  and running standalone EFSD.DLL file, 229
Sub procedures
  and abstraction, 7
  for ClassModule objects, 5, 17-18
  in newly created forms, 147
Subclasses, and inheritance, 8-9
Subroutines
  adding to classes, 82
  within class modules, 89
  as methods, 44, 80
Superclasses, and inheritance, 8-9
Syntax checking, 200-202, 210-212
Syntax error handling, 200-202, 207-210
Syntax error messages
  constructing, 207-210
  documentation of, 266
System Architect, 354-356
System exit, and tracking object references, 145
System objects, as object brokers, 161-162
System variable, in object brokers, 162

T

Tangible objects, 47
Taskbar Icon example.
  See TBIcon ActiveX control.
TBARICON.OCA file, 243
TBARICON.OCX file, 243
TBIcon ActiveX control, 236-244
  events of, 241-242
  general declarations for, 236-237
  methods of, 238-241
  properties of, 237-238
  registering, 236
  settings for, 232-235
  using, 242-244
  Windows Registry entry for, 254-255
TechNet, 329
Template Add menu, 319
Templates, 318-322
Terminate event, 144
  in ClassModule objects, 179-182
  preserving objects in, 143
  reclaiming memory and resources with, 149-150
Terminating objects, 141-145
Text property, as default, 100
theBindingCollection variable, 169
theDataSource variable, 169
theDelimiter constant, and ProcessINIKey sub procedure, 296
Three-tier client/server architecture, 12-15
  of Microsoft Active Platform, 215
Thunking, 279
Title property of ActiveX components, naming scheme for, 180-181
Toolbar Wizard, 116
ToolboxBitmap setting, for TBIcon ActiveX control, 232, 233
Track Record, 356-357
Transitional methods, 52
TrapRunTime method, 182-202
  code for, 184-202
  in Error class, 178
  Help file with, 188-194
  Help topics with, 190-193
  and logging error codes, 197-202
  missing Help topics with, 193-194
  non-VBA error codes with, 191-193
  remapped Help topics with, 194
  specifications of, 182-183
  and splitting error messages, 195-197
  VBA error codes with, 190-191
TrapSyntax method, 202-210
  code for, 202-210

constructing syntax error messages using, 207-210
   in **Error** class, 178
   error handling outside, 210-212
   and **LogError** method, 197
   specifications for, 203-204
   and syntax checking and syntax error handling, 200-202
   syntax checking outside, 210-212
Two-tier client/server architecture, 12
txtFirst box, 85-86
txtInternal box, for data consumers, 170, 171
txtLast box, 85-86
Type names, in object hierarchy, 188
TypeName function, 184
   in object brokers, 162
   and **TrapRunTime** method, 187-188

U

UI objects, 14-15
Underscores, names beginning with, 158
Unicode strings, in Windows API, 273-274
Uninstall feature, of Package And Deployment Wizard, 128
Unload event, 148-149, 150
"Unloaded and referenced while a control is still loaded" state, 146, 150
Unloaded state, 146, 148-149, 150
UnloadMode parameter, in **QueryUnload** event, 148-149
Use cases, 46
User controls, as templates, 318-321
User interface objects. *See* UI objects.
User privileges, implementing, 161-162
User property, in object brokers, 162
UserControl objects, ListBox objects and, 245-246, 250-252
User-defined types, 91-92
   for Collection objects, 155

V

Validation, of data, 41-42
Value method, in **RegIni** class, 285
Value property, of **Address** class, 95-96
Variable parameters, 53
Variables, private, 90-92
Variant data type, 184
   in Collection objects, 16-17, 152, 154, 155
   and generic classes, 309-310
   and "unloaded and unreferenced while a control is still referenced" state, 150
Variant properties, 98-100
ParamArray property as, 108
   and tracking object references, 144
VB Class Builder. *See* Class Builder.
VB6
   ActiveX controls in, 230-232
   ActiveX controls versus servers in, 253-256
   COM components in, 35-36, 215
   compiling ActiveX components with, 259-262
   data-aware classes in, 131, 166-171
   designers in, 231
   extensibility of, 230
   inheritance restrictions in, 9
   object tools in, 115-129
VBA Companion, 120
VBA error codes, displaying, 190-191
VBAssist, 354
   and Visual Basic, 230
vbComplexBound, 169
vbDataSource, 166-167
.VBL files, 219
VBScript, 216
vbSimpleBound, 169
vbSModeAutomation setting, 227
vbSModeStandalone setting, 227
vbSystemModal, syntax error with, 187
VBX custom controls, 229-230, 231.
   See also ActiveX controls.
Verification, with properties, 43
Vertical frameworks, 308

View method, 84, 87
Visible interfaces, 39. *See also* Public interfaces.
Visio Professional 5.0, 357-358
Vision Builder 3.0, 358-359
Visual Basic. *See also* VB6.
   ActiveX components of, 215-257
   classes in, 73-114, 131-176
   ClassModule objects in, 5-7, 17-21
   Collection objects in, 16-17, 151-154
   and contact management system example, 65-69
   developer's resources of, 329-338
   encapsulation with properties in, 41-44
   extensibility of, 229-230
   frameworks and, 305-327
   future of, 34-35, 35-36
   history of, 229-230
   instantiating classes and objects in, 15, 132
   interfaces in, 73-74
   messages in, 4
   and methods and properties, 50-52
   methods in, 44
   Microsoft philosophy for, 229-230
   Microsoft Windows CE Toolkit for, 347-348
   and object-oriented programming, 1-36
   and objects, 46-50
   and OOD, 37-71
   parameters in, 53-54
   polymorphism in applications in, 5, 7-8, 11, 21-33, 62-63, 171-176
   public interfaces in, 37-40, 40-45, 40-45
   reference count in, 144
   Sheridan Software Tools custom controls for, 352-354
   third-party tools in, 339-361
   VBAssist project and, 230
   and Windows, 229-230
Visual Basic 6. *See* VB6.
Visual Basic Books Online, 230

Visual Components, 359-361
Visual Modeler, 48
   and contact management system example, 64-65, 66
VisualSpeller 2.1, 361

W

Whiteboard, 71
   in OOD, 48-50
Width property
   for **Form1** object, 75-76
   within ListBox objects, 250-252, 252
Windows, and Visual Basic, 229-230
Windows API, 271-303. *See also* Registry.
   accessing, 272-279
   encapsulated interfaces and, 271-272
   as horizontal framework, 316-317
   for manipulating INI files, 288
   for manipulating Registry, 287
   and Registry/INI objects, 279-302
WithEvents keyword, 111-113
WndClass structure, 278

Write-once properties, 97-98
Write-only initialization property, 138
Write-only mode, 42
   as property, 51-52
Write-only properties, 97
WritePrivateProfileString function, 274
   and **RegIni** class, 297
WriteProperties event, of TBIcon ActiveX control, 241-242, 244

Y

Yourdon, Ed, 33

Learn More Faster

ISBN: 1-57610-281-5
$49.99 U.S. • $69.99 Canada
Available Now

ISBN: 1-57610-283-1
$49.99 U.S. • $69.99 Canada
Available Now

ISBN: 1-57610-282-3
$49.99 U.S. • $69.99 Canada
Available Now

Regardless of your experience, you'll reach for our books time and time again.

CORIOLIS Technology Press™

Blue, Black, and Gold books. Novice, intermediate, advanced. Easy-to-identify classifications for an innovative new concept in technology publishing.

A completely new series. Each title written to address the specific needs of the system developer, user, or engineer—at the level of his or her concern.

ACQUIRE MORE KNOWLEDGE

When you are learning a new technology, Blue Books are the complete, hands-on tutorials you'll want to reach for first. Their highly interactive, project-based, "learn-by-doing" approach helps ensure that you will learn more at a much faster rate than you can with other tutorials.

USE YOUR KNOWLEDGE

Black Books are indispensable problem-solving guides. Their unique format, which provides very thorough, in-depth, highly technical overviews followed by highly practical "immediate solutions," will help you quickly complete any task: large or small, simple or complex.

EXPAND YOUR KNOWLEDGE

Gold Books are the professional-level guides you'll turn to when you want to expand your horizons. Their highly conceptual but practical approach will teach you how to think in new ways and push your skills to a new level.

Blue, Black, and Gold. They're comprehensive, illustrated, and easy to understand. Experience the difference. Look for these and other soon-to-be-released titles from Coriolis. Of course!

Available at Bookstores and Computer Stores Nationwide

Telephone 800.410.0192 • International callers 602.483.0192
www.coriolis.com

Prices are subject to change without notice. ©1998 The Coriolis Group, Inc. All rights reserved. 8/98

What's On The CD-ROM

The companion CD-ROM contains the following elements, specially selected to enhance the use of this book:

- Source code—All the source code for this book is in the E:\Source Code directory, where E is the CD-ROM drive.
- RoboHELP HTML Edition Version 6.0—An evaluation copy of RoboHELP HTML Edition Version 6.0 from Blue Sky Software.
- ActiveReports—An evaluation copy of ActiveReports 1.0 from Data Dynamics.
- How Learning Edition—An evaluation copy of HOW LE 2.0 from Riverton Software.
- Sheridan Software—An evaluation copy of the entire Sheridan Software product line.
- Formula One—An evaluation copy of Formula One 5.0 from Visual Components.
- VBAdvantage—A powerful VB development utility that enhances the VB design-time environment.

When you install using the DemoShield presentation, the installable disks for the evaluation software are installed on your machine. You can then install the software from the respective folder. Alternatively, you can browse the "\disk1" folder of your CD-ROM to directly install the evaluation software.

See the readme file for descriptions, installation instructions, limitations, and other important information.

Platform Requirements:

- Intel Pentium processor or equivalent is recommended

Operating System:

- Windows 95/98 or NT 4

RAM:

- 16MB memory (32MB is recommended)

Software:

- Visual Basic 6